Critical Theory and Public Life

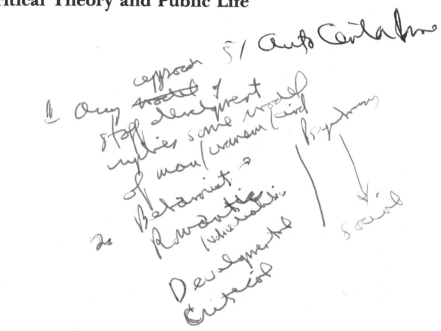

Studies in Contemporary German Social Thought
Thomas McCarthy, General Editor

Critical Theory and Public Life

edited by John Forester

The MIT Press, Cambridge, Massachusetts, and London, England

For my parents and the memory of their parents (JF)

This book was set in Baskerville by The MIT Press Computergraphics Department and was printed and bound by The Murray Printing Co. in the United States of America.

Library of Congress Cataloging in Publication Data
Main entry under title:

Critical theory and public life.

   (Studies in contemporary German social thought)
   Bibliography: p.
   Includes index.
   1. Criticism (Philosophy)—Addresses, essays,
lectures.   2. Social action—Addresses, essays,
lectures.   3. Communication—Social aspects—
Addresses, essays, lectures.   4. Social structure—
Addresses, essays, lectures.   5. Habermas, Jürgen,
Theorie des kommunikativen Handelns.   I. Forester,
John, 1948-   . II. Series.
HM24.C75   1985   361.2   85-15219
ISBN 0-262-06097-3

Contents

Preface

This volume grew out of a correspondence linking several continents and a broad community of students, activists, and scholars. It appears at a time when an increasing number of people are attempting to assess issues of power, policy, ideology, and political action in ways informed by Jürgen Habermas's critical communications theory of society. The diversity of this work can be bewildering to the uninitiated. Moreover, in many cases the temptation to focus on Habermas's theory rather than on specific empirical problems has often been too great to resist; as a result, much work that promises to carry critical theory forward becomes metatheoretical, leaving empirical, historical, and practical issues waiting yet again.

This book was conceived in the hope of showing how critical theory might be applied to issues of public life. By *applied* I refer not to instrumental application but to critical, empirically and historically oriented appropriation. I had begun to make such an appropriation in my own work, and for reasons of politics, solidarity, and practicality, I wanted very much to contact others who were engaged in similar efforts. In particular, I sought authors who paid attention not only to structural issues but also to questions of action and practice. I present the results of this search here in the hope that these essays will provoke criticism, response, and reformulation that will allow us all to advance a critical social theory that concretely addresses issues of domination and emancipation in our public and private lives.

Many people have offered help and encouragement with this project. John O'Neill, Dieter Misgeld, and Tom McCarthy have been consistent supporters. The early responses of Richard Bernstein, Fred Dallmayr, Claus Offe, Jürgen Habermas, Ray Kemp, Jeremy Shapiro, Frank Fischer, and Trent Schroyer gave the project an exciting start. Suggestions, criticism, and other assistance came from C. Fred Alford, Richard Bates, Dudley Burton, Hauke Brunkhorst, Edward McCluskie, Jean Cohen, Peter Dahlgren, Robert Denhardt, William Dunn, Stephen Ealy, Klaus Eder, Brian Fay, Boris Frankel, Gunther Frankenberg, David Held, Trevor Hitner, Axel Honneth, Detlef Horster, Ralph Hummel, Douglas Kellner, David Knights, Richard Lanigan, Tom Long, James Mayo, J. Donald Moon, Bruce Pietrykowski, Michael Pusey, Larry Ray, Rudi Scheidges, James Schmidt, Alfons Sollner, Peter Ulrich, Howard Waitzkin, Peter Watkins, Shierry Weber, Stephen White, John Whiteman, Hugh Wilmott, and H. T. Wilson.

Among my student colleagues, Kieran Donaghy continually pressed me in invaluable ways to balance issues of an applied nature with attention to ambiguous theoretical issues themselves. As a result, our discussions at Cornell of the applied turn in contemporary critical theory had few dull moments as Cathy Campbell, Annette Sassi, Linda Gondim, Charles Rock, Pierre LaRamee, and Diana Mayne, many of them engaged in doctoral research on such problems, explored related issues.

My wife, Betty, was more than patient. Kate and Daniel, our children, grew through infancy as this book took shape and neared publication. My mother and father helped with translations and enthusiasm. My friend Simon Neustein was a continual source of clarity, vision, and hope. I have been very fortunate.

Finally, I would like to thank Tom McCarthy, the series editor, and Larry Cohen of MIT Press for carefully shepherding this project along through its various incarnations. While I bear final responsibility for the shape of the collection, I am certain that the contributors and all those who have supported this project will now look forward with me to the thoughtful efforts of others who, appropriating these essays critically, may further develop the applied turn in the critical theory tradition.

John Forester
Ithaca, New York

Introduction: The Applied Turn in Contemporary Critical Theory

John Forester

"If critical theory is to have a future in the English speaking world it will be through the use of critical theory within various theoretical projects and disciplines and the development of critical theory in relation to contemporary conditions, concerns, and problems. Only then will critical theory be a living force."[1]

This book appropriates Jürgen Habermas's critical communications theory of society to explore issues of public life.[2] The essays that follow examine the research implications and empirical applicability of Habermas's theory.[3] They probe the vulnerabilities and contingencies of everyday life and social action in workplaces, in schools, in planning processes, and in broader social, political, and cultural settings.[4]

The essays are grouped into six parts. Part I investigates the shifting foundations of advanced capitalist economies and recent proposals for reindustrialization. Part II examines subtle and pervasive problems in education, focusing on issues of cultural invasion and the significance of language and speech. Part III analyzes the constitution of everyday practical judgments by considering the institutional development of the news media and the phenomenological character of consumer choices. Part IV explores the planning process, examining public voice in the discussion of nuclear development in Great Britain and city and regional planning practices in the United States. Part V concentrates on problems in the analysis of public policy, asking in what frameworks policies can be best examined when we allow attention to explicitly normative issues as well as to more conventional descriptive ones. Part VI consists of two historical studies that reveal the moments of suppression and appropriation that characterize our inheritance of the emancipatory elements of our political and cultural traditions.

Several major themes recur throughout the volume: (1) the phenomenologically meaningful experience of social action; (2) the structural staging of that action; (3) the institutional contingencies of practical actions; (4) relations of control, authority, and power; and (5) the requirements and possibilities of resistance, of social action cast not simply as instrumental politics but as emancipatory political praxis. These themes represent central research problems for all those seeking to develop critical theory in applied and concretely empirical ways. Let us consider each briefly.

Habermas's action theory can serve as the basis of a politically charged phenomenology.[5] Because it has closer affinities with the work of Alfred Schutz and the late Edmund Husserl than with that of Martin Heidegger or the early Husserl, this critical phenomenological approach allows us to study the meaning-making practices of diverse historical actors. The "real interests" of those actors are not prejudged, nor is their social function known a priori. Their activity is taken to be a matter of contingent, albeit conventionally guided, performance. In John O'Neill's wonderful phrase, "making sense together" is taken to be a structurally staged, yet ever chancy, precarious, and vulnerable social accomplishment—in the workplace, in the home, in political organizations, on the street.[6] Phenomenologists and ethnomethodologists have, of course, scrutinized a variety of sense-making practices, but Habermas connects such practices to issues of power and ideology, hegemony and social reproduction. How does the play of power depend on and work through the fragmentation of meaning and sense, the confusion of issues, the silencing of voice? In the essays that follow, the phenomenological impulse is never divorced from empirical and political concerns; indeed, the political implications of concrete social actions become clearer when an assessment of their effective sociality, their real meaning making and expectation shaping, can be rendered. It is for similar reasons that Habermas has appropriated the work of J. L. Austin and John Searle on "speech acts."[7]

Austin wrote once that the method manifest in his study of speech acts might be called a "linguistic phenomenology, only that is rather a mouthful."[8] He was right about the potential for obscurity: The modifier *linguistic* may create even more confusion than *phenomenology*. Yet Austin meant to, and did, assess what people do when they speak, when they act together by speaking, performing in, their shared language. Thus to read *linguistic* as referring here to abstract sentences and their structures is a serious mistake. We do better to read *linguistic phenomenology* as the phenomenology of performative speech.

A similar problem has plagued those wishing to work with Habermas's "communications" theory. Habermas is not only concerned with communication in terms of deep structure or abstract possibility; he is providing a way to assess social and political action, by considering it generically not simply as instrumental but more fundamentally as communicative, intersubjective, fully social (however contingent, and then at times derivatively instrumental). It helps, then, to understand Habermas's point (and overall project) as quite a bit closer to Antonio Gramsci (or even Michel Foucault) than to Noam Chomsky, for the deep problem that Habermas shares with Gramsci and Foucault (and Paulo Freire, as John O'Neill and Dieter Misgeld here make clear) is this: How can we understand the social construction and management of political consent? This question underlies many of the essays collected here. As a result, we may take Habermas's critical communications theory as the beginning of a critical, empirically sensitive "structural phenomenology."[9]

The stress on action in this book may clarify another area of possible misunderstanding. Significantly, Habermas's attention to the use of language, rather than to its abstract form or structure, marks an analytic shift in focus from disembodied forms of "consciousness" to concrete constellations of action, to specifically situated patterns and instances of claims-making performances (including the claims of management, of so-called experts, or of bureaucratic officials). Habermas has reformulated his early, quasi-transcendental concerns with knowledge-constitutive interests in favor of a far more sociological and potentially historical analysis of social action. As a result, if these essays pay scant attention to the early tripartite division of technical, practical, and emancipatory cognitive interests, they are not making a grievous omission. Instead they are making an applied turn with Habermas to understand such interests in the embodied form of contingently institutionalized learning processes in two dimensions: technical-instrumental (dealing with problems of control and the ordering of the object world) and moral-practical (dealing with problems of legitimacy and the solidarity of social relations). Thus Albrecht Wellmer's earlier use of Richard Rorty's phrase, "the linguistic turn," had ambiguous connotations at best as it applied to Habermas's concerns with language use and communicative action.[10] Had Wellmer called attention to the "performative turn" or the "turn to social action" in Habermas's work, he would have gained in substantive clarity whatever he might have lost in elegance.

The essays, however, are hardly content to assess social action alone, forgoing attention to the stages on which any such action takes its historical place. Here Habermas's own output helps to bewilder his critics. Volume 1 of *The Theory of Communicative Action*, for example, treats action theory at length, but the discussion of systemic social organization comes only in the second (yet to be translated) volume.[11] In *Communication and the Evolution of Society* (1979), the essential action-theoretic "What Is Universal Pragmatics?" was accompanied by two essays dealing with Habermas's reconstruction of historical materialism, yet the complementarity of those essays was only subtly articulated.[12] Too often critics have responded to one focus or the other, the action theory or the historical-structural concerns, ignoring Habermas's attempts to show the systematic connections between the two.

The essays here may help to rectify this problem, not by treating abstractly the problems of relating action to social structure but by showing in substance how consideration of social structure must precede or stage the contextualized assessment of specific patterns of social action. Habermas's essay on modern and postmodern architecture is a short but exemplary example. Ben Agger and Tim Luke and Stephen White also integrate an assessment of structural, political-economic conditions with the action-theoretic focus on radically unequal dialogue chances, the fragmentation, commodification, and professional colonization that turns citizens into consumers, and the resulting silencing of popular voice in the face of concentrated economic power.

Throughout the book are references to the "colonization of the lifeworld." In Dieter Misgeld's assessment of educational practices, in Dan Hallin's analysis of the managed public sphere, and in John O'Neill's account of the ethics of decolonizing the colonized lifeworld, the vulnerability of the lifeworld can be explored only because colonization is a systemic rather than an ad hoc phenomenon. Habermas's notion of colonization is not a matter of voluntaristic action; it reflects the structural effects on people's ordinary lives of systemic developments: the increasing penetration of economic markets into previously nonmarket spheres and increasing concentrations of power in the form of private capital or within the bureaucratic labyrinth of the state.

The catch-phrase *systematically distorted communication* has long suggested Habermas's dual concern with social structure and social action. As Trent Schroyer noted a decade ago, Habermas's notion of systematic distortion is a reformulation of the classical Marxist critique of ideology.[13] It would be as inaccurate to think of Habermas's notion as ad hoc and voluntarist as it would be to suppose that Marx's notion of ideology was simply a matter of conflicting preferences. Habermas's contribution to social research, as these essays help to make manifest, is to pose the structural staging of intersubjectively meaningful action in a particularly fruitful way, enabling experientially and phenomenologically vivid detail to be complemented by equally empirical attention to political-economic and social-structural developments.

C. Wright Mills, of course, posed the challenge of relating action to structure, lived world to system, as that of the sociological imagination.[14] Recently Anthony Giddens has called the reproductive processes by which structurally staged actions re-form social structures, processes of "structuration."[15] Yet if we are to take these problems of structuration seriously, we are driven to bring traditionally Weberian concerns with meaningful social action into conjunction with traditionally Marxist concerns of systemic contradictions, crisis phenomena, power, and ideology. In *Legitimation Crisis* Habermas contrasted system and social integration, linking the two with a theory of contingently displaced crisis phenomena.[16] In *The Theory of Communicative Action* he carries the contingent system–lifeworld interpenetration several steps further, articulating particularly the basic modes of reproduction of the lifeworld and its vulnerabilities to systemic pressures and contradictions. Following the basic impulse set out in *Legitimation Crisis*, and in particular cases the more recent work as well, our essays situate the actors they study within more encompassing structural settings of relations of power and control. The deemphasis of class analysis notwithstanding, this move distinguishes these analyses both from traditionally functionalist and from more voluntaristic, pluralist accounts. Critical theory thus makes possible the concrete analysis of structure and of contingently staged social action.[17]

Nevertheless, attention to systemic pressures often threatens to drive out the careful accounting of the practical contingencies of real social contexts and situations of action. When systems dwarf action, politics vanishes; political events then only mysteriously happen to people rather than being made by them. Frank Fischer's essay is an attempt to integrate phenomenological and structural strategies of policy analysis. Unless critical social research can illuminate the situated, interpretive, and judgmental character of social action, we may never understand politically the very real pragmatic meanings that a simple "no," a simple silence, a simple "it's too complex" might have in the day-to-day play of power in work settings, at home, or in policy processes. To recognize with the ethnomethodologists that the analysis of action benefits from an appreciation of its situated, ambiguous, and multiply interested character need not lead straightaway to pluralist voluntarism, for the social forces that stage and frame situation-definitions must also be taken into account. Thus, for example, Peter Grahame's consideration of practical consumer judgments begins from and extends Habermas's concern with the contingently offered validity claims made in ordinary and institutional speech. Ray Kemp's and my own analyses of planning processes, and John O'Neill's attention to the politics of language as reflected in the writings of Paulo Freire and Frantz Fanon, work to expose the ambiguous structuring of action and its political contingencies. Perhaps more explicitly than Habermas's own writings, these essays seek to link a concern with situated action to research efforts that can assess the interplay of established power and potential resistance.

Indeed, a concern with political power, the ambiguities of authority, and the possibility of concrete action ties together the intentions of all the essays in this book. Power, these essays suggest, is not a simple possession; it must be understood instead as an ensemble of relations in which diverse, historically situated subjects have variously skewed chances, abilities, and capacities for action. These essays work to reveal the power in the maintenance of selective silences, the power manifest in the fragmentation of issue definition, the power manifest in the management of information and the subsequent shaping of popular attention, consent, belief, and trust. Although they explore problems of power in various ways, each essay seeks to clarify how political and economic power is reproduced, consolidated, and maintained in ways that threaten to turn democratic politics into a rhetorical fiction.

What implications for action, for political praxis, flow from these essays? Certainly they draw implications for political practice in their own contexts, yet they can hardly produce recipes for emancipation. In several cases they suggest that questions of power, explored in Habermas's terms, may lead directly to practical questions of resistance. This result follows directly from a strategy of analysis that attends to the contingencies of action, for then even those actions associated with the seemingly monolithic exercise of power can be seen to have their own limits, to be dependent and contingent rather than fully autonomous, inevitably established, and a priori effective. Strategies of resistance may begin from the insight that even political limits have limits. Exploring this relational and dialectical conception of power in diverse empirical circumstances, several of the essays point toward strategies of resistance tailored to specific institutional settings.

Curiously this diversity of strategies and forms of political action suggests a reading of Habermas as less rationalistic in character than traditional, more orthodox Marxism, if either is taken as a source of indications of political praxis and resistance. If the centrality of class or productive relations has at times constricted attention to workplace struggles, Habermas's reformulation of relations of power in terms of lifeworld colonization or penetration suggests a far wider range of sites of resistance, including not only workplaces but also homes, schools, the public sphere, the state, and cultural institutions. Thus the praxis that these essays may inform combines purpose with a vision of freedom from illegitimate power. Resistance to illegitimate power is itself social action, itself interpretive and contingent, itself an offering to others to act together, to learn together, to make possible life in a community. Resistance here does not mean the pursuit of ideal speech; it does mean organizing to make democratic politics a reality.

This discussion allows us to dissolve a recurrent misunderstanding of Habermas's notion of the ideal speech situation as a matter of political strategy. Significantly, none of the essays present the ideal speech situation as a goal to be realized concretely. Nevertheless, deviations from that formal idealization might still be usefully identified and assessed. The obvious fact that an ideal speech situation is never practically realized—that communication is always imperfect—does not yet mean that the analytic concept has no practical importance.

Consider an analogy that is at once medical and political. Our bodily health depends in part on the quality of the air we breathe. Assume that we have just learned that materials containing asbestos will soon be introduced in our workplace. We have several options. We might

simply resign ourselves to this toxic threat by saying, "Well, no workplace is without its risks; the air we breathe is always polluted, imperfect,
never ideal." Taking this position, we do nothing. Alternatively with
a working notion of unpolluted air, however difficult it might be to
achieve ideally, we might still try to assess the potential pollution and
ask: "Can this threat be avoided? How does acting on it depend on
relations of power at the workplace? How might knowledge of the
threat and of alternatives to it enable resistance? How might misrepresentation and obfuscation of the threat thwart resistance?"

Habermas's notions of systematically distorted communication and
the ideal speech situation lead to parallel questions. It is as irrelevant
and ultimately conservative a criticism of Habermas to say that "communication is always imperfect" as it would be a tragically and literally
fatalistic step to resign oneself to exposure to chemical hazards in the
workplace because one might think that "workplaces are never pollution
free."

As Thomas McCarthy has explained, a notion of an ideal speech
situation helps us to give an account of how we might claim a position
to be true or false, right or wrong, in the first place. Lacking that, the
analysis of ideology dissolves into relativist babble. McCarthy writes:

The very act of participating in a discourse, or attempting discursively
to come to an agreement about the truth of a problematic statement
or the correctness of a problematic norm, carries with it the supposition
that a genuine agreement is possible. If we did not suppose that a
justified consensus were possible and could in some way be distinguished from a false consensus, then the very meaning of discourse,
indeed of speech, would be called into question.[18]

The essays that follow, then, are concerned not with the realization
of an ideal speech situation but with specific problems of power and
powerlessness, with ideology, legitimation, and democratic politics.
They are also concerned with social research efforts that will enable
practical analyses of—and political responses to—operative, systemic
distortions of everyday communicative interactions. This concern reflects a pragmatic reformulation of the traditional critique of ideology,
indeed of the specific, concrete social practices and institutionally situated actions by which ideologizing performatively takes place in social
settings and public life. As Trent Schroyer has written, "In every
communicative situation in which a consensus is established under

coercion or under distorted conditions, we are confronting instances of illusory discourses. This is the contemporary critique of ideology."[19]

It is not ideal speech, then, but democratic politics and genuine legitimation that is at stake in a critical theoretic analysis of public life. Concrete critical theoretic research promises to make empirically accessible both the concrete interactions of ordinary life and the contingently opened or foreclosed possibilities of a democratic politics. The following essays are only first steps on this path; they seek to illuminate the intersection of action, structure, and possibility, that intersection where pragmatics and vision may flourish together. Only through such an applied turn, through such labor of applied research, can we develop more powerfully and insightfully the promise of a critical theory of society with a practical, emancipatory intent.

Notes

1. Douglas Kellner and Rick Roderick, "Recent Literature on Critical Theory," *New German Critique* 23 (Spring–Summer 1981).

2. For the most comprehensive review and analysis of Habermas's work, see Thomas McCarthy, *The Critical Theory of Jürgen Habermas* (Cambridge: MIT Press, 1978). The present book focuses on applications of critical theory as reformulated by Habermas. For an introduction to earlier and other formulations, see David Held, *An Introduction to Critical Theory* (Berkeley: University of California Press, 1980). For a more historical treatment, see Martin Jay, *The Dialectical Imagination* (Boston: Little, Brown, 1973). For a collection of earlier writings and commentaries, see Andrew Arato and Eike Gebhart, eds., *The Essential Frankfurt School Reader* (New York: Urizen Books, 1978). A lucid response to the dangers of hypercriticism in the "left-wing samurai tradition" appears in Jeremy Shapiro, "Reply to Miller's Review of Habermas's *Legitimation Crisis*," *Telos* 27 (Spring 1976): 170–176 (the phrase is Shapiro's). See also the cogent volumes by Richard Bernstein: *The Restructuring of Social and Political Theory* (Philadelphia: University of Pennsylvania Press, 1976) and *Beyond Objectivism and Relativism* (Philadelphia: University of Pennsylvania Press, 1983); the collections, *On Critical Theory*, ed. John O'Neill (New York: Seabury Press, 1976) and *Critical Sociology*, ed. J. W. Freiberg (New York: Irvington Publishers, 1979); Fred Dallmayr's *Beyond Dogma and Despair* (Notre Dame: University of Notre Dame Press, 1981; and David Held and John Thompson, eds., *Habermas: Critical Debates* (Cambridge: MIT Press, 1982). Cf. Trent Schroyer's prescient *Critique of Domination* (Boston: Beacon Press, 1973).

3. For an argument comparing earlier formulations of critical theory to Habermas's as potential bases for systematic social research, see Dieter Misgeld's chapter in this book. For related discussions, see the recent reviews of the first volume of Habermas's *Theory of Communicative Action* (Boston: Beacon Press, 1984), including: Dieter Misgeld, "Critical Theory and Sociological Theory," *Philosophy of the Social Sciences* 14 (1984): 97–105; John Thompson, "Rationality and Social Rationalization: An Assessment of Habermas's Theory of Communicative Action," *Sociology* 17 (May 1983); David M. Rasmussen, "Communicative Action and Philosophy," *Philosophy and Social Criticism* 9 (1982); Anthony Giddens, "Reason without Revolution?" *Praxis International* 2 (1982); Thomas McCarthy, "Reflections on Rationalization in the *Theory of Communicative Action*,"

John Forester

Praxis International 4 (1984): 177-191; and compare Albrecht Wellmer, "Reason, Utopia, and the Dialectic of Enlightenment," *Praxis International* 3 (1983).

4. Anticipations of such work may be found, however diffusely, in several fields. In education, see the work of Richard Bates and Peter Watkins of Deakin University, "Towards a Critical Practice of Educational Administration," in T. Sergiovanni and J. Corbally, eds., *Administrative Leadership and Organizational Cultures* (Urbana: University of Illinois Press, 1984), and Michael Pusey, "The Legitimation of State Education Systems," *Australian and New Zealand Journal of Sociology* 16 (1980). Cf. William P. Foster, "Administration and the Crisis in Legitimacy: A Review of Habermasian Thought," *Harvard Educational Review* 50 (1980). In medicine, see Howard Waitzkin, "Medicine, Superstructure, and Micropolitics," *Social Science and Medicine* 13 (1979). In public administration, see Robert B. Denhardt, "Toward a Critical Theory of Public Organization," *Public Administration Review* (Nov.-Dec. 1981): 628-635, and J. Forester, "Questioning and Organizing Attention: Toward a Critical Theory of Planning and Administrative Practice," *Administration and Society* 13 (1981): 161-206. In city and regional planning, see Ray Kemp, "Critical Planning Theory: Review and Critique," in P. Healey et al., eds., *Planning Theory: Prospects for the 1980's* (London: Pergamon, 1982), and John Dyckman, "Reflections on Planning Practice in an Age of Reaction," *Journal of Planning Education and Research* 3 (Summer 1983): 5-12. See also the detailed citations in the chapters that follow.

5. For a probing discussion of the related project of a critical phenomenology, see Dallmayr, *Beyond Dogma and Despair.*

6. See John O'Neill, *Making Sense Together* (New York: Harper and Row, 1974).

7. See Jürgen Habermas, "What Is Universal Pragmatics?" in his *Communication and the Evolution of Society* (Boston: Beacon Press, 1979).

8. John Austin, "A Plea for Excuses," in his *Philosophical Papers* (Oxford: Oxford University Press, 1961), p. 130.

9. The claim here is not that Habermas (or Austin for that matter) already presents an empirically developed phenomenology of performative speech. The claim rather is that Habermas's work makes such critical and empirical sociological analysis possible, as many of the following essays demonstrate. The significance of Habermas's work is not to issue appeals for ideal speech but instead to allow us to assess what social actors do in variously structured situations. Thus, for example, Habermas's *Theory of Communicative Action* does not present an empirically descriptive structural phenomenology; rather it makes such critical research efforts possible in diverse contexts of public, and indeed private, life. For an earlier analysis along these lines, see John Forester, "Toward a Critical-Empirical Framework for the Analysis of Public Policy," *New Political Science* (Summer 1982).

10. See Albrecht Wellmer, "Communications and Emancipation: Reflections on the Linguistic Turn in Critical Theory," in O'Neill, *On Critical Theory.*

11. See Habermas, *The Theory of Communicative Action,* vol. 1: *Reason and the Rationalization of Society* (Boston: Beacon Press, 1984).

12. Habermas, "What Is Universal Pragmatics?"

13. See Schroyer, *Critique.*

14. C. W. Mills, *The Sociological Imagination* (New York: Oxford University Press, 1959).

15. See Anthony Giddens, *Central Problems in Social Theory* (Berkeley: University of California Press, 1979).

Introduction

16. See Jürgen Habermas, *Legitimation Crisis* (Boston: Beacon Press, 1975).

17. See John Forester, "Critical Theory and Organizational Analysis," in Gareth Morgan, ed., *Beyond Method* (Los Angeles: Sage Press, 1983), and "Bounded Rationality and the Politics of Muddling Through," *Public Administration Review* (Jan.-Feb. 1984).

18. See Thomas McCarthy, Translator's Introduction to Habermas, *Legitimation Crisis*, p. xvi.

19. See Schroyer, *Critique*, p. 163.

I

Capitalism with a New Face:
Industrial Policy and
Informational Capitalism

The Dialectic of Deindustrialization: An Essay on Advanced Capitalism

Ben Agger

From Marx to Habermas

This essay traces the evolution within Marxism from the founding thought of Marx to the recent work of second-generation Frankfurt school thinkers like Jürgen Habermas in order to develop a critical perspective on advanced capitalism and, in particular, on the problem of its deindustrialization.[1] I shall argue that the only way for neo-Marxists to address the changing shape of a high-technology capitalism is to abandon significant empirical portions of Marx's original critique of capital while retaining his dialectical method, which vitally links theory and practice. First, the internal transformation of Marxian theory from Marx to Habermas (through Lukács, Korsch, Adorno, Horkheimer, and Marcuse) is examined in order to extract what remains of a valid dialectical approach to capitalism.[2] Second, this essay describes a dialectic of deindustrialization[3] that consists of simultaneous advances and retreats in the processes of class contradiction in this emerging era of high-tech capitalism. Finally, these new (and old) developments within capitalism will be related to the possibilities of emancipatory practice, such as they exist.

This is a project in the tradition of Marx, yet it calls on a reading of Marx's method that views his original critique of political economy as itself historical and requiring revision. It is possible to delineate a Marxian method that essentially separates (albeit dialectically) Marx's immanent critique of the logic of contradiction between capital and labor—the notion that capitalism is torn between the economic progress of capital and the exploitation and alienation of labor—and an empirical theory of the emergence of crises in the real world.[4] Such a separation is necessary lest *Capital* be read not only as an immanent critique (a sketch of an abiding method of dialectical analysis, applicable to later eras) but as a specific empirical theory valid once and for all to describe the irruption of these deep contradictions between capital and labor. *Capital* may be read (against Althusser)[5] as proposing a specific application of dialectical critique to 1860s capitalism in Europe and England and emphatically not as an invariant model of systemic breakdown and emancipatory practice.

Such a reading requires us to accept that capitalism is inherently self-contradictory—with "progress" (profit) in one sector conditioning domination (alienation of labor) in another, thus pointing toward the system's eventual collapse—but to delimit Marx's specific empirical sketch of crisis tendencies in volume 1 of *Capital* as relevant to the entrepreneurial stage of capitalist development in which the welfare state had not yet come to the aid of private capital.

Theorists associated with the Frankfurt school have tried to understand new developments in advanced capitalism both to deflate the authoritarian certainties of the "scientific" Marxists of the Second and Third Internationals and to identify possible agents of socialist transformation.[6] Adorno, Horkheimer, and Marcuse sought individualized transformative agents—even as deep as the instinctual substratum—that could keep alive the memory and dream of liberation.[7]

Marcuse's Freudian Marxism is especially pertinent to this reconstruction of Marxist method.[8] In *Eros and Civilization* (1955) and *An Essay on Liberation* (1969) Marcuse charts the increasing penetration of surplus repression or domination into people's deep sensibilities in a technologically sophisticated corporate era. His argument is that the forces of both external and internal social control mount in this era when workers can otherwise taste the forbidden fruits of their liberation from the regime of scarcity yet are still harnessed to the capitalist division of labor.[9] In his 1969 book, composed during the heyday of the U.S. New Left and counterculture, Marcuse identified a new vehicle of socialist transformation in the "new sensibilities" of individuals who refuse to separate socialist process and product, choosing instead to live as best they can in qualitatively different ways in the here-and-now.[10] By 1973 Marcuse was castigating the New Left for both its rejection of structural theorizing and its spontaneity (leading to irrationalism and authoritarianism),[11] yet his notion of initially individualized modes of rebellion that form a bridge of sorts between private consciousness and full-blown class struggle remains one of the most powerful modifications of Marx's original dialectical method. It is clear that Marcuse does not abandon the whole imagery of nonauthoritarian socialism but rather embeds it in the daily struggles of people and groups who in diverse and eclectic ways are attempting to forge liberation in their immediate lifeworlds, perhaps initially oblivious to the solemnities of the *Manifesto* and *Capital*.[12]

This recalls some of the sentiments expressed in Marx's 1844 manuscripts, where he described the blending of human nature and external nature through creative praxis as a socialist aim. The Frankfurt thinkers returned to the Marx of 1844 to create a twentieth-century agenda of aesthetic politics that projects the possibility of simultaneously self-creative and productive work.[13] Yet from within the Frankfurt tradition Jürgen Habermas in *Knowledge and Human Interests* (1968) challenged what he took to be the original Frankfurt school's indulgence in a vocabulary of liberation that he regards as excessively romantic.[14] Habermas, while certainly not a mechanical Marxist (and indeed the inspiration of much of what is to follow in this essay), feels that Marcuse, Horkheimer, and Adorno went too far in resurrecting the 1844 imagery of creative work, overreacting to the scientism and determinism of the Second International's brand of Marxism.[15]

Habermas in effect reformulates the Marxist critique of ideology as a practical-pragmatic critique of all systematically distorted communications, including asymmetrical conversations and all social relations characterized by the elite monopoly of symbolic and system-steering codes. His argument takes its most systematic form in *The Theory of Communicative Action* (1981; English translation of volume 1, 1984). He believes that capitalism can be shaken to its foundation only if the realm of language and communication is reconstructed so that laypeople share more democratically in the process of system guidance. Habermas's communication theory of society uses the model of discourse—argument governed not by control motives (such as browbeating) but by the search for consensus—as his imagery of substantive socialism or what he calls "rationality." He contends that the ideal speech situation can inform all future social relations in the sense that it represents a process of undistorted speech and action in which every interlocutor shares roughly equal "dialogue chances."[16]

Ben Agger

It is a misreading of Habermas to suppose that he restricts emancipatory projects to the realm of talk, regressing behind Marx to John Stuart Mill. He suggests, rather, that domination has to be reconceptualized (since Marx and the evolution of advanced capitalism) as involving not only economic deprivation but also all distortions of what Marx earlier called the "relations of production." Habermas tries to reenergize the silenced proletariat by appealing to its innate (but currently distorted) competence in self-determining thought and action. Thus his communication theory of society implies counterhegemonic strategies that attempt to uncover and organize our potential for mastering our productive infrastructure and the social relations that underpin them.

In this sense Habermas revises Marx's original critique of bourgeois political economy and transforms it into a critique of all distorted performances in language (which I would call a "socially structured silence"). He broadens Marx's critique of political economy, based on Adam Smith and David Ricardo's original sketch of the laws of an open economic marketplace, into a critique of the technocratic guidance of a complex socioeconomic system, based in large measure on the monopoly not only of capital but also of information and of dialogue chances. In this way Habermas supplements the original critique of political economy with a critique of technocratic guidance, but he does not thereby transcend original Marxism and its emancipatory aims. His goal is still to liberate labor (conceived of as a silenced dialogue partner) from domination.

Thus the new Marxism takes Marx's original critique of political economy as its point of departure. It goes beyond him, however, by suggesting that the monopoly of capital is now reinforced (and occluded) by the monopoly of information and dialogue chances.[17] The aim of the new Marxism from Lukács to Marcuse and Habermas is still to liberate labor from domination, although utopian metaphors and images have significantly changed since Marx. Marcuse's "rationality of gratification" and Habermas's "discourse" flesh out Marx's image of socialism in culturally and historically more relevant terms in order to project qualitative social change in meaningful, nonthreatening ways.

A High-Tech Capitalism?

The recent work of Habermas in particular underlies much of what is to follow in the way of a concrete discussion of the dilemmas of

The Dialectic of Deindustrialization

deindustrialization and its "high-tech" (or "Atari") solution. I draw from him an overall perspective on the displacement of contradictions from the realm of economic class struggle to new socioideological and cultural spheres. Habermas, more explicitly than any other neo-Marxist to date, has extended and deepened Marx's original critique of political economy by applying it to new topics unexamined by original Marxism (either because they were unforeseen or because they simply did not fit Marx's preoccupations with the economic contradictions of early market capitalism). Habermas, beginning in *Legitimation Crisis* (1973), suggests that the contradictions have been displaced from the economy pure and simple and now extend into every sphere of public and private life.[18] He offers a systems-analytic Marxism that helps us bridge between the original political-economic concerns of Marx in *Capital*, on the one hand, and the Freudian Marxism of Marcuse on the other. Habermas's perspective is important because he relates the systemic level of structural contradictions to the microscopic analysis of the lifeworld in a way that helps to explain blockages en route to transformative thought and action.

Habermas also offers an important critique of technology and science as ideology, a central component of my discussion of the contradictions of an Atari capitalism.[19] He suggests that the laissez-faire legitimation of earlier market capitalism has been largely replaced by the scientific-technocratic legitimation that cedes all system-steering authority to an elite of systems managers. Habermas contends that this Atari ideology of impenetrable high technology is even more impervious to radical critique than, earlier, religion and market economic theory because science and technology seem to banish the realm of political values and instead reduce all decision making to pragmatic instrumentality. Habermas contends that this impervious scientific-technical worldview functions as ideology by illegitimately conflating the realms of substantive communication and self-reflection (the proper preserve of informed thought and talk about qualitative values) on the one hand and the realm of technical action on the other. This in effect ensures that system-serving behavior is perpetuated in that we lose our capacity to distinguish among ultimate social values, an exercise banished by positivists since Wittgenstein's *Tractatus* as, literally, non-sense.

This new Marxism, via Habermas, may be turned to the tasks of analyzing the present systemic problem of deindustrialization and then suggesting possible socialist and nonsocialist responses. In particular the mythos of high technology can be challenged both within and outside of Marxism by suggesting a host of new contradictions that a high-tech capitalism will confront in the years just ahead. The notion of deindustrialization has suddenly become prevalent in economic analysis, as well as in the media, pointing to a number of phenomena: the shift in population from northeastern U.S. cities to the sunbelt states; massive unemployment in traditional heavy industries like automobiles and steel; increasing suburbanization, only partly counteracted by urban gentrification on the part of upper-middle-class young professionals; and the aging of the U.S. population, creating a heavy burden on the social security and welfare systems.

In this context, this essay will now examine the dominant technocratic response to deindustrialization and then suggest several contradictions that this response is likely to engender. This analysis will be in the spirit of the new Marxism in the sense that it will examine the shifting constellation of forces in both the base and superstructure that simultaneously hamper emancipatory projects and may trigger subterranean forces of resistance as well.

Three distinctive crises occur increasingly in an advanced capitalism pinched by energy shortage, ecological disruption, and uneven regional development, both domestic and international. The first crisis is the increasing fragmentation of the work force along the axes of skill, unionization, and work style. Flowing from the first, the second crisis is in the increasing personalization of domination as economic pressures and dissatisfactions are introjected into the realm of the personal and the household, seen especially in the increasing subjugation of women. The third crisis is the deepening of the mythos of scientism and technology as we increasingly, if ultimately unwillingly, hand over the reins of power to technical elites, who we (must) trust to keep us off the shoals of economic crisis. Let me address these in turn.

The phenomenon of the dual labor market is often described in terms of a growing gap in skill, income, work style, and occupational prestige between white- and blue-collar workers.[20] The growth of a so-called new working class or new middle class is addressed by both Marxists and Weberian sociologists of work. The former write in terms of a labor aristocracy (Engels's and Lenin's term for internal stratification of the proletariat); the latter speak about the increasing structuration and differentiation of the work force in advanced industrial society.[21] But an important new realm of labor has emerged over the past twenty years comprised essentially of deskilled, low-income, nonunionized and status-poor female pink-collar workers largely found in the service sector of the economy (they are waitresses, maids, keypunch operators, bank tellers). There is now increasingly a tripartite division in the work force along these dimensions of income, work style, unionization, and status. This division can be described in the classic terms of the color of collar: white collar denotes a largely male professional work force with high income and high status; blue collar denotes a largely male unionized manual work force with relatively high income but somewhat lower occupational prestige; and pink collar refers to the characteristics of largely female labor in the deskilled, low-income service sector not protected by unionization.

This analysis of the increasing fragmentation and stratification of the proletariat in high-tech capitalism stems from Harry Braverman's *Labor and Monopoly Capital* (1974).[22] He updates Marx's categories of labor exploitation in a concrete analysis of the modern work force. He suggests that the seeming "embourgeoisement" of the proletariat—the rise of a middle-class mass culture, with higher material standard of living for most in the urban United States—is basically a myth. He argues that certain sectors of the proletariat are more exploited than ever, notably in terms of technological deskilling, unemployment, and lack of unionization. Braverman did not address directly enough the increasingly sexual-political lines drawn between the male white- and blue-collar fractions of the working class and the largely female pink-collar fraction. Braverman's analysis can be extended to show that the rise of a high-tech capitalism in response to the deindustrialization of traditional heavy industry, particularly in the U.S. Northeast, is not likely to bring either the everlasting cornucopia of consumerism or the "pacification" of labor as workers turn from the sweaty din of the industrial shop floor to the creative and antiseptic confines of the computer labs. Instead elite workers are likely to benefit disproportionately, while a whole new cadre of largely pink-collar manual and service workers picks up the slack, as deskilled and economically exploited as ever.

High technology will not upgrade labor in general but only those fractions of labor that stand to gain from the increasing subjugation, exploitation, and deskilling of other larger fractions of labor. These lines are particularly drawn around the issue of gender, as socialist feminists point out. Thus, high-tech capitalism is likely to deepen extant divisions between sex classes as it increasingly fragments the proletariat and creates almost a quasi-managerial class of privileged and relatively powerful professional and technical workers.

It is a mistake to view the embourgeoisement and upgrading of the work force in a monolithic way. In capitalism there is always a trade-off of power and privilege with respect to class formations; some gain where others lose. And those who gain are always a small elite. The people who run computer companies are no less entrepreneurial and narrowly self-interested than the mill owners in Victorian England. It is false to suppose that the computerization of industry, to the extent that it is happening, is a positive augur of a benign postindustrial socialism, except in the dialectical sense that it brings with it new contradictions—such as sex and class struggle—that might one day sound the death-knell of capitalism. High-tech capitalism only sinks the contradictions deeper into the economic and emotional soil of the proletariat.

The second crisis, the increasing personalization and domestication of domination, clearly stems from the growing fragmentation and stratification of the working class. To the extent that women workers are increasingly degraded (earning only about 60 percent of U.S. male workers) and deskilled, tensions between the sexes will rise. In a precarious transition between traditional heavy industry and high technology, with all sorts of interim dislocations such as redundancy and technological unemployment, economic vicissitudes will increase the scapegoating of sexual-political minorities, particularly in the sphere of domesticity. As blue-collar males are thrown out of work, they will bring their resentment home with them and take it out on wives and children who symbolize for them a "feared-because-desired sexual-political Other."[23] Women take the brunt of the quite literal beating as working-class men who come upon hard times mistakenly blame the women's movement (and not transitional capitalism) for their own problems.

Gays and ethnic and racial minorities as well will be increasingly victimized as working-class men join in the collective resentment of allegedly privileged minorities. All this reflects the traditional displacement of rage onto even weaker Others, carefully documented in the study of the authoritarian personality in the late 1940s by Adorno and his colleagues to explain the dynamics of fascist *ressentiment.*[24] In capitalism economic misfortunes among the proletariat are worked through at the expense of even lower and less powerful groups, especially—and this is what is so new and contemporary as an explicit issue—in the realm of domesticity. Ku Klux Klan nightriding is now overshadowed by wife battering as a gesture of rage and desublimation.

This second crisis of high-tech capitalism is addressed in Habermas's recent notion of the colonization of the lifeworld, following from his analysis of system-lifeworld relations and the various pathologies that result from them.[25] He suggests that advanced capitalism founders to the extent that systemic imperatives of domination penetrate too deeply into the pretheoretical realm of lived experience. This is self-contradictory, ultimately blocking the system's own vitality and efficiency, in that the system vitally requires a relatively unencumbered lifeworld as a source of personal creativity and innovativeness. Habermas in this regard follows Paul Piccone's important analysis of "artificial negativity," a major position piece of the *Telos* group.[26] Piccone suggests that the system requires a calculated loosening of the bonds of what Adorno earlier called "total administration" and Marcuse "one-dimensionality" in order to guarantee a supply of economic risk taking and a safety valve for otherwise implosive deviance. Habermas suggests that it is ultimately irrational for the system to colonize the lifeworld if that colonization enforces a false (because impossible) identity between system and lived experience. The system requires nonidentity—incomplete socialization, escape valves for implosive deviance, nonconformity—so that the shell of bondage of capitalism does not become intolerably confining.

In this sense a Habermasian analysis of deindustrialization might suggest that the frightening domestication of sexual and political violence will be ultimately dysfunctional because it allows systemic contradictions to be displaced into the realm of already threatened privacy. If men and women cannot maintain a semblance of civil relations, drawing some succor either from the bourgeois nuclear family ("haven in a heartless world") or from more progressive domestic forms, the already oppressive system will wear them down.[27] Advanced capitalism, Habermas would suggest, requires artificial negativity in order to allow individuals some reprieve from an increasingly administered (or "colonized") work existence.

As both Marcuse and Habermas prefigured in their work in the late 1960s, the third crisis of high-tech capitalism is the deepening of the myth of science and technology. Elites must legitimate their mo-

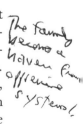

nopoly of system-administering privileges, notably through a theory of problem solving that cedes all conversational and symbolic rights to an allegedly talented technocratic minority. In mainstream sociology, the classic 1945 Davis-Moore theory of the inevitability of stratification is one early example of this deepened scientific-technical mythos. Although Davis and Moore suggested that scarce "merit" must be differentially rewarded, they ignored the obvious questions about the social and economic roots of the definition of merit in a given historical and cultural context.[28]

Habermas in his writings on science and technology as ideology as well as in his more recent writings on communication theory[29] argues that the early market-capitalist ideology of microeconomic laws of supply and demand gradually gives way to laws of the technocratic monopoly of dialogue chances in late capitalism. The system-steering prerogatives of a scientific-technical-economic-political elite are legitimated from the origins of western sociology in Durkheim and Weber through the structural functionalism of Parsons in terms of the "necessity" of technocratic guidance of a complex social and economic system. This is to confuse the ubiquity of differentiation (all specialization, in terms of Durkheim's concept of the division of labor) with the alleged necessity of stratification (in Weber and Marx's sense, the differential distribution of rewards, be they power, prestige, or wealth). This confusion is at the heart of late capitalist ideology rooted in the notion of the necessity of technocratic expertise, unchallenged by the common sense of what Habermas calls the lifeworld (in this regard borrowing from the tradition of critical phenomenology).

Habermas's communication theory thus is a modern version of original Marxism that supplements Marx's critique of the alienation of labor with an analysis of technocratic self-legitimation through unchallenged science and technical guidance. Science and technology function as ideological props of a social system that requires masses to cede all system-steering rights to an elite. Habermas suggests that domination in late capitalism occurs when the rationality of technique (techne) invades the domain of communicative action, replacing the motive of consensus formation, which he contends is the implicit intent of every speech act, with the motive of sheer control. Habermas in effect wants to secure an emancipatory impulse in the grounded structure of speech itself in order to replace the disappointed philosophy of history embraced initially by Horkheimer and Adorno in the 1930s, only to erode into a dismal "negative dialectics" during the post–World War II era of reconstruction.[30] He argues that communication theory helps to explain, simultaneously, the colonization of the lifeworld by systemic imperatives (notably via the media of money and power, the common currencies of sheer control and abstraction), involving the crisis of the domestication of domination, and a guarded optimism about the inherent purpose of consensus formation contained in the structure of speech itself, suggesting a vital basis of counterhegemony that he feels critical theory has lacked since Lukács.

High-tech capitalism is particularly likely to deepen the mythos of science and technology as specialists exude the mystical and esoteric talents of the initiated. Most people recognize that high technology requires a high science that is virtually impenetrable by the practical reasoning of everyday life. Science and technology achieve interface in the high-powered computer, from which ordinary knowledge is excluded. Trends in higher education reflect this development as undergraduates are increasingly taught that computer literacy is quickly becoming as important as the old literacy of reading and writing, and university administrators are rapidly retooling classical liberal arts curricula into curricula heavily weighted in favor of computer science, economics, and engineering.

This shift in educational priorities at both elementary and university levels reinforces the unquestioned faith in scientific and technical expertise. A more subtle effect is to strip the curricula of the potentially critical and subversive knowledge of the humanities and social sciences. While much of this curriculum change is done in the name of financial expediency (falling enrollments and the like), many teachers recognize that as an excuse by administrators and curriculum planners who favor the increasing scientization of education and use economic shortfall only as an excuse to rid the schools and universities of the radicals of the 1960s.

In this climate, including widespread industrial layoffs and economic stagnation, it is no wonder that the mythos of high technology has such a galvanizing appeal. The collapse of the industrial infrastructure of New York, Pennsylvania, Michigan, and Ohio is met with renewed optimism about the various silicon valleys seemingly rising to take their place, fueling public faith in science and technology and giving the mandarins of high technology even more unchallenged power than the fathers of the Enlightenment bestowed on the doyens of

Ben Agger

natural science in the eighteenth and nineteenth centuries. In this climate, against both liberal and orthodox-Marxist appraisals of the Frankfurt school's critique of science—particularly as captured in Horkheimer and Adorno's *Dialectic of Enlightenment*—the critique of bourgeois scientism and technocracy is more than ever on the agenda, particularly in this era of high technology and the prevailing optimism about the technological fix.[31]

The Frankfurt position, now as before, is that faith in science and technology reinforces passive acquiescence to a status quo that is experienced not critically but merely commonsensically, without mediation by overarching categories of qualitative judgment such as justice, truth, and beauty. Faith in high technology reinforces the collapse of what Marcuse in 1964 called the first and second dimensions of experience: the mundane level of Hegel's *Verstand* (everyday understanding, often governed by the technical interest in control) and the transcendent level of *Vernunft* (objective reason, capable of defining the nature of truth, justice, and beauty and unafraid to challenge the relativizing common sense of a one-dimensional society).[32]

High-tech capitalism rests on a further bifurcation of knowledge, with technical specialists at the top of the corporate state usurping even more of the dialogue chances of laypeople, while giving them the illusion of technological and political-economic mastery by offering them home computers. The computerization of education is likely to have the effect of further legitimating the unchallenged system-steering authority of a scientific and technical elite as it works to convince the powerless that they too can have access to the tools and codes of power by enrolling in computer science courses and by using home computers. This pseudo-democratization of advanced technology goes hand in hand with the pseudo-democracy of representative democracy (with periodic mass elections replacing the direct democracy of the Athenian *polis* and the New England town meeting).

In this sense the pseudo-democratization of computer skills and technology reinforces a one-dimensionality of thought and behavior, while in earlier times people experienced a certain critical distance from the esoteric symbolic codes and practices of economic elites. As Adorno and Horkheimer argued in the 1940s, the dialectic of enlightenment works so that superficial advances in general enlightenment (such as the appropriation of home computers and the computerization of college curricula) really betoken knowledge's regression. The more *why does this necessarily follow!*

we rely on canned programs, especially in the realm of domestic entertainment, the less we can think, speak, and write critically about social totality. There may be an inverse relationship between computer knowledge on the level of passive reliance on canned entertainment and a critical literacy that allows us to transcend the pregiven categories of possible knowledge that insinuate themselves into the languages of bytes, text editing, and software. These subtle categories of possible experience are deeply corrosive of our critical sensibilities for we are plugged into machines and mechanical intelligence in a way that reduces us to passivity in our dialogue with microcomputers. The ultimate banalization of this nondialogic relationship is the notion that some computers are user friendly, responding to commands with mechanical languages and convivial nonthreatening graphics and protocols.

The high-tech solution to deindustrialization and uneven regional development in the United States will engender these three original types of class contradiction, unforeseen by Marx. This analysis assumes that the stewards of advanced capitalism can successfully circumvent the increasingly obvious roadblocks that litter the path of gradualist economic expansion. It is clear to most enlightened liberal and conservative economists that the neoconservative administrative strategies of Ronald Reagan and Margaret Thatcher accelerate the tendencies toward serious class confrontation. These strategies reverse the cosmetic but system-serving Robin Hood mechanisms of the Keynesian welfare state that are desperately required in a system that otherwise would experience too much unemployment and thus underconsumption.[33] Reaganomics forgets the lessons taught by Keynes and implemented by every U.S. president since Franklin Roosevelt. Reagan dismantles the safety nets of the U.S. welfare state precisely when they are needed most in order to protect the economic system against both insurrection and starvation.

The high-tech strategy of capitalist survival depends on the transcendence of the very short-term, self-interested administrative strategies of Reagan and Thatcher; instead it substitutes a longer-term incrementalism designed to shore up the U.S. economy's position in the world market (especially in regard to Japan and West Germany). High-tech capitalism transcends the desperation of Reagan and his ilk; it preserves his ultimate aim to save capitalism (the desideratum of all welfare state politicians since Roosevelt), yet it more fundamentally

Ben Agger

attacks the technological irrationalities that underlie the character of U.S. industry, particularly in the urban Northeast.

It may be optimistic, even from the point of view of welfare state liberals, to suppose that the technocratic stewards of the U.S. economy and polity will be able to surmount the desperate tug of war of Reaganomics and its inevitable backlash among the poor and minorities.[34] High-tech capitalism is the best-case alternative to Reaganomics, and it will evolve only if the "executive committee of the bourgeoisie" can temper its immediate class interest and instead recognize its longer-term interest in protecting the world system of threatened capitalism.

The Dialectic of Deindustrialization: Theory, Practice, Research

High-tech capitalism brings a general diminution of collective intelligence as it reinforces the hegemony of state-managed capitalism. It may also intensify struggles within the proletariat among class fractions, notably between ethnic and sexual-political minorities on the one hand and patriarchal males on the other. In addition high-tech capitalism links the realms of work and domesticity, giving us even less space in which to restore ourselves beyond the imperatives of a totally administered world. Thus the process of high-tech reindustrialization is likely to deepen the hegemony of domination.

Yet at the same time a new Marxism inspired largely by Habermas allows us to suggest the emergence of new manifest crises on the basis of this structural evolution, which never ceases as long as deep class contradictions exist at the base of a private enterprise society. The intensification of sexual-political persecution, the splitting of the working class into a dual labor market, and the growing computerization of experience and language might have the unintended consequences of creating new avenues and agents of radical social change, notably (but not exclusively) from within the women's movement.

The most pertinent struggles in this emerging high-tech capitalism will take place on three levels: pink-collar service work, domesticity, and higher education. As increasing numbers of women enter the labor force and find work that is menial, deskilled, and underpaid, the potential grows for socialist-feminist struggle within the ranks of organized labor. Similarly as sexual-political persecution grows (in direct response to the transitional agonies of industrial age capitalism, including widespread male unemployment), there may be increasing struggle on the part of women to take control of the social relations of reproduction and to overcome traditional gender roles in the family. Finally the computerization of higher education might have the effect of prompting educators and students to reevaluate the demise of liberal arts curricula and perhaps even to resist the further linkage of academic production with the requirements of political economy and ideological occlusion. On this last front the struggle by left-wing social scientists to resist the reduction of academic productivity to the system-serving terms of conventionally controlled scholarship (where knowledge is evaluated only in terms of its instrumental relevance) is an example of this mounting resistance.

In this sense the creation of new empirical theory by Western Marxists will be facilitated by the convergence of neo-Marxian political economy and its critique of ideology with the theoretical thrust of socialist feminism, alerting us to some of the emerging contradictions: pink-collar alienation, dual labor market, and sex-political persecution. Above all socialist feminism links the personal and political in a way that allows us to understand the phenomenon of deindustrialization and reindustrialization in concrete terms, notably in regard to the dialectical bond between what happens in (and in between) the realms of work and domesticity. If orthodox Marxism has erred, it has erred most fatally by reducing the relation between work and home to the rigid categories of Engels's *The Origins of the Family*. Socialist feminism alerts us to the important interchange between the contradictions of the workplace (themselves constantly evolving) and their displacement in the realm of domesticity, suggesting liberatory strategies located in both personal and public life. After all, as Adorno recognized, in high-tech capitalism there is no such thing as private life.

What socialist feminism ultimately lacks, and what this essay has attempted to provide, is the dialectic. Socialist feminism is Marxism without the dialectic, a descriptive and moral account of the relationship between alienation "out there" (in capitalist political economy and its social relations of production) and alienation "in here" (the social relations of reproduction in patriarchal society). Western Marxism is Marxism plus socialist feminism, retrieving its important vision of a reconstructed daily life in the context of its analysis of the vicissitudes of advanced capitalism in an age of technological advancement and contraction.

Habermas's recent version of Marxism is a powerful complementary source of dialectical vision in this analysis of deindustrialization, notably in the way Habermas has understood system-lifeworld penetration or what I have called the relationship between the public and the personal. Habermas, like Piccone in another context, points to the inherently self-limiting nature of the colonization and rationalization of the lifeworld in high-tech capitalism, a kind of impervious second dimension that resists complete co-optation and administration.[35] Habermas locates this imperviousness to complete heteronomy in the nonidentity of system and lifeworld, indeed in the social system's requirement of innovative, risk-taking subjectivity formed through the dialogic relations of family, school, and culture. The social system cannot dispense with this inviolate zone in which communicative action takes place lest it lose its dynamism, however irrational and self-contradictory in the long term. For example, the system cannot dispense with the human activity of computer programming, a thoroughly value-laden task that must be carried out according to a substantive rationality of qualitative choice.

The social system in its own terms cannot be self-regenerating; human subjectivity must be vestigially free in order to make systemic on-course corrections (the fine-tuning measures of technocratic incrementalism). A society of robots does not serve the interests of capital, even though the logic of capital (and here all Marxists would agree) tends toward ever-increasing robotization (reification, alienation, domination, and so forth). This suggests inherent dialectical resistance contained in the very activity of dialogue itself, as Habermas has suggested. Short of the full eclipse of reason, our resistance to the artificial intelligence of canned programs is a liberatory act, as are attempts to protect our various lifeworlds (family, school, culture) from rationalization.

This suggests a research program for Habermas-generation critical theory that sheds the quietism of Adorno's pessimistic philosophy of history but refuses to repeat Marx in literal terms. Such research would attempt to locate the weakest links in computer age capitalism as a way of amplifying the possibility and actuality of counterhegemonic activity. If Habermas is right, this counterhegemony will probably spring from attempts to resist the further colonization of lifeworlds in the struggle to secure and protect communicative rationality (as well as to correct the various asymmetries of our lifeworlds). In defiance of system-steering elites who infiltrate and manipulate the lifeworlds of cultural reproduction, education, and family, people will attempt to articulate what has remained unspoken: the human nature of our institutions and thus their susceptibility to reform.

By tracing all institutional objectifications back to their pretheoretical grounds in the lifeworld, we demonstrate the possibility of spontaneous resistances that can be mounted against the lifeworld's further colonization. In showing that people do try to create livable social spaces in which to escape from systemic rationalization and colonization, we can buttress the original Marxian optimism about piercing bourgeois hegemony. A Habermasian research program would attempt to document the instances where people initiate microscopic social change in defiance of the categorical imperative of high-tech capitalism. If in this era of despair such "evidence" is scarce, then critical theory can at least confirm Adorno's notion that the "whole is untrue" without utterly abandoning hope that one day the tide may turn.

Notes

1. For a definitive statement of the problem of deindustrialization from the point of view of a critique of the immanent assumptions of bourgeois economic theory, see Barry Bluestone and Bennett Harrison, *The Deindustrialization of America* (New York: Basic Books, 1982).

2. For a reconstruction of this internal transformation of Marxism, see my *Western Marxism: An Introduction* (Santa Monica: Goodyear, 1979). Also see my "Marcuse and Habermas on New Science," *Polity* 9 (winter 1976): 151–181; and Jürgen Habermas, *Toward a Rational Society* (Boston: Beacon Press, 1970), esp. pp. 81–122.

3. See my "Atari Capitalism: Interpreting the Depression and Its Solutions," *Dialectical Anthropology*, forthcoming.

4. See my *Western Marxism*, esp. chap. 1, and also my "Marxism 'or' the Frankfurt School?" *Philosophy of the Social Sciences* 13 (1983): 347–365.

5. See Louis Althusser, *For Marx* (London: Allen Lane, 1969); also see John O'Neill, *For Marx against Althusser* (Washington, D.C.: University Press of America, 1983).

6. See Georg Lukács, *History and Class Consciousness* (Cambridge: MIT Press, 1971); and Karl Korsch, *Marxism and Philosophy* (New York: Monthly Review Press, 1970). Also see Herbert Marcuse, *Eros and Civilization* (New York: Vintage, 1955); Theodor Adorno, *Negative Dialectics* (New York: Seabury, 1973); and Max Horkheimer and Theodor W. Adorno, *Dialectic of Enlightenment* (New York: Herder and Herder, 1972). Finally, see Robert Antonio, "The Origin, Development and Contemporary Status of Critical Theory," *Sociological Quarterly* 24 (summer 1983): 325–351.

7. See my *Western Marxism*, esp. chap. 6.

Ben Agger

8. See my "Marcuse's Freudian Marxism," *Dialectical Anthropology* 6 (1982): 319–336.

9. See Herbert Marcuse, *An Essay on Liberation* (Boston: Beacon Press, 1969).

10. Ibid., especially the chapter on "The New Sensibility." Marcuse's stress on the political nature of subjectivity shows a remarkable convergence with the contention of both radical and socialist feminists that "the personal is political"; see Alison Jaggar, *Feminist Politics and Human Nature* (Totowa, N.J.: Rowman and Littlefield, 1983).

11. See Herbert Marcuse, *Counterrevolution and Revolt* (Boston: Beacon Press, 1973).

12. See Marcuse, *Eros and Civilization*, esp. pp. 204–206.

13. See my "Marcuse's Aesthetic Politics: Ideology-Critique and Socialist Ontology," *Dialectical Anthropology*, forthcoming.

14. See Jürgen Habermas, *Knowledge and Human Interests* (Boston: Beacon Press, 1971), esp. pp. 32–33.

15. See Jürgen Habermas, *Communication and the Evolution of Society* (Boston: Beacon Press, 1979).

16. See my "A Critical Theory of Dialogue," *Humanities in Society* 4, no. 1 (fall 1981): 7–30.

17. See Claus Mueller, *The Politics of Communication* (New York: Oxford University Press, 1973).

18. See Jürgen Habermas, *Legitimation Crisis* (Boston: Beacon Press, 1975).

19. See Habermas, *Toward a Rational Society*, pp. 81–122.

20. See E. M. Beck, P. M. Horan, and C. M. Tolbert, "Stratification in a Dual Economy: A Sectoral Model of Earnings Determination," *American Sociological Review* 43 (1978): 704–720.

21. See Anthony Giddens, *The Class-Structure of the Advanced Societies* (London: Hutchinson, 1973).

22. See Harry Braverman, *Labor and Monopoly Capital* (New York: Monthly Review Press, 1974).

23. See my "The Dialectic of Desire: The Holocaust, Monopoly Capitalism and Radical Anamnesis," *Dialectical Anthropology* 8, nos. 1–2 (1983): 75–86.

24. See T. W. Adorno et al., *The Authoritarian Personality* (New York: Harper and Brothers, 1950).

25. See Jürgen Habermas, *Theorie des kommunikativen Handelns*, 2 vols. (Frankfurt am Main: Suhrkamp, 1981). An English translation of the first volume has been published: *The Theory of Communicative Action*, volume 1: *Reason and the Rationalization of Society* (Boston: Beacon Press, 1984). See also the useful commentary by Raymond Morrow, "Habermas and Rationalization, Reification, and the Colonization of the Life-World" (paper presented at a joint session of the Canadian Association of Sociology and Anthropology and the International Sociological Research Committee on Alienation Theory and Research, Vancouver, June 1983).

26. See Paul Piccone, "Beyond Identity Theory," in John O'Neill, ed., *On Critical Theory* (New York: Seabury, 1976), and his "The Crisis of One-Dimensionality," *Telos* 35 (1978): 43–54.

27. See Christopher Lasch, *Haven in a Heartless World* (New York: Norton, 1978).

28. See Kingsley Davis and W. E. Moore, "Some Principles of Stratification," *American Sociological Review* 10 (1945): 242–247.

29. See Habermas, *Communication and the Evolution of Society*.

30. See "The Dialectics of Rationalization: An Interview with Jürgen Habermas," *Telos* 49 (1981): 5–31.

31. See William Leiss, *The Domination of Nature* (New York: Braziller, 1972).

32. See *Hegel: Texts and Commentary*, trans. and ed. Walter Kaufmann (Garden City, N.Y.: Doubleday, 1966).

33. See John Kenneth Galbraith, *The New Industrial State* (Boston: Houghton Mifflin, 1967).

34. See, for example, John Rawls, *A Theory of Justice* (Cambridge: Harvard University Press, 1971).

35. For the development of this concept of a second dimension along which critical thought and action take place, see my "Marcuse's Freudian Marxism," esp. pp. 321–322.

Critical Theory, the Informational Revolution, and an Ecological Path to Modernity

Timothy W. Luke and
Stephen K. White

In *Legitimation Crisis*, Jürgen Habermas pointed out how the growth imperatives of advanced capitalism are pressing past the ultimate limits of nature's ecological equilibria, threatening a global environmental crisis that could halt the continuing development of modern society.[1] Although he has not systematically explored these ecological themes, his recent analysis of the "pathologies" of modernity throws new light on the critical theoretical stance of radical ecologists who are working to counter the ecological crisis in the United States.[2] Like Habermas those thinkers are troubled by the dominance of instrumental reason over aesthetic and moral consciousness within advanced capitalist societies. In response the radical ecologists are developing new theories and practices, which emphasize a new balance between humans and nature, as well as the participatory empowerment of producers and citizens. These beginnings constitute concrete guideposts for an alternative future where instrumental reason would be less imperial and the basic structure of society would be more in accord with the criteria of democratic legitimacy Habermas has derived from his communicative ethics.

Any increased concern for the environment and human ecology within it, however, must recognize that contemporary advanced capitalism has not alleviated the threat of environmental disaster. On the contrary it constantly aggravates this threat. In their unending campaign to manage their way out of the economic, legitimation, and motivation problems intrinsic to advanced capitalism, the professional experts and political leaders now steering the advanced capitalist economies are elaborating modernity's core logic of commodification and instrumental reason in radically new ways. These structural innovations are beginning to reconstitute *industrial* capitalism as *informational* capitalism, as the generation, management, and distribution of information has started overshadowing the manufacture of goods in the advanced capitalist centers of Western Europe, the United States, and Japan.[3]

Although Habermas has not specifically taken account of this informational revolution, his analyses of the colonization of the lifeworld and the dominance of technical reason in contemporary capitalism provide a useful conceptual perspective to understand this macrosocial transformation better. More specifically Habermas offers a theoretical framework that links the advances of this complex informational revolution with the aggravation of the ecological crisis as a pathological model of modernity. At the same time, his communicative ethics, when allied with the insights of radical ecology, can also help project the tentative outlines of an alternative model of modernity, which is both ecologically sound and more democratic.

First, we will introduce Habermas's notion of communicative ethics, as well as his theory of modernity and contemporary capitalism. This introduction will set the stage for our supplementary but more concrete analysis, which will focus specifically on three interrelated themes: the new characteristics of informational capitalism, how this informational revolution colonizes the everyday lifeworld, and how the values and practices of radical ecology constitute potential forces for turning informational society down a path of ecological modernity.

Before turning to Habermas's framework, it is important to begin by emphasizing a theoretical point often overlooked by those interested in critical social and political analysis. Habermas's thought frequently is attacked as being too abstract or remote from what should be the concrete concerns of a critical theory. This criticism, however, fails to appreciate the necessarily differentiated character of the theoretical tasks faced by any social theory. A critical theory, which is both philosophically defensible and empirically based, must pursue its traditional goals in two different but complementary dimensions: the Kantian—or better, the quasi-Kantian—and the Hegelian-Marxian.

By quasi-Kantian analysis we mean systematic efforts to develop the basic conceptual components of a model of man, especially the concepts of action and rationality.[4] Theoretical work done in this di-

Timothy W. Luke and Stephen K. White

mension cannot be ignored since every social and political theory will necessarily imply some model of man.[5] The question, then, is how self-consciously this model will be articulated. Habermas, more than any other critical theorist, has pursued this task in a highly systematic fashion, attempting to sketch a model of man that constitutes an alternative to the "possessive individualist" model,[6] which predominates in mainstream social and political theory. His attempts to reconstruct the "communicative competence" of modern man around the concepts of "communicative action" and "communicative rationality" have led him to develop distinctive approaches to democratic legitimacy and the problem of rationalization and modernity.

Although these approaches open up broad new moral-political and theoretical foundations for critical theory, they are inadequate unless supplemented by more substantive analyses of the conflictual character of contemporary capitalism, the constraints it faces in reproducing itself, the specific forms of class ideology and contradiction it generates, and the types of social movements and values that offer genuine alternatives to such a system. Such concerns constitute the Hegelian-Marxian dimension of critical theory. Although Habermas in fact has presented some provocative hypotheses that fall into this dimension, his work in these areas remains relatively abstract and needs to be supplemented by more concrete analyses. Our paper is intended to do just that.

Habermas's Theoretical Project

One of Habermas's central claims is that social theory needs a more adequate conception of action. Specifically it needs a conception that provides a better account of the centrality of language in the reproduction of sociocultural life. With this goal in mind, he has attempted to unpack systematically what is implied when subjects engage in "communicative action," especially what conceptual capacities they display and what accountability they owe to each other. Communicative action is action oriented toward "reaching an understanding" of an initially unclear situation, with the goal of "coordinating action" consensually through persuasive argumentation. A communicatively competent actor has the cognitive capacity to differentiate reflectively a natural world of objects and states of affairs, a social world of legitimate interpersonal expectations between subjects, and a subjective world constituted by his own wishes, feelings, and hopes. Corresponding to each of the three components of this "commonly imputed system of coordinates" that agents have at their disposal to aid in interpreting a given situation is a respective type of validity claim. Communicatively competent actors have the capacity not only to dispose reflectively over the three types of possible "world relations" but also to raise the respective types of validity claims in their own speech acts, as well as to evaluate critically the claims made in the speech acts of others: truth or success (in relation to assertions about a world of objects and states of affairs), legitimacy (in relation to a world of social norms), and truthfulness or authenticity (in relation to a world of subjectivity).[7]

An actor who uses these conceptual capacities in ongoing communicative action necessarily takes on a particular sort of responsibility: a "speech-act immanent *obligation*" to be accountable for justifying the claims he raises in interaction. It is this idea of mutual accountability for differentiated validity claims, as well as the associated idea of what constitutes proper justification for the different types of claims, that constitute Habermas's conception of "communicative rationality."[8] He has been particularly interested in explicating the structure of a universally valid "ideal speech situation" for assessing the legitimacy of *normative* claims; and this in turn forms the basis for his notion of a "communicative" or "discursive ethics." Such an ethics does not provide an institutional blueprint for a particular interpretation of the good society.[9] It simply provides general procedural criteria, on the basis of which one can make claims about the kinds of directions a society might take to increase its democratic legitimacy. Given the traditions and material level of Western industrialized societies, it is fair to say that the criteria of a communicative ethics would be met well by the sort of participatory and decentralized institutions proposed by radical ecologists. Before looking more closely at this topic, it is first necessary to elaborate Habermas's conception of modernity and why it is integrally linked with the concept of rationality.

Because the communicative competence from which Habermas begins his analysis is most fully displayed in modern societies, it is necessary for him to offer an account of modernity that locates the precise sense in which it represents a systematic increase in the rationalization of life. This task, however, puts him in a somewhat uneasy relationship with his mentors in critical theory, especially Max Horkheimer and Theodor Adorno. In the *Dialectic of Enlightenment*, Horkheimer and

Adorno accepted the idea that modernity and the rationalization of life have indeed gone hand in hand, but they maintained that rationalization has been a thoroughly destructive phenomenon. Horkheimer and Adorno equated rationalization with the expansion of instrumental rationality, and to them that meant an ever-increasing degree of domination in more and more areas of man's relationship to nature, to others, and to himself.[10]

The challenge Habermas has taken is to offer a more complex account of modernity, one that can accommodate the insights of earlier critical theorists about the destructive effects of instrumental reason and yet locate a sense in which modernity can be identified with an increase in the *potential* for a nondestructive, communicative rationalization of life. This dimension is central to our evaluation of the ecological potentialities imbedded in the informational revolution. Habermas meets this challenge by first offering a way of conceptualizing the crucial initial step in the development from premodern societies to modern ones. This step is taken with the rise of what Max Weber called "world religions." They offered a cognitive framework within which the "sociocentric" consciousness of magical-mythical thinking could begin to differentiate itself into a "decentered" consciousness, which recognizes demarcations among the natural, social, and subjective worlds, as well as the relative autonomy of corresponding value spheres in which knowledge can be accumulated as science and technology, law and morality, and aesthetics. The evolutionary importance of decentration (in the sense of an increase in learning potential) is that it gives actors the conceptual means for constructing a self-critical perspective; that is, it provides for the possibility of entertaining and evaluating alternative interpretations in all three dimensions.[11]

A decentration of consciousness through the "rationalization of world images" (*Weltbildern*) allows agents a degree of reflexive penetration of the hitherto impenetrable horizon of their "lifeworld" (*Lebenswelt*). The "formal scaffolding" provided by the system of natural, social, and subjective worlds, as well as the corresponding types of validity claims, can increasingly be used by each agent as a medium in which to accommodate new experiences to the stock of unproblematic background convictions that constitute his lifeworld. As this occurs, each agent's own critical capacities are increasingly integrated into the ongoing reproduction of his lifeworld. Hence the rationalization of world images opens the potential for "a rationalization of the lifeworld" in the sense that the latter's reproduction comes to depend more on the exercise of interpretive and evaluative skills displayed in arriving at a "communicatively attained understanding" in problematic situations and less on normative prescriptions grounded in opaque sources of authority.[12]

The rational potential that Habermas identifies with modernity becomes concrete and systematically effective, however, only to the degree to which it is progressively incorporated into social institutions. One of Habermas's basic intentions is to show how this process of incorporation, or "social rationalization," developed in the West in a "one-sided" manner. "Capitalistic modernization," he contends, represents a process of "selective" utilization of the potential offered by modern structures of consciousness.[13]

Habermas's attempt to think in terms of different levels of rationalization owes much to Weber. And yet Weber did not use his own insights in a way that could illuminate adequately the one-sidedness of modernization. Specifically his paradigm conception of purposive action led him to equate social rationalization with the institutionalization of *Zweckrationalität* rather than seeing this institutionalization against a background of what was *"structurally possible,"* given the potential of modern structures of consciousness.[14]

This contrast between cognitive potential and selective social institutionalization is crucial to Habermas's project in two interrelated ways. First, it provides the possibility of a perspective located within modernity that at the same time can yield a critical analysis of social rationalization, or modernization, as it has proceeded in the West. And in providing such a perspective, this contrast offers a potentially persuasive way of lessening a suspicion that is rightly directed at any argument associating modernity with universalistic claims about rationality. This suspicion assumes that such arguments inevitably end up providing "Whiggish" stories of Western self-congratulation.[15] Habermas tries to meet this suspicion with a story whose plot is somewhat more complex.[16]

Habermas identifies the one-sidedness of capitalistic modernization with that "rise to dominance of cognitive-instrumental aspects [of rationality], through which everything else is driven into the realm of apparent irrationality."[17] This general focus is hardly new to critical theory; in fact it could be said to constitute that tradition's central preoccupation. The problem with earlier critical theorists, however,

Timothy W. Luke and Stephen K. White

was that the one-sidedness (in a normative sense of being distorted) of modernization was always identified in an ambivalent way. Although they thought that much in modernity was valuable, the perspectives from which they located one-sidedness made it difficult not to see modernity as somehow totally condemned. What Habermas's conception of different dimensions of rationalization can provide is a more adequate way of differentiating the "pathologies" of modernization from the potential of modernity.[18] This distinction will be useful to our analysis because it provides a basis for separating out of the informational revolution those tendencies that merely intensify the pathological characteristics of modern society from those that might form the nucleus of a more balanced, ecologically sound society.

Modernization since Weber has been closely identified with a progressive increase in the percentage of social interactions organized according to the imperatives of a market economy and an administrative polity. Habermas conceptualizes this as an expansion of social subsystems reproduced through the media of money and power, respectively. Although this formulation has a Parsonian cast to it, the divergence between the two thinkers is clear in the way Habermas interprets social rationalization. The accumulation of cognitive-instrumental knowledge and its systematic application to increasing segments of social life represents an overdevelopment of one value sphere of a rationalized lifeworld at the expense of the other two: the moral and the aesthetic. Stated so baldly this hardly sounds very profound or provocative. After all what criterion is there for saying that the sphere of science and technology is out of balance; that is, why does the idea of balance constitute a norm that condemns the greater institutionalization of one sphere?

The answer to this question is that a rationalized lifeworld is not only one in which different spheres of value have been distinguished but also one in which each actor's critical communicative capacities play an expanded role in the ongoing process of reproducing that lifeworld. The viewpoint then from which the idea of imbalance or one-sidedness is constituted is that of a *lifeworld* reproduced through the *medium of communicative action* that finds itself increasingly invaded by *subsystems* reproduced through the *media of money and power*. It is this phenomenon that Habermas refers to as the "colonization of the lifeworld."[19] This colonization has an impact within three dimensions: the transmission of knowledge and carrying on of traditions, the social integration of individuals, and the formation of personalities. These processes reproduce the basic symbolic structures of the lifeworld: culture, society, and personality.[20]

Our analysis will link up with Habermas's framework at the point at which he delineates this colonization problem. First, we will supplement his own analysis of colonization in the dimension of social integration by outlining how the development of informational capitalism has invaded the dimensions of cultural reproduction and identity formation. Habermas has argued that the role of *citizen* is losing ground to that of dependent *client* of the welfare state.[21] We will analyze the complementary process through which the role of *producer* loses ground to that of *consumer*—but not just the "old" consumer of goods and services; rather one whose ideas, images, motivations, and even identity are packaged to meet the needs of *informational* capital. It is the colonization of cultural reproduction and identity formation by informational capital that gives the "new" consumer his character.

One crucial aspect of this colonization process is that it needs no ideology in the traditional sense. It invades and undercuts the very grounds on which individuals try to formulate their own convictions about what is the case, what is legitimate, and what is authentic. The problem today, as Habermas and others have noted, is less that of false consciousness than that of "fragmented consciousness" beset by "expert cultures."[22] Hence one of our goals in analyzing informational capitalism will be to highlight the expanded role of professional experts as agents of colonization.

Although the expansion of informational capital extends in new ways the loss of freedom and loss of meaning in modern life, it nevertheless has an ambivalent character, at least in relation to some of its new technologies. These, under radically altered conditions, could become supportive of greater human autonomy. An inquiry into such conditions forms the second part of our analysis. The increasing breakdown of the ecosystem, entailed by an infinitely expanding industrial civilization, may come to play a role as significant in reorienting human life as the one Marx felt the internal breakdown of capitalism would play. Ecological crises might function as the material catalyst for an economic and political transformation that could reverse the state-corporate colonization of the lifeworld and create forms of life in which the potential of modernity could be utilized in a more balanced fashion.[23] The moral-practical sphere could expand in the sense of greater participation and control by average citizens of economic and political decisions. And the aesthetic sphere could expand as the need for nondestructive ways of tending to nature became increasingly imperative.

Concrete possibilities along these lines are embedded in the ideas and practices of radical ecologists. Our third concern is to speculate as to how the informational revolution, in combination with an ecological crisis, could create the context in which these ideas and practices might coalesce into a modernity that is both ecologically balanced and oriented toward a communicative ethic. If relating radical ecology to critical theory can thus help concretize some of Habermas's ideas, it can also serve as a corrective for some of the more romantic ideas of the ecological movement. Here we mean that Habermas's framework for differentiating the rationality of modernity from that of modernization reveals the weakness of blanket condemnations of modernity as being totally inimical to a proper relationship of humans to nature. Proposals to resubjectify nature, liberate animals, or accord rights to trees are, if taken literally, mostly misconceived. The real challenge, as we see it, is not to cast about for ways of obliterating the cognitive-objectivating attitude toward nature (out of which science and technology arise), but rather to rethink the way in which that attitude relates to the aesthetic and moral-practical attitudes at the level of everyday practice. Going in this direction means reconceptualizing, rather than simply blurring, the relationships between the moments of a modern, decentered consciousness.[24]

On Informational Capitalism

Since the late 1940s, U.S. transnational firms have shifted capital and jobs to other continents, forging a transnational industrial regime out of their largely untapped natural resources, labor reserves, and consumer markets. In turn the character of U.S. capital—as it has developed new managerial, communications, transportation, and engineering techniques to administer this global economy—has shifted profoundly. Traditional industrial goods-producing activity in the United States itself has fallen behind informational knowledge-producing activities in economic and political importance.

By elaborating on the impact of this informational revolution on the U.S. industrial economy, one can explore the possibilities for an ecological transformation emerging out of the contradictions between informational and industrial society. Ironically the economic interests of the experts, managers, and professionals guiding informational capital through these deindustrializing trends now may partially parallel the political agendas of ecological activists, who seek to build new, ecologically sound communities to coexist with nature in diverse habitats without qualitatively lowering most material standards of living.

Some observers already see a postindustrial informationalized society as an environmentally sound economic order.[25] Still, their high-tech solutions for the current industrial malaise, like the construction of massive solar collectors in earth orbit to generate electricity or the relocation of polluting industries abroad, must not be mistaken for an authentic ecological revolution. The ecological crisis is a global problem that is growing worse with this informational revolution. It can be only aggravated by internationalizing industrial pollution or microwaving megawatts of electricity through the atmosphere. Instead informational capital's program for cybernetically managing the earth's ecological collapse from space must be recognized as an environmental false promise that implies an increasingly pathological mode of modernity tied to the uncontrolled imperatives of capital accumulation. These same informational means of production, however, could be combined with a discursive ethic of participatory democracy. This fusion of participatory management, administration, and governance with decentralized informational tools of labor might lay down an institutional foundation for an increasingly ecological mode of modernity based on a new emphasis on the moral and aesthetic dimensions of everyday life.

Informationalization represents the new dominance of data-intensive techniques, cybernetic knowledge, and electronic technologies as the strategic resources of corporate production. The invention, production, management, and distribution of information—as words, numbers, images, or audio—now overshadows the manufacture of goods or provision of services in the truly advanced capitalist economies. This qualitative shift toward informational productivity separates the United States, Japan, and West Germany from other advancing industrial systems in the USSR, Spain, Italy, Taiwan, Brazil, or South Korea, which still measure their advances in terms of industrial activity. Informational society has been defined partially as deindustrialization, the service economy, the technological society, or postindustrialism.[26]

Timothy W. Luke and Stephen K. White

Each of these incomplete notions, however, does not fully account for the total transformations wrought by the informational revolution of U.S. industrial society.

An entirely new social formation tied to the production, interpretation, and distribution of information has emerged from within U.S. industrial capitalism since the mid-1950s. These trends were launched in the 1920s and 1930s as telecommunications and electric power grids were extended throughout the nation. The primary centers of informational activity accounted for 18 percent of national income in 1929 and 17 percent in 1948. In the 1950s, informationalization rapidly accelerated, with widespread growth in education, computerization, technical services, and mass media. The annual growth rates in knowledge production in primary informational activities from 1949 through 1958 are astounding: 16.4 percent in research and development, 10.9 percent in telephone systems, 77.2 percent in television station revenues, 104.2 percent in electronic computers, and 10.6 percent for total knowledge production.[27]

In 1956 white-collar workers in technical, clerical, and managerial positions outnumbered blue-collar industrial workers for the first time in U.S. history.[28] With the Sputnik challenge in 1957, an unprecedented mode of technologically intensive industrial production, based on these white-collar workers' generating data-intensive scientific knowledge and complex electronic technology, came together in U.S. aerospace, defense, telecommunications, computer, and electronics industries to produce new genres of technological information. With these technological innovations, U.S. industrial capitalism has been greatly augmented, if not nearly displaced, by informational capitalism. In this period of transition, most information production still can be tied to the programming and management needs of complex government or corporate operations. Similarly many informational jobs are undemanding, repetitive, low paid, and essentially uncreative. Nonetheless job definitions, skills, and duties increasingly have been defined in both the blue-collar and white-collar strata by their relation to informational activity.

As the computer console has replaced the factory smokestack as the determinant sign of economic power, informationalization has reconstituted labor and management. Indeed, white-collar, blue-collar, and pink-collar labor rapidly is being either augmented or displaced by "steel-collar" robotic mechanisms and "silicon-collar" informational processors. By the late 1960s, the primary information sector of the economy—computer manufacturing, telecommunications, mass media, advertising, publishing, accounting, education, research, and development as well as risk management in finance, banking, and insurance—produced 25.1 percent of the national income. The secondary information sector—work performed by information workers in government and goods-producing and service-producing firms for internal consumption—produced 21.1 percent of the national income. Already by the late 1960s, prior to widespread computerization of the 1970s, informational activities produced 46 percent of the U.S. national income and earned 53 percent of total national wages. By the mid-1970s the primary information sector's overall share of national income production alone rose from 25 percent to 30 percent, and all information workers in both sectors surpassed noninformation workers in number.[29]

Informational capital has not eliminated industrial or agricultural capital; rather its managers have begun to "informationalize" industrial production (using computer-assisted design/computer-aided manufacturing, group technology, and automated assembly) and agricultural production (using biotechnology, genetic engineering, and computer-assisted farm management) just as industrial capital industrialized agriculture in the early twentieth century. Industrial and agricultural products still remain vital to U.S. overall economic output. Yet with the transnationalization of manufacturing and food cultivation in second and third world export platforms, the informationalized production of words, images, audio, and numbers increasingly dominates the U.S. workplace as the anchor of its niche in the world economy.

The collapse of the U.S. industrial economy will be followed by additional employment losses as the informationalization of economic life becomes more pervasive. Current projections hold that 40 percent of all economic productivity can be improved by microprocessing technology. Data-intensive production could mean that at least 50 percent of the current shopfloor workers will be replaced by highly skilled technicians and robots by 1990. With over 130,000 workers laid off in 1981 and 1982, General Motors began buying 14,000 industrial robots in March 1982; 40,000 to 50,000 jobs will be lost once the robots are on line, which equals the Chrysler Corporation's total hourly U.S. labor force in 1982.[30]

Some of these displaced workers will be retrained as informational workers to return to private sector jobs or will be absorbed into service occupations in public employment. Nevertheless neither the private nor the public sector can entirely absorb the tremendous displacement of labor brought about by robotization and informationalization. Most of the displaced workers will not get jobs of equal status or pay as they fall into the high-turnover, low-wage niche of the labor markets. With informationalization, hundreds of thousands of stable, medium, and high wage jobs will by lost forever, while only thousands of new high wage professional jobs in the informational industries can be developed to replace them.[31]

Consequently some corporate planners argue that the informationalizing economy and the contracting welfare state must develop a third sector (beyond the private and public sectors) or a third system (beyond the market system and planning system) to accommodate the deindustrialized work force of the coming decades.[32] Being unable to maintain the incomes of the unemployed and underemployed through either transfer payment schemes or full employment programs, the "technologically competent" elites now in control of the informationalizing industrial state and transnational firm are promoting—in the familiar rhetoric of Yankee ingenuity, free enterprise, and self-reliance—a hybrid package of structural unemployment, volunteerism, soft energy paths, frugality, voluntary simplicity, decentralization, and local actionism to meliorate the deteriorating situations of the "technologically obsolescent" and "technologically superfluous" classes.[33] Within this third sector, Illich's notions of the "subsistent household," "useful unemployment," and "vernacular economics" might come to prevail. Downwardly mobile consumers will be encouraged to produce their own goods and services for their own frugal consumption as the larger informational economy discredits the ideas and infrastructure of mass consumerism on the lines of post–World War II suburbia.[34]

According to a corporate forecast generated by the Values and Lifestyles program at SRI International in 1980, U.S. consumers fall into three groups: need-driven consumers living at the poverty level and buying bare necessities are 11 percent of the adult population or 19 million persons; outer-directed consumers living affluent middle-class life-styles and buying the complete package of consumer society are 69 percent or 110 million persons in the total adult population; and inner-directed consumers living "consciously" or "voluntarily" simple lives, or nonconsumeristic life-styles compared to outer-directed consumers, add up to 20 percent or 33 million persons in the total adult population.[35] Although the inner-directed consumers do not see their life-styles as forming an austerity or downward mobility movement, its ultimate impact, in the context of the deindustrialization and ultrainformationalization of the U.S. economy, is that of forced austerity. With scores of millions of these outer-directed consumers losing their industrial or service jobs to informational technology and only a few million jobs being created in the new informational sphere of production, it becomes imperative for the system's continual functioning to legitimize this new materially deprived era as a morally desirable quality of life revolution.

Most consumers will not fall into the underclass of need-driven consumption. Yet they cannot hope to have in material wealth or symbolic fashions what outer-directed consumption has promised to Americans since industrialization in the 1890s. The high-volume, low-cost, down scale marketing of mass consumption of the 1950s and 1960s that always stressed accessibility is giving way slowly in corporate product demography to the low-volume, high-cost upscale markets of elite consumers that primarily emphasize exclusivity. Outer-directed consumption will continue under informational capitalism, but it will center increasingly on smaller enclaves of elite consumers.

Hence, "voluntary simplicity," "frugality," "ecological life-styles," "conspicuous conservation," "small is beautiful," "conserver society," and "simple living" are the new master codes of mass consumption in the age of informational capitalism, which produces less goods at higher costs for fewer people in specialized markets. Yet image systems, value codes, knowledge bases, and information networks are readily produced under informational capitalism to ground an inner-directed consumption tied to innovative information packages of postaffluence, such as personal fulfillment, physical fitness, self-actualization, and spiritual awakening.[36]

The managers of transnational informationalizing capital want to break down outer-directed consumeristic dependencies in the mass population on national industrial capital and the welfare state. Needing capital for rapid informational development, informationalized firms do not want their backward industrial competitors to fritter away financial resources on consumer goods production or the overextended welfare state to redistribute the social surplus.[37] Informational capital instead seeks to displace old-line industrial capital and welfare states from financial markets. The management of informational firms, then,

Timothy W. Luke and Stephen K. White

can invest in the new producer goods of informational economies, soaking fresh financial reserves out of contracting consumer production and the public sector. As a short-term substitute for affordable, diverse consumer goods and dependable, substantive welfare payments, transnational informational firms are backing volunteerism, frugality, and spiritual reawakening to take up the slack during the informationalizing transition. Hence the technologically competent experts, managers, and professionals who are now largely in control of informational capital urge the technologically obsolescent consumer and superfluous client strata to muddle toward frugality and voluntarily simplify their lives.

To restratify U.S. society along the lines of technological competence, however, the managing groups within informational capital must contradict many of the egalitarian-democratic myths underpinning mass electoral politics. Contained within this sort of contradiction are the seeds of potential legitimation problems. So far, though, even the new politics of redistribution aggressively pursued by the Reagan administration have not resulted in anything like Habermas's legitimation crisis.[38] Although the emerging informational society promotes massive unemployment, urban decay, social dislocation, and international inequity, these complex trends and their new interconnections are as yet poorly understood by the average citizen. Moreover, they are not fully understood by many political leaders, and as a result, most existing political strategies for easing the informational transition are unrationalized, open-ended, and disorderly. The ambiguity of this state of affairs is important because ecological movements may gain thereby the opportunity to appropriate some of the institutional, technological, and cultural possibilities of informationalization for the purposes of organizing a new ecological form of modernity.

Colonization of the Lifeworld

The influence of informational capitalism can be witnessed most explicitly in the colonization of the everyday lifeworld. Through the production, circulation, and consumption of information, advanced corporate capital has directly modified the processes of cultural reproduction and identity formation in modern society. Consequently our analysis of informational capitalism, as a new mode of social rationalization, must explore the origins and processes of this ongoing reconstruction of the identity formation and cultural traditions during the transition from entrepreneurial to corporate capitalism. In understanding how informational capitalism colonized the inner and outer lifeworlds, we can begin to outline how an ecological mode of modernity might emerge from informational capitalism.

First, however, this analysis must elaborate the essential logic of corporate capitalist consumption that anchors this entire system. It is the main strategy used by corporate capital for colonizing the everyday lifeworld. Instead of maintaining an irreducible tension between the public and private spheres that classical bourgeois economic and legal theory implies, public and private increasingly have become identical under advanced corporate capitalism as the needs of the state and/ or the firm are internalized by individuals in the family, firm, and mass public.[39] Such identity linkages, in turn, allow professional experts in the state and firm to regulate individuals more closely inasmuch as they define the needs extended to individuals as reified scripts of normal behavior through the media, mass education, or professional expertise and through packages of material goods provided by corporate manufacture and commerce. Still, these needs of individuals simultaneously are needed by the state and firm inasmuch as the aggregate economic growth and specific commodity claims implied by these needs are a demand-side productive force guaranteeing the further development and legitimacy of the supply-side state-corporate delivery system. Thus, corporate capitalist production in informational economies is largely the obverse of socializing its clients and consumers to accept the necessity of corporate capitalist consumption.

From this vantage corporate capital purposely stimulates the propagation of consumption, not as the rewarding outcome of material abundance in an affluent society but as a constant investment in a new productive force. This growth imperative is the *ultima ratio* of the everyday lifeworld's colonization. "The *consumption* of individuals," as Baudrillard states,

mediates the *productivity* of corporate capital. It becomes a productive force required by the functioning of the system itself, by its process of reproduction and survival. In other words, there are only needs because the system needs them. And the needs invested by the individual consumer today are just as essential to the order of production as the capital invested by the capitalist entrepreneur and the labor power invested in the wage laborer. It is *all* capital.[40]

Under corporate capitalism, all individuals qua consumers become capital assets. This mobilization of consumers through the colonization of their fragmentary consciousness directly boosts the productivity, profitability, and power of corporate capital's increasingly intensive, automated, and monopolistic industries.

By defining certain behavioral and material needs as appropriate for particular groups of private individuals to internalize, the expert public authorities and corporate professionals in the state and firm can liberate new demographic segments—women, children, teenagers, racial minorities, blacks, senior citizens, gays, ethnic minorities—to expect and acquire need fulfillments once mainly reserved for straight, affluent, middle-aged men. Specific prepackaged need fulfillments continually can be defined by the means of consciousness engineering in advertising, formal schooling, or the entertainment media. In turn the aggregate access of these individuals to their need satisfactions can be mandated through legal entitlement or job creation. To deny that such consciousness engineering occurs, one must ignore such obvious forces of everyday life as the highly processed informational packages of ego administration circulated daily in the mass media, public school curricula, and popular culture.

In commercially colonizing the traditional processes of ego formation and rituals of domestic reproduction, neither the corporate firm nor the modern state has respected the sanctity, privacy, or autonomy of the family. Bourgeois notions of frugality, sexual propriety, personal trust, parental authority, private property, family status, and household autonomy only place irrational limits, inefficient constraints, and non-productive obstacles before the total commodification of personal re-lations. The bourgeois individual and family systems, then, necessarily have had to be dismantled from without as professional experts in health care, childbirth, nutrition, education, fashion, morality, elder care, shelter, leisure, and funerary services expropriated these functions from individual producers in the family, where they had been organ-ically provided for use, to return them in exchange as commodified goods and services. These instrumental interventions, in turn, have enabled the aggregate planning system of corporate production to more effectively "organize the entire society in its interest and image."[41]

Having made the real decisions about how these satisfactions would be provided, the experts, managers, and professionals who direct corporate capital have turned to the state to make this mass acceptance of exchange-based reproduction compulsory through coercion and legislation. As a result an administrative regime formed to provide public health regulation, minimal nutritional requirements, mass education, mandatory retirement, urban planning, national recreation areas, and a bevy of other mandatory public welfare services and transfer payments.[42] Starting first in the affluent middle-class suburbs of the major industrial cities and then spreading into more marginal market zones in the inner-city ethnic neighborhoods, racial ghettos, small towns, and rural areas, the new model of the corporate capitalist individual has emerged from within the wreckage of the older bourgeois individual ideal.

The managers of corporate capital and the bureaucratic state's service providers have decided what particular material packages and behavioral scripts will be produced and provided along a spectrum of quality- and quantity-graded alternatives made available to consumers. The first principle of this order is the fragmentation of consciousness through experts' definition and design of the lifeworld. In turn, consumers can exercise their "free choice" over the predesigned alternatives, which will deliver the need satisfactions required to fulfill their need definitions as they have been socialized under this colonizing regime to define them. This interconnection of choice and design, production and consumption, freedom and administration boosts aggregate growth and productivity. Seemingly the corporate family and ego ideal serves as a "halfway house" that inculcates the formal skills of adaptive role performance in its members but leaves the ever-changing substantive definition of those roles to new authorities in the school, television, specialty magazines, the workplace, peer groups, or professional societies.[43]

The means of cultivating passive consumption, social dependence, and cultural submission through the controlled emancipation of personal self-seeking and sensual fulfillment serve at least in part as the regulatory apparatus for managing personal and family life under corporate capitalism. The logic of mass consumption effectively enables corporate firms and the state to plan the basic level of aggregate demand and to manage the general scope of specific demand for goods and services by turning the psychic need for these satisfactions into a dynamic productive force.

By usurping the decision-making power once held by families and individuals, professionals, managers, and experts employed by the firm and the state increasingly regulate mass and individual behavior. In the colonization of the lifeworld, group autonomy and personal liberty are reduced to sets of highly structured, predetermined choices from varied menus of prepackaged material goods and conventionally scripted behavior options. The authorities increasingly define each individual's alternatives and refine the individuals' choice-making faculties through counseling, advertising, education, therapy, marketing, and gatekeeping. The informational revolution thus brings with it new and potent ways of "systematically distort[ing] communication."[44] As consumers and clients accept their preprocessed choices, they simultaneously accept their status as colonial subjects.

This description of the increasing colonization of the lifeworld might seem to point in the direction of a society that is becoming progressively more "one-dimensional" in Marcuse's sense.[45] In other words, as long as the economies of advanced capitalist societies do not falter drastically, the preprocessing of choice will manifest itself in ever-more effective ways; however, we agree with Habermas that the colonization of the lifeworld, even under relatively favorable conditions of material growth, is a phenomenon that generates new forms of protest and resistance as increasing numbers of people react against "a culturally impoverished and unilaterally rationalized praxis of everyday life." This reaction occurs in a "colorful mixture of groups," some of which manifest a blind defensiveness, but others of which have a real emancipatory potential. The latter, Habermas argues, are groups "for which a critique of growth based on *environmental and peace concerns* provide a common focus."[46] In the next section, we will elaborate on some of the ideas and practices espoused by such groups, as well as on some of the broad trends entailed by the informational revolution that enhance their prospects.

Before turning to these questions, however, a few remarks must be made about the differences between these new oppositional forces and the old ones that arise more directly from the antagonism of labor and capital. The latter, more sharply class-based opposition may continue to lie relatively dormant, particularly if the welfare state can manage to stimulate tolerable levels of economic growth without having its actions clearly perceived by broad segments of the population as illegitimate in the light of democratic values. But while this state of affairs may continue for a number of years, it becomes more uncertain as one expands the time frame. For one thing, as we have indicated, the likelihood of permanently high levels of unemployment comes along with the shift of investment into informational capital. This phenomenon, combined with resource shortages and other environmental constraints on unlimited economic growth, may eventually constitute a material crisis situation out of which new levels of working-class opposition will arise. It would take us beyond the limits of this chapter to speculate further about this possibility or about the sorts of relationships that might develop between this opposition and the new forms we delineate. But it can at least be noted that if working-class opposition does reemerge, it will do so in a situation where ecologically sound ideas and practices will be well developed and thus available to be creatively appropriated in a fashion that points away from models of socialism tied to blind growth imperatives and overcentralization.

Ecological Potentials of Informationalization

With the growth of the informational revolution, the systematic contradictions involved in colonizing the everyday lifeworld on a transnational scale express themselves most destructively in the expansion of advanced corporate capitalism. Informational capitalism can intensify existing abuses of the ecosystem by universalizing their effects in scores of new third world export platforms, producing both manufactured components for new "world products" and new industrial pollutants for these myriad offshore "local markets." Transnational capital also promises to despoil natural systems in qualitatively new ways, introducing new informational pollutants—new supertoxic herbicides, rogue recombinant viruses, bioengineered livestock—into the already ecologically stressed environment. By transposing the "immiseration of the proletariat" on to the "immiseration of nature," corporate informational capital has created limited material opportunities for a small, privileged number of consumers mainly in Europe, Japan, and North America. Their current enjoyment of material abundance is generated by stealing ecological goods from the future, despoiling the natural inheritance of the past, and robbing resources from other less technologically intensive economies in the present.

While Habermas's social theory points out these problematic pathological tendencies in modernity, his communicative ethics also can lend coherence to the untested ecological potentialities of informational captialism by providing bench marks for organizing an economy based on alternative technologies, a democratic-communitarian society, and a new exurban culture as the alternative modernity of ecological reason. Such forms of alternate modernity are direct challenges to capitalist ideology, modes of liberating the lifeworld, and critiques of informational domination.

Since the Industrial Revolution the technical advances of capitalist economies progressively have robbed individuals and communities of their rights to self-definition, self-determination, and self-direction. This colonizing process of rationalization without representation has engendered new modes of human and ecological domination in everyday life, which are the institutional roots of the "pathologies" of modernity.[47] The authority of technical experts and their specialized knowledge exerts itself as a "fragmented consciousness" through the material artifacts and organizational processes of corporate culture, benefiting its anonymous controllers and designers in the technologically competent classes, who manage the state and corporate bureaucracies. It is this anonymous authoritarianism and its fragmentary consciousness that an ecological modernity would overturn. Still, in beginning and being grounded in a modern welfare state that tends toward an increasingly extensive administration of economic and political life, any meaningful ecological critique also must recognize that transnational capital, at least at first, inescapably will moderate, limit, and define its revolutionary thrusts.

Informationalization, particularly when mediated through decentralized microprocessing technology, can promote its own version of an ecologically viable society. Informational developments have advanced the growth of exurban and rural communities by downsizing and automating industrial plants. New communications and cybernetics media keep these farflung smaller factories under centralized management. The older industrial cities and regions, in turn, are decaying as they lose population, industries, tax base, and services to new informational communities and regions.

Microprocessing technology has been heralded as the true avantgarde of a democratic decentralization of society. In 1975 a microprocessing chip cost $360. By 1980 the same chip cost $5, making computer processing capacity virtually free. Its coinventor, Robert Noyce, predicted in 1973 that computerization after the microprocessor implies radical decentralization rather than the complete centralization characteristic of early mainframe systems. Microprocessing units, in turn, are diffusing rapidly. Use estimates rose from under 1 million in 1975 to 60 million in 1980 (compared to 100 years to reach 440 million telephones) worldwide.[48]

For the first generation of critical theorists, phenomena such as computerization and cable television could only be understood as new instruments for more effective domination. Just as this view is overly pessimistic, so also is the view that such phenomena will promote a more decentralized and democratic society. From the perspective of communicative ethics, however, these sorts of phenomena have no predestined role to play; rather they have an "ambivalent potential."[49] This potential can be used either to enhance systematically distorted communication and the blind imperatives of growth or to facilitate the establishment of decentralized, democratic communities. For example, microprocessing units can be used equally well to generate power on a handful of massive orbital solar satellites or in millions of tiny rooftop solar panels. And cable television can be used equally well as an instrument for more effective marketing of products and images or as a local informational device for helping producers and citizens to take greater control over their lives. The problem is to guide informational technologies into uses more suited to ecologically reasonable forms of production and democracy. Otherwise the power centers of industrial capitalism will continue to divert informational development to reinforce their centralized transnational hierarchies.

The institutional framework for an alternative modernity exists in nuce in certain tendencies of advanced corporate capitalism. Yet it exists in fragments, unrealized possibilities, and unchosen options that need to be fully identified, correctly implemented, and openly practiced. A concrete objective basis for ecological action in the United States might be found in six developing trends: recent population patterns, the growth of political action groups centered on local or regional politics, the expansion of cooperative exchange and social services, the development of alternative communal institutions, the rise of an anticorporate-antistate underground economy, and a growing population of persons, perhaps as many as 10 million in the United States alone, already practicing aspects of anticonsumerist ecological lifestyles.

One critical trend is the overall return of population to small cities and rural areas. From 1820 to 1970 large cities grew faster than small cities and country regions. By 1920 the United States was predominantly urban. Yet since the early 1970s small towns and rural areas have grown faster than large cities. For every 100 people who moved into cities from 1970 to 1975, 131 people moved out. Over 42 percent of the population (95 million persons) now live in small towns, small cities, and the country, providing the solid possibility for developing a new exurban mode of existence since towns under 2,500 people are now the fastest-growing form of settlement.[50]

These population movements reflect a developing interest in the pace, aesthetics, and stability of rural living. Similarly they accord with the population decentralization implicit in informationalization and deindustrialization. Along with this rapid growth in the rural population, many new jobs have moved into exurban regions as urban industrial jobs diminish in number. Over 700,000 new manufacturing jobs and 3.5 million new informational and service slots were created in non-metropolitan areas from 1970 to 1978 alone.

With this growth in exurban communities, a new trend toward localism in economic activity, political decisions, and social structures also has developed. State, county, and local governments are being and can be pressured to be more responsive, participatory, and effective. Nearly 20 million citizens belong to single issue or comprehensive action groups tied into local political agendas. Citizen action groups like Arkansas Community Organizations for Reform Now, Virginia Action, Campaign for Economic Democracy, Carolina Action, and the Illinois Public Action Committee have formed to put local and regional economic, political, and social issues on their public agenda.[51] Much of this change has been manipulated from above to legitimize and rationalize the emerging system of informational administration. Nonetheless, these new localist citizens' movements also are providing the structural possibilities for realizing an ecologically sensible politics.

In the economic sphere 70 million Americans participate in some kind of producer, credit, or consumer co-op. These alternative economic institutions are augmented by a tremendous underground economy that amounts to hundreds of millions of dollars. Nearly 15 percent of the U.S. GNP turns over underground off the books. Four and a half million people get all their income and 15 million more obtain part of their incomes off this noncorporate shadow economy. Similarly, over 32 million households engage in backyard or commons home gardening—a 100 percent increase since the 1950s—and produce $13 billion in agricultural commodities.[52]

Apart from and completely outside of corporate capitalism and the welfare state, the self-production of goods and services has started in free schools, food co-ops, free clinics, women's groups, community media, credit unions, community day care, neighborhood councils, flea markets, health foods, counterculture publishing, law clinics, co-operative housing, and localist politics. These tendencies are central to the abolition of domination by experts and the fragmented consciousness of consumer-client relations. Consumer movements must become producer movements in order to liberate the everyday lifeworld from its corporate colonization through increased self-production of goods and services. Single-issue action groups and citizens' movements now have more contributing members (1.4 million to 520,000 in 1976) and funds ($16.6 million to $13.6 million in 1976) than the two major political parties. Of course, many of these groups and their members have been and can be instrumentalized by mainstream politicians and public agencies. Still they indicate a new tendency for engaging in local direct action and a possible basis for moving toward ecologically sound institution building at a regional level. Studies conducted in 1977 and 1980 argue that 4 million or 5 million people in the late 1970s and nearly 10 million in the early 1980s have withdrawn from consumer society to pursue "voluntary simplicity."[53] In other words 5 to 6 percent of the adult population in the United States already may be working toward some of the goals of an ecologically reasonable society.

Within such a new institutional order, it is technically possible, particularly with present-day informational technology, to design technical instruments that are simple, durable, useful, and accessible to individual, household, or community use in this self-production of need satisfactions.[54] Such tools, once disengaged from the constraints imposed by corporate control, can provide the inorganic energy and the mechanical efficiency needed for a humane standard of living. Virtually every tool possesses some self-subversive dimension in its corporate deployment that ecological activists can tap to serve the purposes of ecological development.

The alternative technology groups, which formed concretely as a movement only in the mid-1970s, already have developed into a considerable technical community and are promoting several viable technologies. Many journals, including *RAIN*, *Appropriate Technology*, *Solar Energy*, *Undercurrents*, and *Appropriate Technology Quarterly*, have a circulation of nearly a million and constitute both a developing technical discourse and a public sphere for articulating ecologically sound technical alternatives. In addition to these journals and the publication of hundreds of related pamphlets and books, over 2,000 alternative technology groups have formed to popularize these techniques. These technologies have not yet transformed economic production in the United States. Still, their development can provide a potential technological basis for living a labor-intensive, self-sufficient, ecologically sound existence for millions of households.

An ecologically grounded politics also necessitates a transition to a spatial-practical setting that ecologically fuses the rural and urban into a new mode of exurban existence.[55] This deconcentration of urban resources would bring "urban" commerce, art, society, letters into balance with "rural" crafts, culture, community, customs. In such an exurban culture, both the anthropocentrism of orthodox urban leftists and the nature chauvinism of traditional romantic rebellion could be lessened.

Large U.S. cities, which have developed with advanced industrialization, often have expanded quantitatively with little qualitative improvement in cultural benefits, social services, public utilities, or physical infrastructure for most people. Rather size itself imposes a cost on these collective goods, making them less accessible, enjoyable, and useful except for an affluent few as more people are concentrated around them. Yet these changes do not imply massive rustication of most urban populations in the reconstitution of corporate society. Rather transport, communications, and land use could be reordered to reconnect the rural and urban economy through small-scale interdependent linkages. The benefits of rural and urban life can be unified in new spatial-practical forms to eliminate the personal costs imposed by rural isolation and urban giganticism.

These new spatial-practical institutions in turn would guarantee popular participation and operational accountability in the management of the localist economy and community. The municipalization of industry, agriculture, and services rather than the nationalization of the corporate economy emerges as the optimal mode for socializing the means of production to produce use values locally in the ecological revolution of everyday life. To create a postconventional ethic of natural cooperation, balanced manual and mental labor close affinal association, and skilled craft practice, a communicative ethic for situating people in nature and reintroducing nature's balance into social reproduction could emerge in the discursive social integration of these communities.

Combining a participatory democracy with a communitarian ethos will demand tremendous exertions to ensure that the obligations and benefits of producership, managership, and consumership are not unequally distributed. Municipal and household production must not create new class or gender, age, or status contradictions. An ecologically viable institutional order can go beyond these class-specific conventions by demanding a balance of manual and mental labor from all producers and an equitable sharing of resources within the communal networks of an ecological society. Such change implies the adoption of a lifestyle grounded in "voluntary simplicity." Yet these strategies do not imply an uncritically embraced austerity, which mystifies the falling rate of material satisfaction in informationalizing U.S. society. On the contrary, it defines itself in the self-creation and self-realization of postconventional needs independent of corporate capital's "coercive complexity" of commodified goods and services.

Ultimately, however, the political goals of the many communal ecological revolutions and structural directions intrinsic to the trends of the transnational corporate informational revolution only coincidently complement each other. One must not presume that the ecologically minded new citizens' movements or the rise of localism are simply stalking horses for transnational capital. These ideas and the new institutions grounded on them can be reappropriated and redeployed to serve progressive ends. Specifically the decentralizing, humanizing, and empowering possibilities implicit in such new ideas and institutions can be fostered so as to develop in ways that accord less with the imperatives of capital and more with those of a communicative model of democratic legitimacy.

In the short run corporate capital and the welfare state might stimulate the advent of free schools, neighborhood councils, backyard gardening, or frugality philosophies to compensate for the withering away of familiar public goods and consumer commodities as capital flows into informationalizing firms, as jobs are exported abroad, and as mass consumer markets shift into specialized upscale boutiques. Yet in the long run these alternative institutions and techniques hold the potential for developing a more rational, equal, and participatory society through self-reliance and communal interaction. Thus ecological activists must nurture the emancipatory potential of corporate capital's "third sector," "new volunteerism," or "voluntary simplicity." Ecological politics represents an emancipatory dimension: an oppositional possibility within the informationalizing corporate order that can be organized to reorder everyday life.

Such ecological activism delimits the class conflict of informational societies as the members of consumer and client groups, socialized as conventional egos of corporate fragmentary consciousness, struggle locally to gain greater communal use and benefit from the informationalized means of production now controlled by corporate producers and professional expertise providers. By refusing to accept the corporate and professional administration of informational capital, consumers and clients can organize to reappropriate their alienated energies and skills communally from the technologically competent classes, thus overcoming their technological obsolescence. The motivational basis for pushing forward such radical practice is already taking shape in the developments we have outlined. Old democratic traditions, stressing localism and citizen independence, can play an important role here. In the context of an ecological crisis, these traditions can be appropriated in ways that universalize the responsibilities of democratic citizens. Recently these traditions too often have been melded with the preferences of outer-directed consumption, resulting in a regressive form of localism—articulating concerns like "dump that chemical waste in someone else's community" or "site that nuclear reactor in the next state, not our state." As the shortsighted and ultimately self-destructive character of this mode of thinking becomes evident, however, the opportunities expand for combining localist democratic traditions with a consciousness that we are all members of one global community, or "fictive world society," as Habermas calls it.[56] The recent successes of the nuclear freeze movement lend concrete plausibility to this idea of a collective identity that emphasizes both the local and the global dependencies of human life on ecologically sound political interactions.

Conclusion

Informational capital and ecological activists are working in different ways to dismantle advanced industrial society in order to create a less centralized, hierarchical, and environmentally destructive economy in the United States. Still the management of informational capital stops short of an authentic ecological transformation at the definite limits imposed by transnational capitalist exchange. It simply seeks to reconstruct industrialized manufacturing and agriculture along informational lines, making them more data intensive, robotized, numerically controlled, and downsized. It does not, however, end the domination of man and nature. Instead informationalized technology promises to extend and elaborate that domination. Individual producers and consumers are to be reduced further to word processors, number crunchers, and image consumers in their cyberneticized frugal households, while nature is bioengineered or genetically technologized to unfold along corporate-planned lines of evolution. The politics of informationalization, now forming inchoately in the United States as neoliberalism, neoconservatism, or high-tech democracy, must not be mistaken for a progressive new wave of the future.

On the contrary, the many local revolutions working for an ecological modernity can push beyond these state-corporate limits to resist the ongoing domination of man and nature, challenging both industrial and informational capital. In the process of elaborating new ideas and forms of life, ecological activists can help initiate in broad segments of society the kind of reflective processes, based on Habermas's notion of communicative ethics, that have the potential to demystify, decode, and repossess the material packages and behavioral scripts being produced by informational capital.[57] This deconstruction of managed meanings will help open the way for rethinking what autonomy in everyday life can mean for average producers and citizens in an informational age. The new form of ideological struggle thus centers on the different meanings being reassigned to acts and artifacts in modern industrial life by informational capitalism. One set of alternatives, based on corporate capital's instrumental rationality, points toward an informational transformation of labor and leisure that would revitalize the reification of labor in the production and consumption of information. Another range of ecological alternatives, based on communicative rationality, decentralized institutions, vernacular cultures, and global moral consciousness, can empower producers and citizens with the competence to decide for themselves the meaning and direction of the informational revolution.

Notes

Excerpts from this article have appeared previously in *Telos* 56 (Summer 1983) and *New Political Science* 11 (Spring 1983).

1. Jürgen Habermas, *Legitimation Crisis*, trans. Thomas McCarthy (Boston: Beacon Press, 1975), pp. 40-41 (hereafter cited as *LC*).

2. See Tim Luke, "Radical Ecology and the Crisis of Political Economy," *Telos* 46 (Winter 1980-1981): 97-101.

3. See Tim Luke, "Informationalism and Ecology," *Telos* 56 (Summer 1983): 59-73.

4. Stephen K. White, "The Normative Basis of Critical Theory," *Polity* (Fall 1983).

5. J. Donald Moon, "Values and Political Theory: A Modest Defense of a Qualified Cognitivism," *Journal of Politics* 4 (November 1977): 900, and "The Logic of Political Inquiry," in F. Greenstein and N. Polsby, eds., *Handbook of Political Science* (Reading, Mass.: Addison-Wesley, 1975), vol. 1; Martin Hollis, *Models of Man: Philosophical Thoughts on Social Action* (Cambridge: Cambridge University Press, 1977); William Connolly, *Appearance and Reality in Politics* (Cambridge: Cambridge University Press, 1981), chaps. 2-3.

6. See C. B. Macpherson, *The Political Theory of Possessive Individualism* (Oxford: Oxford University Press, 1970); and Timothy W. Luke, "Regulating the Haven in a Heartless World: The State and Family under Advanced Capitalism," *New Political Science* 8 (Winter 1981): 51-74.

7. Jürgen Habermas, *The Theory of Communicative Action*, vol. 1: *Reason and the Rationalization of Society*, trans. Thomas McCarthy (Boston: Beacon Press, 1984), pp. 75-101 (hereafter cited as *TCA 1*). Also Habermas, *Communication and the Evolution of Society*, trans. Thomas McCarthy (Boston: Beacon Press, 1979) (hereafter cited as *CES*).

8. *TCA* 1, pp. 8, 28, 44, 110-113, 198-199; *CES*, p. 64; Habermas, "Zwei Bemerkungen zur praktischen Diskurs," in *Zur Rekonstruktion des Historischen Materialismus* (Frankfurt: Suhrkamp, 1976), p. 339 (hereafter cited as *ZUR*).

9. *LC*, pt. 3; "Wahrheitstheorien," in *Wirklichkeit und Reflexion* (Pfüllingen: Neske, 1973), p. 252ff.; "Diskursethik," in *Moralbewusstsein und kommunikatives Handeln* (Frankfurt: Suhrkamp, 1983) (hereafter cited as *Moral*); "A Reply to My Critics," in John B. Thompson and David Held, eds., *Habermas: Critical Debates* (Cambridge, Mass.: MIT Press, 1982), pp. 261-262 (hereafter cited as "Reply"). See also Stephen K. White, "Reason and Authority in Habermas: A Critique of the Critics," *American Political Science Review* 4 (December 1980):1014-1016.

10. Max Horkheimer and Theodor Adorno, *Dialectic of Enlightenment* (New York: Seabury Press, 1972). See White, "Normative Basis," for a discussion of what Horkheimer and Adorno thought might constitute a negation of the totalization of instrumental reason.

11. *TCA* 1, pp. 48-50, 159-164, 166-180, 194-217.

12. Ibid., pp. 70-71, and Habermas, *Theorie des kommunikatives Handelns*, vol. 2 (Frankfurt: Suhrkamp, 1981), pp. 191, 518 (hereafter cited as *TKH 2*).

13. *TCA* 1, pp. 139-141, 167-168, 233-242.

14. Ibid., p. 233; *TKH* 2, p. 449ff.

15. Richard Rorty, *Philosophy and the Mirror of Nature* (Princeton: Princeton University Press, 1979) chaps. 7-8.

16. For arguments as to why this story is not susceptible to Rorty's criticisms, see *TKH* 2, p. 586ff., and "Die Philosophie als Platzhalter und Interpret," in *Moral*.

17. "Interview with Jürgen Habermas," *New German Critique* 18 (Fall 1979):43; *TKH* 2, p. 451.

18. *TCA* 1, p. xl, and *TKH* 2, pp. 349-422.

19. "Reply," pp. 280-281; see also *TKH* 2, p. 489ff.

20. *TKH* 2, pp. 208-209, 391, 427; "Reply," p. 227.

21. *TKH* 2, p. 514ff.

22. Ibid., pp. 520-522.

23. "Reply," p. 262.

24. Ibid., p. 250.

25. See Lester C. Thurow, *The Zero-Sum Society* (New York: Basic Books, 1980), for the classic example of neoliberal thought. See also Barry Bluestone and Bennett Harrison, *The Deindustrialization of America* (New York: Basic Books, 1982), and Hazel Henderson, *The Politics of the Solar Age: Alternatives to Economics* (New York: Anchor Press, 1981), for the neoliberal program for a cybernetic "reindustrialization with a human face."

26. Daniel Bell observes, "A postindustrial society is based on services. What counts is not raw muscle power, or energy, but information." See Bell, *The Coming of Post-Industrial Society* (New York: Basic Books, 1976), pp. 126-127; Victor C. Ferkiss, *Technological Man* (New York: New American Library, 1970); and Alan Gartner and Frank Riessman, *The Service Society and the Consumer Vanguard* (New York: Harper and Row, 1974). For further discussion, see Christopher Evans, *The Micro Millennium* (New York: Viking 1979); Fritz Machlup, *The Production and Distribution of Knowledge in the United States* (Princeton: Princeton University Press, 1962), pp. 362-400. Also see John Rose, *The Cybernetic Revolution* (New York: Barnes and Noble, 1974) Wickham Skinner and Kishore Chakraborty, *The Impact of New Technology: People and Organizations in Manufacturing and Allied Industries*, Work in America Institute Studies in Productivity: Highlights of the Literature, no. 18 (Scarsdale, N.Y., 1982); and Ronald Stamper, *Information in Business and Administrative Systems* (London: Batsford, 1973).

27. Marc Uri Porat, *The Information Economy*, vol. 1: *Definition and Measurement*, Office of Telecommunication Special Publication 77-12 (Washington, D.C.: Office of Telecommunication, 1977), pp. 64-65.

28. Bell, "Notes on the Post Industrial Society," *Public Interest*, nos. 6, 7 (Winter and Spring 1967): 24-35, 102-118.

29. See Porat, *Information Economy*, pp. 65, 119-123, and also vol. 2: *Sources and Methods for Measuring the Primary Information Sector* (Washington, D.C.: Office of Telecommunication, 1977).

30. John Stansell, "The Social Impact of Microprocessors," *New Scientist*, October 12, 1978, pp. 104-106. By 2000 nearly all industrial workers could be displaced by robotic units, while 50 to 75 percent of all industrial jobs could be lost in the process. By 1990 the United States, which is lagging behind Japan and some European Economic Community nations, could be producing 17,000 to 20,000 robots a year to augment a robotic base of 80,000 to 160,000

52

Timothy W. Luke and Stephen K. White

units. U.S auto producers today already employ 1,000 complex robots to increase their productivity. The most sophisticated units cost $50,000 each; they work two shifts a day for eight years in normal work span, or $5 per hour versus $15 per hour for human workers. Along with manufacturing, informational technology is predicted to displace 30 percent of the human workers and up to 50 percent of all middle-level corporate and industrial management. Already the relatively low capital intensitivity of office work—$2,000 to $6,000 per worker in 1980—will rise to over $10,000 per worker by 1985 as informational capital displaces labor. The labor-displacing qualities of informational capital can be seen, for example, in New York Telephone's handling of 30 percent more calls in 1980 than 1969 with 15,000 fewer employees. "Info City," *New York*, February 9, 1981, p. 28; Skinner and Chakraborty, *New Technology: Manufacturing*, p. 2; *New York Times*, September 3, 1981; John Naisbitt, *Megatrends: Ten New Directions Transforming Our Lives* (New York: Warner Books, 1982), p. 74; Dirk Hanson, *The New Alchemists: Silicon Valley and the Microelectronics Revolution* (Boston: Little, Brown, 1982), p. 263; Skinner and Chakraborty, *Impact of New Technology*, p. 6; and "Jobs: Putting America Back to Work," *Newsweek*, October 18, 1982, pp. 80–81.

31. One labor analyst noted in 1981, for example, as the Ford auto plant in Mahwah, New Jersey, closed with a loss of 6,000 jobs, that 6,000 new hotel rooms in New York would open in 1981. In-house projections suggest that one domestic helper is needed for each room; thus 6,000 new jobs were being created—at lower pay and with less status—for those displaced autoworkers. See "Info City," p. 29.

32. For a discussion of the third sector, see Richard C. Carlson, Willis W. Harman, and Peter Schwartz, *Energy Futures, Human Values and Lifestyles: A New Look at the Energy Crisis* (Boulder, Colo.: Westview, 1982).

33. For a discussion of technology as the basis of class formation and conflict, see David Apter, "Ideology and Discontent," in *Ideology and Discontent*, ed. David Apter (Glencoe, Ill.: Free Press, 1964), pp. 15–43.

34. These alternative social and economic institutions are discussed more completely in Ivan Illich, *Toward a History of Needs* and *Shadow Work* (Boston: Marion Boyars, 1981).

35. See *Leading Edge* 1, no. 1 (Summer 1980); and Duane Elgin, *Voluntary Simplicity: Toward a Way of Life That Is Outwardly Simple, Inwardly Rich* (New York: Morrow, 1981).

36. For one pollster's efforts to chart these changes, see Daniel Yankelovich, *New Rules: Searching for Self-Fulfillment in a World Turned Upside Down* (New York: Bantam, 1981). A handbook for the new rules might be Warren Johnson, *Muddling toward Frugality: A Blueprint for Survival in the 1980s* (Boulder: Shambala, 1979).

37. See "The Reindustrialization of America: Special Issue," *Business Week*, June 23, 1980, pp. 126–134 on the central importance of finding new pools of capital in wasteful government and consumer spending to meet the needs of "reindustrializing" America; also Timothy W. Luke, "Rationalization Redux: From the New Deal to the New Beginning," *New Political Science* 2, no. 4 (Spring 1982): 63–72.

38. *LC*, p. 62.

39. Galbraith, *New Industrial State*, pp. 119–128.

40. Jean Baudrillard, *For a Critique of the Political Economy of the Sign* (St. Louis: Telos Press, 1981), p. 82.

41. Herbert Marcuse, *Counter-Revolution and Revolt* (Boston: Beacon Press, 1972), p. 11.

42. See Norman Furness and Timothy Tilton, *The Case for the Welfare State: From Social Security to Social Equality* (Bloomington: Indiana University Press, 1977), pp. 22–49.

43. See Morris Janowitz, *The Last Half-Century: Societal Change and Politics in America* (Chicago: University of Chicago Press, 1978), pp. 320–363.

44. *LC*, p. 27.

45. Herbert Marcuse, *One-Dimensional Man* (Boston: Beacon Press, 1964).

46. "New Social Movements," *Telos* 49 (Fall 1981): 33–35.

47. *TKH* 2, pp. 489–547.

48. Hanson, *New Alchemists*, p. 159; "Microcomputers Aim at Huge New Market," *Business Week*, May 12, 1973, p. 180; and "The Microprocessor/Microcomputer Industry," Industrial Analysis Service, Creative Strategies, Inc. (San Jose, Calif., 1977), quoted in Hanson, *New Alchemists*, p. 144.

49. *TKH* 2, p. 571.

50. Naisbitt, *Megatrends*, pp. 126–127, and Kirkpatrick Sale, *Human Scale* (New York: Coward, McCann & Geoghegan, 1980), p. 44.

51. See Harry C. Boyte, *The Backyard Revolution* (Philadelphia: Temple University Press, 1980), pp. 100–102. For a discussion of how such movements have been purposely stimulated to provide much needed administrative rationality, also see Tim Luke, "Culture and Politics in the Age of Artificial Negativity," *Telos* 35 (Spring 1978): 55–72.

52. Sale, *Human Scale*, pp. 45–46, 236. Also see John Case and Rosemary C. Taylor, eds., *Co-ops, Communes and Collectives* (New York: Pantheon, 1979).

53. Elgin, *Voluntary Simplicity*, p. 132; and Milton Kotler, "Citizen Action: New Life for American Politics," *Nation*, October 30, 1976, pp. 429–431.

54. See Richard C. Dorf and Yvonne C. Hunter, eds., *Appropriate Visions: Technology, the Environment and the Individual* (San Francisco: Boyd and Fraser, 1978).

55. For a suggestive treatment of how to rebuild rural society, see Wendell Berry, *The Unsettling of America: Culture and Agriculture* (San Francisco: Sierra Club Books, 1977); and Murray Bookchin, *The Limits of the City* (New York: Harper and Row, 1973).

56. "On Social Identity," pp. 99–103; *ZUR*, pp. 95–96; and "New Social Movements," *Telos* 49 (Fall 1981): 34–35.

57. For an introduction to this process of critically identifying emancipatory possibilities, see Jacques Donzelot, *The Policing of Families* (New York: Pantheon, 1979); Stuart and Elizabeth Ewen, *Channels of Mass Desire* (New York: McGraw-Hill, 1982); Ivan Illich, *Disabling Professions* (Boston: Marion Boyars, 1978); and Christopher Lasch, *The Culture of Narcissism* (New York: W. W. Norton and Co., 1979).

II

Critical Studies of Education

Decolonization and the Ideal Speech Community: Some Issues in the Theory and Practice of Communicative Competence

John O'Neill

Language and politics are each the terror of the other.[1] The man of politics cannot rule through deeds that merely beat on the air like words. Yet few political regimes ignore the power of language. The man of literature is faced with the same dilemma. Anyone who writes and reads and speaks is enslaved once language serves order at the expense of freedom, and yet freedom must be serviced by more than words. Silence is the ultimate political tragedy of language. Silence is the special fate of colonial societies; and thus philosophers like Jürgen Habermas, Frantz Fanon, and Paulo Freire have been deeply concerned with the crucial relationship between politics and language in the struggle for decolonization. Men and women are ruled by silence so long as they lack political poets to give names to the things and relations that rule their lives. The oppressed are ruled in silence so long as they do not have a name even for themselves but are forced to speak of themselves as others speak of them—as niggers, as natives, as poor people. As long as three-quarters of the world's men and women refer to themselves in terms of the theory of inhumanity[2] through which the other quarter of the world dominates them, they live in enforced silence.

I

Karl-Otto Apel[3] and Jürgen Habermas[4] have attempted to reconstruct the ethics of a communicative community as the implicit norm of any society concerned with human development and collective emancipation. In view of the availability of these ideas and their extensive critical evaluation, I shall introduce them briefly with the purpose of locating them in the less abstract setting of a colonial society. Speech and literacy are vital to the emergence of a self-determining community. However, there is no analogue in the colonial context to the psychoanalytic model of nonrepressive dialogues[5] or parliamentary debate and its extensions in the media. Nor indeed can there be any presumption on even a bare structure of civil rights designed to foster free inquiry and discussion. In turn, it is well to remember that the specific issues that we shall identify as the problem of linguistic decolonization need not be restricted to exotic colonial settings. Insofar as we are all colonized by the specialist languages of the social science agencies of the administrative state, we need to think of a creative pedagogy that will help to emancipate relatively literate urban and industrialized citizens.[6]

With this in view I want to show that the principles and applied pedagogy to be found in the work of Fanon and Freire are equally relevant to the problems of repressive communication in socialist and capitalist societies whatever their degree of literacy.[7] Their work provides a vital extension to critical theory and its implicit pedagogy. The core of Habermas's search for a rational principle that could function at once as nature and norm in the human community is articulated in his theory of communicative competence. To this end he has attempted to reconstruct the logical analysis of language, restoring its pragmatic and semantic dimensions relative to the triple domains of the external world, the speaker's lifeworld, and the social world.[8] In effect Habermas's linguistic turn shifts the function of the proletariat as nature and norm of society off the historical stage in favor of a universal communicative competence that on each occasion and circumstance of its exercise implicitly invokes a civil community of truth, equality, sincerity, and freedom. This ethical matrix bears a striking resemblance to the moral foundations of the pedagogy of the oppressed developed by Freire. Habermas is, of course, aware that there are complex historical and political developments involved in the institutionalization of three domains of discourse, which may be represented as science, ethics, and politics, as well as in their distinctive relations over the course of Western history.[9] Nevertheless he considers that there exists a historical trend that raises the ethics of communication to the level of an evolutionary universal, to employ Parsonian language.

Along the same lines, although with a less sweeping reconstruction of the logic of the social sciences than undertaken by Habermas, Apel has argued against the split between the value-neutral rationality of the sciences and the subjectivization of group morals. This split, which Habermas has done much to identify, really moves in a direction that subordinates the need for universal communicative ethics to the public dominance of technical rationality over private, family, and local values. Apel's solution, however, does not provide any discussion of the institutional processes that would realize the a priori of the communication community of argument, which is the transcendental pragmatic ground of the peculiarly Western goal of science-based emancipation. Moreover, in Apel's version of the reconstruction of historical materialism and proletarian ethics, Marxism survives only as a "humanitarian, emancipatory and, to some extent, hypothetical, experimental Marxism or—more correctly—neo-Marxism."[10] Not only is Marxism severely reduced as the transcendental nature and norm of human history, whatever Habermas's view, but its real political institutionalization will, as Maurice Merleau-Ponty observed, bring Marxist humanism to Marxist violence.[11] Until very recently Habermas and Apel have restricted their discussion of the conflict between the stategy of emancipation and its necessary scientific base to the problem of the accountability of experts in bourgeois society.[12] But it is obvious that the same problem exists in avowedly socialist societies. In other words, socialist political parties and their technical apparatus must find ways of bringing the proletariat, artists, and intellectuals into the full enjoyment of a democratic polity. The fate of Solidarity in Poland is surely evidence of this problem. The Communist party turned away from its chance to learn to talk with the trade unions. Against a background of imperial Russian tanks, the junta turned to martial law and the suspension of Solidarity, crushing the new hopes for even a minimal practice of communicative socialism.

In his latest work Habermas has been concerned with the problems of reproducing life-work structures eroded by the logic of the generalized media of power and money as a force in all systems of cultural reproduction—society, personality, and culture. This represents an important step away from the analytic problems of the normative foundations of the ideal speech community toward the treatment of the contingent problems of the expropriation and alienation of lifeworld communicative competences. As Habermas now sees it, the problem of cultural reproduction is to maintain a double exchange between the lifeworld (folk culture, village, family, and neighborhood values and knowledge) and the social system (economy and polity) such that the lifeworld structures remain lively enough to participate in the broader social system and healthy enough to resist the colonization of the lifeworld. To a considerable extent this welcome move involves a reappraisal by Habermas of the phenomenological contribution to critical theory. It involves a recognition of the critical function of the lifeworld for which I have argued for several years.[13] The present essay represents a further step in this inquiry since it brings to bear the ethical problems of responsibly introducing critical communicative competences into a colonized lifeworld in which mind, self, and society have been brutalized.

II

With such concerns in mind we turn to the work of Frantz Fanon and Paulo Freire because of the way each radicalizes the political issues and the methodological tasks in the construction of a viable communicative community in the first stages of political emancipation. We shall first consider Fanon's analysis of the institutions and social psychology of colonialism and the role that Marxist diagnosis and political leadership can play in overcoming the fundamental linguistic alienation of a colonial people before and after their revolution. Fanon's observations contextualize and show how the evolutionary process that Habermas reconstructs may be repressed, if not turned to self-oppression. In short we shall be concerned with the politics of silence on the other side of the communicative community. Such silence, so far from being empty, is the harsh and cruel work of those who refuse to name the political institutions through which they own other men and women. Thus colonial medicine, psychology, and economics are essentially racist. They diagnose the lives of the oppressed in abstraction from the political conditions of which they are themselves an integral practice. The oppressor's language can locate political differences racially only if the social scientist is willing to conspire with the dominant political culture. The "North African syndrome," the "negro personality," and the "lower-class attitude" represent the twisting of language into the stereotypes that rule men and women who are not free to analyze their political culture as the principal source of the differences in the lives of the oppressor and the oppressed. In calling for a situational diagnosis[14] of the colonial sickness, Fanon's purpose was not simply to substitute sociological analysis for medical analysis. Fanon's diagnosis of the colonial world, of its ecological and economic divisions, was intended to serve the classical Marxist purpose of revealing the moral structure of the colonial world by naming its protagonists in the light of the historical drama that will make the last first and the first last. Like Marx's classical analysis of capitalism, Fanon's analysis of colonialism was not intended to become the instrument of a scientific or party elite.

The Wretched of the Earth is at once a great work of politics and literature because it takes up the calling and the praise of those famous men and women whose anonymous labor and suffering has borne the weight of Europe's noisy humanism from which so much of humanity is shut out:

When I search for Man in the technique and style of Europe, I see only a succession of negations of man, and an avalanche of murders.

The Human condition, plans for mankind and collaboration between men in those tasks which increase the sum total of humanity are new problems, which demand true inventions.

Let us decide not to imitate Europe; let us combine our muscles and our brains in a new direction. Let us try to create the whole man, whom Europe has been incapable of bringing a triumphant birth.[15]

Many have read *The Wretched of the Earth* as a eulogy to revolutionary violence. I believe that this interpretation is misled by the shouting and noise of revolution and overlooks Fanon's patient concern with building new institutions, among which is first of all language through which men and women test their freedom and equality. For this reason, Fanon was a severe critic of that narcissistic dialogue engaged in by colonial intellectuals in their belief that Western values can bridge the transition from a colonial society to independent nationhood. He is equally the critic of demagoguery and silent expertise on the ground that both exist only where native communal constitutions are in decay. Indeed if violence had any attraction for Fanon, it is because it is the ground of common experience that reintegrates traditional institutions and strengthens them against both their colonial oppressors and their own internal counterrevolutionary expropriation by new nationalist parties and leaders:

An isolated individual may obstinately refuse to understand a problem, but the group or the village understands with disconcerting rapidity. It is true that if care is taken to use only a language that is understood by graduates in law and economics, you can easily prove that the masses have to be managed from above. But if you speak the language of every day; if you are not obsessed by the perverse desire to spread confusion and to rid yourself of the people, then you will realise that the masses are quick to seize every shade of meaning and to learn all the tricks of the trade. If recourse is had to technical language, this signifies that it has been decided to consider the masses as uninitiated. Such a language is hard put to it to hide the lecturer's wish to cheat the people and to leave them out of things. The business of obscuring language is a mask behind which stands the much greater business of plunder. The people's property and the people's sovereignty are to be stripped from them at one and the same time. *Everything can be explained to the people, on the simple condition that you really want them to understand.* And if you think that you don't need them, and that on the contrary they may hinder the smooth running of the many limited liability companies whose aim it is to make the people even poorer, then the problem is quite clear.[16]

My argument is not intended to minimize the necessity of revolutionary violence in the achievement of decolonization. But it is important not to overlook the educational value that Fanon attributed to the experience of common dangers and problems. A national culture is not built by violence so much as what men and women learn together in dealing with the capacity for oppression that lies in themselves and their own people, as well as in the foreign bourgeoisie. We need to distinguish the earlier stages of revolution, where violence may be a necessity, from the later stages of revolutionary social reconstruction in which permanent violence is debilitating. In the early stages of the colonial revolution, violence may be a step through which individuals come to terms with the internalization of economic and political oppression. Marxist sociodiagnosis facilitates the externalization of aggression and is a step toward the rejection of the colonialist sickness. But as the revolution faces the task of rebuilding native institutions, its strength lies not so much in its capacity for violence as in its efforts to deal maturely with the experience of differences in moral strength, political knowledge, and ability to speak and act. Revolutionary leaders face their greatest trial in the seductions of political success and the constant temptation to treat their own people once again as the material of wealth and privilege.

Fanon was insistent that the task of building national culture lies in encouraging the voice and common sense native to the people wherever there are sound traditions and institutions. This is not simply populist romanticism. The argument is that sound local institutions are essential to good sense, not that politics is an affair of the untutored mind. Nothing is achieved by the revolution if the people merely exchange the oppressor's language for the language of a revolutionary elite that expropriates the meaning and purpose of the revolution as an exercise in technical planning. The revolution can be strengthened only so long as its will and reason are exercised through communal arrangements whose health and maturity in turn are strengthened through the exercise of functions that otherwise is only atrophied by the appropriations of centralized planning and control. Fanon expressly rejected any false preservations or shouting of native culture since this reflects once again the internalization of cultural racism.[17] The vitality of native culture is threatened by elitist aestheticism, that is, by the subjectivization of culture and its expropriation as the sensibility of a small, urban elite that preserves its distance from the rural interior and presumes always to speak on behalf of people whom it silences.

Clearly Fanon was opposed to the cult of leaders and to the single-party state. His ideal was a peasant-oriented party that would not harden against the masses in favor of its own power and maintenance. Fanon sought to separate the party from its inevitable role as a committee on behalf of the dictatorship of the state and its police.[18] Similarly the party should avoid becoming the instrument of leaders, for this shows its conception of the people only as a herd to be driven. The revolution becomes another sickness of the people where every meeting serves only to harangue them with the speech of their leaders. Such occasions serve to hide the failure to achieve forms of political decentralization Fanon believed to be the only means of preserving the popular vitality and intelligence of a revolutionary society:

The people must understand what is at stake. *Public business ought to be the business of the public.* So the necessity of creating a large number of well-informed nuclei at the bottom crops up again. Too often, in fact, we are content to establish national organizations at the top and always in the capital: the Women's Union, the Young People's Federation, Trade Unions etc. But if one takes the trouble to investigate what is behind the office in the capital, if you go into the inner room where the reports ought to be, you will be shocked by the emptiness, the blank spaces, and the bluff. There must be a basis; there must be cells that supply content and life. The masses should be able to meet together, discuss, propose and receive directions. The citizens should be able to speak, to express themselves and to put forward new ideas. *The branch meeting and the committee meeting are liturgical acts.* They are privileged occasions given to a human being to listen and to speak. At each meeting, the brain increases its means of participation and the eye discovers a landscape more and more in keeping with human dignity.[19]

In *Black Skin White Masks* Fanon remarks on the importance he attached to language as a central feature of colonial culture.[20] The black men and women who speak the white man's language cannot achieve anything beyond the place assigned to them in the white society. Negritude, as Fanon learned in a shattering comment from Jean-Paul Sartre,[21] cannot achieve the positive negation of the master-slave relationship. Negritude is the beautiful song of the experience that whites have laid on black men and women. But it is not the everyday language of blacks working out their own fate in the midst of institutions for which they are themselves responsible.

III

We now turn to Paulo Freire in order to see how Fanon's conception of the role of language in decolonization can be made an empirical instrument of participant social change and yet not lose its Hegelian ties with the concept of metaphysical rebellion. Without exploring this relationship in Hegel,[22] let us simply observe that what Fanon and Freire have grasped from Hegelian Marxism is that the problem of alienation requires a theory of education. A theory of socialist education is therefore a theory of the education of socialist educators, as Marx stated so clearly in his third thesis on Feuerbach:

The materialist doctrine that men are products of circumstances and upbringing, and that, therefore, changed men are products of other circumstances and changed upbringing, forgets that it is men that change circumstances and the educator himself needs educating. Hence, this doctrine necessarily arrives at dividing society into two parts, of which one is superior to society (in Robert Owen, for example). The coincidence of the changing of circumstances and of human activity can be conceived and rationally understood only as revolutionary practice.[23]

Freire's critique of the "banking" concept of education as an instrument of oppression is a necessary extension of Marx's critique of the inevitable elitism in socialist educational theory that develops from the moment the masses are made the instrument of party ideology and leadership.[24] In short it would be mistaken not to take the opportunity of combining the observations of Fanon and Freire to lay the foundations of the positive theory and practice of socialist education among oppressed people. It is part of this recommendation that such a theory of education would be an instrument of revolutionary practice in industrial as well as colonial societies. Here a number of attempts to recommend the deschooling of industrial society come to mind, though they cannot be taken up at this point.[25] I regard the remaining discussion of Freire's views on language and decolonization as an essential ingredient in the educational theory of any society, whether it is industrialized and whether it is a socialist society—though how a revolutionary society could be instituted without the pedagogical practices recommended by Fanon and Freire is hard to see.

Freire and Fanon are political writers because they are aware that all culture is political. This is so not because culture is simply ideological but because it involves competences and resources that are unevenly distributed. Worse still, even leftist, radical, and humanitarian culture defends itself as a form of property. Thus a constant struggle is necessary to make reading, writing, listening, and speaking essential to the life of free people and to see that they are never practiced apart from the solicitation of a community in which cultural activity is not the work solely of exceptional individuals.[26] By this standard the humanitarian and leftist sloganizing of the masses merely continues their oppression because it still excludes the people from their vocation of naming and transforming their own world. Not every revolutionary will find himself or herself capable of abandoning the ambition to stand out even in a community of free men and women:

Those who authentically commit themselves to the people must reexamine themselves constantly. This conversion is so radical as not to allow of ambiguous behavior. To affirm this commitment but to consider oneself the proprietor of revolutionary wisdom—which must then be given to (or imposed on) the people—is to retain the old ways. The man who proclaims devotion to the cause of liberation yet is unable to enter into *communion* with the people, whom he continues to regard as totally ignorant, is grievously self-deceived. The convert who approaches the people but feels alarm at each suggestion they offer, and attempts to impose his "status," remains nostalgic towards his origins.[27]

It would be a separate although closely related topic to explore the implications of Fanon and Freire's pedagogical views with respect to the role of socialist parties and the education of the masses. Their position seems to be largely a humanist one, at least as we understand it from Georg Lukács and Maurice Merleau-Ponty.[28] The practical concerns of Fanon and Freire with the colonial context of language lie with its deconstruction. In this sense they deepen Habermas's own analysis of the process of distorted communication, of manipulated trust and consent, that occurs in the colonization of the lifeworld. Although I think it necessary to consider these values as relevant to the deschooling of socialist society, I would like to describe in some detail Freire's theory of conscientization (*conscientizaçao*) because it lies at the basis of any resolution of the tragedy of language and politics in which socialist humanism is caught, no less than that European humanism on which Fanon's brothers may turn their backs.

The oppressed are the instrument of a culture of silence, which is maintained by the political control of language and education that excludes the poor from critical reflection and its revolutionary practice.[29] At first the oppressed are as fearful of their own freedom as are their masters, for they have internalized or, as Fanon says, "epidermalized," the oppressor's opinion of their incompetence. The oppressed believe obedience to be their destiny. Thus it is difficult to persuade them that their historical and ontological destiny is to become men and women who answer to the call of the name of man and woman in their own way and in accordance with their own capacity to name and to analyze their world. At best the oppressed are likely to believe that their freedom can only be a gift, and in this their humanitarian leaders are just as much deceived:

The central problem is this: How can the oppressed, as divided, unauthentic beings, participate in developing the pedagogy of their liberation? Only as they discover themselves to be "hosts" of the oppressor can they contribute to the midwifery of their liberating pedagogy. As long as they live in the duality in which *to be* is *to be like*, and *to be like* is *to be like the oppressor*, this contribution is impossible. The pedagogy of the oppressed is an instrument for their critical discovery that both they and their oppressors are manifestations of dehumanization.[30]

Conscientization is not the work of cultural and political leaders alone, for they are prone to sloganize the people, to lead them by the hand, and to hide their own elitism behind a populist rhetoric that has a hollow ring. Cultural and political leadership merely continues the people's alienation from the uses of language, thought, and action. Wherever some men or women think and speak and act on behalf of others, thought and action are separated from genuine praxis; thought degenerates into verbalism, and action is misled into activism. True speech holds thought and action together; it speaks in order to alter the world, to move men and women and to be moved by them in true dialogue:

Human existence cannot be silent, nor can it be nourished by false words, but only by true words, with which men transform the world. To exist humanly, is to *name* the world, to change it. Once named, the world in its turn reappears to the namers as a problem and requires of them a new *naming*. Men are not built in silence, but in word, in work, in action-reflection.

But while to say the true word—which is work, which is praxis— is to transform the world, saying that word is not the privilege of some few men, but the right of every man. Consequently, no one can say a true word alone—nor can he say it *for* another, in a prescriptive act which robs others of their words.[31]

Science names the world without any concern for the world's response. For this reason it cannot be a model for social scientists and their political leaders. The human world is essentially a spoken world. Wherever some men or women presume to speak for others, they make the world less human. In the human world there is no counterpart to the silence of nature—except where oppression rules.[32] To the extent that political leaders and their advisers talk in a language beyond the people, they make of science a crafty instrument for the expropriation of human dialogue and its rule of community. Human dialogue cannot exist except where men and women love the world and human society. Such a love cannot be one-sided; it belongs neither to the giver nor to the receiver. Dialogue therefore cannot grow where love is sentimental or manipulative, for then it fails to generate freedom from which it in turn grows. Dialogue cannot grow where men or women are arrogant and domineering; it can be sustained only in humility. Such humility cannot be present where a few people consider themselves wise and the rest ignorant or where men and women set themselves apart and unwilling to bend in the service of the people. Of course, the capacity of men and women for dialogue may be thwarted and overpowered by their oppressors, but this will not destroy the faith in men and women that "dialogical man" has. This is not because the dialogical person is naive but rather is critical and regards oppression as the positive occasion for struggle and liberation. Thus insofar as dialogue is grounded in love, humility, and faith, it cannot do anything less than foster trust, that is, a partnership in naming the world. By the same token the humility and trust conveyed in dialogue cannot be exercised without hope. But hope is not waiting in silence. Hope is fighting belief in our essential incompleteness, which makes injustice not a thing for despair but a reason to search for communion and greater humanity. Hope is therefore necessary to critical thinking because it temporalizes the dead spaces of culture and makes them virtual dimensions of human action and obligation.

IV

Conscientization is achieved by critical thinking, which makes language the instrument of decolonization. The task is to bring into play the dialectical mediation of the concrete and theoretical contexts of the word by problematizing such generative words as *slum, ignorance, re-develop, progress.*[33] Thus literacy becomes a dialogical exercise through which social reality is decoded in order to lay bare the overdetermination of the word by the infrastructure of political power and exploitation. In this process learners seek to test the objectification of their social world against their existential experience and to reevaluate the objective institutional order in terms of subjective relevances. However, rather than devalue their own experiences in favor of the ruling codification, they judge the latter in the light of the alternative community generated by critical understanding. At first the oppressed man and woman will be afraid of critical knowledge because they have internalized the oppressor's hostility to anything that challenges the dominant order. Their temptation is silence. For this reason the generative themes of domination and liberation can be presented to the people only through a pedagogy founded on love, faith, and humility.

An elitist knowledge hides its paternalism behind imitative and rote learning, which never opens up the generative themes of daily life in the colonial world. Conscientization, however, from the first works with the people to reach an understanding and transformation of the oppressive elements in their lives. So far from remaining a matter of principled declaration, the praxis of conscientization may be summarized in the following practical steps:

1. The investigators may not enter an area or village without the informal consent of the local people. Consent is to be reached through a meeting in which the purposes of the thematic investigation are explained and local members recruited to participate. Without local participation the investigation cannot achieve its pedagogical end, for "thematic investigation is justified only to the extent that it returns to the people what truly belongs to them; to the extent that it represents not an attempt to learn about the people, but to come to know with them the reality which challenges them."[34]

2. In order to decode the reality facing the people, the investigators must observe and record every idiom of the people's daily life, their work and conversation, always seeking to avoid discounting its value in terms of their own preconceived notions.

Meetings should be held in the area of the investigation in which each of the team presents its decoding essay for consideration by other members, including representatives of the local inhabitants. At issue is the decoding of the total social situation into nuclei of principal and secondary contradictions, with the aim of eliciting dialogically a program of educational action in the community.

3. "Since they represent existential situations, the codifications should be *simple* in their complexity and offer various decoding possibilities in order to avoid the brain-washing tendencies of propaganda. Codifications are not slogans; they are cognizable objects, challenges towards which the critical reflection of the decoders should be directed."[35]

4. Once the interdisciplinary team has reworked the codification, they must return to the area of investigation in order to set up a number of thematic investigation circles, each with twenty participants. The participants from the area must be challenged to engage in the dialogue that produces a decodification relevant to the practical interests

of the people. A psychologist and a sociologist should be present to record the responses and reactions of the decoders.

5. All the materials gathered in the thematic investigation circles are then subject to analysis to discover the themes that can be broken down and presented in the form of learning units, which will convey the sense of the total theme, say, of nationalism or development. In the dialogical atmosphere of these culture circles, it is likely that certain hinged themes will have to be introduced either by the people or the educators in order to preserve the connections between the part and the whole or else to preserve the anthropological concept of culture as the work of men and women who actively transform the world and do not simply adapt to their surroundings.

6. Finally, it is necessary to choose the best mode of communication for each theme. Codification will make use of pictorial, graphic, tactile, and audiovisual channels. Dramatizations, reading of magazine articles, newspapers, and passages from books may also be used in order to cultivate critical reading, watching, and evaluating by the men and women who have participated in the thematic investigations from the beginning.

Freire's method of thematic investigation makes language the basic tool of that true educational dialogue in which the human world is subjected to the same question that men and women are for themselves. Freire's literacy method integrates the historical and ontological task of naming the world with the everyday tasks of education and social transformation. At every turn Freire exposes how methodology and rationality become ideological instruments of paternalism and of expert-lay control and manipulation. For there is a risk that socialist talk and analytic competence may constitute yet another form of proletarian exclusion. Literacy campaigns, land reform, agricultural development, nationalism, and party leadership, until proved otherwise, represent new instruments of oppression. Unless they can be subjected to a genuine popular educational praxis designed to encourage critical use and evaluation, the instruments of modernization merely serve as new contexts of domination.[36]

The evil of our time is the domestication of men and women's intellect, will, and imagination. Both Fanon and Freire are utopian socialists for the reason that neither appears to have lost hope. The pedagogy of the oppressed is the educational instrument of an anthropological hope that is neither idealist nor impractical. Rather it is realistic because it denounces existing reality on the basis of a scientific analysis and decodification of its dominant themes, and it is practical because its analysis already identifies the mechanisms and consciousness of change.[37] A revolutionary society must avoid the historical fatalism of the so-called advanced industrial countries that decree that Third World history shall only repeat their own. By the same token revolutionary leaders must struggle against the temptation to initiate. Therefore, they cannot:

Denounce reality (capitalism) without knowing how it really operates.

Proclaim a new reality (socialism) without having a draft project that, although it emerges in the denunciation, becomes a viable project (a farm or school) only in praxis.

Know reality (colonialism) without relying on the people as well as on objective facts for the source of its knowledge.

Denounce and proclaim by itself (mere propaganda).

Make new myths out of the denunciation and annunciation; denunciation and annunciation must be anti-ideological insofar as they result from scientific knowledge of reality.

Renounce communion with the people not only during the time between the dialectic of denunciation and annunciation and the concretization of a viable project but also in the act of giving that project concrete reality.[38]

Ignorance is the instrument of domination. Revolutionary leadership must always discipline itself against the seduction of scientific expertise, which only breeds a new culture of silence. Men and women may be oppressed as much by knowledge as by violence, even though liberation is impossible without scientific analysis and critical reflection. The people are not to be mystified by slogans and channels of communication that bypass the everyday contents of popular action and reflection in order to prefabricate the people's will in accordance with the ambitions of this political elite. Leaders who think without the people lose their vitality and soon borrow their ideas from the oppressor culture. It is a paradox of the revolution that whereas there is surely someone oppressed by the oppressor, there is no certainty that anyone is freed by the liberator. Thus the education of men and women always calls forth the education of the educators themselves:

Scientific revolutionary humanism cannot, in the name of revolution, treat the oppressed as objects to be analyzed and (based on that analysis) presented with prescriptions for behavior. To do this would be to fall into one of the myths of the oppressor ideology: the *absolutizing of ignorance*. This myth implies the existence of someone who decrees the ignorance of someone else. The one who is doing the decreeing defines himself and the class to which he belongs as those who know or were born to know; he thereby defines others as alien entities. The words of his own class come to be the "true" words, which he imposes or attempts to impose on the others: the oppressed, whose words have been stolen from them. Those who steal the words of others develop a deep doubt in the abilities of others and consider them incompetent. Each time they say their word without hearing the word of those whom they have forbidden to speak, they grow more accustomed to power and acquire a taste for guiding, ordering, and commanding. They can no longer live without having someone to give orders to. Under these circumstances, dialogue is impossible.[39]

V

There is a considerable complementarity between the practical aims of Fanon and Freire and the analytic and emancipatory enterprise of critical social theory. The importance of human freedom and enlightenment is such, however, that we must treat every social institution as potentially strange if it does not foster participant understanding. In this light the institutions of so-called advanced societies will be just as exotic, will require just as much anthropological vigilance, as colonial or so-called underdeveloped societies. But this means that the educators themselves need to be educated. In order not to become the latest class of oppressors ruling through bureaucratic institutions—political parties, universities, hospitals, corporations, and welfare institutions— all who exercise professionalized linguistic competence must be especially vigilant. There is enormous work to be done in cities and neighborhoods and on behalf of the natural environment. The nature of human discourse is challenged as men and women, parents and children begin to reconstruct their relations in the family, in law, medicine, and the workplace. In all these areas they have to learn to handle information and misinformation, to understand that power resides in innumerable discursive strategies, as Foucault has shown.[40] Inevitably such discursive competence will be taught over as property and will be observed under adversarial rules. The liberal professions are morally bound to treat circumspectly the knowledge, consent, trust, and sincerity of those who place their hopes in them. Habermas to the contrary, there is no ideal speech community. All there can be is that strenuous ethical commitment to the practice of communicative participation that Freire has improvised. We otherwise risk imposing on the people all the vices of what Alvin Gouldner aptly calls the "flawed universal class."[41]

Neither Fanon nor Freire can be accused of overlooking the pitfalls that lie in the path of anyone who seeks to transform the culture of silence and oppression. Both writers evidence an eloquence that cannot be appreciated apart from its echo in the voice and assembly of men and women who confer on it a profound and serene force. Fanon and Freire are exemplary cultural critics. They reveal the power of language to witness, in pleading for the integrity of speech and action, while assuming the common risks of living in the world and loving it enough to dare to transform it so as to make it more just and to strengthen human faith in itself. The task they set for the political imagination of men and women opposed to the modern administrative state is to find a pedagogy that will begin to unlock its discursive dominance.[42] The bureaucrat's office administers us in writing and in officialese. It requires that we conscript ourselves to its tasks as evidence of our literacy, thereby trading on the surplus value of mass education in the process of social control. The most urgent task for socialist educators is to begin the work of decolonizing urban and industrial communities. We need no more idealism and no more materialism than this—to see that there is misery in every corner of the earth and that a revolution that is not well made at home is poorly suited for export.

Notes

1. George Steiner, *Language and Silence, Essays on Language, Literature and the Inhuman* (New York: Atheneum, 1967); Susan Sontag, "The Aesthetics of Silence," in her *Styles of Radical Will* (New York: Dell, 1967); Ihab Hassan, *The Literature of Silence: Henry Miller and Samuel Beckett* (New York: Alfred A. Knopf, 1967); John O'Neill, "Violence, Language and the Body Politic," in his *Sociology as a Skin Trade, Essays towards a Reflexive Sociology* (New York: Harper and Row, 1972).

2. Frantz Fanon, *Toward the African Revolution*, trans. Haskon Chevalier (New York: Grove Press, 1969), p. 3.

3. Karl-Otto Apel, *Towards a Transformation of Philosophy*, trans. Glyn Adey and David Frisby (London: Routledge and Kegan Paul, 1980); and *Analytic Philosophy and Geisteswissenschaften* (Dordrecht: D. Reidel Publishing Company, 1967).

4. Jürgen Habermas, "What Is Universal Pragmatics?" in his *Communication and the Evolution of Society*, trans. Thomas McCarthy (Boston: Beacon Press, 1979); Thomas McCarthy, *The Critical Theory of Jürgen Habermas* (Cambridge: MIT Press, 1978), chap. 4; Jürgen Habermas, *The Theory of Communicative Action*, vol. 1: *Reason and the Rationalization of Society*, trans. Thomas McCarthy (Boston: Beacon Press, 1984); *Habermas: Critical Debates*, ed. John B. Thompson and David Held (Cambridge: MIT Press, 1982).

5. See Jürgen Habermas, *Theory and Practice*, trans. John Vietel (Boston: Beacon Press, 1973), pp. 23–32, for a discussion of these objections.

6. John O'Neill, "Language and the Legitimation Problem," *Sociology* 2 (May 1977): 351–358; and "Mutual Knowledge," in *Changing Social Science: Critical Theory and Other Critical Perspectives*, ed. Daniel R. Sabia, Jr. and Jerald T. Wallulis (Albany: State University of New York Press, 1983).

7. Claus Mueller, *The Politics of Communication: A Study in the Political Sociology of Language, Socialization and Legitimation* (New York: Oxford University Press, 1973); and "Notes on the Repression of Communicative Behavior," in *Recent Sociology No. 2, Patterns of Communicative Behavior*, ed. Hans Peter Dreitzel (New York: Macmillan, 1970), pp. 101–113.

8. Habermas, "What Is Universal Pragmatics?" pp. 67–68.

9. Jürgen Habermas, *Strukturwandel der Öffentlichkeit. Untersuchungen zu einer Kategorie der bürgerlichen Gesellschaft* (Neuweid und Berlin: Luchterhand, 1962); "The Classical Doctrine of Politics in Relation to Social Philosophy," in *Theory and Practice*, pp. 41–81.

10. "The *a priori* of the communication community and the foundation of ethics: the problem of a rational foundation of ethics in the scientific age" (Apel, *Towards a Transformation*, p. 283).

11. Maurice Merleau-Ponty, *Humanism and Terror: An Essay on the Communist Problem*, trans. John O'Neill (Boston: Beacon Press, 1969); John O'Neill, "Merleau-Ponty's Critique of Marxist-Scientism," *Canadian Journal of Political and Social Theory* 2 (Winter 1978): 33–61.

12. John O'Neill, "The Mutuality of Accounts: An Essay on Trust," in *Theoretical Perspectives in Sociology*, ed. Scott G. McNall (New York: St. Martin's Press, 1979).

13. John O'Neill, *Making Sense Together: An Introduction to Wild Sociology* (New York: Harper and Row, 1974); and *Five Bodies: The Human Shape of Modern Society* (Ithaca: Cornell University Press, 1985).

14. Fanon, *Toward the African Revolution*, p. 10.

15. Frantz Fanon, *The Wretched of the Earth*, trans. Constance Farrington, with a preface by Jean-Paul Sartre (Harmondsworth: Penguin Books, 1967), p. 252.

16. Ibid., p. 152 (emphasis added).

17. Fanon, "Racism and Culture," in *Toward the African Revolution*.

18. Fanon, *Wretched of the Earth*, p. 146.

19. Ibid., p. 157 (emphasis added).

20. Compare Eldridge Cleaver, *Soul on Ice* (New York: McGraw-Hill, 1968); Albert Memmi, *The Colonizer and the Colonized*, trans. Howard Greenfeld (Boston: Beacon Press, 1967).

21. Frantz Fanon, *Black Skin White Masks* (New York: Grove Press, 1967), pp. 132–135.

22. John O'Neill, "Hegel and Marx on History and Human History," in Jean Hyppolite, *Studies on Marx and Hegel*, trans. John O'Neill (New York: Harper and Row, 1973); Alexandre Kojève, *Introduction to the Reading of Hegel*, ed. Alan Bloom and trans. James H. Nichols, Jr. (New York: Basic Books, 1969).

23. Karl Marx, "Theses on Feuerbach," in *Selected Works*, vol. 2 (Moscow: Foreign Languages Publishing House, 1951), pp. 365–366.

24. Paulo Freire, *Pedagogy of the Oppressed*, trans. Myra Bergman Ramos (New York: Herder and Herder, 1972), chap. 2.

25. Ivan Illich, *Deschooling Society* (New York: Harper and Row, 1971); Paul Goodman, *Compulsory Miseducation and the Community of Scholars* (New York: Vintage Books, 1962).

26. Jean-Paul Sartre, *What Is Literature?*, trans. Bernard Frechtman (New York: Harper and Row, 1965); Roland Barthes, *Writing Degree Zero*, trans. Annette Lavers and Colin Smith (Boston: Beacon Press, 1970); Maurice Merleau-Ponty, *The Prose of the World*, trans. John O'Neill (Evanston: Northwestern University Press, 1973); David Gross, "On Writing Cultural Criticism," *Telos* 16 (Summer 1973): 38–60.

27. Freire, *Pedagogy*, p. 47.

28. Georg Lukács, *Lenin, A Study on the Unity of His Thought*, trans. Nicholas Jacobs (Cambridge: MIT Press, 1970); Merleau-Ponty, *Humanism and Terror*.

29. Paulo Freire, "The Adult Literacy Process as Cultural Action for Freedom," *Harvard Educational Review* 40 (May 1970): 205–225; and "Cultural Action and Conscientization," *Harvard Educational Review* 40 (August 1970): 452–477.

30. Freire, *Pedagogy*, p. 33.

31. Ibid., p. 76.

32. Of course, silence is constitutive of life and language when it is not a sullen imposition. See, for example, Ivan D. Illich, "The Eloquence of Silence," in *Celebration of Awareness, A Call for Institutional Revolution* (Garden City, N.Y.: Doubleday, 1970).

33. For detailed descriptions of the words, pictures, and questions employed in this method, see Cynthia Brown, "Literacy in 30 Hours: Paulo Freire's Process in Northeast Brazil," *Social Policy* 5 (July–August 1974): 25–32; Elisabeth Angus, "The Awakening of a People: Nicaragua's Literacy Campaign," *Two Thirds, A Journal of Underdevelopment Studies* 2 (1980–1981): 6–32.

34. Freire, *Pedagogy*, p. 102.

35. Ibid., p. 107.

36. Paulo Freire, *Education for Critical Consciousness* (New York: Seabury Press, 1973).

37. Freire, "Adult Literacy Process," pp. 220–221.

38. Freire, "Cultural Action," p. 468.

John O'Neill

39. Freire, *Pedagogy*, p. 129.

40. Michel Foucault, *Language, Counter-Memory, Practice*, ed. Donald F. Bouchard (Ithaca: Cornell University Press, 1977); see also John O'Neill, "Sociological Nemesis: Parsons and Foucault on the Therapeutic Disciplines," in *The Dissolution of Sociological Theory? Morals, Politics and the Transformation of Sociological Discourse*, ed. Mark L. Wardell and Stephen Turner (London: George Allen and Unwin, 1985).

41. Alvin W. Gouldner, *The Future of the Intellectuals and the Rise of the New Class* (New York: Seabury Press, 1979), p. 83.

42. John Forester, "Listening: The Social Policy of Everyday Life (Critical Theory and Hermeneutics in Practice)," *Social Praxis* 7 (1980): 219–232; "Planning in the Face of Power," *Journal of the American Planning Association* (Winter 1982): 67–80.

Education and Cultural Invasion: Critical Social Theory, Education as Instruction, and the "Pedagogy of the Oppressed"

Dieter Misgeld

The transformation of cultural resources for understanding social activities into technically planned courses of action is the topic of this chapter. It addresses education as a field in which this transformation is attempted. Critical social theory will be discussed as a theory that has had this kind of cultural change occurring in industrial societies as a general theme since the 1930s. From the perspective of a critical theory of society, the technical reorganization of modes of social understanding appears as a form of cultural invasion. By this I mean the suppression of capacities for cultural and social criticalness, which had begun to become part of the design of education since the Enlightenment. These capacities are being pushed aside by the technical rationalization of social interaction in particular organizational spheres of developed industrial societies. Education is one of these spheres. The phenomenon of cultural invasion is further illuminated with respect to the project of a critical-interpretive pedagogy, which places the development of critical competences into the context of dialogical communication.

These topics will be discussed in four sections. In the first I discuss education as a field increasingly subject to pressures arising from the forms of advanced (or late) capitalist social organization. Critical social theory is introduced, because it has claimed in its arguments regarding the relation between society and philosophy that in advanced capitalist (and bureaucratic socialist) societies, the promise of the philosophy of the Enlightenment (from D'Alembert and Diderot to Kant, Fichte, Hegel, and Marx) has either been obscured or defeated. I primarily address Horkheimer and Adorno's position in their *Dialectic of Enlightenment* and apply their arguments to the field of education (while also reviewing some basic features of their critique). Throughout I stress connections linking scientific method, beliefs in social progress, and universal compulsory schooling as the object of the critique.

In section 2 I discuss proposals for the rationalization of instruction connected with the instructional objectives movement. At issue are plans and programs for the reorganization of education grounded in behavioral techniques and in a managerial and administrative approach toward education. Arguments derived from critical social theory are developed in order to illuminate the implications of an unrestrained adoption of this position.

In section 3, by following Jürgen Habermas's reformulation of critical social theory as a theory of communicative action, I attempt to establish a vantage point most relevant for a critical consideration of the developments considered in section 2. In applying Habermas's communications theory of society to education, I bring the position of critical theory up to date regarding the possible transformation of education and schooling into technically controlled courses of action.[1]

In the final section I compare and integrate Habermas's theory of communicative rationality with the Brazilian educator Paulo Freire's *Pedagogy of the Oppressed*. Their conceptions are used to criticize more cogently the transformation of education into the technical planning of instruction.

1. Education and Critical Social Theory

Discussions about education and its aims are subject to a number of political and administrative influences and pressures. They are exposed to the strategic and tactical manipulations of pressure group politics as are other major public goods in developed welfare state societies, such as health care, unemployment insurance, and, most of all, major economic policies. It follows that philosophical ideals of educational value or educational ideals of learning, knowledge, and reason have become submerged in political interpretations of the meaning of education or have been subjected to the rules constitutive of processes of social planning.[2] Thus the meaning of education and of educational activities increasingly is defined by organizational exigencies arising from the educational system (on all its levels) and the political-governmental order on which it is dependent. Thus the educational value of autonomy in the pursuit of knowledge, for example, which was regarded as a supreme value indispensable for any kind of inquiry in educational philosophies since the Enlightenment, is no longer supported by a philosophy enjoying broad public support. It becomes a stock-in-trade phrase of teachers' associations, which are acting as bargaining units: they are concerned with defending the right of teachers to professional self-control against an encroachment on this freedom by public agencies for the administration of schooling, especially ministries of education and other powerful governmental agencies. On the other hand, these agencies, intermediate levels such as boards and their supervisory personnel, and the representatives of research and development may basically want to subordinate teachers to their purposes and to what they regard as significant values—for example, increasing the effectiveness of teachers' performances and their accountability to agencies located outside the classroom.[3] Therefore they can hardly give much play to teachers' need for professional self-control.

It is clear that the meaning of autonomy in inquiry as a value normative for educational transactions barely plays a role. It is pushed aside altogether or becomes subject to reformulations emanating from organizational processes and from organized pressure politics, the essence of a bargaining society (Heilbroner 1976). Insofar as these conflicts are resolved at all, however, resolutions usually take the form of a compromise between increasing monetary rewards to teachers and their relinquishing some of their professional self-control. So far there does not seem to have been a major teachers' strike in developed capitalist societies fought purely on the grounds for the need of professional self-control, on the basis of teachers insisting that they must have greater control of their working conditions. Most labor conflicts in this field concern monetary compensation and job security.

Therefore it can be argued that the notion of autonomous inquiry no longer is foundational (if it ever was) for the practice of education in the organized system of schooling (and of postsecondary education in all probability). It has been transformed into a bargaining item and subordinated to organizational goals themselves, not controlled by the force of the idea of autonomy as an ideal standing above these processes and requiring means of realization adequate to it.

Critical social theory is one of the few theories of society that made the contrast between reason in its ideal sense and the actualities of social life a central topic of their analysis. Critical theory has examined the development of rationalization in industrial societies by focusing on the elimination of the distinction in these societies between the ideal of a rational society as an ideal of human emancipation and actual social arrangements. By affirming the ideal of reason, critical social theory has attempted to show what is needed for critical thought to remain separate from and thus critical of the actual organization of the society. But it has also been critical of philosophical ideas. It has interpreted the philosophical ideals of the Enlightenment (such as that of reason) as having the sense of social emancipation from ignorance, unreflected force, and suffering, thus giving much play to social ideals of full self-possession and nonrepressiveness, of individuation and autonomy, on the part of individuals. The ideal of autonomy and of the pursuit of reason in inquiry has its place in this context.

Critical theorists have also argued that in industrial societies, both capitalist and bureaucratic socialist, knowledge is integrated into a social process, which has as its central content the alienation and reification of social relations. They argue that education at present is not, as was Enlightenment thought, the vehicle for emancipation from ignorance and the suffering caused by the latter. It has become a major means of social control, reconciling people to the reified understanding they have of themselves and of their possibilities of social action, as well as of the historical development of the society. Education, like the mass media and ultimately the market, is part of an organized system to subvert the critical powers of insight and imagination. Students (learners), for example, are to be reconciled to a market society by accepting the possible choice between an array of goods as a real choice and by not contrasting it with an altogether different conception of choice or of relations between people and the products of their work.

In order to determine to what extent critical theory is right in its highly skeptical, often relentlessly pessimistic analysis of advanced capitalist societies, it makes sense to inspect proposals for the technical rearrangements of teaching and learning. They are to be contrasted with the kind of critical inquiry required by an ideal of reason. The latter is a notion of the center of the idea of critical inquiry, which has been derived from the philosophy of the Enlightenment and of German idealism by the critical theorists.

In their *Dialectic of Enlightenment* (1947, 1972) Horkheimer and Adorno argued that the inheritance of Enlightenment philosophy is ambiguous. One must consider the ideal of reason and the notion of critical inquiry connected with it in this context. For them, the notion of emancipation that has emerged from Enlightenment thought has a practical meaning: It requires the removal of force and suffering caused by ignorance and the persistence of traditional authority, unshaken by new possibilities of knowledge. But the Enlightenment has also enthroned a conception of reason and of method that can be interpreted as a new form of domination, subjecting societal members to new modes of regimentation. In reporting these claims, I use the term *Enlightenment* to refer to the historical process of the generation of scientific rationality and universal principles of practical judgment. I do not merely speak of the seventeenth and eighteenth centuries.[4]

The ambiguity of the Enlightenment notion of emancipation is best explained by reference to Kant's suggestive formulation in his *What Is Enlightenment?* His formulation displays the interconnectedness of ideas of emancipation, reason, and education. For Kant, Enlightenment is the "emancipation of man from a state of self-imposed tutelage, of incapacity to use his own intelligence without external guidance."[5] Education here must be seen as self-education; the very act of becoming educated, of daring to use one's own intelligence, is the essence of Enlightenment emancipation.

Kant's formulation indicates that emancipation is also a political act and not just cognition. The removal of conditions of force and repressiveness, standing in the way of the use of one's own reason, is not merely a matter of using one's will intelligently; it is also a matter of using one's will. The emphasis on the cognitive indicates why the Enlightenment's concern with education must follow from its interest in emancipation.

The Enlightenment's confidence in cognitive learning, in both the theoretical disciplines and practical-moral ones, is the normative basis for the view that universal schooling can become the basis of social and political emancipation. My assumption is a judgment based on the predominant historical effects of Enlightenment thought. It is important to note, however, that Kant's emphasis on reason, science, and the possibility of disciplined cognitive learning in both the theoretical and practical spheres declares knowledge to be a matter of universal human interest. This interest is an interest in autonomy, assumed to be universally available to rational creatures. Knowledge is not to be handed over to specialists. In fact the philosopher speaks for all when formulating knowledge as a right.

Today conceptions of education having social emancipation as an end remind us of goals of liberation once connected with the introduction of universal education. Universal education's failure to meet such goals may result from the dialectical transformation of such goals and the institutionalizations designed to implement them. This is the topic of Horkheimer and Adorno's critique.

It is also important to remember that ideas of emancipation such as Kant's were connected with the emergence of a notion of revolution (Habermas 1973, pp. 82–141). An interest in education for the Enlightenment must coincide with an interest in emancipation from natural circumstance and those modes of social authority and power sanctioned by cognitively defective beliefs. Traditional beliefs are defective because they do not permit the autonomous pursuit of insight or will and because they inhibit the public discussion of insights. The Enlightenment, especially when it became a revolutionary political force, was interested in more than just individual autonomy and the concomitant rule of rational methods of discovery and learning.

Enlightenment authors, such as the ideologues of the French revolution (Habermas 1973, p. 89), Thomas Jefferson, and Thomas Paine, were also interested in the creation of a sphere of public debate and of a public will based on such debate. The concern with universal schooling can then be interpreted as resulting from an interest in the development of an enlightened public opinion. Social emancipation requires a concept of reason that has three features: (1) knowledge must be self-discovered, (2) this discovery occurs when thought is based on universal principles of reason, and (3) reason must be public. In adopting universal principles of reason, we subject ourselves to procedures that everyone else must follow as well. Historically what we may vaguely call scientific method has been viewed as the guarantor of the publicness of rules and principles and their universality. For Kant and others its uninhibited operation becomes one major benchmark for the achievement of emancipation, and the notion of reason that it represents becomes the model of individual autonomy. The publicness of reason clearly has a political meaning, although it reaches further than public debate in legislative bodies and other institutions typically established during the Enlightenment. It suggests the formation of a political will to organize the enlightenment of a citizenry beyond all traditionally known bounds. It is probably the very impersonality of scientific method that was seen as supporting the publicness of reason. The progress of science becomes the great leveler of traditional authority and makes education a public concern.

On this basis, a new dialectic of universal principles and individuality arises. Yet for Horkheimer and Adorno, this dialectic has issued once more in a system of domination. Here I once more refer to Kant: "dare to know" for him means removing the conditions that keep people in a state of immaturity. Yet they themselves are responsible as individuals for this immaturity. Education is the act of removing it. Kant understood immaturity as the inability to make use of one's reason, a capacity available to everyone. Yet this faculty, although describable only in concepts expressing a universality ("categories"), is also what allows individuality. Once one "dares to know," one has established one's sovereignty as a person (Adorno and Horkheimer 1972, p. 3) and has become free of the fear of authority. Yet in doing so, Enlightenment ideals demand the individual's acceptance of a cognitive order, which aims at a system, a collective unity of concepts.

Adorno and Horkheimer (1972, p. 25) call this process the self-objectification of thought, which in the end would make thought over into an automatic process. It makes objects universally interchangeable (p. 10). In the course of this process, human beings subject nature to human will yet become subjected even more to one another. Human beings are treated one just like the other. Individuation is denied as a worthwhile human goal. Conformity to rule is required above all. And people, just like things, are apprehended "under the aspect of manufacture and administration" (p. 84).

If one puts Kant's dictum into the context of his philosophy as a whole and interprets it in terms of the evolution of Enlightenment thought into utilitarianism, positivism, and pragmatism (Horkheimer 1972), Kant's concepts of Enlightenment and emancipation become ambiguous:

As the transcendental, supraindividual self, reason comprises the idea of a free, human social life in which men organize themselves as the universal subject and overcome the conflict between pure and empirical reason in the conscious solidarity of the whole. This represents the

Dieter Misgeld

[handwritten annotation: The will to technical competence + knowledge take precedence over emancipation, liberty, from authority + dominance.]

idea of true universality: utopia. At the same time, however, reason constitutes the court of judgment of calculation, which adjusts the world for the ends of self-preservation and recognizes no function other than the preparation of the object from mere sensory material in order to make it the material of subjugation. (Horkheimer and Adorno 1972, pp. 83–84)

Given this interpretation, the adequacy of which it seems idle to deny in terms of contemporary developments in the practical exploitation of scientific knowledge, Francis Bacon's foreshadowing of the modern era's proccupation with a use of knowledge directed toward the mastery of nature seems to have become the cornerstone of an idea of emancipation that makes the mastery of nature its dominant aim. In it is implicit the will to self-preservation of human collectivities, which are determined to master their natural environments by asserting their supremacy through technical knowledge. In Horkheimer and Adorno's judgment this aim has taken precedence over that of general human emancipation from authority and dominance.[6] It has required the repression of impulses suggesting harmony with nature in the experience of an uninhibited and artful display of the unity of consciousness and libidinal impulse (Marcuse 1965). Thus the utopian promise contained in Kant's notion of the autonomy of reason has not been fulfilled.

Knowledge, Horkheimer and Adorno claim, has become social power because of the rule of scientific method that "knows no obstacles: neither in the enslavement of men nor in compliance with the world's rulers" (p. 4). When people are in its thrall, nothing will escape its routinizing and schematizing function. Science becomes operative in society as a particular mode of production, which includes even the planning and direction of consumption, tastes, and preferences. And the increase in rationality provided in the historical achievements of the Enlightenment turns into its opposite, the destruction of critical capacities.[7] The pursuit of human sovereignty in the mastery of nature has turned into the domination of people, not least because of the Enlightenment's concept of reason having been transformed into a factual mentality, a conformist stance of thought. The emergence of totalitarian modes of social control (initially explained with reference to the phenomenon of nazism) is detected as present even in the "culture industry," Horkheimer and Adorno's term for the mass media culture of Western societies (pp. 120–168). These modes of control cannot be viewed merely as contrary to the Enlightenment; they are its legitimate and illegitimate heirs. Enlightenment thought, inseparable for Horkheimer and Adorno from social freedom, must retain its capability to be relentlessly negative over and against the prevailing realities of the organization of social life. Thus is detected in modern education, the Enlightenment institutionalized in universal compulsory education, a serious fault. Education in the new societies of mass production and consumption is a perversion of the intentions of the Enlightenment itself.[8] In many instances it has produced "technologically educated masses" who have "an enigmatic readiness to fall under the sway of any despotism" (p. xiii). What Horkheimer and Adorno have in mind is a manifest phenomenon for anyone who is not struck by ideological blindness—the most advanced societies, in terms of the development and application of scientific knowledge, have also been the most ruthless in the use of such power to dominate and destroy people. Horkheimer and Adorno's reflections suggest that the impersonality of scientific method, its indifference to how it is used, is a factor contributing to the demise of the Enlightenment. It does so by denying difference and individuation, not only in nature but in the human world. Their examination of the manipulation of personality and individuality in the culture industry illustrates the point.

The point can be put even more forcefully: what I globally call the Enlightenment had an interest in education motivated by a basic nonspecialist conception of worthwhile aims of human life hitherto frustrated. Those aims encompassed freedom from want and suffering, as well as intellectual and moral-political autonomy. The model case for autonomy had been provided in natural science. There philosophers and scientists could acquire a sense of their own authority and independence from tradition and of their ability to question and criticize. Science therefore becomes a politically important example.

Yet since the Enlightenment, an unresolved ambiguity has remained: is the resolution of bonds of dependency on others, especially in the sense of subjection to the will of others exerted in the form of political and economic control, the aim of an idea of education connected with a concern for emancipation from dogma and tradition? Or are the liberation from dogma and tradition as well as the removal of political and economic inequality viewed as instrumentally useful for the development of scientific knowledge?

If the latter conception has prevailed, then education, having come under the control of specialists (its being defined by techniques of research no longer responsive to broad philosophical conceptions), is only the latest step in the self-denial of the Enlightenment, once on a course toward social and political emancipation. This is the sacrifice of emancipation for the sake of the most efficient acquisition of knowledge believed to be instrumental in the achievement of general welfare. What has resulted is in some senses even worse. We are faced with a situation wherein general welfare may become indistinguishable from the most efficient administration of society's affairs or the practice of social control by agencies especially designated to engage in controlling and influencing. Should this be so, the Enlightenment's emphasis on the emancipatory function of cognitive learning would have degenerated to the practice of domination in various forms, but especially to the domination of the specialist, and, if so, often in the name of economic and political elites resisting public control of their decisions and actions.

The very existence of elites, to which some Enlightenment authors were antagonistic and which offends the notion of reason's autonomy, would have become an inoffensive fact which we, through education, must become adjusted to rather than emancipated from.

2. The Ideal of Reason and a Technical Conception of Instruction

Horkheimer and Adorno's (as well as Marcuse's) diagnosis of science and enlightenment rationalism as a new form of social power, as well as their endorsement of a comprehensive conception of reason as I discussed it (based on the connections linking ideas of rational autonomy, self-directed inquiry, and education as emancipation from ignorance), rest on the difference between philosophical ideals and the instrumentalization of science in its social use. There cannot be a critique of instrumental reason (as another word for critical social theory) without philosophy. Thus critical social theory attempts to revive a philosophical discourse, which contained the sciences within philosophy. Knowledge can be critical, it is argued, only if it is entered into a comprehension of the entirety of the society in its rationality or, what comes to the same, into a critique of its irrationality. Thus critical theory employs the ideal of reason as an idea of the rationality of the entire society and human history (Jay 1984). It turns it against conceptions of rationality, stressing its procedural nature (Benhabib 1982), that emanate from the specialized sciences. Therefore critical theory is not merely a critique of reified social relations, attacking the latter directly. As such it would only be moralizing indictment. It contains proposals for analyzing the transformation of social relations due to the rule of applied social science. Procedures first arising from industrial production are topical, which "reach into the spheres of material production, administration and of distribution, as well as into the sphere, which calls itself culture. They do so with economic necessity" (Adorno 1979, p. 361).

Education is a field in which one can observe the increasing preponderance of conceptions of managerial rationality initially attached to industrial production. As this happens, the relation of particular instructional activities, pedagogy (which is their theory) and the totality of the society is removed from the center of educational theory. Systems analyses of the functioning of educational institutions can prevail, which place the latter in the context of organizational forms developed for the commercial production and distribution of goods. There remains little room for the formulation of a normative concept of education and of its place in society and culture. Education, just as other practical disciplines such as medicine and law, separates itself from philosophy.[9]

Not even a philosophical theory such as John Dewey's can still serve as a framework for the interpretation of education as a general social concern and the employment of research in the furtherance of educational change. In *Democracy and Education* (1916), Dewey had integrated the theory of education into a theory of democracy (and vice versa). In his case the development of education and of democracy was still accounted for with reference to an idea of social emancipation: they were seen to contribute to the growth of social intelligence as the overcoming of a blind obedience to customary habit. This was the last philosophical theory of education to have generated a major movement of educational reform in industrial societies (Feinberg 1975).

In the contemporary study of education, pragmatic commitments of a much simpler kind come first. One is primarily concerned with the technical improvement of teaching and learning and of administration, supervision, or the use of expert advice. Although Dewey's theory was much more pragmatic than older theories of pedagogy in philosophy and although it regarded education as a form of social intervention that could take the place of more direct political intervention in the society, it would appear as too comprehensive in scope and too principled in intent when viewed from the perspective of contemporary research and theory in education. In other words, although Dewey thought that social science and education could become a new basis for social intervention, he still embedded this conception in the formulation of a comprehensive social ideal, which could serve as a critique of the adaptation of education to criteria derived from the organization of industrial work, of an economic market, and of managerial conceptions of institutional rationalization. By becoming increasingly preoccupied with detailed methods for improving the efficiency of instruction (rationalization), educational research, and frequently theory, are increasingly integrated into the administrative organization of education. As educational research becomes more specialized, more task oriented ("pragmatic"), and closed to principled reflection, applied social science, rather than philosophy and theory, dominates the field. Education is treated as one socially organized activity among others, from the production of goods to the provision of welfare (Illich 1977, 1978, 1981). This orientation in the study of education has little to do with a theory of knowledge in the broadest sense or with a reflection on education as a central concern in all human activities.

Take the example of the planning of instructional objectives (and the related cases of programmed learning and competence-based instruction). Authors of one book in the field, *Objectives for Instruction and Evaluation*, state that "a first step in preparing instructional objectives is to determine what kinds of learning outcomes are desired for a given unit of instruction" (Kibler et al. 1980, p. 81). One does not know when one reads the book where these units come from or why they must be there other than that they are the best thing to have for the sake of accountability, of improving the efficiency of teaching and of providing guarantees for learning success (defined as mastery of a unit as determined by a taxonomically organized evaluation of learning outcomes—in terms of a relation between learners' "entry behavior" and "terminal behavior"). They are also to help avoid "confused" (too broad, too "insecure") ideas of learning.

The reader is told to subordinate the learner and him/herself to a process of instruction centering on the instructional unit concept, such that beginning and end, the parameters of educational activity, are already visible before learning has happened. What has been conceived outside the pertinent interactional situation will determine this situation.

The instructional objectives movement is representative of a rationalizing attitude toward education. The very notion of reflection on education and what education could be in an ideal sense is alien to it. This attitude to education cannot be committed to the mediation of the ideal with the practically feasible, as John Dewey's still was. Dewey was an intermediary, by now of an almost classical cast, between an efficiency-oriented education and an orientation to full realization and self-possession of humanity through education. He still regarded the achievement of practicable arrangements, which both represent and effect a shared ("democratic") concern with social efficiency and social cooperation, as something to be reflectively enjoyed by societal members. Any increase of social intelligence in behavior was to be valued as a case of the self-achievement and self-realization of humanity (Dewey 1916, p. 248).

The instructional objectives movement along with programmed learning and competence-based instruction no longer employ the notion of education in such an emphatic sense. If education occurs at all, it refers only to the business of instruction. Thus teaching and learning, the center of any conception of education corresponding to the classical concept of reason, are redefined to consist of the systematically monitored delivery of instructional units to a client-target group. This group is described as capable of producing anticipated and planned results ("terminal behavior," Kibler et al. 1981, p. 123) by showing on the appropriate range of diagnostic-evaluative tools applied that they have mastered an instructional unit. In this sense only can the group be called "learners." Indeed it would be more correct to say that learners (in this restricted sense) can be documented to have achieved the mastery required. No passionate phrases are used for this achievement. Dewey still employed them when he defined discipline in education as "power of command, a mastery of the resources available for carrying through the action undertaken" (Dewey 1916, p. 129). He also linked discipline to interest, which is "the depth of the grip which the foreseen end has upon one in moving one to act for its realization" (ibid., p. 130).

The classical conception of education placed learners and teachers in their interaction at the center of the educational transaction. Education was sanctioned by an idea of knowledge (of what demands knowing) that required of teachers and learners that they reciprocally engage each other in the examination of some subject matter. They were to help each other to be adequate to the idea.[10] But for the instructional objectives movement, learners appear to be only objects of instruction. They are not constructors of the learning process or co-initiators of a learning experience. From the point of view of those making policy in the instructional objectives mode, learners can be taken for granted. They are a captive audience. Teachers are more prominent, of course, for they are to implement the policy in the classroom. They do the daily work of specifying instructional objectives and checking student progress along the evaluative dimensions provided for them by the constructors of tests and of other diagnostic tools (such as taxonomies of learning outcomes). But they are often little more than the lowest-level implementers of the policies they themselves do not determine. The policies do not arise out of their interaction with the learners. Thus the book we are discussing as an illustration of this position (*Objectives for Instruction and Evaluation*) was not written in order to convince teachers of the value of specifying instructional objectives. Rather it aims to shape their behavior. They are to become favorably disposed toward the policy without having been convinced on the basis of a consideration of pertinent alternatives (Kibler et al. 1981, p. vii).

The active reflection of teachers (and learners) on the meaning and significance of educational work is no longer solicited. Policymakers, planners, and testing specialists take charge of the entire educational process in a supervisory and managerial capacity. In effect teachers are in the same position as a manager of the local supermarket who cannot determine policies for the distribution of food supplies on the basis of his or her knowledge of the real needs of the local population (if he or she still possesses it). The manager may be asked occasionally, of course, for an opinion. And so are teachers.

Advocates (they may sometimes sound like marketing agents) for the specification of measurable instructional objectives in programmed learning and in other instructional technologies warrant their advocacy by referring to possible improvements in the efficiency of instruction. They claim that lessons—the presentation of instructional units—can be better planned by being broken up into separate, controllable segments. Learners' and teachers' behavior can be divided into elements that provide for the possibility of increased predictive control. By limiting teaching to the activity of monitoring (assessing-evaluating) the presentation (by teachers) and reproduction (by learners) of these segmented elements of instructional activity, other possible questions about instruction are blocked, questions, for example, concerning reasons and principles, purpose and ends, origins and motives, the legitimacy of educational activity in particular. These questions are determined by public authorities in any case. Educators may not mislead students into believing that they "can 'democratically' deviate from socially mandated goals" (Kibler et al. 1981, p. 13). It is not their right or privilege, nor that of learners, to call into question what "society" requires that they carry out. Most of all "society" requires that the individual teacher or school system be able to demonstrate that students have learned as a result of their instruction (cf. p. 3).

Thus the instructional objectives movement can pretend that it is not really addressing questions of educational value at all. It is not concerned with the formulation of new educational aims. In fact, it does not talk of education at all. It is concerned only with the improvement of instruction. Statements of aims remain the prerogative of policymaking agencies. Theirs is the privilege to raise issues of educational philosophy. Thus, the issue of what is worth knowing and why and who one is to become by learning to know is sidestepped and also taken out of the hands of teachers and learners, for whom education or even just schooling are daily concerns. But when our concern with education is transformed into the problem of organizing instruction so that its efficiency can be demonstrated, a teacher's interest in and involvement with education can only become wholly external. David Riesman (1979, p. 47) has noted that education may become a concern with appearing to be doing something rather than with doing something. This is a form of the self-objectification of thought Horkheimer and Adorno had observed. They had noted that it would make thought over into an automatic process (cf. 1947, pp. 10, 25). The use of scientific method has grown beyond the limits of rational autonomy and critical insight. It leads to the use of technology and science for purposes of social dominance, a "one-dimensional society" according to Marcuse (1964). The problem of social science is found here.

The social sciences frequently usurp the process of reasoning and deliberation societal members can jointly engage in by presenting themselves as policy sciences or as committed to the furthering of

[handwritten at top of page: Education / Teaching / Reasons with critical / knowledge + critical / self-knowledge]

purposes of social control and administrative planning.[11] The social sciences thus uncritically endorse those very aims that the most powerful institutions in industrial societies, the institutions of the state and large corporations, already have.

When the social sciences have become planning sciences, no longer kept in check by a normative ideal of reason (as I discussed it), progress in planning rationality has been paid for with social regression. Social regression is the indifference to conditions that provide for the distinct identities of societal subjects. Insofar as the instructional objectives movement does not have a conception of the autonomy of teachers (and learners) to be exercised over against the technical rationalization and the administrative reorganization of instruction, individuation in and through one's chosen profession can no longer be a significant goal for teachers. They are transformed into employees of a large organization, the purposes of which they do not define.

Thus the replacement of philosophy by social science and the subjection of critical reasoning capacities to the exigencies of technically efficient action stand for the new forms of domination, which are addressed by critical social theory under the term of a critique of instrumental reason. It becomes a critique of a "positivistically bisected" (Habermas 1976, p. 198) concept of reason, for the latter has the preparation of the world as the material of administration as a consequence. I had argued that the Enlightenment concept of reason is important for a concept of education in accord with critical social theory because "one's sovereignty as a person" (Horkheimer and Adorno 1947, p. 3) was a central feature of this idea. Critical knowledge entailed critical self-knowledge as a necessary feature of the concept of reason. Philosophy from Plato to Rousseau and from Kant to Hegel has always reflected on education with reference to such an idea of self-knowledge: reason could be emancipatory only if teachers and learners engaged in the pursuit of knowledge out of their own volition and for the sake of their own self-recognition.[12] Education as the process of gaining insight into the requirements of reason as an ideal could occur only if a sense of a learner's (and teacher's) own involvement was preserved, a strong sense of self-responsibility. Autonomy and self-responsibility were values for education because without them there could be no development of critical faculties. Detailed pedagogical (and political) prescriptions were derived from this conception.

Advocates for the reformulation of education as the planning and administering of instructional objectives may believe that their programs indeed serve the development of critical abilities. They believe their programs have the advantage of avoiding confused goals and practices. They could not readily conclude that the programs merely make educational processes administratively controllable. They invoke clarity as a virtue, thus calling on science as the form of reasoning that sanctions their enterprise. Yet they can conflate science and technology, thus separating science from the spirit of criticalness, which the Enlightenment conception of science had also contained, largely by drawing on a philosophical ideal of knowledge. When science and technology are conflated, as the advocates for the behavioral formulation and evaluation of instructional objectives intend it, clarity is no more than the predictability of a learning outcome. It has little in common with self-certainty or the reflective achievement of self-knowledge in the course of acquiring objective knowledge. Without embarrassment instructional objectives technologists can therefore admit that their technology is based on research and development "in experimental psychology, military training, and programmed instruction" (Kibler et al. 1981, p. 34).[13]

Thus education is entirely assimilated to training.[14] Research and training have in common that they do not require self-initiated insight into the purposes of the research or of the training program. They require that the interest in self-generated insight be put aside. The risk-burdened enterprise of critical self-reflection is replaced by a program for the avoidance of conflict and uncertainty. This is why the behaviorally organized reform of instructional practice places much emphasis on evaluation.

Evaluation by means of standardized tests and the systematic segmentation of learning tasks and corresponding learning outcomes amounts to a standardization of instructional activities. Research, technology, administration, planning, and finally teaching coalesce into one functionally organized system, with the learners at the bottom and teachers close to it.[15]

Classical educational thought could not have countenanced such a systematically organized rationalization of educational activities because it could not have envisaged the total externalization of conduct into the production (some say "emission") of various goal-directed behaviors.

Dieter Misgeld

3. The Communication Theory of Reason and the Colonization of the Lifeworld

The opposition of critical social theory to these developments amounts only to their indictment as long as it merely charges advanced capitalism (and bureaucratic socialism) with perpetrating universal forms of regimentation and with having eradicated the difference between what is and what might be by having transformed the transcending power of an ideal of reason into a factual mentality and a socially conformist stance of thought. Can the critique of critical social theory be more than indictment and protest?

The interest in socially critical inquiry represented by critical social theory can best be advanced, I believe, by addressing modes of reasoning not yet overwhelmed by the technical rationalization of social activities and by analyzing the rules and principles operative within these modes. The difference between them and the policies and rules operative in planning programs for technical rationalization is to be made manifest.

Habermas has taken this step in his recent work (1979b, 1981). He makes use of the concept of a "sociocultural lifeworld," which has played a major role in phenomenology, by adapting it to the theoretical-critical interests of a critical theory of society.

In *Theorie des kommunikativen Handelns* (1981) he operates with the distinction between system and lifeworld, thus pointing to two different modes for the rationalization of social action. They are a communicative and a purposive rational (or instrumental mode) form of rationalization: we understand society as a system when we focus on the factors underlying social action not known to social actors in their world of everyday communication (the lifeworld). We understand the society as social-cultural lifeworld when we address it with reference to the rules of discourse that establish social relations as relations of communication among societal members who also know that they partake in these relations. Habermas uses these distinctions for identifying the problematic features of rationalization in developed industrial (or late capitalist) societies. Their major conflict is the clash between social action systems having become independent from the generally shared lifeworld and the lifeworld itself as the ground for the communicative organization of commonly held beliefs.[16] These action systems are formed around the axes of increasingly successful intervention in the environment (technologies, economy) or of increasing efficiency in the coordination of social interaction (economy, administration). The rationalization of these action systems is a partial rationalization of the lifeworld at most. At worst it may be destructive of the lifeworld because this process may tend toward making the communicative organization of social interaction superfluous. Thus the terms *lifeworld* and *system* serve as a contrast. A theory that has this contrast as its theme is committed to showing the difference between types of rationalization.

The increasingly complex organization of the economy, for example, or of systems of public administration is exclusively responsive to an interest in increasing the efficiency of these action systems. In the history of systems rationalization, they become functionally more adequate to particular requirements by becoming more differentiated. But their unbridled development may occlude the possibility of further reaching and of more fundamental processes of rationalization. The latter can only arise—therefore the importance of a theory of communicative action—from the social generation of possibilities for making the consensual foundations of social life problematic in a second-order form of consensual validation: a critical discursive examination of claims. A very pointed formulation, admittedly not Habermas's own, might even suggest that a society only follows a path of comprehensive rationalization insofar as the routine grounds of everyday actions in society become increasingly interpretable as claims, just as much as possibilities increase for assessments of the efficiency of its economic and administrative institutions:

A greater degree of cognitive-instrumental rationality produces a greater independence from limitations imposed by the contingent environment on the self-assertion of subjects acting in a goal-directed manner. A greater degree of communicative rationality expands— within a communication community—the scope for unrestrained coordination of actions and consensual resolution of conflicts. (Habermas 1981, 1:15)

One notices already how the discussion of the relation between communicative and instrumental rationality quite naturally leads into an examination of the origins and consequences of societal rationalization. Thus, although Habermas proceeds initially as if a general philosophical argument regarding the dimensions of rationality achievable in speech (discourse) could provide foundations for a theory of societal rationalization, he clearly intends this argument to come into its own by employing it in order to open up the problem of societal rationalization. In his most recent work Habermas systematically addresses the relation between societal development (modernization) as an increase in the efficiency of goal-oriented action (instrumental rationality) and social emancipation (as second sense of rationalization) as a process of freeing communication both from its unreflective reliance on tradition (traditional worldviews, customs) and its being overpowered by the untrammeled and therefore irrational growth of instrumental rationalization.

The rationalization of action systems such as the economy, the financial markets, and corporate and govermental bureaucracies can proceed only if they manage to be indifferent to the cultural resources (including language) usually employed for the organization of everyday life in communication. There may be a threat of these resources drying up. This is what is meant by the phrase "colonization of the lifeworld," which Habermas uses. I have also referred to it when speaking about education as "cultural invasion." By this is meant, the less it becomes possible to hold planning policies and proposals for increasing the efficiency of teaching and learning, for example, accountable to the understanding of these activities arising from their ordinary, policy-independent organization, the more the lifeworld of educational activities is colonized and the more the cultural resources for critical reflection on the organization of social relations have been extinguished. The realities of institutional planning must remain accountable to practices of reasoning and communication that precede planning. These practices consist of the ongoing interpretation of cultural traditions in daily situations. Their subjection to the exigencies of planning may lead to the suppression of societal members' competence to put their interests and needs ahead of the imperatives of planning agencies.[17] The colonization of the lifeworld can succeed if the reasoning typical of planning agencies and bureaucracies is entered into the very processes of deliberation societal members engage in who do not normally undertake the explicit task of policy planning and policy execution. People's ability to be critical of policies and planning designs cannot find adequate expression if the language of everyday communication and common deliberation is undermined with reference to normative conceptions of predictability, controllability and exactitude not readily available in everyday communication but quite entrenched in the organizational practice of planning.

Habermas's theory is a new phase in the development of critical theory because it addresses these new realities. Besides addressing the issue of cultural invasion, it ranges from studies examining the conditions for the full development of the general reasoning capacity of societal members and of their communicative competence (Habermas 1979a, pp. 1–95) to the development of suggestions for participatory planning and for the maximization of democracy in policy deliberation. We can claim, therefore, that with Habermas critical theory has moved beyond its merely philosophical phase. It has become more research oriented and more political. Its aim is to establish limits and orienting values for processes of planned institutional change by critically examining the values subscribed to in this planning and by recognizing and forcefully documenting the place of people and of their administratively untutored reasoning in all this.

When considering education, for example, one begins with questions that may arise between learners and teachers as to what could warrant the kind of social intervention that education is. One begins with questions that proclaim every step to be taken in a process of teaching and learning as a step toward the achievement of mutual recognition of their capacities (competence) by and for teachers and learners. Whatever else the rule of reason may mean here, it requires that teachers and learners confirm one another in their identity as inquiring selves in the very process that generates what they are jointly committed to: an acknowledgment of one another as equally significant participants in the process. This is the central idea of Paulo Freire's influential *Pedagogy of the Oppressed*. My formulation of his position will indicate that I regard his enterprise as akin to aspects of Habermas. Both are critics of cultural invasion and advocates of participatory processes of inquiry.

A synthesis of Habermas's and Freire's ideas (Misgeld 1975, pp. 31–36) offers a productive possibility for a revitalized interest in education as a matter of common (shared human) concern. My interest is in those fundamental modes of reflection and action-orienting understandings that permit people to entertain the kind of reasoning about education with which we began. It raises questions about the whys (reasons, grounds, principles), wheretos (purposes, ends), and wherefroms (origins, motives) of being involved in educational work.

It makes the grounds for being so involved available as what everyone can understand.

Because the older tradition of critical social theory did not unambiguously endorse the radically democratic and egalitarian position typical of Habermas's work, one must show this to be the basis and guiding idea of the newer phase of critical social theory.[18] Otherwise the encounter with Paulo Freire's radical *Pedagogy of the Oppressed* (a pedagogy in action in literacy education in the Third World from Guinea Bissau to Nicaragua) would be far less compelling.

I therefore discuss the issues of cultural invasion and language in Habermas's thought also pertinent to Freire's pedagogy. The program for the specification of instructional objectives stands as an instance of cultural invasion because it requires the subjection of pedagogic-educational reasoning to the exigencies of administrative rationality. Horkheimer and Adorno's analysis of the concept of reason reached its conclusion with their prognosis that in technological society reason might lose its ideal sense and become a mere cipher for a "world adjusted to purposes of self-preservation." The sciences bring about this adjustment. There no longer is any need for an idea of reason. As a consequence objects are subjugated to the purposes of self-preservation. The importance of the notion of reason had been that it preserved an idea of a life to be lived beyond the purposes of self-preservation. But once the development of the sciences, and the increasing powers of technical control issuing from them, have succeeded in reconstructing anything that can stand opposite to human understanding, self-preservation automatically becomes the purpose of increasing technical control. And it is not even well understood anymore as self-preservation. Technical progress having become automatic does not permit societal agents subjected to it any perspective beyond itself; they can no longer assess what it is there for (cf. the discussion of true and false needs in Marcuse 1964, pp. 4–5).

This is where Habermas begins. He describes the development of the sciences — the transformation of reason into the means of collective self-preservation — as did Horkheimer and Adorno and Marcuse.[19] He also interrogates this development so as to make it visible as a practical problem (a topic for a future-oriented analysis, as well as for practical intervention). This is how it becomes a problem of cultural invasion.

In one of his earlier texts Habermas says, "Whether it is a matter of rationalizing the production of goods, management and administration . . . the professional practice in question will always have to assume the form of technical control of objectified processes" (1970a, p. 55). Habermas's efforts concentrate on the distinction between the "capacity for control made possible by the empirical sciences" (ibid., p. 56) and the "capacity for enlightened action" (emancipatory action and reflection). It is just as distinctive for him, however, also to introduce the issue of democracy; when one begins to consider technology, the ever-expanding and scientifically rationalized power of control (ibid., p. 57) over both natural and social environments, the issue of democracy arises in a particularly forceful way: is democracy just the environment conducive to the further expansion of this power, or is it representative of the effort of people (citizens) communicating and acting together to establish a consensus on "how men can and want to live" (ibid., p. 57) under these novel conditions? Habermas argues that the latter is its significance: democracy is not just a system of government. It stands for a kind of society (McPherson 1976, p. 5). In these times it stands for the need to establish the capacity of people to deliberate on their possible aims so that they will not be overtaken by technical-technological progress itself. The intensity of the development of science and technology requires the most intensive pursuit of the ideal of rational (discursive) will formation achieved by people joined in communication.

But the discourse needed for the rational will formation of societal collectivities requires cultural resources that are in jeopardy, when the social lifeworld has become colonized, for the moral-practical and the aesthetic practical meaning of cultural action and communication have been penetrated by forms of economic and administrative rationality that suppress this meaning. Habermas speaks of "an impoverishment in possibilities of expression and communication, which as far as we know are still required, even in complex societies, so that individuals can learn to find themselves, to come to terms with their own conflicts, and to cooperatively solve conflicts which they have in common, i.e., by collectively forming their will" (Habermas 1979b, p. 28).

The concept of the lifeworld suggests the generation of shared understandings underlying the orientation of action, which cannot be made fully explicit either by theoretical analysis or by following the model of technical knowledge (control over objectified processes). The concept's strength (Misgeld 1983c) lies in reminding us of ways for understanding and interpreting one's culture that have little or nothing to do with controlling them. Matters of moral and aesthetic sensitivity, for example, to which Habermas alludes, never suggest that they can be understood without some investment on the part of the one devoted to them. These kinds of values make demands on us that transcend purposes of self-preservation. Indeed they and the objects ("creations") they stand for suggest possibilities of personal and cultural development that establish limits to self-preservation. They show why the latter cannot be the exclusive cultural value.

One might also say that these cultural values set limits to the possibilities of planning; values that can be planned for totally, such as increase in leisure, are not equal to the values they are instrumental for, such as happiness. Yet with the penetration of the lifeworld by the administrative rationality of total planning and the corresponding manipulation of needs and desires, increases in leisure time may become equated with happiness. (Marcuse explored this dialectic with much force. Compare his concept of repressive desublimation: Marcuse 1964, pp. 56–83.)

Yet the concept of the lifeworld as such (or the corresponding concept of social integration; see Habermas 1975, p. 4, 1981, vol. 2) cannot sustain the needed distinction between the action (knowledge) of technical control and emancipatory action (and discourse). The normative ideal of increasing democratization of processes of will formation in "complex" (a phrase Habermas occasionally employs) societies cannot be derived from the distinction between administratively regulated and administratively unregulated comunication processes.

Rather, for the ideal to be theoretically defensible and to be politically persuasive, it must be shown—this is the argument preferred by the later Habermas—to be rooted in the very idea of communication underlying actual processes of communication in the world of daily life and cultural understanding as well as administrative systems.

An analysis of presuppositions for the possibility of communication is proposed. It organizes all speech actions (communicative actions) into types in order to show how the intention of reaching agreement is their animating force. It analyzes "the process of understanding from the dynamic perspective of bringing about an agreement" (Habermas 1979a, p. 3). Habermas states therefore that speech actions can be understood as the raising of claims insofar as they point to the possibility and necessity of reaching agreement (shared understanding). This is the project of universal pragmatics, the systematically developed theory of communicative competence (Habermas 1970b, pp. 114–150, 1979a, pp. 1–68; McCarthy 1978, pp. 272–357). An even more ambitious argument is employed in order to show that the claims supportive of an orientation to agreement in ordinary language communication are "universal claims to validity." This means that speakers, in the course of making utterances, have an implicit grasp of what rational agreement-consensus could look like in a number of cognitively and practically (morally, politically) consequential cases. They have implicit mastery of the idea of rational agreement or of an "ideal speech situation," as Habermas sometimes says. We notice that the theme of the ideal of reason returns, placed into the context of a discussion of language. Reason becomes the telos of communication.

The construction of an ideal situation of discourse (a situation free from internal compulsion and externally imposed domination, to mention merely one feature of it) represents, in somewhat elusive generality, what communication and deliberation could look like between participants certain of their identity and willing and able to come to agreement with one another without the invocation of privilege, the use of force, or the employment of manipulative strategies. It is a situation in which they are sincerely willing to seek agreement, fully committed to the search for theoretical truth and normative consensus, when discussing contested claims. They are also committed to the equality of all participants in the discussion or to full reciprocity in the initiation of question and response (cf. Habermas 1970b, p. 143).

I want to choose a formulation that makes Habermas's construction appear to represent adequately some of the intuitions people have when they enter into serious discourse and debate. This implies that we must put all technical formulation, qualifications, and concessions to contemporary theories in linguistics and philosophy (speech-act theory) aside; they make the design of universal pragmatics too complicated. But we gain the advantage of being able to avoid many criticisms that address the construction as too idealist, abstract, or "liberal" (Schmidt 1979, p. 39; O'Neill, 1973, p. 3). For one may rightly claim that something like the idea of unconstrained discourse and communication is available to us when we experience that conversation or debate is unexpectedly cut off by one side or another—or when a rule is imposed restricting communication without explanation, just on the basis of invoking the privileges of authority or by means of procedural trickery.

I have already examined programmed learning and instructional objectives orientations to learning and teaching as examples of restricted communication. They seem so insidious or stultifying because they streamline instruction. They make it secure, as Michael Apple says, thus removing the creative power of "dissent, discordance, disagreement" (1979, p. 119), and fit teaching and learning into a frame that leaves no room for a reflection on the why and whereto of learning and teaching as part of the content of both. They might allow for such why questions, for example, in a particular segment of instruction, as when the reasons for studying history are reviewed. But the instructional units and the outcomes they are meant to achieve produced by instructional objective technicians, curriculum testers, and evaluators, for example, do not make the raising of why questions a continuously present theme (at least in a latent form) in teaching and learning. A concern with such questions, however, is entailed by Habermas's construction: if any more elaborate case of communication in a natural (nonformal) language can be interpreted as the raising of claims (such as claims to truth, to adequacy to social norms or conventions, to truthfulness; see Habermas 1979a, p. 3) in the set of utterances in question, it becomes not just plausible but necessary to interpret a pedagogic speech exchange from this point of view. No teacher can present something he or she takes to be an item of knowledge without believing that it is true.[20]

A particularly compelling way for teachers and learners to raise the issues of truth or normative rightness is to ask, "Why teach that [a topic or a field of inquiry]?" Any possible answer, by offering some ground, will point to the issues of truth and/or normative rightness in some sense. Yet clearly that is not all. Raising the question of why something is taught does not just raise the issue of the usefulness of what is taught in terms of the truths it teaches. It also raises the question of at least the teacher's and also the learner's involvement in the discovery of this truth. Thus an additional claim to validity comes into play: the issue of truthfulness. A teacher must truthfully represent himself or herself to learners, while presenting something he or she regards as true. Learners must be able to trust the teacher's commitment to teach what is true. Thus the issue of personal authenticity—or of identity, autonomy, self-responsibility—is raised.

A rigorously implemented program for the specification of instructional objectives, however, would make it impossible for a teacher to raise the issue of commitment to what he or she teaches. Nor could learners. The language of instruction would have to be adjusted to the delivery of instructional units as information to be passed on. It might require a reduction of various speech actions to a language stating mere cognitive content enforced by commanding authority. Freire has severely criticized this orientation to learning, calling it the "banking concept" of education (Freire 1970, 1971, pp. 57–68). Here the language of communiqués and edicts prevails. What is fundamentally missing in it is what Habermas calls the two-fold character of communication in language. Speakers do not just communicate cognitive content (propositions). They also indicate how they want to take up interpersonal relationships to one another in addition to and through the communication of this content (Habermas 1979a, p. 42).

To describe both levels of communication as the implicit raising of validity claims makes it possible to reflect on any pedagogic practice as a relation of presenting a content (a subject matter) to the speaker's (teacher's, learner's) commitment to the communication of this content. One can raise the issue of teacher's sincerity, for example, as a question of his or her intentions. They are present in and codetermine the manner of the presentation. This is a matter of great concern to Freire. A teacher-student or coordinator of educational groups, called culture circles, can only properly inform about the givens of a culture by indicating that he or she intends any description of the facts of the culture to be available for evaluation (that is, criticism). This includes the evaluation or criticism of the teacher's own role by learners.

Now we can see that the notion of the lifeworld, as Habermas employs it, suggests the shared understandings (including an understanding of conflict) that societal members achieve through discourse and action. By claiming and expressing a distinctive identity of one's own based on the competence and readiness to give reasons for one's actions and beliefs, one calls on a similar expressiveness and display of identity and competence by others. One can also legitimately expect their respect for one's competence and one's concern to be a distinctive "I." The normative concepts of identity and competence thus belong to a characterization of what is required of people if they are to engage in dialogue (communication). The discovery of truths and adequate norms is connected with the interpersonal recognition of dialogue participants as subjects. Insight into impersonal truths and interpersonal norms is not separated from the development of a practical social consciousness based on the reciprocal affirmation and endorsement of speakers as equally significant participants. This is the communications-theoretical ideal of reason and liberation. It weds the commitment to truth with a commitment to free interpersonal recognition.

The instructional objectives movement is just one example among many of present tendencies to render this mode of socialization through discourse and communication superfluous. Thus Habermas's construction of an ideal speech situation is not just a theoretical construction, at least in its core. It resonates with the cultural past in which acquisition of cultural membership through communication was not yet in question, even if older cultural traditions were far removed from understanding the issues underlying Habermas's construction or its ideal sense. Habermas's idea also points to the future insofar as it can compel us to consider to what extent we want the existence and growth of a cultural form that recognizes open argument, uninhibited self-expression, and reciprocal recognition of and by participants in discourse (dialogue) as values.

In the end Habermas's reflections on the relation between our insertion into a preobjective (and unobjectified) social lifeworld, linguistic communication and the achievement of (rational) personal and group identity (through the transformation of conflictual experiences into arguments) are so important because they reveal tendencies in technological societies that lead to a repression of the category of ethics (Habermas 1970b, p. 112). Ethics is repressed in the sense that a practical orientation treating conduct as rooted in the recognition of a moral order has become unavailable. "With the dissolution of the practical orientation, the interpretive framework on which ethics essentially relies is no longer available" (Grahame 1981, p. 22).

A more extended analysis of the text serving to illustrate the program for the specification of instructional objectives could show how the organization of this text (in the detail of its practices) requires readers to suppress the inclination to treat the idea of instruction formulated in the text as fundamentally problematical.[21] They are not to examine that and how the concept of instruction proposed may be incompatible with any idea of education that requires searching dialogue with others. The specification of instructional objectives cannot include the reflective procedure of making this very aim (specification) problematic. It therefore favors procedures of specification (such as the formation of behavioral objectives) that tie the process of specifying instructional objectives from the beginning to the purpose of evaluation by means of standardized tests, an essentially unreflective procedure that is primarily useful to controlling and planning agencies.

4. Education as Critical Pedagogy: Freire, Habermas, and Critical Social Theory

Paulo Freire's *Pedagogy of the Oppressed* is an enterprise akin to Habermas's. Freire's pedagogy is not only eminently practical (and in this it differs from Habermas's) and expressive of its moral and political commitments, it is also philosophical. Although some of Freire's ideas and pedagogical practices have been anticipated by both Dewey and revolutionaries with a strong sense of the educational requirements of a revolution, neither Dewey nor these revolutionaries have integrated the emancipatory content of their ideas into practical steps to be taken as much as Freire. Freire presents a thorough mediation of emancipatory-philosophical ideas and pedagogical steps in his design of an educational practice of freedom. Any step in the pedagogy of educating for literacy (this is Freire's primary focus) is to be monitored and to be examined by all participants in the pedagogic process for its contribution to the self-recognition of participants as active subjects. Thus, the first steps of the pedagogy require the "teacher" (Freire or his coworkers) to dispel any declarations of incompetence the learners (for example, Third World peasants) may make. When they "call themselves ignorant and say the 'professor' is the one who has the knowledge and to whom they should listen" (Freire 1970, p. 49), the educator encourages them to make this statement problematic. Instead of accepting it as a true description, the educator invites them to examine it as a response to the situation in which they have not yet assumed responsibility for their learning. All depends on the learners' learning to interpret their situation as other than immutable. They must learn to regard their situation as requiring intervention, especially their own intervention. The very learning of "generative themes," the central terms to be decoded in a program of literacy education, is organized in such a way that the cultural realities of the learners are brought into play. They can begin to conceive the possibility of their own intervention in their situation. Indeed their learning is such an intervention. This is why literacy education in Freire's sense is not literacy training but cultural action (for freedom). It aims at a "becoming," one of Freire's favorite terms.

Because interventions in one's situation can be a problem for anyone who does not embrace technicist visions of constant progress, teachers and learners are united by a common concern.[22] They must always make certain that educational interventions are in the interest of all participating in the process. Freire identifies what teachers and learners have in common by employing a quasi-ontological, essentialist vocabulary reminiscent of the philosophical anthropologies of the early Marx (as interpreted by Erich Fromm), Marcel, Buber, and Sartre. "Men emerge from their submersion [their succumbing to their actual situation in society, which to them seems a "dense enveloping reality"] and acquire the ability to intervene in reality as it is unveiled. Intervention in reality—historical awareness itself—thus represents a step forward from emergence, and results from the conscientizacao [conscientization] of the situation. Conscientizacao is the deepening of the attitude of awareness characteristic of all 'emergence'" (1970, pp. 100–101).

There is no question that Freire's pedagogy is not just committed to emancipation from this or that instance of oppression or ignorance as an aim. It intends to awaken an interest in "emancipation as such," to speak with Habermas, through unceasing struggle against imposed and self-imposed ("tranquilizing," as Freire calls them) definitions of the situation. Critical reflection as intervention in reality includes both social critical and existential elements. Social transformation includes and requires self-transformation. One is reminded of Habermas's discussion of the notion of self-formation in *Knowledge and Human Interests* (1971) coming from German idealism. Thus the identity of learners and teachers is just as much at issue and to be discovered through the pedagogy they cooperate in as the content of what they learn (for example, materials they use in order to learn to read). In fact they have learned to read only if they have learned to assert their identity through the reading. They claim their place in their world and the world as theirs, at least in part. The teacher, by joining them in the enterprise, no longer takes reading for granted as a routine activity. Thus the teacher has learned as well—that is, transformed himself or herself. Yet none of this would happen were the pedagogy in process (Freire 1978) not an endeavor of social collaboration and communication—of "dialogue."

Freire's pedagogues (teacher-students or initiators of activities in culture circles) can therefore allow themselves to learn, and they must learn from their students.[23] The learning we speak of is not merely incidental. It is not a question of merely monitoring student performance so that a learning task can be presented with greater teaching efficiency. Rather the purpose of the educational enterprise is learned and relearned from and with the students. The students (student-teachers) remind the teachers of the essential learning task: that learning and teaching are meant to bring about self-knowledge with knowledge of one's culture (and "the world" as Freire sometimes says). One learns to understand, appreciate, and affirm membership in the culture. One is one of those for whom culture is there. One learns about oneself as a "being of decision," an "active subject of the historical process" (Freire 1971, p. 156).

In his *Pedagogy* and in his more applied writings, Freire warns against the intervention he calls cultural invasion, connected with the employment of professionals in education and in other enterprises of social reform (he even discusses the figures of the revolutionary and the revolutionary leader from this perspective). In fact we may refashion Freire's discussion of this particular issue and state for our purposes: professionalism in education may characteristically rely on a lack of respect for the view of the people (Freire 1971, p. 154). By people I mean any student population.

Professionalism can be distinguished from expertise (Freire allows for expertise, 1971, pp. 115, 156–157). Expertise is special knowledge of some field of activity that can be entered into the common knowledge of a cultural group under two conditions: the appropriate vehicles of translation and interpretation must be available (here one might consider supplementing Freire's account with hermeneutical reflections on the transmission of culture and cultural meaning), and those possessing special knowledge must be accountable to the cultural group with which they work.

For this second purpose Freire makes a practical recommendation: members of a cultural group (consisting of peasants from northeast Brazil, for example) who are not specialists or experts in the context of their culture are to participate in deliberations about the applicability of special knowledge to the educational (learning) problems posed by the group. This provision is meant to guarantee that specialists and their knowledge remain accountable to the general cultural knowledge and to the interests of the cultural group whom they are advising. The competence of the average member of the cultural group matters most in the end, for the average member's knowledge is the morally-practically and politically most consequential knowledge. Without its remaining the basis of communication and deliberation, a community cannot exist. *Pedagogy of the Oppressed* aims at the generation of a critical community, not merely at strengthening the critical reasoning capacities of individuals. It concentrates on the awakening and practical acknowledgment of the cognitive beliefs, affective dispositions, and existential attitudes needed for the community to have a critical sense of its existence and its capacities.

Professionals are representative of a case of cultural invasion because they will proceed as if there was no need for this basic knowledge and as if the basic knowledge they also possess (prior to their so-called professional knowledge) did not matter. They will therefore not only show no respect for the people's (students') views; they will also ignore how their own basic beliefs and attitudes due to general membership in their own culture (as a culture different from that of the people or of clients) enter into the interaction with their client group. Professionalism thus permits the neutralization (or the obliteration) of differences in cultural membership that arise out of different cultural and social locations. Because the professional (a Third World agronomist, let us say) does not construct his or her idea of knowledge around an acknowledgment of these differences, he or she can be said to be more ignorant than the "people."

Consider how this applies to a teacher well trained in the formulation and specification (categorization) of instructional objectives. Among other so-called techniques, he or she may have mastered for purposes of specifying learning outcomes taxonomies of educational objectives in "the three domains of behavior with which education typically has dealt—cognitive, affective and psychomotor" (Kibler et al. 1981, p. 82). When this professional teaches an "instructional unit," such as a poem, requiring "higher-level behavior" as a response, such as being able to understand (recite, comment on, and appreciate) the poem, he or she will divide up the understanding required into several components and then check to see if the student has mastered each component. The teacher will then declare whether the student has achieved mastery of the unit.

Clearly a student may have mastered everything from reciting to appreciation (this latter phrase to be replaced by more specific ones according to the procedure) without at all knowing that he or she has mastered them unless he or she trusts (or is made to trust) what the teacher says. Nothing in the process indicates that there is to be an autonomous ground of judgment available to the student. Nothing indicates either that the teacher still knows why this subject matter is taught rather than another or what indeed the subject matter, poetry, is. The teacher cannot engage in the reasoning—for example, of linking a poem to a literary genre (poetry) or raising questions of meaning and form—except insofar as it is planned into the process of instruction. But because the process of instruction is planned in such a way that a general procedure is available in advance for any program of instruction, independently from the particularity of content of a subject matter, any reflection on the particular subject or content taught cannot be a reflection on what makes it something that requires or needs to be taught. The only rationale available is administrative decision. Thus, the teacher has lost his or her own cultural grounds for the activity of teaching when teaching becomes a technology of instruction. The learning of this technology suppresses the need to learn about the cultural grounds of learning and teaching—for example, why certain subjects and contents are valued more than others.

Now we can see why Freire regards professionalism and professionalization as contrary to the dialectically conceived process of education (pedagogy) as a process of cultural learning. We can also see how Freire's critique of professionalism (as we developed it to be applicable to the situation in North American education) as "cultural invasion" resembles Habermas's critique of technology and science as ideology and his theme of the "colonization of the lifeworld."

Where do we stand, then, with respect to the ideal of reason and the critique of the transformation of education into instruction (as well as the reduction of educational theory to a theory of instruction and evaluation)? And in what way can we be said to have left the older tradition of critical social theory behind?

It is probably no exaggeration to say that Habermas's theory of the claims (to truth, normative rightness, and truthfulness) made with speech as presuppositions for bringing about agreement is a theory of reason in its practical linguistic form. The achievement of (rational) agreement in discourse is the ideal of this communications-theoretical conception of reason. In fact establishing the conditions of discourse for the raising and reconciling of controversial claims, either of knowledge or of the warrantability (Habermas says "generalizability") of an interest or need, is the achievement of reason. It stands for liberation from all those regulations of social intercourse and interaction that suppress the principle of the debatability of claims.

A program for the specification of instructional objectives is an instance of such suppression because it transforms the critical-pedagogic concern with the warrantability of assertions, beliefs, and need dispositions into an attitude of controlling the efficient delivery of instruction. A program of this kind may contain units for teaching comprehension skills or for the appraisal of theories, but it does not provide for teachers and learners as inquirers working together. The teacher must be firmly in control of what is to be delivered and of whom it is to be delivered to. The learner is the target insofar as learners are to acquire a skill. Learners, in fact, appear to their teachers and to those designing instructional packages for teachers as bundles of skills. There is no recognition of an identity to be achieved through reflection, a continuity of purpose and understanding to be maintained through the particular tasks set on target toward the acquisition of skills.

Habermas's theory of discourse joins those participating in discourse in multiple relations; they do not only refer one another to a topic to be comprehended. They also affirm one another as needed for the consideration of the topic, which in turn is linked to what they need—what for them needs understanding or examination.

Freire's pedagogy as a program for cultural action also places learners and teachers into a context in which they must be attentive to one another as agents in the culture. What culture could mean as the sustenance (ground) of human activity and what it aims at, the reaffirmation of the generative power of people, is the content of the pedagogy. The pedagogy is the enactment of this content insofar as it extricates teachers and learners from the anonymity of professional role identities or the submissive speechlessness of cultural submersion.

We might say that Habermas and Freire do not just have their criticism of cultural invasion (colonization) in common. The criticism rests on their having made the invader and invaded recognizable. Yet this task, on which they agree, depends on their having established that inquiry and education (learning, teaching) belong together. Inquiry is the discovery and identification of critical claims, which forces the one making and the one debating the claim out into the open, into the reciprocity of a formative (educational) process in which not only beliefs or convictions change but also those who hold them.[24] Both Habermas and Freire know that inquiry (discourse, dialogue) succeeds only if those engaging in it commit themselves to it. Their autonomy, self-responsibility, and cooperation with one another are needed for it. We may say that the topics of cultural invasion and of the colonization of the lifeworld bring the idea of reason back to earth. It is no longer removed from daily concerns and the struggle for autonomy, responsibility, and mutuality carried out in the institutional worlds of late capitalism or in the depressed and subjected regions of the Third World. Critical social theory may become politically effective, when Habermas's metacritically and metatheoretically organized communications theory of society (and of liberation) is entered into a pedagogy, a praxis of critical reflection, that formulates the removal of barriers to communication and the realization of the identity of those inquiring into these barriers as a practical project, for a critical pedagogy places the critical emancipatory concerns right into the world of daily life (the lifeworld) among the daily realities of institutional suppression. It can put Habermas's distinctions among emancipatory, communicative, and administrative (technical) action to work in the interventions of those who feel the need to act on the institutional realities of late capitalism. These interventions need a situation in which to begin. They cannot be derived from the generality of a comprehensive theory of society and from metatheoretical deliberations. Habermas's theory will have transcended this built-in limitation of critical theory (the legacy of its tradition) the more it permits us to identify situations in need of critical address. Much of his work points in such directions.

Notes

I wish to acknowledge the support of the Social Sciences and Humanities Council of Canada (grant no. 431-77006) for the completion of this essay. Some of the arguments presented here arose from the research supported by the grant, which had the relation between classical social theory and contemporary social science (sociology) as its topic. I was one among five faculty members participating in the research.

Dieter Misgeld

I thank John Forester as the editor of this volume for having encouraged me to reexamine ideas expressed in an earlier paper (1975). His friendly remarks about this paper and his resistance to some of my criticisms of Habermas expressed elsewhere have helped me considerably.

1. My discussion in this section does not take account of Habermas's recent appraisal of the history of critical social theory. In *Theorie des kommunikativen Handelns*, vol. 2 (1981), pp. 548–594, Habermas clearly distinguishes his position from that of his predecessors in the evolution of the critical theory of society. He argues that reliance on the philosophy of history (the Hegelian inheritance) had misled Horkheimer and Adorno into a thorough devaluation of the Enlightenment as a whole (especially in the *Dialectic of Enlightenment*). He also argues that as a consequence Horkheimer and Adorno, and also Marcuse, no longer could take a position on the possible completion of the modern project. By continuing to rely on the classical unitary concept of reason, they failed to recognize existing possibilities for the development of society. See also vol. 1 (English translation 1984), pp. 366–402, regarding the implicit dependence of the classical critical theorists on Weber. For other revisions and critiques of the classical position of critical social theory, see Cohen (1982) and Benhabib (1984). In this chapter I express some reservations regarding the tradition of critical theory that predates Habermas. But I am also concerned with stressing the continuity of some themes such as that of reason.

2. Traces of an interest in the normative force of educational and political ideals can still be found in the philosophical theory of education (Peters 1966; Crittenden 1973; Passmore 1980), although hardly elsewhere in educational theory. One may note, however, that the interest is only realized at the price of neglecting an examination of the potential for deliberate social change implicit in education. The contemporary philosophy of education can frequently be read as a retreat from Dewey's demanding and provocative position onto safer, more easily surveyable ground. Only Freire still expresses the visionary hopes also animating Dewey's theory of education (and democracy).

3. Apple (1979) believes that the "ideological place of science in curriculum can in part be explained by the promise of better control, of greater ease of prediction and manipulation" held forth by "the language of science and technology" (p. 79). It is this very language that is frequently employed by supervisory personnel, justifying their efforts to monitor classroom activities in the schools.

4. Horkheimer and Adorno (1972, pp. 43–81) extend the Enlightenment back to Homer's *Odyssey*. For them the Homeric hero is the prototype of the bourgeois individual (p. 43), and "the venerable cosmos of the meaningful Homeric world is shown to be the achievement of regulative reason, which destroys myth by virtue of the same rational order in which it reflects it" (p. 44). They also extend the Enlightenment forward to include its critics, such as Hegel and Nietzsche, in order to document a double aspect of the Enlightenment "as a historical principle" (p. 44). It has always paid the price of new forms of domination for having shown the way out from under previous ones.

5. I am using Popper's translation (1968, p. 177). The lines subsequent to the ones quoted are: "Such a stage of tutelage I call 'self-imposed' if it is due, not to lack of intelligence but to lack of courage or determination to use one's own intelligence without the help of a teacher. Sapere aude! Dare to use your own intelligence! This is the battle-cry of the Enlightenment."

6. Benhabib (1984) has identified major shortcomings in the notion of emancipation employed by Horkheimer and Adorno. She identifies the background to these shortcomings in Hegel's and Marx's philosophy of history and in the notion of the human species as the subject of its own history. Benhabib extends and refines critical remarks made by Habermas in a thorough manner. She also applies them to Habermas's own position and with surprising results.

7. Habermas (1975) therefore speaks of the "end of the individual" as a possible outcome of the application of scientific technique to the management of social affairs. The possibility of

organizing human conduct by manipulating situational contexts and by suppressing motives for action resulting from the internalization of norms (p. 141) leads to the abolition of an autonomous ego organization and thus to the abolition of all historicaly generated paradigms for the establishment of self-identity.

8. In making this claim with Adorno and Horkheimer, I go further than Lasch (1973), who has summarized much research critical of compulsory public schooling. Lasch states that Enlightenment (eighteenth-century) ideas "still have something to teach us . . . as a social theory of education," since they stated "the two objectives a democratic system of education might reasonably expect to accomplish." These are to give everyone the resources "to distinguish truth from public lies" and to "train scholars, intellectuals, and members of the learned professions." These objectives are to be preferred to "mass education" or to the "ideology of school reform as the motor of social progress" (p. 24). My argument is that you cannot have Enlightenment ideas without supporting mass education and the respective ideology of social progress and school reform. Enlightenment ideas no longer are sufficient in themselves for the formulation of a historically adequate idea of social progress, since the very means derived from them in order to achieve them, such as universal schooling or mass higher education, have made a travesty of the eighteenth-century social theory of education (Lasch 1973). We need a theory critical of the Enlightenment while giving a sympathetic hearing to its basis conceptions.

9. Habermas has examined this process with reference to the philosophy of German idealism. He has also argued that in the contemporary situation education as the formation of critical capacities (Bildung) can take place only in the context of the sciences. This requires a different (and more modest) role for philosophy. See Habermas (1963).

10. Here I am thinking of the practice of Socratic inquiry, as Plato has represented it. It stands for an ideal of inquiry and of education. The ideal has remained a powerful force in intellectual and moral inquiry, even if it hardly reflects the daily routines of education and moral reasoning. It may not be entirely coincidental that Freire's Pedagogy has been developed for adult learners. It is Socratic and committed to humanization as an ideal. For a contemporary interpretation of Socrates' practice, see A. Blum, Socrates: The Original and Its Images (London: Routledge & Kegan Paul, 1978).

11. One example for this role of social science is its propensity to proceed in an abstract conceptual mode, thus making ordinary communicative understanding of social situations over and transforming natural language terms, having their own history, into technical terms (for example, socialization once meant making people fit to live in society by teaching them polite behavior). Dorothy E. Smith (1979) has analyzed the tendency of sociology to proceed in this way. As a feminist theorist she has argued that the place to begin for a sociology for women is the local and particular, corresponding to the primary location of women in production relations (domestic labor and care). With the local and particular, the everyday becomes the sociological problematic. Sociology that does not begin with it is like a policy science proceeding in an ideological mode from the start.

12. I am not arguing that an egalitarian theory of education existed in philosophy from Plato to Hegel. Clearly much of this theory was quite authoritarian. I am only arguing that with its conception of inquiry, the idealist tradition from Plato to Hegel was committed to the ac-knowledgment of the self-motivated or autonomous pursuit of philosophical knowledge as a principle.

13. For historical background on the the convergence of these three forms of research and development, see Neumann (1979, pp. 67–88): "The efficiency and effectiveness of military training" was seen to constitute an "open challenge" to civilian educators in the United States during and after World War I.

14. In forthcoming publications Misgeld, Grahame, and Jardine are attempting to identify the consequences of the introduction of life-skills training programs into education in the schools. Life-skills training programs have been developed to help the handicapped, "chronically unemployed," and other economically and socially weak social groups to overcome their condition. They are extremely practical programs and make no effort to introduce students to the major intellectual and cultural traditions of their society. As soon as these programs become a partial model for school education, education is transformed into training. But as we shall attempt to document, such programs also have an ideological function because they often can only purport to be practical but are too primitive to match the knowledge of practical skills acquired in practical situations.

15. It is not at all farfetched to expect a synthesis of the "instructional objectives" position with something like N. Luhmann's systems-theoretical sociology. Such a synthesis would prove to be a powerful tool for the complete entrenchment of managerial administrative conceptions of social organization in everyday life in postliberal industrial societies. Cf. Habermas's critique of Luhmann (Habermas and Luhmann 1971). For some remarks on the relation of systems theory, phenomenology, critical theory, and education, see Misgeld (1983b).

16. See Misgeld (1983a).

17. Pusey (1980) has analyzed the tensions between the tradition-based understanding of cultural competence and of educational aims that school personnel (especially classroom teachers) possess and conceptions of instructional objectives dictated by the instrumental and political logic of governmental planning agencies. His article is a significant application to education of Habermas's theory of a legitimation crisis in late capitalism (1975).

18. Even if all of critical theory can reasonably be called a critique of domination, the critical theory of Horkheimer and Adorno and of Marcuse is unconcerned with the tradition of democratic theory. Liberal democracy and its ideals are not given much thought because they are regarded as empty. They are the mere ideological facade of mass society. The latter is mostly described as if the daily realities of its political practice were already akin to those of a totalitarian society. And socialist democracy is not given consideration either. Habermas is both more moderate and more radical. He is more moderate by recognizing the possible force of democratic ideals even in advanced industrial societies. He is more radical by arguing for ongoing democratization as a possibility in these societies. This is why examinations of the public sphere are central for him. They are integral to his early and his later work.

19. I do not claim that Habermas endorses every detail of their analysis, but he inherits the problem of the relation between the production of knowledge in the sciences and social systems as orders of domination from the older tradition of critical social theory. His conceptions of the sciences and of politics are clearly more differentiated, however. The clearest statement available on the issue is his famous discussion of interests constitutive of knowledge in *Knowledge and Human Interests* (1971).

20. Wexler, Whitson, and Morkowitz (1981) have developed an interesting argument regarding the relation between schools and truth. In the past public schooling could be used in capitalism to reproduce and transmit existing production relations (a class-divided society) only if it recognized a simultaneous obligation to provide liberal education. Public schools are legitimated by a claim to truth. Present-day capitalism tries to remove this broader cultural commitment from schools. They say, "Skills-training, narrowing of the curriculum, and the institutional disassembly of schools are all methods by which the technical aspects of labour-power are produced in schools without the occasion for self-conscious production of social cognitions and cultural attitudes in traditional general education" (p. 32). Therefore present-day opposition to capitalism may paradoxically require a defense of the public school (and of traditional liberal education) rather than further arguments for deschooling.

21. Kibler et al. (1981) begin every chapter in their text with a list of learning outcomes or instructional objectives a reader should have "achieved" after completing study of a chapter. It does not occur to the authors that the first question a reader might have concerns the validity of thinking in these terms. They refuse to involve the reader in argument and thus to risk their own assumptions. The authors seem to want to fashion a reader who obediently memorizes the learning objectives stated at the beginning of each chapter. A reader thus is not even invited to examine the chapter for its internal consistency. The chapter will have just the content the list of objectives at the beginning says it will have. One needs neither hermeneutics nor deconstructionist criticism in order to realize that the authors do not want readers who are fully engaged. This is incompatible with the "shaping" of readers' responses the authors intend.

22. Grahame (1981) has formulated the issue of grounds for intervention as the problem of the warrantability of critical inquiries. He has used Freire's critical pedagogy, aspects of Habermas's work, as well as ethnomethodological studies of mundane reasoning and its "natural competence" in order to develop a "hermeneutic of critical practice" in his dissertation.

23. A cultural circle consists of investigators (let us say, of a region for which an adult literacy campaign is planned) and the people (who would normally be considered objects of that investigation) as coinvestigators. Together they identify a theme generative of their cultural reality, thus taking possession of that reality (Freire 1971, p. 97). This is why literacy education is a continuation of popular struggles in Third World nations, which Freire calls people's struggles for their word (1978, p. 72). It is a way of collectively achieving consciousness of a culture in a process of participatory inquiry.

24. I have addressed the theme of common convictions as the ground held in common by phenomenology, hermeneutics, and critical theory as critiques of scientific sociology (Misgeld 1983c). I have also pointed to the centrality of education (self-formative processes) in the development of common convictions.

References

Adorno, T. W. 1979. "Spaetkapitalismus oder Industriegesellschaft?" In T. W. Adorno, *Soziologische Schriften*, vol. 1 (Frankfurt: Suhrkamp, 1979).

Apple, M., 1979. *Ideology and Curriculum*. London: Routledge & Kegan Paul.

Benhabib, S., 1982. "The Methodological Illusions of Modern Political Theory: The Case of Rawls and Habermas." *Neue Hefte für Philosophie* (Spring 1982): 47–74.

Benhabib, S., 1984. "Critique, Norm, Utopia," manuscript.

Cohen, J., 1982. *Class and Civil Society*. Amherst: University of Massachusetts Press.

Crittenden, B., 1973. *Education and Social Ideals*. Don Mills, Ontario: Longman Canada.

Dewey, J., 1916. *Democracy and Education*. New York: Free Press.

Feinberg, W., 1975. *Reason and Rhetoric: The Intellectual Foundations of 20th-Century Liberal Educational Policy*. New York: John Wiley.

Freire, P., 1970. *Cultural Action for Freedom*. Harvard Educational Review Monograph Series.

Freire, P., 1971. *Pedagogy of the Oppressed*. New York: Herder and Herder.

Freire, P., 1978. *Pedagogy in Process: The Letters to Guinea-Bissau*. London: Writer and Readers Publishing Cooperative.

Grahame, P., 1981. "Critical Practice: Toward a Hermeneutic of Critical Social Inquiry." Ph.D. dissertation, University of Toronto.

Grand, G., et al., 1979. *On Competence*. San Francisco: Jossey-Bass.

Habermas, J., 1963. "Vom sozialen Wandel akademischer Bildung." *Merkur* 17 (1963): 413–427.

Habermas, J., 1970a. *Toward a Rational Society*. Boston: Beacon Press.

Habermas, J., 1970b. "Toward a Theory of Communicative Competence." In P. R. Dreitzel, ed., *Recent Sociology*, no. 2 (New York: Macmillan).

Habermas, J., 1971. *Knowledge and Human Interests*. Boston: Beacon Press.

Habermas, J., 1973. *Theory and Practice*. Boston: Beacon Press.

Habermas, J., 1975. *Legitimation Crisis*. Boston: Beacon Press.

Habermas, J., 1976. "A Positivistically Bisected Rationalism." In T. Adorno et al., *The Positivist Dispute in German Sociology* (London: Heinemann).

Habermas, J., 1979a. *Communication and the Evolution of Society*. Boston: Beacon Press.

Habermas, J., ed., 1979b. *Stichworte zur "Geistigen Situation der Zeit,"* 2 vols. Frankfurt: Suhrkamp.

Habermas, J., 1981. *Theorie des kommunikativen Handelns*, 2 vols. Frankfurt: Suhrkamp.

Habermas, J., 1984. *The Theory of Communicative Action*, vol. 1: *Reason and the Rationalization of Society*. Boston: Beacon Press.

Habermas, J., and N. Luhmann, 1976. *Theorie der Gesellschaft oder Sozialtechnologie*. Frankfurt: Suhrkamp.

Heilbroner, R., 1976. *Business Civilization in Decline*. New York: W. W. Norton.

Horkheimer, M., 1972. "Traditional and Critical Theory." In M. Horkheimer, *Critical Theory* (New York: Herder and Herder).

Horkheimer, M., and T. W. Adorno, 1972. *The Dialectic of Enlightenment* (New York: Herder and Herder; original German edition, 1947).

Illich, I., 1977. *Disabling Professions*. London: Marion Boyars.

Illich, I., 1978. *The Right to Useful Employment*. London: Marion Boyars.

Illich, I., 1981. *Shadow Work*. Boston: Marion Boyars.

Jay, M., 1984. *Marxism and Totality*. Berkeley: University of California Press.

Kant, I., 1965. "What Is Enlightenment?" In K. Popper, ed., *Conjectures and Refutations* (New York: Harper). (Original German publication, 1785.)

Kibler, R. J., et al., 1981. *Objectives for Instruction and Evaluation*. Boston: Allyn and Bacon.

Lasch, C., 1973. "Inequality and Education." *New York Review of Books*, May 17, 1983, pp. 19–25

Luhmann, N., 1969. *Legitimation durch Verfahren*. Neuwied: Luchterhand.

Marcuse, H., 1964. *One-Dimensional Man*. Boston: Beacon Press.

Marcuse, H., 1965. *Eros and Civilization*. Boston: Beacon Press.

Marcuse, H., 1969. *An Essay on Liberation*. Boston: Beacon Press.

McCarthy, T., 1978. *The Critical Theory of Jürgen Habermas*. Cambridge: MIT Press.

McPherson, C. B., 1977. *The Life and Times of Liberal Democracy*. Oxford: Oxford University Press.

Misgeld, D., 1975. "Emancipation, Enlightenment, and Liberation: An Approach Toward Foundational Inquiry into Education." *Interchange* (Toronto) 6(3): 23–36.

Misgeld, D., 1983a. "Communication and Rationalization: A Review of J. Habermas's *Theorie des kommunikativen Handelns*." *Canadian Journal of Sociology* 8: 433–453.

Misgeld, D., 1983b. "Phenomenology, Social Science, and the Social Service Professions: The Case for the Integration of Phenomenology, Hermeneutics, and Critical Social Theory." *Phenomenology and Pedagogy* 1(2): 195–216.

Misgeld, D., 1983c. "Common Sense and Common Convictions: Sociology as a Science, Phenomenological Sociology and the Hermeneutical Point of View." *Human Studies* 6: 109–139.

Misgeld, D., 1984. "Critical Theory and Sociological Theory." *Philosophy of the Social Sciences* 14: 97–105.

Misgeld, D., P. R. Grahame, and D. Jardine, 1985. "The Life-World Colonized: Life-Skills Instruction and the Transformation of Education and Everyday Life." *Phenomenology and Pedagogy* 3(1–2).

Neumann, W., 1979. "Educational Responses to the Concern with Proficiency." In G. Grand et al., *On Competence* (San Francisco: Jossey-Bass), pp. 67–88.

O'Neill, J., ed., 1975. *On Critical Theory*. New York: Seabury Press.

Passmore, J., 1980. *The Philosophy of Teaching*. Cambridge: Harvard University Press.

Peters, R. S., 1966. *Ethics and Education*. London: George Allen and Unwin.

Pusey, M., 1980. "The Legitimation of State Education Systems." *Australian and New Zealand Journal of Sociology* 16(2).

Riesman, D., 1979. "Society's Demand for Competence." In G. Grand et al., *On Competence* (San Francisco: Jossey-Bass).

Dieter Misgeld

Schmidt, J., 1979. "Offensive Critical Theory: Reply to Honneth." *Telos*, no. 39.

Smith, D. E., 1979. "A Sociology for Women." In J. A. Sherman and E. Torton Beck, eds., *The Prison of Sex: Essays in the Sociology of Knowledge* (Madison: University of Wisconsin Press).

Wexler, P., T. Whitson, and E. J. Morkowitz, 1981. "Deschooling by Default: The Changing Social Functions of Public Schooling." *Interchange* (Toronto) 12(2–3): 133–151.

III

**The Constitution of Judgment:
The Informed Citizen and the
Critical Consumer**

The American News Media:
A Critical Theory Perspective

Daniel C. Hallin

Critical theory is concerned with the ability of human beings to reflect on their social life for the purpose of discovering, as Tolstoy once put it, "what we should do and how we should live." For this reason it has devoted a good deal of attention to the institutions of what Habermas calls the public sphere: the arena, formed as the liberal political order was replacing the feudal, in which private individuals come together to discuss the public affairs of the community.[1] At the heart of the critique of contemporary capitalism advanced by Horkheimer, Adorno, Marcuse, Habermas, and others is the thesis that the capitalist form of social organization that brought the public sphere into being nevertheless distorts and limits its development to the point that the society is unable to establish the process of dialogue and collective self-reflection that the advent of liberal institutions seemed to promise.

From the beginning the newspaper was among the key institutions of the emerging public sphere. "We should underrate their importance," wrote Tocqueville, "if we thought [newspapers] just guaranteed liberty; they maintain civilization."[2] And the young Marx, in the wonderfully overblown style of German romanticism, called the fledgling press "the omnipresent open eye of the spirit of the people . . . the ruthless confession of a people to itself . . . the mind of the state that can be peddled in every cottage, cheaper than natural gas."[3] Both expected the newspaper to assist in the birth of a fundamentally new political order, to enable the society as a whole, for the first time in human history, to open a dialogue about itself and decide in a public way the direction of public life. But this, according to critical theory, is not how it has turned out. The public sphere has given way to the "consciousness industry," the press as a potential medium of public dialogue to the "mass media," deeply embedded in a structure of domination.

Critical theorists have offered two types of explanation for the distortion of political dialogue in liberal capitalist societies. The first and more familiar concerns the structure of power in a class society. Unequal distribution of political and economic power gives to some members of society greater access and control over the institutions of political communication and organization than others. All interests and perspectives are not equally represented. Power intrudes upon discourse, and the outcome of debate can neither be considered a genuine consensus or compromise, nor can it be expected to reflect an assessment of all the information or insight potentially available.

The second argument is less familiar but more original to critical theory, and I will take it as my primary focus here. This argument, summed up by Habermas's phrase the "scientization of politics," concerns the type of social action and discourse characteristic of capitalist society. There are, according to Habermas, two types of action fundamental to human life. First, human beings must interact with nature to produce their material means of subsistence. This type of action, involving the manipulation of nature and of human beings as "forces of production" to achieve established purposes, Habermas calls purposive-rational action. Second, human beings must interact with one another to produce the frameworks of reciprocal expectation that make it possible for them to live as members of collective social institutions. This Habermas calls communicative action. Habermas draws these concepts in part from Aristotle's distinction between techne— "the skillful production of artifacts and the expert mastery of objectified tasks"[4] —and praxis—action directed toward human education and the realization of human potential. He accordingly distinguishes between two types of knowledge, technical and practical, which correspond to the two types of human action. Capitalism, Habermas argues, develops the capacity for purposive-rational action to a degree never approached by any previous social order. But it also tends to universalize that form of action and the standards of discourse and knowledge that correspond to it. All questions come to be framed as essentially technical or strategic questions, questions of the most effective means by which a given end can be attained. As a result society is unable to develop a capacity for communicative action through which it could resolve practical questions, those that have to do not with means but ends, not with techniques but standards of human conduct.

This, then, is the perspective from which I will examine the American news media. I will begin by making the argument that modern American journalism does in fact take technical knowledge as a model for the reporting of news. This conception of news reporting, I will argue, is a relatively recent historical development, connected with the rise of commercial mass media—and thus with capitalist forms of social organization—and with the professionalization of journalism. I will conclude by discussing the political implications of this transformation of journalism. As we shall see critical theorists have taken two very different positions on the political role of mass media. Marcuse, Horkheimer, and Adorno, writing in the 1940s, 1950s, and early 1960s, argued that the media were capable of producing an ideological consensus tight enough that the possibility of opposition to the existing structure of society became extremely problematic. Habermas, on the other hand, has cast doubt in his recent writings on the possibility of any such centralized production of social values and in fact has argued that liberal capitalist societies are susceptible to conflict and crisis precisely in the sphere of ideology and culture.

In discussing this debate over the media's ability to legitimize the existing social order, I shall introduce Habermas's recent work on the pragmatics of human communication, which points toward important new ways of approaching the study of the mass media. For Habermas all forms of human communication, however asymmetrical the social relations may have become, are essentially derived from the basic form of dialogue and must be seen as relationships between active human subjects. This suggests that we must direct our attention not only to the content of media messages but also to the character of the relations established between communicator and audience and the message that relation implies about the nature of social relationships generally. The news tells us not only what happened in the world today but who we are in relation to that world. I shall argue that the crucial consequence of the scientization of journalism, the shift to a technical angle in the reporting of news, may well lie in the message this form of journalism conveys about the nature of politics and the citizen's relation to it. The grounding of mass communication in dialogue also suggests that there may be limits beyond which the process of communication may not be stretched without destroying the legitimacy of the communicator. This point is important to understanding the relation of the mass media to the structure of social power: the ability of the media to support that structure ideologically is limited by their need to maintain the integrity of the process of communication on which their own legitimacy depends.

This argument is very preliminary. One might think, given the centrality to critical theory of the problem of public dialogue, that critical theorists would by now have produced a substantial body of research on the institutions of political communication. In fact, critical theory, which has been preoccupied for most of its history with the philosophical critique of positivism and the effort to develop a nonpositivist conception of social inquiry, has so far produced relatively little in the way of extended analysis of concrete social institutions, and the news media are no exception.[6] What follows, therefore, should be taken not primarily as a report on research already undertaken but as a proposal for future work in an area where most of the interesting questions remain to be addressed.

Technical Angle in News Reporting

A few examples will illustrate how the modern journalist reports political events. In December 1968 *CBS Evening News* featured a two-part special report on "pacification" in Vietnam. The series, which totaled an unusually long thirteen minutes in length, reflected the growing maturity of the American news media. A couple of years earlier Vietnam coverage had been primarily a chronicle of daily battlefield events. By late 1968 the media were beginning to make a conscious effort, at least occasionally, to offer background, analysis, and perspective. CBS had chosen well the topic for this particular background report. Pacification involved the struggle for political support or hegemony in the villages of South Vietnam, which was what the war was ultimately about. By this time, too, the media were beginning to venture beyond official sources of information. The CBS pacification report included a lengthy interview with a critic of administration policy (John Tunney, a senator from California); a few years earlier use of information from critics had been extremely rare in foreign policy coverage.

How did CBS provide background on the complex and controversial struggle for South Vietnam's countryside? Here are Walter Cronkite's introduction to the report and correspondent Murray Fromson's wrap-ups to the two segments:

Cronkite: American officials in Saigon came out with their most optimistic pacification report of the war today. They said that almost three-fourths of South Vietnam's seventeen million people now live in relatively secure areas controlled by the Saigon government. According to those officials Vietcong control has dropped to just over thirteen percent of the population with the remaining South Vietnamese living in contested areas. Tonight we get a look at one of those contested areas. . . .

Fromson [concluding part I]: So pacification does not stand still. It moves forward, it moves back. But what is the balance? What is the trend. . . ? An effort is being made to measure this, and we'll look at the measurements in our next report.

Fromson [concluding part II]: Another offensive by the Communists would undermine the program. . . . But the momentum seems to be in the other direction. Since the November 1 bombing halt government and U.S. troops have taken over nearly 800 hamlets previously regarded as contested. The goal is to occupy another three hundred of these hamlets by the anniversary of the Tet offensive.[7]

The story, in short, was structured from beginning to end around the question of effectiveness; each element was explained within this framework. A U.S. tank, for instance, had recently fired into the village in response to small arms fire, killing two civilians. "What may be regarded as a military necessity," Fromson reported, "also creates problems for the pacification team." The whole of part II was devoted to the computerized Hamlet Evaluation System (HES), which produced the official figures on the progress of pacification. That was where Senator Tunney came in; he was not there to discuss the wisdom or justice of U.S. policy in Vietnam but to offer an opposing view on the accuracy of the figures produced by the HES.

The tendency to frame and analyze events in terms of strategy and tactics, success and failure is characteristic of modern U.S. journalism. In Vietnam coverage, even stories about the political debate at home were shaped to this pattern. Reports about the antiwar movement, when they were not preoccupied with the possibility of a violent disruption of social order (another common focus in coverage of political controversy), focused heavily on the issue of whether the movement was gaining or losing ground: would as many people participate in this year's demonstration as in last year's? Would the demonstration have any impact on the president's decision, or would the president be watching a football game? Indeed only 40 percent of television reports on the antiwar movement contained any discussion of the war in Vietnam.[8]

Studies of election coverage have shown a heavy preponderance of attention to the horse-race angle and the strategic battle of wits.[9] "The Presidential debate produced no knockout blow, no disastrous gaffe and no immediate, undisputed victor," wrote the *New York Times*'s Hedrick Smith, analyzing the Reagan-Carter debate. "It was a contest of content against style, of a President repeatedly on the attack to put his challenger on the defensive while Ronald Reagan used his calm demeanor to offset Jimmy Carter's contention that he was 'dangerous,' "[10] In November 1981, when President Reagan's budget director in a published interview termed the administration's budget policy trickle-down economics and conceded the numbers on which it was based were dubious, the media's handling of the affair was not surprising. "The question all day at the White House," reported Lesley Stahl of CBS, "was: Can Stockman survive? Will he be fired?" And from congressional reporter Phil Jones: "The question is: Can Stockman regain credibility in Congress? If today's Senate Budget Committee hearing is any indication, it will be difficult for Stockman to be effective again."[11]

What I have called here the technical angle in news reporting is by no means the only way contemporary journalists frame political events. Journalism, like any other long-standing cultural institution, is intricate in its complexity. But the technical angle does tend to dominate political coverage, particularly when background and analysis are offered.[12] It also serves well to illustrate what is distinctive about contemporary journalism as a form of political communication. In order to understand why this form of journalism has become dominant and to assess its implications, it is necessary to trace the transformation of the news media from the small-scale political press of the eighteenth and early nineteenth centuries to the large-scale commercial mass media of today.

Displacement of the Political Press by Commercial Mass Media

When Benjamin Franklin in 1749 outlined the curriculum for a proposed Pennsylvania Academy, he stressed the importance of political oratory, noting that this required a knowledge not only of the rhetoric of the ancients but of the craft of newspaper publishing, "Modern Political Oratory being chiefly performed by the Pen and the Press."[13] Alexis de Tocqueville, writing in the 1830s, saw the American newspaper as catalyst of collective political action, essential for maintaining an active political life under conditions of mass democracy. Tocqueville wrote,

The leading citizens living in an aristocratic country can see each other from afar, and if they want to unite their forces they go to meet one another, bringing a crowd in their train. But in democratic countries it often happens that a great many men who both want and need to get together cannot do so, for all being very small and lost in the crowd, they do not see one another at all and do not know where to find one another. Then a newspaper gives publicity to the feeling or idea that had occurred to them all simultaneously but separately. . . . The newspaper brought them together and continues to be necessary to hold them together.[14]

The U.S. newspaper of the eighteenth and early nineteenth centuries was a vehicle of political debate and action. Neither objectivity nor political neutrality, the key values of contemporary journalism, was considered a virtue.[15] The main purpose of a newspaper, to the extent that it concerned itself with public affairs (newspapers also provided entertainment, commercial information, and religious and moral edification), was to express a particular point of view as forcefully and eloquently as possible. In the early nineteenth century as political parties were established, the press became primarily partisan. Most newspapers were backed financially by parties or politicians whose politics they represented and whose followers they served to mobilize. The press of this period was also relatively decentralized. Newspapers were small, numerous, and, given the small amount of capital required, relatively easy to establish; Franklin began as a printer's apprentice. The early American newspaper was both public and political: public in the sense that it was neither an official agency of the state nor primarily a private business venture but an organ established by citizens to communicate with one another; political in that it took a stand on the issues of the day. It was a quintessential institution of the public sphere, a means by which the ordinary citizen could be involved in the discussion of political issues.

The public sphere in the eighteenth and early nineteenth centuries, however, was restricted to a relatively small segment of the population. It was not until the 1820s and 1830s that property qualifications were dropped and the franchise extended to the entire white male population, nor until then that the newspaper became fully accessible to the masses. The papers of the pre-1830 period cost six cents an issue, nearly 10 percent of a wage worker's average daily income. They were read primarily by commercial and political elites. It was the penny press of the 1830s, the forerunner of today's commercial mass media, that first put newspapers in the hands of the mass public on a regular basis. This transformation of the American press was to prove paradoxical: on the one hand it democratized the market for newspapers, but on the other it centralized the means of political communication in the hands of large corporations and caused the atrophy of the mobilizing and advocacy roles previously fulfilled by the newspaper.

The penny papers and their successors were commercial rather than political enterprises. Introducing newly developed steam-powered cylinder presses, they lowered prices and expanded circulations by an order of magnitude. This gave them a new but very valuable product to sell: the attention of a mass audience. Advertising became the solid economic foundation of the new mass circulation papers, and the newspaper became a major commercial undertaking, requiring substantial capital investment and promising handsome profits. These profits had important political implications; they meant that the mass circulation newspaper, unlike its less lucrative predecessor, had no need of political subsidies to stay afloat. The economics of advertising, in fact, not only made it possible for the newspaper to free itself from political entanglements but probably created substantial incentives for the abandonment of politically committed journalism, especially of the partisan variety. A paper intent on maximizing its circulation could not afford the restriction of its audience that would result from identification with a particular political position.[16] The penny papers for the most part broke with the political tradition of the early American press, proclaiming their independence and their distaste for "political discussions of a merely partisan character," turning from "oratory" to news in the modern sense of the term.[17]

After the rise of the penny papers, the commercial press consolidated its hold on journalism, and the political journalism of the pre-1830 period gradually died out. Partisan newspapers continued to play an important role in journalism into the latter half of the nineteenth century, but by about the 1870s most had folded or converted to non-partisanship. The demise of the partisan press was followed by a period when the press was nonpartisan but nevertheless often activist, presenting itself as a defender not of a partisan viewpoint but of "the public good" in general, and crusading for everything from municipal reform to war with Spain. The great muckrakers of the progressive era belonged to this period in American journalism, as did the sensationalism of Pulitzer and Hearst. The modern American news media, committed not only to nonpartisanship but to the ideal of a professional, "objective" journalism, began to take shape roughly in the 1920s, becoming fully entrenched by the 1950s or early 1960s.

It is the ideal of objectivity that explains the emphasis on technique and efficacy in the news stories cited. The rise of commercial mass media transformed not only the institutional structure of political communication but also the structure of discourse itself. Commercial or professional journalism employed standards of truth and of the writer's proper relation to the audience very different from those of the political journalism. It had entirely changed standards for what needed to be said in a newspaper and how it should be said.

At the heart of this conception was the respect for "facts," which the penny papers proclaimed along with their political independence and which grew in importance as the commercial media developed. Just as the changing organization of the press paralleled the central change taking place in the wider economy, the growth of large-scale capitalist organization, the changing conventions of journalism paralleled the rise of science as a cultural paradigm against which all forms of discourse came to be measured. "We shall endeavor to record facts on every public and proper subject, stripped of verbiage and coloring," wrote James Gordon Bennett in his 1835 prospectus for the *New York Herald*.[18] The *Herald* was by no means free of verbiage or coloring, but it did emphasize news and the gathering of information rather than the political "oratory" that had been the stock-in-trade of the "six-penny" papers. By the 1920s Walter Lippmann and others would be speaking explicitly of scientific method and "the habit of disinterested realism" as a model for journalism. The journalist of the late nineteenth century, despite a commitment to factual reporting, did not yet radically separate fact and value; one could be a realist and yet a moralist, a recorder of facts and yet a political crusader. But by the early twentieth century realism had become objectivity: "a faith in 'facts,' a distrust of 'values,' and a commitment to their segregation."[19] And journalists came to think of themselves not as participants in a process of political discussion, even of a nonpartisan character, but as professionals, standing above the political fray.

The precise meaning of objective journalism has changed considerably over the course of the twentieth century. From about World War II through the early 1960s, objectivity was assumed to require strict separation not only between fact and value but between fact and interpretation. This was the heyday of straight journalism; news analysis for the most part was restricted to the signed column, and the ordinary reporter was supposed to tell "who, what, when, where" and leave it at that. The naive realism of straight objective journalism was shattered by the political conflict of the 1960s and 1970s, which produced both a credibility gap (a questioning of traditional sources of political information) and a clash of interpretations unknown in the years of wartime and cold war consensus. The stories examined above represent a concern for analysis and investigation born of the disillusionment and confusion of the 1960s. They offer the audience not just facts, not just a record of latest press releases, but perspective and summation, an interpretation of how the facts fit together and what they mean. But the 1960s and 1970s did not produce a questioning of objectivity itself; the "new journalism," which harkened back to the committed journalism of earlier periods, never gained more than a slippery toehold in the commercial media. In some ways, in fact, the 1960s and 1970s, precisely because the interpretation of reality had become subject to political debate, increased the journalist's and the news organization's need to appear strictly objective. The journalist had to provide analysis without appearing to depart from disinterested professionalism. And the easiest way to accomplish this was to focus on questions of strategy, effectiveness, and technique, questions that did not touch directly on conflicts of interest or clashes over the ends and values of political life. The political future of David Stockman is easier to assess with an attitude of detached realism than the actual policy of trickle-down economics, which inevitably raises the issue of how the interests and values affected by economic policy are to be weighed.

One-Dimensionality or Legitimation Crisis?

What are the consequences of the commercialization of the press and the scientization of journalism? Critical theorists have given two very different answers. The prevailing view in the 1940s, 1950s, and early 1960s held that the mass media had become fully integrated into a form of welfare state capitalism, which was rapidly expanding technical rationalization from the sphere of production into all aspects of social life.[20] The media had been stripped of the independent position the early press had held regarding the dominant social interests and had become not merely policemen of the ideological realm but something more sinister than that (policemen, after all, are only necessary to the extent that people resist social control). The media had become producers of consciousness. The consciousness they produced, moreover, was what Marcuse called a "one-dimensional" consciousness; it accepted the existing social order as defining the limits of rationality and sought merely to reflect that order, rejecting any attempt to speak of values or possibilities beyond it as inherently meaningless.

Centralization of Control over the Production of News

This perspective was never developed within critical theory beyond a few provocative essays or applied very systematically to an analysis of news reporting. But clearly there is a good deal of truth to it. The rise of the commercial media reversed the decentralization that had prevailed in the early days of the press, placing political communication once more under the control of established institutions, albeit institutions very different from those that had regulated political discourse before the advent of the newspaper and the pamphlet. It is interesting to look at the rise of commercial media in Great Britain, where the political implications of that development were more directly evident than in the United States.[21] The British newspaper was burdened by onerous political restrictions until well into the nineteenth century, including heavy taxes designed to keep newspapers too expensive to be either published or purchased by the lower classes. But repression proved not only ineffective but possibly counterproductive. Working-class papers published illegally, and the taxes, which they therefore did not have to pay, gave them a competitive edge over the respectable papers. Repression, in other words, ensured that the working class would continue to control its own press. By 1836 the growing illegal press exceeded the legal press in circulation. The liberal campaign for repeal of the "taxes on knowledge," which triumphed in the 1850s, made use of all the familiar arguments for freedom of the press, but the reformers did not leave their case simply to noble sentiments. To these they added the argument that a free market in information would place the education of the masses in the hands of men of "wealth and character." Said one reformer in Parliament, quoted in a fascinating article by James Curran, "We have made a long and fruitless experiment with the gibbet and hulks. Is it not time to consider whether the printer and his types may not provide better for the peace and honor of a free state, than the gaoler and the hangman. Whether in one word, cheap knowledge may not be a better political agent than costly punishment."[22] Freedom of the press meant not merely the lifting of censorship but the transformation of knowledge into a commodity, and the small-scale political press, like the independent petty producer of the precapitalist era, soon had to face the devastating economic power of highly capitalized mass production.

The radical press never attained a political importance in the United States comparable to its importance in Britain in the 1830s.[23] Perhaps this was in part because the United States had for a long time given market forces free reign in the sphere of information; no doubt it was largely due to the differing political and economic structure of the two societies. But when the penny papers appeared in the 1830s, there was nevertheless a growing labor press in the United States, and the penny papers played precisely the role described by the English reformers: they spoke to the cultural and political needs of the constituents of the labor press, artisans who in the 1830s were facing loss of economic independence. But they spoke to those needs from a consensual, reformist, and often a relatively apolitical perspective, emphasizing what the artisans had in common with the other and probably the primary constituency of the new commercial press, the rising middle class. "An emerging American working class," writes Dan Schiller, ". . . confronted newspapers that accepted and amplified belief in individual property, the market and the state, and that simultaneously drew heavily on its own experience. . . . The American working class had barely begun to employ the press as an agency of class identity when the commercial penny papers began to enlist the interest and identification of the laboring men."[24]

The liberal conception of a free market in ideas rested on the principle that the exchange of ideas should be insulated from the structures of wealth and power. In fact the rise of a market in ideas tied the production and dissemination of political information closely to the centers of economic and political power. There is a deep historical irony here. The coming of mass production, which so democratized the market for news, making the newspaper, as Marx put it, "cheaper than natural gas," at the same time centralized the production of news, placing the press under the control—today, in fact, generally monopoly control—of the corporation.[25] The American news media, moreover, have also come to have an intimate institutional connection with the state, despite the absence of formal state control. Modern American news organizations are so strongly geared toward reporting the activities and perspectives of government officials that one journalist gave his influential book the ironic title, *The Fourth Branch of Government*.[26] The news generally reflects the views of political elites faithfully enough that in a period like the 1950s and early 1960s, when conflicts within that elite are relatively insignificant, the political discourse that filters through the media to the public does come very close to the one-dimensionality described by Marcuse. There has, incidently, been relatively little research on the reasons for this historical connection between the rise of a commercial mass media and the institutionalization of relations between the news media and the state.

The Role of Ideology

There is also another, more impersonal but perhaps ultimately more significant face of power: the power of ideology. This is where the technical angle on politics and the principle of objectivity enter the picture. The scientistic model of political discourse is a deeply rooted element of modern capitalist culture, which imposes itself on political discourse without any direct or conscious political intervention for the most part. I introduce the qualification "for the most part" because there have been times when this model of journalism has been emphasized for directly political reasons, and these are revealing. Objectivity was stressed by editors and publishers during the 1930s, for instance, when the Newspaper Guild was strong and relatively political, and there was concern reporters would slant the news toward the interests of labor.[27]

What are the implications of this use of the technical angle? Again, they are not simple, and I shall discuss some of the complexities below. But certainly that model of journalism does have the effect that Marcuse decried; it tends to exclude from political discourse all discussion of the ends of public policy. It conveys, moreover, along with the news of particular events, a general conception of politics more or less compatible with the prevailing low level of popular mobilization. It portrays politics either as a matter of administration or as a more or less sordid personal struggle for power (as in the story on the Reagan-Carter debate), and not, to use Habermas's phrase, as a process of "collective will-formation" and not therefore as a process in which the average citizen need be involved. It conveys to citizens a message about their own role in politics, and that message is essentially one of exclusion.

The News Report as a Speech Act

This last point touches on a dimension of communication much neglected in the study of the media. It is a basic principle of pragmatics, stressed by Habermas, who borrows it from J. L. Austin and John Searle, that any "speech act" has a twofold structure: it contains both a propositional and a "performative" content. It makes a statement about the world and simultaneously invokes or solicits a relationship between speaker and hearer.[28]

Consider the contrast between a modern news broadcast and an eighteenth-century newspaper. Let me take as examples the CBS broadcast containing the special report on pacification and an edition of the *New-England Courant*, an early American newspaper published by James Franklin and later Benjamin Franklin. The CBS broadcast analyzes for the audience in a factual and authoritative tone the progress of the pacification program. It contains virtually no statements that address the audience members directly; they are treated as strictly anonymous. It ends with Walter Cronkite's famous sign-off, "And that's the way it is, Tuesday, Dec. 16, 1968."

The *New-England Courant* dealt with political material of entirely different kind. One fairly typical edition contained a tract on the philosophical basis of law: "Law is right Reason, commanding Things that are good, and forbidding Things that are bad. . . . The Violation therefore of the Law does not constitute a Crime when the Law is bad; but the violation of what ought to be a Law, is a Crime even where there is no Law."[29] Along with this different kind of content went a different way of addressing the audience. The political tract, which was reprinted from a London journal, was introduced to the readers by a letter to the editor, signed in the fashion of the time, "Your Humble Servant, &c." It may in fact have been a contribution sent in by a reader, or it may have been written by the publisher. Most major articles were presented in the form of open personal letters.

In the two cases, very different relationships are established between speaker and hearer. The *New-England Courant* speaks to its readers in a personal tone, at an equal level. It invites them to participate in political discussion. CBS speaks to its audience as a provider of authoritative information. It solicits nothing beyond their attention, solicits of them no active role regarding the political material reported; indeed the authoritative and detached style of the report and the finality of the sign-off leave the impression that the matters discussed are essentially closed, at least until the next broadcast.

The technical angle is only one element of the ideology that shapes modern U.S. journalism. The role of ideology in political communication is a subject that cries out for more systematic investigation. A number of recent studies of the media have addressed the question perceptively, but there is as yet little systematic theory in the area. Most discussions of the role of ideology tend, for lack of theory, to slip by default into functionalism. They tend, that is, to identify certain ideological assumptions, supportive of the capitalist social order, which seem generally to dominate the news, and sometimes to show how these assumptions are effective—how, for example, they are built into the routines of journalism. But they then generally default the question of why these particular ideological principles become dominant, why a congruence develops between the ideological structures of capitalism and its political and economic structures, assuming that the fact of congruence is explanation enough.[30]

Legitimation Crisis?

One reason functional assumptions can be dangerous in the study of the media and of ideology generally is that cultural institutions do not always develop in ways that are functional for the established social order. This brings us to Habermas's theory of legitimation crisis, which departs sharply from the picture of ideological integration painted by the critical theory of the 1940s, 1950s, and early 1960s. The critique of late capitalist society advanced by Horkheimer, Adorno, and Marcuse is based largely on the "closing of the universe of discourse," which they believed that society had produced. Habermas's critique of late capitalism rests on the impossibility of this very ideological closure, the impossibility of an "administrative production of meaning." This argument, which Habermas presents in an admittedly sketchy and preliminary form in his *Legitimation Crtisis*, runs essentially as follows.[31] Liberal capitalist societies have been able to maintain political stability largely because they have permitted the state to intervene increasingly in the workings of the market, softening the social disruptions it produces and ensuring a level of private satisfaction high enough that the mass public will remain generally uninterested in politics. But state action to maintain an orientation of civil privatism has an ironic consequence; it results in an increasing "politicization of the relations of production": more and more areas of social and economic life, previously regulated by the market or by traditional institutions like the family and the church (whose functions, threatened by the tradition-shattering rationality of capitalist production, the state often takes over), are drawn into the political arena. Politicization creates an increased need for legitimation, for justification of social decisions that had previously seemed inevitable products of the market mechanism or expressions of cultural tradition. But legitimation is becoming increasingly hard to come by, precisely because the institutions that have borne the burden of cultural "production," the family, the church, and to some extent the market itself, are on the decline. And the resulting deficit of legitimation cannot, at least ultimately, be made up by any sort of managed production of ideology, for the latter is incompatible with the communicative action essential to the creation of shared normative structures.

It might seem that the media would be the logical institution to fill the legitimation gap, especially in the United States where they are

almost entirely independent of the state and enjoy a much higher
level of public trust than most other institutions. Habermas himself
does not address the role of the media in *Legitimation Crisis*. But I
would like to outline here, in a preliminary way, several reasons why
it seems unlikely that the media could be counted on to play this role
adequately and consistently.[32]

The anarchy of ideological production
Corporate control of the mass media does not guarantee that the
media's cultural products will consistently serve the interests of the
capitalist system as a whole, any more than corporate control of energy
guarantees against an energy crisis. Certainly no major news organization is ever likely to become an open critic of capitalism, but the
purpose of a news organization is to make profit, not politics, and
there is no reason to assume that the narrow economic interest of the
corporation will always coincide with the political interest of the system.
If the anarchy of production leaves the capitalist system vulnerable
to economic crisis, why should the anarchy of ideological "production"
not leave it similarly vulnerable to cultural crisis?

Tensions within the dominant ideology
Neither does the hold of ideology over the journalist seem likely to
guarantee that the media will consistently serve to legitimate the dominant institutions of capitalist society, though here we run up against
the primitive state of knowledge about the structure and dynamics of
ideology. Ideologies are as fraught with contradiction as are any other
historical phenomena. Certainly that is true of the ideology that dominates U.S. journalism. The ambivalence of U.S. journalism is especially
acute with respect to the state. Modern journalism is characterized by
a great reverence for political authority, expressed in explicit terms
at times of ceremony or crisis (the transition of power from Nixon to
Ford, for example), and, perhaps more important, manifested implicitly
in the whole focus and organization of the news-gathering process,
which revolves like a satellite around the center of political power.
But the U.S. journalist is also traditionally cynical about the holders
and seekers of power, and that tradition has been reawakened and
perhaps deepened by the political conflicts of the 1960s and the drift
and ineffectiveness of the 1970s. This cynicism may itself be functional
for the system in that it demobilizes the public, lowering what political

scientists call the sense of political efficacy.[33] But that does not mean it could not simultaneously be hollowing out the myths that have sustained the welfare-national security state of the postwar period. When it comes to the economic structure of modern capitalism, the journalist is much less likely to express doubts. But even here there are ideological tensions. The American journalist believes in "free enterprise" and the rationality of modern capitalist technology and social organization; at the same time she or he clings to an ideology of traditional individualism that predates the corporate era and coexists with it somewhat awkwardly.

Universal pragmatics and the limits of ideological manipulation

The media, finally, have a need for legitimation of their own, which may conflict with the legitimation of the system. Here it will be useful to return to Habermas's pragmatics. Critical theory is concerned with developing a form of social inquiry that will be able to bridge the gap between is and ought, enabling us to offer rational answers, grounded in the analysis of human experience, to practical questions, questions of how we should live and act. Habermas believes the solution to this puzzle is to be found in the analysis of communication. The effective use of language presupposes certain relations of reciprocity between human individuals; these conditions for the possibility of effective communication, which can be established by a reconstructive science of speech acts, provide a basis for both normative discourse and for empirical analysis of the dynamics of human history. It is this "universal pragmatics" that provides the justification for the central premise of *Legitimation Crisis*, the premise that there can be no "administrative production of meaning." The use of communication as an instrument of domination, Habermas argues, violates the conditions of trust and reciprocity essential to the achievement of shared meaning. This is not to say communication cannot be used successfully for manipulative purposes. On the contrary, what Habermas calls instrumental or strategic communication is a routine fact of social life and certainly a central characteristic of contemporary political history; one need only to recall the effectiveness of government management of the news in the early years of the Vietnam war.[35] But it follows from Habermas's theory that there are limits beyond which the basic structure of human communication cannot be stretched.[36]

The idea of a universal pragmatics is fraught with theoretical dif-
ficulties, far too numerous and fundamental to be discussed here. But
Habermas does seem to have stated a simple but neglected truth
crucial to the analysis of ideological institutions. Every process of communication involves a social relationship, in fact, a network of relationships, among active human subjects.[37] the maintenance of these
relationships imposes demands on institutions like the media that may
conflict with the need of the system for legitimation. The media have
to attend to their own legitimacy. They must maintain the integrity
of their relationship with their audience and also the integrity of their
own self-image and of the social relationships that make up the profession of journalism.[38] Maintaining these relationships requires a certain
minimum of honesty, which, especially in periods of political crisis,
can lead to conflicts of considerable ferocity between the media and
other major social institutions and may seriously conflict with the
legitimation requirements of the system. To a limited extent, this did
in fact occur in the United States during the 1960s and 1970s.[39] We
do not yet know how substantial the ideological consequences have
been. It has often been observed that the fact of conflict between the
media and other institutions does not necessarily mean the media are
playing a delegitimating role in relation to the political and socioeconomic system, and this is clearly true. Indeed the media often see
themselves in such cases as upholders of that system and present the
correction of abuse as the ultimate proof of its soundness.[40] One study
of the impact of Watergate coverage found that those who followed
Watergate on television were more likely than others to lay the blame
on individuals rather than the political system.[41] There is, however,
no theoretical reason to assume this will always be the case, and the
potential for disjunctions between the needs of the media and the
needs of other institutions deserves more attention than it has gotten
from critical analysts of the media.

To the extent that the media do not maintain the integrity of their
relationship with their audience, moreover, legitimation may break
down in another way: the media may become ineffective ideological
institutions. This may in fact be one important consequence of the
scientization of journalism. The shift to an attitude of detached realism
places the ends and values of political life outside the normal bounds
of political communication; and this is functional for the system. But
at the same time it may render the media incapable of contributing

to the establishment of new legitimating values if the old ones are beginning to break down. The modern mass media and the professional journalist clearly have great power (subject to the many political, economic, and social constraints within which they operate) to set the agenda of political discussion and to determine the context within which day-to-day events will be perceived. As purveyors of authoritative information, their strength is great indeed. But their ability to establish positive social values and political commitments may be another matter altogether.

Concluding Comments

The rise of commercial mass media, which began in the United States in the 1830s, had paradoxical political consequences. It democratized the market for newspapers; at the same time it centralized the production of political information and ruptured the connection between the press and an active public. It led to the decline of politically committed journalism and its replacement by a professional journalism that claimed to stand above politics. Professionalization transforms the nature of political discourse. It narrows discussion to questions of technique and effectiveness that can be approached with detached realism. It also changes the performative content of journalism; it transforms the newspaper from a political message addressed from citizen to citizen, inviting the reader to participate in political debate or action, into an authoritative account of the state of the world, addressed to an audience whose own role in that world normally is not at issue. For these reasons, the modern news media do not produce the kind of active, critical public debate that the newspaper seemed to promise when it first emerged as an institution of the public sphere. The American news media may, in fact, communicate to the public a conception of politics and of their own political role that strongly discourages active political involvement. Beyond this the precise consequences of the commercialization and scientization of journalism are not easy to judge. There is no simple answer, in particular, to the much-debated question of whether a commercial-professional news media can be expected to serve as an effective ideological support for the power structure of advanced capitalism.

This argument I put forward simply as a research proposal; all the links in the chain of development I have outlined here need to be investigated more thoroughly. I have suggested, for example, that the technical angle in news reporting results from professionalization, which in turn results from commercialization. In fact little is known about the interconnections among these three aspects of American journalism, and these most likely are considerably more complex than I have presented them here. Professionalization, for instance, no doubt has cultural and political as well as economic roots; it is particularly advanced in the United States and much less so in other advanced capitalist states.[42] And the technical angle is no doubt to some extent a reflection of the general political culture of the twentieth-century United States, not a result purely of the structure and ideology of the news media. Little is known, similarly, about how the public actually responds to the underlying messages about politics, embedded in the form of news presentation, which I have stressed. And the problem of legitimation is still shrouded in ambiguity. We do not know, for example, to what extent a system of political and economic power actually needs a coherent legitimating ideology that penetrates the consciousness of the mass public. Perhaps passivity and pragmatic acceptance of power are sufficient; in that case Habermas's strictures about administrative production of meaning would be more or less irrelevant to assessing the role of mass media in the maintenance of structures of power.

The mass media are an institution with a dual social identity. They are both an economic (or in Western Europe, often political) and a cultural institution; they are a profit-making business and at the same time a producer of meaning, a creator of social consciousness. Much research has been done in recent years on the political economy of the news media, the structure of the media as economic institutions, and the impact of that structure on their cultural product. This, however, is only part of the story: the "production" of culture—to use a common but misleading metaphor—also surely has imperatives of its own, which must be understood if we are to capture in its full complexity the functioning of an instituion like the news media. It is for this reason that I have placed such heavy emphasis on Habermas. Habermas seems to offer at least the beginnings of a systematic approach to the dynamics of ideological production, conceptualized in such a way that those dynamics can be linked with the economic and other processes that also shape the news media.

Daniel C. Hallin

Underlying Habermas's contribution to the understanding of political culture and communication is the concept of dialogue, which is crucial in two respects. First, it is the concern with dialogue that leads Habermas, like others in the critical theory tradition, to focus on the character of political debate, the fate of the public sphere in liberal capitalist societies. But Habermas also uses the concept of dialogue in a new and powerful way: as the heart of a method of analysis of communication and culture. For Habermas, all forms of human communication, even under conditions of mass dissemination, are essentially relationships between human subjects, derived ultimately from the elementary structure of dialogue. The structure of dialogue therefore provides a basis for a theory of communicative action and hence of the "production" of culture. Whether one accepts the idea that a universal structure of dialogue underlies all communication, communication is clearly a relationship, not merely a product. It is essential to grasp not only the effects of mass communication (the focus of the positivist tradition) and the economic and political constraints under which it operates but also the specifically communicative or interactive constraints involved in the creation of shared meanings.

Discussions of the media and public policy are traditionally closed with exhortations to the media to provide the public with more and better information, "an informed and active public being essential to a vigorous democracy" (as the phrase goes). This is sensible enough advice, subject of course to the problem of saying what is to count as better information about public affairs. But it is also insufficient. The problem with the American news media, if one does in fact value active public participation, lies not so much with the quality of the product being offered the consumer as with the fact that the major relation of political communication has indeed become a relation of seller and consumer.

The modern mass media are relatively good at collecting and disseminating information. When one compares them with the news-gathering efforts of the precommercial, premass press, the organizational, technological, and even cultural advances are staggering. The mass public today receives an unprecedented quantity of information. Even the scientism of contemporary journalism represents a significant—and in certain ways democratizing—cultural advance. The shift from the oratory of early political journalism to the commercial media's focus on news and "facts" meant a shift of attention from abstract principles (the "right Reason" of the *New-England Courant*'s discussion of law) to the real historical events and social conditions that touched the mass public in their daily lives.

What the modern mass media cannot do is to play the role of sparking active public participation in deciding the direction of public policy. I use the word *cannot* deliberately. Individual journalists working in established news organizations can certainly from time to time break out of the focus on technique and strategy to raise the direction of public policy as an issue; they can be sensitive to the underlying message their reporting conveys about politics and the citizen's relation to it; they can give a hearing to those who do seek to play a mobilizing role. But all of this must remain within relatively narrow limits; the antipolitical tendencies explored here are deeply rooted in the structure and the professional ideology of the American news media. Few of us, in fact, would want the established news media to presume to play the mobilizing role of the decentralized press of Tocqueville's day. It is not a role appropriate to institutions with such massive social power.

To the extent, then, that life is to be breathed into the public sphere of liberal capitalist societies, the initiative must come from outside the institutions now dominating that sphere. The "Habermasian" analysis I have stressed suggests reason for at least cautious optimism that citizens' organizations can make themselves heard despite the centralization of control over the channels of political communication. However powerful they may have become, the mass media must maintain some semblance of a dialogue with the public. There is always, therefore, some degree of openness, of two-dimensionality in the communication porcess: when an active public challenge to the limits of political discourse arises, the media can ignore it only at the peril of their own legitimacy.[43]

Notes

1. Jürgen Habermas, "The Public Sphere: An Encyclopedia Article (1964)," *New German Critique* 1 (Fall 1974).

2. Alexis de Tocqueville, *Democracy in America* (Garden City, N.Y.: Doubleday, 1969), p. 517.

3. Karl Marx, "Debates on Freedom of the Press and Publication" [1842], in Saul K. Padover, ed., *Karl Marx in Freedom of the Press and Censorship* (New York: McGraw-Hill, 1974), p. 31.

Daniel C. Hallin

4. Jürgen Habermas, *Theory and Praxis* (Boston: Beacon Press, 1973), p. 42. See also his *Knowledge and Human Interests* (Boston: Beacon Press, 1971).

5. I will not be concerned here with presenting a critique of the positivist tradition in media research, which is focused on the effects of media messages, primarily on individual attitudes. For such a critique, see Todd Gitlin, "Media Sociology: The Dominant Paradigm," *Theory and Society* 6 (September 1978).

6. One work that does attempt an empirical analysis of political communication from a critical theory perspective is Claus Mueller, *The Politics of Communication* (New York: Oxford University Press, 1973). Mueller's work, though, contains relatively little discussion of the media.

7. CBS, December 11 and 16, 1968.

8. See my *The Uncensored War: The Media and Vietnam* (New York: Oxford University Press, forthcoming); also Todd Gitlin, *The Whole World Is Watching: Mass Media in the Making and Unmaking of the New Left* (Berkeley: University of California Press, 1980).

9. Thomas E. Patterson and Robert D. McClure, *The Unseeing Eye: The Myth of Television Power in National Politics* (New York: Putnam, 1976).

10. *New York Times*, October 29, 1980, p. 1.

11. CBS, November 12, 1981.

12. One might object: "What about the editorial, the 'op-ed' page and the specialized press of political opinion? Doesn't modern American journalism merely differentiate news and political commentary?" Political commentary certainly survives in the modern media, but it survives in a subordinate and restricted status. It is no longer considered the primary task of journalism. It is banished from the front page. It also tends to be restricted to the prestige press. The *New York Times*, the *Washington Post*, and a few other papers with relatively elite readerships have fairly substantial "op-ed" pages, most U.S. newspapers do not, and television, which is the major source of information for the mass public, places a particularly low value on political commentary. The "op-ed" page itself is not unaffected by the growing importance of the technical angle in news analysis.

13. Benjamin Franklin, *The Autobiography and Other Writings* (New York: Signet, 1961), p. 213.

14. Tocqueville, *Democracy*, p. 518.

15. In discussing the early American news media, I draw heavily on two fine studies: Michael Schudson, *Discovering the News* (New York: Basic Books, 1978), and Dan Schiller, *Objectivity and the News* (Philadelphia: University of Pennsylvania Press, 1981).

16. Political neutrality is a long-run tendency, not an immediate demand of commercialism. At certain times, when competition among newspapers was intense, political crusades were a good way to sell papers. Once a newspaper aspires to cover an entire market, however—as advertisers prefer and as most papers (and television) do today—identification with a particular political position becomes much more problematic.

17. *Baltimore Sun*, quoted in Schudson, *Discovering*, p. 22.

18. Quoted in Schiller, *Objectivity*, p. 87.

19. Schudson, *Discovering*, p. 6.

20. The most important statements of this perspective are Max Horkheimer and Theodor W. Adorno, "The Culture Industry: Enlightenment as Mass Deception," in *The Dialectic of Enlightenment* (New York: Seabury Press, 1972), and Herbert Marcuse, *One-Dimensional Man* (Boston: Beacon Press, 1964).

21. See James Curran, "Capitalism and Control of the Press, 1800–1975," in James Curran, Michael Gurevitch, and Janet Woollacott, eds., *Mass Communication and Society* (Beverly Hills: Sage Publications, 1979); and George Boyce, "The Fourth Estate: Reappraisal of a Concept," and James Curran, "The Press as an Agency of Social Control: An Historical Perspective," both in George Boyce, James Curran, and Pauline Wingate, eds., *Newspaper History: From the 17th Century to the Present Day* (Beverly Hills: Sage Publications, 1978).

22. Curran, "Press as an Agency," p. 55.

23. There has been relatively little research on the radical press in the United States. See Joseph R. Conlin, ed., *The American Radical Press, 1880–1960* (Westport, Conn.: Greenwood Press, 1974), and Robert Armstrong, *A Trumpet to Arms: Alternative Media in America* (Boston: Houghton Mifflin, 1981).

24. Schiller, *Objectivity*, p. 74.

25. By the late 1970s fewer than 4 percent of U.S. cities had competing newspapers. See Ernest C. Hynds, *American Newspapers in the 1980s* (New York: Hastings House, 1980), p. 139.

26. Douglass Cater, *The Fourth Branch of Government* (New York: Vintage, 1959). An enormous literature bears on this point. Two of the most important works are Bernard Cohen, *The Press and Foreign Policy* (Princeton: Princeton University Press, 1963), and Leon V. Sigal, *Reporters and Officials* (Lexington, Mass.: D. C. Heath, 1973).

27. Schudson, *Discovering*, pp. 156–157.

28. Jürgen Habermas, "What Is Universal Pragmatics?" in *Communication and the Evolution of Society* (Boston: Beacon Press, 1979). A similar point is made by a little-known but extremely important Russian philosopher of language, Bakhtin. Bakhtin published under the name of a friend: V. N. Volosinov, *Marxism and the Philosophy of Language* (New York: Seminar Press, 1973). A good introduction to his work is Michael Holquist, "The Politics of Representation," in Stephen J. Greenblatt, ed., *Allegory and Representation* (Baltimore: Johns Hopkins University Press, 1981).

29. *New-England Courant,* May 7–14, 1722.

30. The most glaring example of this kind of functionalism is Luis Althusser, "Ideology and Ideological State Apparatuses," in *Lenin and Philosophy* (New York: Monthly Review Press, 1971). The best work on ideology and the media makes use of Gramsci's concept of hegemony. See especially Stuart Hall, "Culture, the Media, and the 'Ideological Effect,' " in Curran *et al.*, *Mass Communication,* and the concluding chapter of Gitlin, *Whole World.* For Gramsci's own discussion of hegemony, see *Selections from the Prison Notebooks* (New York: International Publishers, 1971).

31. Jürgen, Habermas, *Legitimation Crisis* (Boston: Beacon Press, 1975). See also "Legitimation Problems in the Modern State," in his *Communication and the Evolution of Society.*

32. Cf. Douglas Kellner, "Network Television and American Society: Introduction to a Critical Theory of Television," *Theory and Society* 10 (January 1981).

33. Political scientists have tried, without success, to demonstrate a connection between the media and the level of political efficacy. But no one has devised a way to assess long-term

Daniel C. Hallin

media effects through the use of quantitative methods. See Michael J. Robinson, "Public Affairs Television and the Growth of Political Malaise: The Case of 'The Selling of the Pentagon,'" *American Political Science Review* (1976); Arthur H. Miller, Edie N. Goldenberg, and Lutz Erbring, "Type-set Politics: Impact of Newspapers on Public Confidence," *American Political Science Review* (1979); and my critique of both in "The Media, the War in Vietnam, and Political Support: A Critique of the Thesis of an Oppositional Media," *Journal of Politics* 46 (February 1984).

34. Much of the ideology of the modern American journalist can be traced back to the progressive era, when the journalistic profession was just beginning to take shape. It is, it seems to me, the ideology of an independent middle class absorbed into corporate capitalism but not entirely comfortable with the new order. This is a connection that deserves more attention than it has gotten. There is some discussion of the importance of progressivism in Herbert J. Gans, *Deciding What's News* (New York: Pantheon, 1979).

35. See Hallin, *The Uncensored War*.

36. There is considerable ambiguity in Habermas's writing on this point, as there is in general on the relation between the normative and the empirical sides of his argument about legitimation. When Habermas writes in "Legitimation Problems in the Modern State," "Only the rules and communicative presuppositions that make it possible to distinguish an accord or agreement among free and equals from a forced or contingent consensus have legitimating force today," he is falling into a purely normative concept of legitimation (or perhaps confusing intellectual history with the history of actual legitimation processes), for the actual process of legitimation is in fact much more complex, involving, for one thing, a continuing importance of tradition.

37. Again Bakhtin is also relevant.

38. On the possibility of disjunction between the media professional and the structure of power, see Alvin W. Gouldner, *The Dialectic of Ideology and Technology: The Origins, Grammar, and Future of Ideology* (New York: Seabury Press, 1976).

39. See my "The American News Media from Vietnam to El Salvador, A Study of Ideological Change and Its Limits," in David Paletz, ed., *Political Communication* (Norwood, N.J.: Ablex, forthcoming).

40. David L. Paletz and Robert Entman, *Media Power Politics* (New York: Free Press, 1981).

41. Jack McLeod, Jane D. Brown, Lee P. Becker, and Dean A. Zieke, "Decline and Fall: A Longitudinal Analysis of Communication Effects," *Communication Research* 4 (January 1977).

42. A number of European countries are trying to find ways to preserve a political press, despite strong economic tendencies toward the elimination of such a press. See Anthony Smith, ed., *Newspapers and Democracy: International Essays on a Changing Medium* (Cambridge: MIT Press, 1980).

43. Gitlin discusses the interaction of the media and citizen activists in *Whole World*, and "News as Ideology and Contested Area: Towards a Theory of Hegemony, Crisis and Opposition," *Socialist Review* 9 (November–December 1979). See also Paletz and Entman, *Media Power Politics*, chap. 8.

Criticalness, Pragmatics, and Everyday Life: Consumer Literacy as Critical Practice

Peter Grahame

In "The Culture Industry: Enlightenment as Mass Deception," Adorno and Horkheimer carried out a relentless attack on the transformation of culture into a sphere of empty satisfactions geared to elicit consumers' participation in their own victimization. Their emphasis was on the irrationality of the prevailing mode of consumption as a cultural form. About twenty years later, Marcuse renewed the attack on consumer culture in *One-Dimensional Man*, denouncing Plato in the drugstore book rack and Bach at the breakfast table with the same vehemence that Adorno and Horkheimer had used to denounce jazz and Hollywood films. These attacks, which show critical theory in its role as a critique of satisfaction, proceeded from a common posture: critique from above, from outside, from a morally or epistemologically superior position. To be sure, Adorno had in principle rejected reliance on either immanent (from within) or transcendent (from outside) critique in favor of a third option: "The dialectical critic of culture must both participate in culture and not participate."[1] Nevertheless, in their critiques of consumer culture, Adorno, Horkheimer, and Marcuse seem committed to a standpoint radically outside the everyday world of consumption. David Held has summed up this posture lucidly:

The critique of ideology, as the immanent critique of an object—a critique which (to put it crudely), assesses an object in terms of its own standards and ideals—is possible only in so far as "ideology contains a rational element with which the critique can deal". Capitalist exchange, for example, can be assessed in light of its own, substantial claim to be just. But when people become "objects of calculation," as the consumers of the culture industry, then the ideology which informs this calculation is no longer simply false by its own standards—for it has none.[2]

Again and again the emphasis is on consumers' victimization and their utter lack of opportunities for rational participation in the achievement of satisfactions. Thus, for example, "There is nothing left for the consumer to classify. Producers have done it for him," and "Capitalist production so confines them, body and soul, that they fall helpless victims to what is offered them."[3] This posture of radical condemnation has also informed subsequent, often popularized critiques of consumer culture, which have tended to regard consumerism nondialectically, as the bad fruit of capitalism or mass society, rather than as a complex sphere of lived experiences, of competences and situations in which contradictory elements are conjoined.[4] Meanwhile new developments in critical theory have hinted at the possibility of putting the analysis of consumer culture onto a different basis. Habermas's work on communication theory has opened up new possibilities for developing more adequately the immanent aspect of critiques of mass or popular cultural forms.

This chapter aims to continue the investigation of the pragmatics of communication Habermas initiated in order to illustrate possibilities for making critical theory more responsive to the task of examining mundane forms of criticism or "mundane critiques."[5] These are critical practices within everyday life, often connected with elements of popular culture, in which societal members take some step toward a critical analysis of their situation. To study such practices seriously would require the development of a stance different from that exemplified in the often dazzling diatribes of the earlier Frankfurt school. The other side to the presumption of absence of criticalness (or, indeed, rationality) that animates so much critical theoretical work would therefore be a willingness to consider respects in which the development of criticalness is, however inchoately, already underway in the present society.

In particular I propose to focus on one of the various forms of literacy through which persons develop their membership to consumer culture. As Stuart Ewen has shown, basic features of the consumer culture familiar to us emerged in the early twentieth century. A prominent aspect was the introduction of forms of consumer education that proposed making the consumer an active participant in the development and rationalization of mass markets.[6] This "education" was carried out on several fronts, including advertising, public school education, and the appearance of a new kind of popular periodical literature, of which *Consumer Reports* is probably the best-known exemplar. In terms of these developments, the consumer is not a passive victim but rather a willing accomplice in the overcoming of traditional, local forms of satisfying material needs and the creation of an entirely new kind of material culture. Of course, Adorno and Horkheimer would point out that such "education" illustrates precisely what is so appalling about consumer culture: it promotes forms of consciousness that are the very betrayal of enlightenment. But that view endorses the notion that consumer culture is monolithic and that it is still firmly in the hands of those who conspired to create it. Insofar as consumer culture is contradictory, analysis must refrain from either endorsement or denunciation as its habitual stance.

Consumer culture is worth studying closely because it contains within it some of the most familiar popular notions of criticalness, for example, the ubiquitous "Don't get ripped off!" Such notions illustrate what can count mundanely (as an attitude of everyday life) as being critical. It is probably not unreasonable to say that the world of consumption is the commonsense sphere par excellence in which we may be critical or fail to be critical, so thoroughly have notions of criticalness in the marketplace penetrated popular consciousness. In part this consciousness has developed through the influence of the popular literature exemplified by *Consumer Reports*. This literature occupies a unique position as a critical interlocutor of mass market definitions of satisfaction, exerting an influence no doubt reaching far beyond its direct readership.[7] Here I intend to initiate an analysis of the pragmatics of this literature, giving special attention to the critical moments it supports.

The Standpoint of Pragmatic Analysis

The point of departure for my analysis of mundane consumer criticism is Habermas's universal pragmatics. I will give a short outline of his position, emphasizing the conception of critical potentials it affords and then introduce a complementary strategy I propose to pursue.

Following the model of psychoanalysis's "depth hermeneutics," Habermas proposed to develop an analysis of repression at the social level in terms of a theory of systematically distorted communication. Just as the psychoanalyst must rely on a model of normal communication in order to interpret the patient's deviant utterances, a model of undistorted communication would be needed to analyze deformations of communication at the social level, for example, the false consensus secured through the working of an ideology. Universal pragmatics is intended to furnish the needed model of pure, undistorted communication by means of a clarification of what is presupposed for using language in order to reach agreement.

Habermas observes that the normal state of linguistic communication lies between the extremes of secured consensus and clear-cut cases of its absence or violation. Instead the more usual cases have to be analyzed from the point of view of what it is to bring about an agreement. Habermas analyzes the process of reaching an understanding in terms of the satisfaction of validity claims. He proposes that there are four types of universal validity claims we unavoidably raise when we act communicatively:

The speaker must choose a comprehensible [verständlich] expression so that speaker and hearer can understand one another. The speaker must have the intention of communicating a true [wahr] proposition (or a propositional content, the existential presuppositions of which are satisfied) so that the hearer can share the knowledge of the speaker. The speaker must want to express his intentions truthfully [wahrhaftig] so that the hearer can believe the utterance of the speaker (can trust him). Finally, the speaker must choose an utterance that is right [richtig] so that the hearer can accept the utterance and speaker and hearer can agree with one another in the utterance with respect to a recognized normative background.[8]

Habermas thus universalizes speech act theory's interest in instances of "doing something in saying something" in order to argue that whenever we act communicatively, we must do these four things. The point of this universalizing treatment, which is carried out as a formal reconstruction of presuppositions, is to give an analytically compelling account of the basic qualifications—the competence—on which we must rely in reaching agreement, an account that has implications for the analysis of systematically distorted communication. Thus acting communicatively to reach an understanding is not just a matter of making ourselves clear (comprehensible expression) or exchanging propositions and assessing their truth value. In addition we make claims concerning the legitimacy of our utterances (their rightness with respect to a recognized normative background), as well as their truthfulness (thus we make reference to trust as a condition of reaching understanding, and to deception as a condition of its frustration). The communicative achievement of understanding depends not only on the cognitive use of language (*re* propositions) but also on its interactive use (*re* the normative context) and on its expressive use (*re* the speaker's trustworthiness).

The specification of these three uses of language fundamental to communicative action in turn furnishes a basis for analyzing distortions. When we act communicatively, we suppose that the validity claims associated with these uses are satisfied or could be vindicated. In effect we anticipate a pure form of communication in which uncoerced consensus is possible. In this pure form, no structural constraints produce unequal advantages for raising and testing validity claims; instead there prevails a symmetry between speakers with respect to each aspect of language use. Habermas has characterized the structure these symmetries comprise as the "ideal speech situation."[9] In normal cases speakers can thematize a problematic validity claim and submit it to appropriate tests. The crucial cases are those in which attempts to test claims break down. According to Habermas's scheme the presence of systematic distortion can then be analyzed with respect to disturbances of the structural symmetries associated with each validity claim. The analyst must review each of the fundamental dimensions of language use for possible distortion in the light of the model of pure communication.

Through pragmatics the perspective of the participant in social action acquires a new meaning for critical theory. Whereas Adorno and Horkheimer emphasized the forms of victimization entailed through participation in broad sectors of cultural life, Habermas shows how resources for critique are built into the communicative competence that the participant uses even under conditions of distorted communication. However, Habermas does not assume that this critical potential is automatically translated into effective critical practices. Instead the reconstructed validity basis of speech is to be used as a scheme to decode the blockages and impedances that govern particular communicative actions.

Since pragmatics is to contribute to the analysis of actual cases of communication, it seems important to distinguish between two possible directions in pragmatic analysis: toward investigation of the universal and the particular. In Habermas's elaboration of the basic features of universal pragmatics, a reflection on anonymous competences (masteries of rule systems) is the condition for analyzing the rational basis of consensus. This reflection aims at a rational reconstruction of the intuitive knowledge presupposed for using ordinary language to reach agreement. Habermas's basic procedure is to review analyses of speech acts (in particular, those worked out by J. L. Austin and John Searle) that already spell out what any competent speaker knows about how to make promises, give orders, and so forth. He then distinguishes between what is particular to a speech act type (such as promising) and properties universal to the utterance of any speech act (for example, the raising of the four fundamental validity claims). Analysis is thus directed to the most general features of communicative competence rather than to specifics of particular speech acts and their performance in concrete settings. The latter enter only to illustrate universal pragmatic properties. Universal pragmatics thus deals with properties of language use that are universal and anonymous, rather than tied to particular cultural activities.

The application of insights won by universal pragmatics to clarify particular cases of distortion requires, however, a complementary strategy, which shows how the situation of the participant is understandable not only in terms of general qualifications for speech but also in terms of membership to particular cultural practices. I propose to call this complementary strategy "cultural pragmatics."[10] In cultural pragmatics reflection on cultural membership is the condition for analyzing particular determinations of validity. Insofar as critical theory aims to clarify culturally located participants' potential for critical insight, the critical theorist cannot remain indifferent to the particular cultural practices through which societal members make their situation understandable to themselves. One must, for example, consider what possibilities for thematizing validity claims are built into the relevances that organize a particular cultural practice. Thus critical theorists must use not only their basic communicative competence but also their specific cultural competence in order to locate critical tasks and potentials for enlightenment. In this sense the critical theorist must in part proceed as an ethnographer who uses his or her pregiven, tacit cultural competence in order to locate and analyze features of participation in a specific cultural practice. In this way features of the cultural competence specific to the practice are delineated. Cultural pragmatics complements universal pragmatics by clarifying the particular horizon within which the fundamental validity claims become articulated.

The Standpoint of Mundane Criticism

If universal pragmatics furnishes a scheme for the analysis of distorted communication, its most immediate application might be thought to be to communications that are commonly recognized as cases of distortion, manipulation, and deception. In the sphere of consumption, advertising would be a likely target. But just as such distortions are already mundanely recognized, there are also mundanely recognized forms of critical practice, such as those associated with consumerism and environmentalism. Not only do these practices claim to ground critical interpretations of the everyday life of which they are a part, but they also furnish indications of what can count practically as critique for the participants concerned.

Adorno and Horkheimer were not alone in recognizing the prominence of the consumer in American public life. At about the same time they were drafting their indictment of the culture industry, the U.S. National Association of Secondary-School Principals was issuing, through its Consumer Education Study publication series, vigorous and wide-ranging proposals concerning not only the need for consumer education but also the policies required to guide it. In 1945 an association publication cited "the flowering of professional literature on the subject" and "the accelerating speed with which consumer education is sweeping into the schools."[11] And it could trace its origins to a consumer movement developing early in the twentieth century. One can scarcely imagine, however, that Adorno and Horkheimer would have shared the association's enthusiasm for improving consumer decision making. Adorno and Horkheimer were critical to the point of contempt of the characteristic self-understanding of consumers, and there is little reason to doubt that they would have extended this attitude to the promotion of consumer education, which they might have viewed as further evidence of the system's power to incorporate all forms of opposition. As they wrote of the culture industry,

the necessity inherent in the system [is] not to leave the customer alone, not for a moment to allow him any suspicion that resistance is possible. The principle [that needs should not be satisfied] dictates that he should be shown all his needs as capable of fulfillment, but that those needs should be so predetermined that he feels himself to be the eternal consumer, the object of the culture industry. Not only does it make him believe that the deception it practices is satisfaction, but it goes further and implies that, whatever the state of affairs, he must put up with what is offered.[12]

In this spirit, one might be ready to say that these consumer education efforts, which already received national attention in the 1930s and were dramatized further as matters of national urgency in the 1960s, are properly viewed as organized efforts to ensure the continued domestication of the consuming public.[13] Yet that would scarcely account for the substantial impression of opening up critical perspectives that has almost always accompanied these efforts. If for the moment we set aside the special motives of critical theory, the striking and recurrent feature of consumer education efforts is their promise of enlightenment. Instead of being passive recipients of messages directed at them, consumers are to become active, critical interpreters of those messages. When "The Culture Industry" was being written, the need for such enlightenment was already becoming established as a social fact, a reality whose validity, however questionable from the perspective of critical theory, continues to govern popular notions of the consumer's criticalness.

In seeking to clarify the standpoint of mundane criticism, my purpose is not to vilify or endorse mundane critical practices with respect to a more adequate concept of critique but rather to consider the commonsense basis of the appearance of criticalness that such practices achieve. The term *mundane* is thus not intended in a pejorative way. Rather it is intended to call attention to how consumer reasoning must appear to a participant who practices it.[14] Mundane reasoning is reasoning in its everyday, worldly aspects, reasoning as it appears (socially, interactionally) as a feature of the accomplishment of practical activities. The emphasis is on the performative attitude of the participant rather than on the attitude of the neutral observer.[15] A contrast with speculative or theoretical reasoning is thus implied. To be sure, the scene of theorizing has its own practical features, some of which—for example, its basis in interests—have been emphasized by critical theorists. The contrast remains useful, however, if it is understood as signifying the aspect under which reasoning is viewed rather than a difference between types of substantive reasoning activities. In its mundane aspect, the guiding constraints on reasoning are deeply practical: it is not a question of deciding what, according to an externally imposed principle of adequate scientific method (or the like), could in theory be done but rather of what it makes sense to do in terms of what can have a point within the activity underway. In contrast theorizing is detached from the relevances that are constitutive for the participant. The mundane character of consumer reasoning can be seen both in its preoccupation with getting on with the task at hand (choosing products, making complaints, weighing satisfactions) rather than pondering abstract questions (what is a consumer? what is a rationally grounded validity claim?) and also in the fact that it is carried out in everyday circumstances, in the marketplace rather than under idealized conditions of reflection and deliberation. Somehow consumer reasoning—like other kinds of mundane reasoning—is able to proceed without benefit of cultivation of a theoretical attitude toward its preoccupations. We might be inclined to view this stance as a function of the ignorance of consumers. We could, for example, view this in the light of the common observation, typical of consumer education literature, that consumers fail to be adequately scientific in dealing with their problems, as in the following:

There is a wide gap between the best scientific knowledge relating to consumer commodities and the beliefs held by most of the people. Not only are many consumers prevented by lack of scientific understanding from making fully intelligent choices and use of foods, vitamin products, and medicines—to mention only a few products—but even the little science they do know can be, and not infrequently is, exploited by pseudoscientific advertising and sales promotion.[16]

But the attempt to see consumer reasoning in its mundane aspect requires a different attitude. It is not a question of viewing consumer practice as a defective version of scientific practice but rather of understanding its exclusion of all motives (such as ideals of consistency and comprehensiveness) that do not respect the primacy of its practical concerns.[17] The paramount property of consumer reasoning is its practical adequacy, its adequacy-in-use to the practical contingencies of the activities of consumers.

The objection that consumer reasoning in its mundane aspect cannot be genuinely critical must be acknowledged. Here two notions of being critical need to be distinguished. On the one hand, the term *critical* may be applied to the cultivation of modes of resistance and opposition indigenous to mundane reasoning—part of the cultural competence of consumers, for example. Consumer criticisms of particular products and marketing practices seem to belong here, as well as attempts to "improve consumer decision making" insofar as they merely provide remedies and improved versions of the same kind of reasoning consumers already use. On the other hand, the term *critical* may be reserved for the adoption of a special attitude that breaks with the apparent naturalness of such a domain of criticism and exposes its unexamined assumptions. Critiques designed to show that consumerist criticisms serve only to reproduce the victimization of the consumer seem to belong here. Such critiques depart from the relevances of mundane reasoning in order to propose alternative—usually philosophically or scientifically clarified—conceptions of adequacy in reasoning. The stance of these two senses of criticism is thus radically different, but Habermas's universal pragmatic approach appears to suggest an underlying link between the two since the orientation to unimpeded discursive testing that could expose the false limits determining mundane practices has its basis in the acquisition of competence for participating in ordinary language communication. In this respect the move from mundane criticism to critical theorizing would require consumers to appropriate reflectively the communicative competence they already possess. But it would also require them to take up a new relation to the particular cultural competence they have as consumers. We must therefore try to do justice to the distinctive reasoning practices that are constitutive of membership in consumer culture.

The Domain of Consumer Literacy

"The consumer" is such a pervasive and familiar figure in contemporary public life that it is perhaps useful to remind ourselves of the diverse sources from which this figure has been built up. In fact, we owe "the consumer" to several discourses, which, in one sense, have co-constituted this actor-type but also continue to compete in claiming authority over its definition. Each of these discourses projects its own version of the consumer and the world consumers inhabit. They include public policymaking, law, public education, the social sciences, market and motivational research, and cultural criticism in a broad sense, ranging from muckraking journalism to elevated discourses on the tastes and manners of the masses. There are also diverse discourses specifically directed to consumers and in relation to which consumers can recognize themselves to be the addressees. These include advertising, product instructions and guarantees, demands for or declarations of consumer rights, consciousness-raising campaigns, boycotts and other protests, consumer alerts and product recalls, and advice and assistance dispensed by better business bureaus, ministries of consumer affairs, and newspaper columns and television shows that dramatize consumer problems. They also include the burgeoning array of consumer guides, ranging from the lore and science of using a particular kind of product (the recent explosion of magazine literature directed to video and computer enthusiasts, for example) to the ubiquitous product testing and rating literature. The latter occupies a special position among these discourses because it both addresses a mass public of consumers and routinely grants consumers an active role in the construction of a relationship between their needs and the satisfaction of them. In this section close attention will be given to the use of this literature as an example of mundane criticism.

In the North American context, the magazine *Consumer Reports* is only the most well-known example of a considerable body of periodical and monograph publications that share typical features related to the provision of product ratings.[18] Our concern here will be with what it is to use a typical individual report. (The terms *consumer report, report, ratings*, and so on will not refer specifically to *Consumer Reports* but rather to any typical report in terms of the particular, situated competence implied, relied on, and elaborated by recurrent features of the report design. This will involve setting aside much of what actual, individual consumer-readers might know in addition or otherwise, in virtue of an acquaintance with critical theory, for example.)

The working assumption underlying the treatment of report use ventured here is that texts have a design that orders their possible readerly (literate) uses. The focus on the design of a text implies setting aside any notion of one correct, authoritative reading of a text in favor of the idea of a field of possible, sensible readings. Further, the kind of design at issue here is not one that is decidable by interviewing some privileged group of readers (including the text's producer), nor is it reducible to the perceptions of actions of particular empirical readers. Rather what is required is to clarify those features of the text that project a community of possible readers-users. To be sure a text's actual uses may turn out to be quite other than those uses the text's order projects; its design may be used or ignored or violated by empirical readers. The extreme case of this can be seen in "bricolage," practices through which the text is used opportunistically and in a way which is either incidental to or in violation of its designed-for use.[19] Although the possibility of bricolage is itself intriguing, that is not our concern here; indeed the very possibility of recognizing such counteruses points back to the horizon of use projected in and through the text's design. Our question concerns what it is to use the consumer report "properly," that is, in accordance with what its typical features require. This will also involve a reconstruction of the reader required to operate the text properly, the reader who is a member to the cultural practices encoded in the text and who is thus its entitled reader.[20]

The Discursive Production of Consumer Advice

Let us begin by considering some features of the background to consumer report readership. A common feature of many mundane discourses that compete for the consumer's attention is a concern with reexamining the alternatives available for satisfying a need. Often this takes the form of a direct or implied comparison of specific products within a product genre as means for satisfying a given need. The idea of choosing the best means lies behind many forms of advice, including both advertisements and product ratings. It has been widely observed that advertising does not stop at influencing choices in relation to given needs but both modifies present needs and creates new ones (of course, it may prove that other forms of advice do this too).[21] For example, domestic cleaning tasks mark out a sphere of conventional needs to which a great deal of advertising effort is directed. Typically advertisements addressed to this sphere do not rely solely on the tacit criteria of adequate cleanliness used by persons doing housework but rather promote additional criteria that are often regarded as spurious by other consumer advisers. For instance, perfumes are routinely added to cleansers. The perfumes add nothing to the product's cleaning effectiveness but are used to warrant claims to the effect that a "fresh-as-outdoors" (or lemon- or pine-fresh) scent will be obtained, an effect that is then adduced as a further criterion of adequate cleanliness.

Even when claims are limited to more traditional criteria, ads often mislead. A common type of claim used for cleaning products consists of variations on the following: "Nothing cleans better than X!" A little probing shows that this claim can be perfectly true without affording any useful grounds for choice, for the proposition "Nothing cleans better than X" is fully compatible, in the logic of ordinary language use, with the propositions "Everything cleans just as well as X" and "X cleans no better than anything else." The first proposition does not rule out the second two, and all three can coexist as true descriptions of the same world. Yet neither of the latter two claims would be likely to inspire us to dash out and stock up on X. The first invites an uptake, albeit one based on faulty logic, that is clearly ruled out by the other claims. We might say that the first is an apparent superlative. While the first seems to say, "X is best," lying behind the exclamation is a disguised comparative, "X is as good as the others." None of the propositions is adequate for grounding the conclusion, "Choose X"; at best, they ground the conclusion, "Choose X or any other equivalent to it." The relevance of this conclusion can be seen by considering another claim with which the first is compatible: "Many products (but not necessarily all) clean just as well as X." The issue here is familiar: the advisers that compete for the consumer's attention claim what it is in their interest to claim while suppressing additional information required to furnish adequate grounds for choice. The consumer's interest in grounding choice rationally is thereby frustrated.

Consider, then, that "consumers" are those who must make choices in the context of communication situations with features such as those sketched. Evidently what they need is a rational form of advice, advice adequate to the tasks of choosing with which they are faced. The consumer report furnishes a discourse in which consumers can find their problems of consuming constituted within a format "adequate" to the practical conditions of choice. Yet like other kinds of advice, the report form is not neutral, for it constitutes consumers and their problems in its own distinctive way. The typical report will include at least the following features: (1) a formulation of the consumer's problem as a problem of rational choice, (2) the provision of suitable, empirically testable criteria of product performance, and (3) ratings, according to the criteria, of competing products within the genre being examined.

A consumer choice is "adequately" grounded when it can be made in accordance with this format.

What does one have to know in order to use such a report? Suppose that dishwashing liquids are being examined.[22] One has to know how to apply what is provided within the ratings format to a recurrent task of everyday domestic life (washing the dishes) and how to use that information in the context of shopping, itself a distinctive practical task. The report mediates the consumer's relation to both home and market in a unique way. To begin with, the consumer must set aside the folk knowledge he or she already possesses pertaining to both dishwashing and shopping. The report will probably assist in this by debunking popular myths related to each. Further the consumer learns to separate moral and technical features of the problem. This will often consist of thematizing technical features of a product's use to the exclusion of other features. In the home "washing the dishes" is practically constituted through moral, technical, and aesthetic relevances. It is a question of who will be required to wash the dishes how and with what effect. For example, is dishwashing regarded as "women's work"? Is rack or towel drying preferred? Is lemon or another scent desired? The particular way in which these and other considerations are handled will make up the dishwashing customs of a home, and the handling of other considerations will make up shopping customs. One may be inclined to shop according to product loyalties, sales and specials, or the advice of friends or shopkeepers. The hold of these customs over the consumer must be neutralized so that "cleaning" can be properly operationalized. Then the consumer can attend strictly to the product's performance features.

A shift in attitude is involved, bringing with it a new set of requirements. Before, use of the product was situated in a network of routine practice and commonsense knowledge. Now, the consumer may need to change everything about his or her relation to the task of dishwashing in order to make it more rational, more in conformity with the clarified version in the report. In effect the consumer is required to shift from a grasp of product use as something familiar and unquestioned to seeing product use as a problem and as an occasion for critically reexamining his or her practice. Other requirements govern the report form itself. The overriding concern is that performance differences be established. The testing strategy used may be varied until differences are found. If differences fail to appear, additional performance criteria may be adduced in order to locate relevant differences that make it possible to organize product ratings into a hierarchy.[23] Exceptions to this procedure turn out to be an inversion of the basic principle: where popular prejudice holds that real differences exist among products of a genre, the test may be used to show that in fact there are no performance differences. Yet in the report context, this "surprising" finding serves to reinforce the appropriateness of the testing and rating format by standing as an instructive exception to the expectation that differences permitting a rating will be located.

While the body of the report prefaces ratings that in themselves might be regarded as the decisive feature, the significance of this preface should not be underestimated. The report body prepares the consumer for using the ratings by deconstructing the prejudices through which he or she had previously known the product. It is here that product use appears in its new guise, as a problem of rational action. Yet using the report is not a matter of repeating the experimental format of the test design but rather—given the rearticulation of one's needs established in the report and coded into the ratings—using the report as a map of possibilities for rational satisfaction afforded by the market. Following the report's reconstruction, one proceeds as if these (cleaning power in its operationalized aspect, convenience of dispensing, and so forth) are the product's rational features, and the local particulars—price fluctuations, location of retail outlets with stocks suitable for comparisons, acceptability to the user of unrated product characteristics, and so on—are to be fitted to the deliberative procedures supported by the report's reconstruction. However, the point is not to use the report to produce perfectly rational action. Indeed the report could not without incongruity be used that way for very long, for even the ratings-supported achievement of a "best buy" can be undone by tomorrow's sale, which makes the same product available at half the price. Nor is it a matter of using the report as if it were an advertisement for some best buy, although that might be tempting since the report can dramatize a certain product's superadequate features as a commendable solution to some everyday problem. The point is rather an exercise of intelligent practical judgment, a judgment motivated by the need to resist manipulative, deceitful, irrationalizing forces. Yet it is also a judgment based on the transformation of familiar needs and satisfactions into a technically articulated problem. The ratings are simply the textual culmination of this transformative process. Their salience depends on the reconstruction of need and satisfaction worked out in the body of the report.

The Textual Organization of Validity

With respect to Habermas's universal pragmatic scheme, one can observe that the entitled, competent user of the report (the reader who complies with what the text requires) has at his or her disposal a discourse within which validity claims relevant to consumer choice can be handled. Thus the typical report will include claims to provide useful, reliable, relevant, factual information (truth), to be in conformity with normative conditions of advice giving (rightness), and to be sincere and free from improper influences (truthfulness). Yet it is not just that validity claims are handled that is noteworthy but rather that the handling of claims is organized in a way that permits readers actively to take up a new relation to need interpretations that had hitherto defined their possibilities.

The significance of consumerist criticism lies to a great extent in the production of counterdiscourses that depart from the marginalization of consumer judgment promoted through dominant definitions of consumers' needs. The counterdiscourses signify organized attempts at reappropriating the power to interpret needs. In the midst of the contest between producer-oriented discourse (such as advocacy advertising) and popular consumerist counterdiscourses (such as journalistic exposés of consumer problems), the consumer report discourse genre has achieved a unique position by virtue of the special claim to advise it has won. The use of a consumer report to marshal true propositions about a potential purchase signifies its cognitive use. In its cognitive aspect the report must distinguish itself propositionally from competing claims to advise, such as producers' advocacy advertising, as well as the "consumer chic" orientation of superficial consumerist advice and exposé. In this dimension the report demonstrates the testability of product claims and performance features and the applicability of test results to problems of choice. Hence the report's accountable basis in a testing procedure grounds a claim to provide consumers with correct information. In a similar way the reporting publication's professed lack of any ties with commercial or other conflicting interests grounds claim to trustworthiness. In the expressive dimension the report claims to act only in the interest of the consumer. Thus it distinguishes itself from both commercial interests and from positions, such as those of governmental agencies, that have to mediate the conflicting interests of the various parties to which they are responsible. In my view, however, the most distinctive aspect of the report's claim to advise lies in the interactive dimension. The rightness of its advice lies not only in the provision of information that is "correct" and "unbiased" but also in the use of a format that requires the consumer's active collaboration. The report furnishes not a completed decision but rather an "objective" set of grounds for decision. A concrete consumer decision cannot be arrived at without the judgmental work of the reader, who enlists these grounds in weighing up the choices. The competent reader is one who uses this advice to enhance the autonomy of his or her deliberations. Unlike the instillation of prejudices typical of other mass forms, what is required is a deliberation that leads to individuation, not massification. Above all it is this design whereby the user's active collaboration is required that distinguishes the consumer report's special claim to advise.

It should be clear from these considerations that the dimensions of validity and language use each have a different status within the report form. Each kind of validity is not equally open to examination on the occasion of reading a particular report. In the expressive dimension trustworthiness is stabilized not at the level of the individual report but rather through avowals of freedom from bias that appear in a ritualized form in each issue as part of the magazine's identifying apparatus (often as part of its masthead). In the interactive dimension the special legitimacy won through participant critique does not vary in its essentials from report to report; rather it is encoded into the very form of the report. While the special advisory relation of reader and report furnishes a device for debunking other attempts to influence consumers, the relation itself is treated as stable rather than as something to be questioned within each report. Both the expressive and interactive characteristics of the report have thus been institutionalized as recurrent, ongoing features of the magazine as a reporting medium. It is the interactive features that are actually encoded at the level of the text in that reports are routinely organized to invite reader collaboration in reaching a decision. While trustworthiness is established on the level of the reporting medium rather than within particular reports, the reports themselves will include features (debunking, testing, and rating devices) that support the accomplishment of advising on the occasion of a particular reading. Yet on the level of individual reports, it is only in the cognitive dimension that clear-cut tests of validity are carried out: the factual examination of product claims and characteristics. It is not my purpose to suggest that this asymmetry in the textual organization of validity in consumer reports is invidious, that asymmetry itself is somehow a bad thing. Rather the asymmetry is a built-in characteristic of the consumer report as a concrete cultural form. However, this recognition need not prevent us from addressing some of the limitations of report use, both on its own terms and with respect to broader critical concerns about consumerism.

The Limits of Consumer Literacy

Attempts to use the report's advice involve the consumer in a redis-covery of particularities that resist its rationalizing sphere of influence. Critical consumers will need to recognize when the advice directs them to do something they cannot practically do or do only at the cost of producing unacceptable conflicts. Thus they cannot expect to reproduce the ideal situation of comparison depicted in the report, nor can they expect to impose a purely legal definition of the situation on those with whom they deal in the marketplace. They have to realize that attempts to make provocative use of the report's findings are likely to involve risks. Furthermore, readers, who had shifted their perspective to take into account the ratability of the product, must shift their perspective again when they return to the scene of consumption and discover what it is to use the product they had known previously only in terms of its reconstruction in the report. They will have to reconcile themselves to differences between the potential for satisfaction implied in the report and the outcome that has resulted from using its advice in a particular way. They will have to discover the concrete fit between the product they have purchased and the need to be satisfied, a need whose character and intensity may now be felt even more pressingly than before. A "best buy" can be more disappointing than a routine purchase precisely because one now expects *real* satisfaction rather than the looser fit between product and satisfaction one had tolerated in other cases. The product I use is not ideal but particular. Back home, what occupied a certain mathematized place in the ratings has at last become something that is mine. I now know the product as something that enters into my life and becomes part of it in a concrete way. In short, use of the report permits consumers to work out a relation to certain validities that are part of the culture of consumption they inhabit.

Thus, while our concern has been with what the achievement of a competent user of a consumer report is, such reports can also be viewed as providing a questionable basis for rational action. The sphere constituted by the report format projects through its relevances a delimited version of rational action. Consumers must translate their prejudices (the sphere of routine practice in which they begin) so as to ensure the applicability of the report. On the one hand, it is consumers qua readers who achieve and carry out this applicability. On the other hand, it is the testing-rating format that articulates the relevant model of rational action to be applied. It is commonly admitted that the consumer can expect problems of application (normal, local troubles) beyond the report's power to aid or ameliorate.[24] Application of the report is a real achievement, but it is also a possible source for an exaggerated sense of being in control of factors that still resist adequate analysis.

What is provided for in the consumer report format is a deliberation regarding a codified array of products that all claim to satisfy the same need in the same way. What is not provided for organizationally, even though it creeps into the commentary from time to time, is the question of whether the need in question is adequately defined in the first place by such a commodity. In other words, what is left largely unquestioned is the commodification of needing, which has already been worked out in such exquisite detail by the market that we recognize our needs largely through the product arrays that claim our attention. In order to address this broader issue of need interpretation, other kinds of discourses are needed, discourses that permit moves excluded by the report format. For example, ecological discourses may direct us to reconsider our choice of a detergent but not on the basis of its ratable proficiency as a cleanser. Rather the concern will be to avoid products that could cause damage to the environment, and this might lead us to reappraise the wisdom of adhering to popular notions of adequate cleansing. It may even lead us to consider the relative wisdom of a life-style in which there are fewer dishes to wash because cooking and eating are organized differently. We may also be directed to moral and political discourses in which, for example, the question of who washes the dishes is much more important than the question of how, technically, they are washed (with what economy and effectiveness). It may be a matter of reappraising the importance of dishwashing in the household economy (for example, questioning the view that dishwashing is "women's work"), or of questioning whether one should rely on corporate empires to provide the relevant product array, versus participating in a co-op that produces or arranges production of a basic and unmystified product. Consumer report discourses do not tend to question the rules of the game in the ways permitted by these other discourses. In the latter, it is no longer sufficient to adhere to the consumer per se as the central figure for collecting an appropriate image of human satisfaction. Thus in a crucial way, the consumer report leaves claims associated with interactive language use unthematized. For while the legitimacy of the report's intervention is asserted, the legitimacy of the marketplace as an instrument of satisfaction remains largely unquestioned. The report encourages a deliberation about propositional claims, about the facts of satisfaction, but not about the correctness of the norms that determine that, in societies like ours, the marketplace functions as the chief arena of satisfaction. Indeed, it is this underlying accord with market culture that grounds the consumer report's production of alternative facts.

While this failure to probe implicit normative claims suggests the consumer report's limits with respect to a broader view of satisfaction, there are also indications of limits from within. The aura of criticalness attached to the report is all too easily undone in the course of its application to a concrete task of consumption. The alternative product turns out to have its own problems; it too is a particular thing with limited power to satisfy. The "best buy" may turn out to be little better than what was bought previously, by habit, impulse, or chance. In this way, satisfaction will still elude consumers. For them the hope for power to see through the market's deceptions may seem to be little more than self-delusion. They are also likely to encounter popular commentaries that remark on their foibles and inevitable disillusion, holding up a ridiculous image of what all their efforts at criticalness have amounted to. On this point, the popular commentaries and the elevated critiques appear to agree: as critics, consumers are undone by their very preoccupation with consumption.

Conclusion

In one sense, the explication of a cultural competence leaves everything as it is. But in showing what specific power to pose questions is achieved by use of the consumer report, we have already begun to indicate what is left unquestioned. Universal pragmatics indicates the need to review the validity claims that govern not just manifestly distorted communications but also everyday forms of criticism. Following Habermas, we might say that insofar as the demands of consumer criticism remain focused on rationalizing the circulation of goods by improving the conditions of personal choice, such criticism remains committed to the form of life of possessive individualism. The consumer report user's instrumental attitude toward personal satisfaction even takes on an archaic appearance in the face of the increasingly public character of social wealth (represented, for example, in the growth of infrastructure—transportation, leisure, health care, education, and so forth). Although the model of private accumulation of commodities can no longer convincingly represent "the expanded horizon of possible satisfying alternatives," the consumer report still locates the achievement of satisfactions in terms of the preferences of private individuals. In contrast, the increasingly public character of wealth, represented in collective commodities, means that

the constant interpretation and reinterpretation of needs has become a matter of collective will-formation. In this process, free communication can be replaced only by massive manipulation, that is, by strong, indirect control. The more freedom the preference system has, the more pressing become the problems of market policy for the suppliers. This is true, at least, if the appearance that consumers can decide privately and autonomously—that is, according to monologically certain preferences—is to be preserved. Opportunistic adaptation of consumers to market strategies of monopolistic competition is the ironic form of the consumer autonomy that is supposed to be maintained as the façade of possessive individualism.[25]

Beyond the vestiges of consumer autonomy, which hinder the develoment of processes of collective will formation, Habermas can glimpse a more positive prospect: "The 'pursuit of happiness' might one day mean something different—for example, not accumulating material objects of which one disposes privately, but bringing about social relations in which mutuality predominates and satisfaction does not mean the triumph of one over the repressed needs of the other."[26] From the alternative perspective of collective need interpretation and mutuality of satisfaction, the consumer report's emphasis on propositional knowledge permitting the "monological ascertainment of preferences" appears in a negative light, as a move designed to shore up the faltering legitimation of possessive individualism as a form of life. The rationalization of consumer experience effected by the consumer report is centered on improving the information environment of consumer activities. A key weakness is the failure of this genre to scrutinize the interactive dimension, to examine, in Habermas's words, "whether the validity claims connected with norms of action, and recognized in fact, are legitimate (or whether the existing normative context does not express generalizable or comprehensible interests, and thus can be stabilized in its de facto validity only so long as those affected can be prevented by inconspicuous restrictions on communication from discursively examining the normative validity claim."[27] From the standpoint of universal pragmatics, then, one can detect serious flaws in the form of criticalness encouraged by the consumer report insofar as it helps to stabilize the de facto normative validity of private accumulation rather than provoking a reflection on the centrality of private accumulation in contemporary images of satisfaction.

From the standpoint of mundane criticism, however, the consumer report grounds a definite form of critical activity, one that invites the participation of the consumer addressees. Of course, the student of universal pragmatics is entitled to respond, "So much the worse for mundane criticism!" since the standpoint of universal pragmatics calls attention to the distinct weaknesses of this kind of critical activity. What, then, is the benefit of a detailed examination of the cultural competence that grounds such activity?

First, examination of a cultural competence can lead to the discovery of potentials for and impediments to critique, which is beyond the power of an abstract scheme to anticipate in any substantial way. Even if use of the consumer report begins within an instrumental attitude toward private satisfactions, the critical activity involved is still a first step in interrupting the massive manipulation through which preferences are steered. Report use involves a refusal to go along with marketing strategies that channel desires away from any significant possibility of testing claims to satisfy. The test shows that a different standpoint is possible, one that begins to overturn the closure to opposition contrived by monopolistic competition. The report also partially disrupts the normative basis of market manipulation by establishing a location in which a special advisory relationship is possible, one which—even if it does not challenge the market culture of private accumulation per se—still exemplifies the possibility of genuine rationalization of satisfaction that would challenge its continual deferment in favor of pseudo-gratifications that all admit to be phony.[28] Further the consumer report is designed to permit local applications, to enable consumers to begin to reclaim some of the "schematizing activity" denied to them by marketing strategies.[29] Thus even if the more provocative practical questions concerning alternative cultural bases of satisfaction are left latent, the consumer report at least helps to put technical questions on a new basis by placing them into a discourse that encourages serious doubts toward the communication environment of the marketplace.

The focus on a cultural competence, then, can supplement universal pragmatics by revealing features of the concrete cultural form into which the fundamental forms of validity are inscribed. At the level of cultural competence, one encounters the particular, contradictory position from within which interpretation of one's situation has to begin. Critical consumerism can be treated neither as an unproblematic strategy for reintegrating disaffected consumers nor as the realization of an adequate critique. One may consider, for example, the ambiguous pressure that consumerism exerts on policymaking. On the one hand, consumerism becomes the focal point of policy initiatives that use its themes and orientations in order to extend administrative control over the sphere of consumer action (think of ministries of consumer affairs, consumer advocacy organizations, and consumer education programs introduced into the schools). In this way consumerism functions as an instrument for extending state control over sectors of everyday life. On the other hand, consumerism can become the basis for grassroots, locally generated policy initiatives, based on mundane critical orientations and practices, that challenge the administratively organized appropriation of power over the interpretation of needs (think of environmental groups that organize consumer protests, for example, of energy policies). While one could conclude, in the spirit of Adorno and Horkheimer, that critical consumerism has become a sphere of legitimized dissent that continues to domesticate oppositional impulses, one must also be ready to acknowledge that a system that produces new legitimations at the cost of providing wider scope for critical activities cannot guarantee stability in the long run. In practice critical consumerism can be expected to become increasingly contradictory so long as it must balance the imperative to maximize access to system-conforming rewards with demands to rationalize satisfaction that increasingly take into account the social effects of consumption and growing distrust of commercial manipulation of interpretations of need and satisfaction. The cultural competence that grounds consumer report use has already mastered, or rather accommodated itself to, this contradictory situation and can, along with universal pragmatics, be used as a scheme for investigating features of it.

Such investigation need not limit itself to accurate description or speculative assessments of delegitimation potentials. For the emphasis on a cultural competence can also bring attention to the possibility of a pedagogy in which that competence could be the starting point for developing a more genuinely effective critique. In this respect the cultural competence to use a consumer report can be viewed as an instance of what Paulo Freire has called the "game of the people"— concrete activities that already engage the attention of a group whose members are potential addressees of an enlightening praxis.[30] The standpoint of universal pragmatics already implies that critique becomes effective only through a dialogue in which previously unquestioned validity claims can be thematized and tested. Freire adds that such a dialogue must always respect the "particular view of the world held by the people," the concrete, lived experiences through which a group knows and understands its situation. From this perspective, the cultural competence to use consumer reports represents a contradictory, "semi-transitive" consciousness, which, precisely because it contains both regressive and progressive elements, can be the point of departure for more adequately problematizing the experiences of consumers.[31] The point would be to engage consumers in an immanent critique of the form of rationality through which they understand needs and possibilities for their satisfaction. While the enlightening dialogue represents the possibility of undistorted communication, it has to deal with the facticity of validity claims, with the contradictions encoded in a focalized view of the world.

In a certain way mundane criticism provides a ready-made illustration of what can count as being critical in the situation under review. In the impetus toward problematization the dialogue seeks to kindle, it can benefit by building on the forms of resistance already developed through mundane critical practices. For example, the activity of "seeing through" whose potential the consumer report so vividly illustrates in the case of propositional claims could also be applied to a reflection on normative structures governing satisfaction. In this way the existing cultural competence would be used as the starting point for addressing the dimensions clarified by universal pragmatics as a horizon of untested possibilities. Such a pedagogy might support insights capable of de-centering satisfaction away from the role of private consumer. It would not be a question of using universal pragmatics in order to refute cultural competence or codify its weaknesses but rather of showing how the "partial penetrations" achieved by that competence can be taken up with a different force and engaged in a broader problem-atization of the cultural situation of the addressees.[32] The pedagogy thus reverses the habitual direction of theorizing. Rather than using theoretical insights to review the defects of present consciousness, it directs attention to cultural competence as the practical horizon for recognizing emancipatory alternatives. The critical moves of such a problematizing pedagogy challenge and shift this horizon from within rather from a vantage point alien to everyday understandings.

In short, just as universal pragmatics indicates the possibility of reflective access to the fundamental aspects under which validity claims can appear, cultural pragmatics indicates the possibility of more em-pirically oriented investigations of the concrete forms of validity within which impulses toward critical questioning arise and find their limits. Thus cultural pragmatics can provide a supplementary strategy for the immanent critique of cultural forms that universal pragmatics grounds in a formal manner. Such a strategy could bring universal pragmatics into closer contact with the analysis of concrete experiences and materials and furnish indications for its linkage with an enlightening pedagogy.

Notes

A draft of this chapter was completed as part of my activities as a postdoctoral fellow on the project "Critical Social Theory, Practical Reasoning and Communicative Competence," in which Dieter Misgeld was principal investigator. (This was one of four related projects included under Social Sciences and Humanities Research Council of Canada Program Grant 431-770006: "The Problem of Self-Reflection and the Study of Children's Culture.") A revised draft was prepared as part of my further research made possible by a postdoctoral fellowship from the Social

Peter Grahame

Sciences and Humanities Research Council of Canada during 1982–1983. I thank John Forester and Dieter Misgeld for their comments on the earlier drafts.

1. Theodor W. Adorno, "Cultural Criticism and Society," in *Prisms*, trans. Samuel Weber and Shierry Weber (London: Neville Spearman, 1967), p. 33.

2. David Held, *Introduction to Critical Theory* (Berkeley: University of California Press, 1980), p. 106.

3. Max Horkheimer and Theodor W. Adorno, "The Culture Industry: Enlightenment as Mass Deception," in *Dialectic of Enlightenment*, trans. John Cumming (New York: Seabury, 1972), pp. 125, 133.

4. This tendency is evident in diatribes such as Vance Packard's *The Hidden Persuaders*; it reappears in more sophisticated form in recent social criticism such as that of Christopher Lasch and Ivan Illich. An important contribution that has sought to moderate this tendency without losing its critical edge is William Leiss's *The Limits to Satisfaction* (Toronto: University of Toronto Press, 1976).

5. The point of this designation is elaborated in my doctoral dissertation, "Critical Practice: Towards a Hermeneutic of Critical Social Inquiry" (University of Toronto, 1981).

6. Stuart Ewen, *Captains of Consciousness: Advertising and the Social Roots of the Consumer Culture* (New York: McGraw-Hill, 1976).

7. One should consider not only the prominence this literature achieves in relation to news coverage, legal actions, and use in the schools but also through its contributions to the critical vernacular (such as use of the expression *best buy* or the somewhat outdated *buymanship*) and a distinctly critical posture that has been popularized in countless magazine articles, books, and television shows, thereby entering into the general culture.

8. Jürgen Habermas, "What Is Universal Pragmatics?" in *Communication and the Evolution of Society*, trans. Thomas McCarthy (Boston: Beacon Press, 1979), pp. 2–3.

9. See Jürgen Habermas, "Toward a Theory of Communicative Competence," in *Recent Sociology No. 2*, ed. Hans Peter Dreitzel (New York: Macmillan, 1970).

10. This usage is suggested by Habermas's declared intention to exclude culturally specific features of communication from universal pragmatics, as in his assertion that "universal pragmatics is distinguished from empirical pragmatics, e.g., sociolinguistics, in that the meaning of linguistic expressions comes under consideration only insofar as it is determined by formal properties of speech situations in general, and not by particular situations of use" (*Communication and the Evolution of Society*, p. 31). Speech act analysis per se is caught in the middle of this distinction since the focus is on formal properties and constitutive features, which, however, are not universal but particular to a type of speech act. The constitutive features of particular activities, encoded in the language games associated with them (such as conducting an interrogation or using clinic records), also fall between the cracks of this distinction. By *cultural* pragmatics I wish to emphasize a concern with features of language use that are both constitutive and culturally specific (to a speech act, practice, or setting).

11. National Science Teachers' Association, *The Place of Science in the Education of the Consumer* (Washington, D.C.: Consumer Education Study, 1945), p. 1.

12. Horkheimer and Adorno, "Culture Industry," p. 142.

13. For example, in President Kennedy's "Special Message on Protecting the Consumer Interest" of November 15, 1962, and subsequent initiatives by Presidents Johnson and Nixon.

14. In speaking of "consumer reasoning" and "mundane reasoning," I do not intend "reasoning" in the sense of the mental processes of a solitary subject but rather in its outward aspect as it is displayed in communications, public deliberations, speech acts, and so forth. The point of considering mundane reasoning is sociological rather than narrowly epistemological and can be thought of as part of a phenomenology of the social world that focuses on situated practices and socially constructed competences. For a more elaborate discussion of mundane reasoning, see Melvin Pollner, "Mundane Reasoning," *Philosophy of Social Science* 4 (1974): 35–54.

15. Compare Habermas's discussion of these contrasting roles in *Communication and the Evolution of Society*, p. 200. Habermas acknowledges that the facticity of validity claims is apprehended within the performative attitude, but he then uses this mundanely recognized claim to be right to introduce the notion of a rational basis for appraisals of legitimacy, which in turn could be systematically clarified. I do not disagree that this is a necessary step for a critical theory but only wish to propose that the leap to the rational justification of norms, for example, is premature if a more sociological account of the particular forms of participation surrounding the facticity of the validity claims being examined has not been worked out. Otherwise the social possibility of the appearance and recognition of just those validities is not taken into account. Taking facticity seriously involves the hermeneutical recognition that even rationally clarified norms must make their way into the world against the background of interpretive practices through which notions of validity adequate "for all practical purposes" are already at work. In part the critical theorist must develop a mode of participation through which existing practical purposes and notions of adequacy can be contested, but such participation presupposes a cultural competence through which the facticity of validity claims is understood.

16. National Science Teachers' Association, *Place of Science*, p. 1.

17. The problem of distorting sociological descriptions by assimilating practical activities to norms of scientific conduct is a major theme in Harold Garfinkel's *Studies in Ethnomethodology* (Englewood Cliffs, N.J.: Prentice-Hall, 1967), esp. pp. 279–281.

18. Many of these are indexed in the *Consumer's Index to Product Evaluations and Information Sources*. Canadian examples include *Canadian Consumer* and *Protect Yourself*, both appearing monthly. There are also a number of European equivalents, including *Which?* in Great Britain.

19. See Dick Hebdige, *Subculture: The Meaning of Style* (London: Methuen, 1979), pp. 102–106.

20. In devising this account of readership, I have learned much from Garfinkel's treatment of the clinic record in *Studies in Ethnomethodology*, pp. 186–207, as well as from Dorothy Smith's account of what it means to "operate" a text. For Smith's version of textual analysis, see her unpublished manuscript, "The Active Text" (Ontario Institute for Studies in Education, 1982).

21. For example, John Kenneth Galbraith, *The Affluent Society* (Boston: Houghton Mifflin, 1958), pp. 152–160.

22. The report on dishwashing liquids in the February 1981 *Consumer Reports* exhibits the features being discussed here and includes, as well, a "real-cost calculator" to be used by the consumer in the store to work out the local best buy.

23. An example of this approach can be found in the treatment of dishwasher detergents in the June 1980 *Consumer Reports*.

24. See, for example, G. L. Bush, *Science Education in Consumer Buying* (New York: Teachers College, Columbia University, 1941), pp. 63–81.

25. Jürgen Habermas, *Legitimation Crisis* (Boston: Beacon Press, 1975), p. 83.

26. Habermas, *Communication and the Evolution of Society*, p. 199.

Peter Grahame

27. Ibid., p. 119.

28. Adorno and Horkheimer strikingly capture the character of a "seeing through" that remains incapable of seeing something other in the following: "The triumph of advertising in the culture industry is that consumers feel compelled to buy and use its products even though they see through them" (*Dialectic of Enlightenment*, p. 167).

29. As Adorno and Horkheimer observe, industry has in effect preempted the schematizing function that Kant's formalism accorded the individual. Thus: "There is nothing left for the consumer to classify. Producers have done it for him" (ibid., p. 125).

30. This point concerning the "game of the people" was elaborated by Freire during his lectures at the Ontario Institute for Studies in Education in the summer of 1976.

31. For a discussion of this concept, see Paulo Freire, *Cultural Action for Freedom*, Harvard Educational Review Monograph Series, no. 1 (Cambridge, Mass.: Harvard Educational Review, 1970), pp. 32–42.

32. Paul Willis, in *Learning to Labour* (Westmead, U.K.: Gower, 1977), uses this term to indicate an accomplishment very much akin to what I have been describing as the achievements of mundane criticism: " 'Penetration' is meant to designate impulses within a cultural form towards the penetration of the conditions of existence of its members and their position within the social whole but in a way which is not centred, essentialist or individualist. 'Limitation' is meant to designate those blocks, diversions and ideological effects which confuse and impede the full development and expression of these impulses. The rather clumsy but strictly accurate term, 'partial penetration,' is meant to designate the interaction of these two terms in a concrete culture" (p. 119).

IV

Planning Practice, Power, and Public Participation

Planning, Public Hearings, and the Politics of Discourse

Ray Kemp

Public hearings into a wide variety of sociopolitical issues have become accepted practice in the majority of Western industrialized societies, part and parcel of the everyday fabric of democratic life. Activists and politicians of every political persuasion often argue for recourse to a public hearing or inquiry in order to settle particular disputes in an objective, rational, and egalitarian manner. This chapter seeks to provide an alternative to this traditional, pluralistic interpretation of such forms of decision making, and it argues that, in the main, public inquiries rather serve to legitimize the actions and interests of dominant groups in advanced capitalist societies. Outcomes of public hearings are rarely objective, rational, and egalitarian; they are manipulated to further the interests of both state and capital. Following Jürgen Habermas, I contend that a primary mechanism through which this is achieved is the systematic distortion of the communication process that takes place at public inquiries.

The argumentation will begin with a brief description of the historical background to the British public inquiry process and the contemporary role of public inquiries for the execution of controversial government policies; this will be shown to be especially the case with respect to the development of nuclear energy in Britain. Next a detailed exposition of certain critical theoretic concepts developed by Habermas will be followed by a section that seeks to apply them in an analysis of the Windscale Inquiry, which was held in 1977 into a proposal by British Nuclear Fuels Ltd (BNFL), to construct a thermal oxide reprocessing plant at Windscale, Cumbria, England. The chapter will conclude with some observations on the relevance and implications of the arguments presented for both future research and for political action.

Public Inquiries: The British Experience

Public hearings into diverse areas of planning activity have become increasingly commonplace in Britain in recent years. For example, the implementation of transport policy has been hampered, on the one hand, by numerous controversial "motorway inquiries" dating from the mid-1960s and, on the other hand, by the lengthy inquiry conducted by the Roskill Commission in 1968 into the possible site for a third London airport. Perhaps the most significant area of governmental planning to be so affected concerns the development of nuclear energy. Energy policy has had to proceed, in fact, subject to public inquiry outcomes: first with respect to individual development proposals, such as those relating to the construction of particular power stations, and second with respect to more wide-ranging issues, such as those contained in the proposal to reprocess waste nuclear fuel and considered at the Windscale Inquiry in 1977. More recently plans to construct the U.S.-designed pressurized water reactors (PWRs), as opposed to the British-designed advanced gas-cooled reactors (AGRs); to develop the first British commercial fast breeder reactor (FBR); and also to proceed with test drilling for appropriate sites for the dumping of nuclear waste in the British Isles; have all been pronounced suitable matters for consideration by public inquiry.[1] With respect to the first two of these proposals, members of government now appear to imply justification for their decisions in advance by claiming them to be subject to the outcome of a relevant public hearing. That is, their decisions are thought to gain justificatory force through association with the supposedly open, democratic characteristics of the public inquiry process. This would appear to be a questionable extension of established political rhetoric, which tends to emphasize the impartial nature of public hearings by stating that government decisions by no means preclude the outcome of individual inquiries, which thereby remain fully independent. Such an approach was adopted by Tony Benn, energy secretary at the time of the Windscale Inquiry, who later defended the inquiry and the subsequent decision to proceed with reprocessing, by stating that "no one in his senses could describe all this as a charade" (Benn 1979, p. 85). Similarly Peter Shore, then environment secretary, stated in the House of Commons, "I doubt whether any country in the Western World has had a more open and thorough examination of a major nuclear proposal than we have had at Windscale" (Hansard, March 22, 1978).

By contrast, objectors to the establishment of test drilling sites for the possible dumping of nuclear waste at Ayr in Scotland held their own alternative "people's inquiry," fearing a lack of impartiality at the official proceedings.[2] Thus despite raising certain doubts about the formal inquiry process, this comparatively recent and novel form of protest nevertheless still relied on a similar inquiry procedure to that provided by the state. Objectors may therefore be said to have demonstrated their implicit faith in the public inquiry as an appropriate means for the resolution of sociopolitical disputes, provided that overt state interference is excluded.

Clearly the public inquiry or hearing, in the expressed view of central government politicians and in the expectations of opponents and objectors, is generally held to provide an open, objective, and rational, that is, a truly democratic form of practical decision making. Furthermore this lends justificatory force to government decisions and policies that are reached subject to the public inquiry process; public inquiries are seen to legitimize controversial decisions taken in several important areas of governmental planning activity. This leads us to consider the extent to which public inquiries are in fact open, objective, rational, and by implication legitimate decision-making procedures. In order to do this, it will first be necessary to understand the historical development of the British public inquiry process.

It is arguable that the genesis of the public inquiry process is closely related to the process of the enclosure of open fields and common land that took place in Britain primarily during the eighteenth and nineteenth centuries. One major form of enclosure was carried out through the authority of Private Acts of Parliament. Individual enclosures of land each required, until 1845, a separate Act of Parliament, and although diverse provisions were embodied in more than 4,000 Acts, certain central features did in fact become uniform over the years. First, public meetings in the area in question were held at the outset in order to draw up a petition for Parliament to endorse the proposed enclosure and then again later in order to settle any outstanding objections to the proposals once Parliament or the relevant parliamentary committee had considered them. Second, the all-important final public meeting, held to consider disputes and make awards, was conducted by enclosure commissioners who were usually named in the original petition. There could be as many as fifteen such commissioners, but more often only three were appointed. Third, by 1760, the enclosure commissioners became bound by an oath of impartiality, and in 1774 they were further ordered by Parliament to render accounts. Finally, various provisions were introduced to ensure publicity for the proposed enclosure plans, especially within the local parish.

After 1845 greater central government control was exerted over the process. The 1845 General Inclosure Act made provision for two permanent enclosure commissioners, appointed by the Board of Agriculture, who were to place all proposals before Parliament in one bill each year. An assistant commissioner, publicly appointed and accountable to the board, would be sent, on receipt of an application to enclose land, to hold a public meeting in the area concerned in order to hear objections. Following this he would submit a report, upon which a provisional order for enclosure would be issued. A further local public meeting would then be held to discuss the provisional order and the assistant commissioner's report, following which an award would be made subject to acceptance by two-thirds of those eligible to so decide.

Thus it can be argued that in an area of decision making specifically related to planning matters—the allocation and reorganization of land—there arose a political process utilizing public local inquiries, which attempted to display characteristics of openness, impartiality, and justice. Furthermore, with the onset of the 1845 Act came increased state intervention and control over the whole process, leading to increased uniformity of application. Perhaps the most important feature that evolved was that of the public nature of the process—various means were employed to ensure that in each case an inquiry took place that was both public and local—the forerunner of the present public local inquiry process.

Care must be taken to acknowledge the class-based nature of this process. Enclosure was generally carried out by the propertied class in order to reap the benefits of a more efficient use of agricultural land and to increase the amount of such land in their possession. An enclosure commissioner before 1845 was usually proposed by one of the following: the local clergy, the lord of the manor, or the local landowning (middle) class. Voting rights at local public meetings were restricted, as with other issues, to those enfranchised according to existing, property-based qualifications. Furthermore, Parliament itself was at that time a class-based institution, and parliamentary committees often displayed a less than impartial interest in the passage of enclosure legislation: "Eighteenth century committees were by no means impartial, and it was said in 1825 that 'under the present system it has been found that the members to whom bills have been committed have been generally those who have been most interested in the result' " (Curtler, 1920, p. 156).

It is possible to argue, therefore, that especially prior to 1845, the process of public local inquiries arose under a system that worked to further the particular interests of the propertied class in British society while maintaining the appearance of an open, impartial, democratic procedure. To be sure, it is uncertain whether the reforms of 1845, resulting in increased central government control over the enclosure movement, served to mitigate the worst effects of the existing system. Rather the post-1845 period may be seen as a time when enclosure could be carried out much more efficiently, with certain palliatives being offered to the disaffected working class in order to subdue their disquiet. Thus, for example, Sir Robert Peel, in supporting a House of Commons motion requiring enclosure commissioners to provide open space for recreational purposes in all future plans, argued that

it was most desirable that the neighbourhood of manufacturing towns, and indeed of all towns, should have some place where the population might find the means of innocent recreation. Such an arrangement would have a most beneficial effect, not alone on their health, but also on their morals, by gradually withdrawing them from scenes where their time was likely to be much less innocently employed. He was sure that such an effort on the part of the local authorities would insure to them the lasting gratitude of the working population. (Parliamentary Debates, 3d ser., vol. 37, March 9, 1837, 163)

A critical theoretic interpretation of this move would be that such an offer served as a defusing, legitimizing device to enable the continued domination of the interests of the propertied class over those of the working population. At a period of popular unrest throughout Europe, this measure sought to divert the activities of potential political dissenters toward innocent activities. Somehow the exchange of recreational land for what previously would have been subsistence-providing land was thought to be a generous provision.

This, then, is the historical background to the development of the public inquiry process in Britain. It displays characteristics of open, impartial, and rational decision making, somewhat compromised by the dominant interests of the era.

Political Discourse in the Public Sphere

The term *public sphere* (*Öffentlichkeit*) is employed by Habermas to refer to that area of public life in which intersubjective agreement on values and standards can be reached in order to solve sociopolitical or practical questions. In a historical account of its development during the seventeenth and eighteenth centuries in Western Europe, Habermas describes the public sphere as an area of society that arose between the absolutist state and bourgeois society, in which discoursing private citizens could freely and critically discuss practical issues and the role of the state. Institutionally the public sphere took the form of participatory democracy based on property, the independent fuctioning of free competition, and the balance of supply and demand. With an increasing franchise based on property, the public sphere was evidenced in the English House of Commons and furthermore in the independent press. At the same time certain rules applied to the public sphere, which were reflected in regulations concerning the conduct of open court proceedings and the form public inquiries should take. Thus general accessibility to all citizens, the elimination of all privileges, and the discovery of general norms and rational legitimations became paramount. Habermas is careful to stress the importance of the concept of rationality to decision making on practical issues, when he describes the public sphere as "a public body who as citizens transmit the needs of bourgeois society to the state, in order, ideally, to transform political into 'rational' authority" (Habermas 1974a, p. 54). However, Habermas readily points out that access to the public sphere was restricted to bourgeois society. It was a class-specific phenomenon, and any emergent consensus from the liberal public sphere should be judged in that light: "Public discussions about the exercise of political power . . . grew out of a specific phase of bourgeois society and would enter into the order of the bourgeois constitutional state only as a result of a particular constellation of interests" (Habermas 1974a, p. 50).

Clearly from the description of the development of the public local inquiry process during the enclosure movement of the eighteenth and nineteenth centuries, it can be seen that although Habermas does not in fact refer to this particular aspect of political life during that period, the process nonetheless displays exactly those characteristics of supposed openness, impartiality, and rationality that allow us to describe it as a paradigm case of practical decision making in the public sphere. Furthermore, Habermas develops this thesis by claiming that the latter part of the nineteenth century saw an increase in state involvement in the public sphere, which resulted in its eventual disintegration. The rise of organized capitalism with concomitant conflicts of interests between the working population and the landowning class led to the alteration of the public sphere by the bourgeoisie in order to disguise the particularistic nature of its interests. It is clear that my description of the changes in the process of enclosure brought about by the introduction of central government control lends some support to Habermas's interpretation of the disintegration of the public sphere, albeit at a slightly earlier period in the nineteenth century than Habermas suggests.

According to Hohendahl (1979), this account of the development and subsequent disintegration of the public sphere forms a central thread in the extension of Habermas's work to later and much more theoretically sophisticated arguments. Habermas's major concern has been to reformulate Marxian theory to account for what he sees to be major changes in the nature of advanced capitalism. The central problem of capitalist society remains as originally formulated by Marx: the fundamental contradiction of the continued private appropriation of socially produced wealth. For Habermas, however, the logic of the situation no longer leads to an inevitable politicoeconomic crisis but rather to its displacement into other realms of society as a result of increased state intervention. Thus rationality and legitimation crises are posited as potential disturbances in the administrative subsystem, while motivation crises are possible outcomes in the sociocultural subsystem of advanced capitalism (Habermas 1976a).

The crux of Habermas's argument centers on the notion of increased state intervention, which resulted in the structural depoliticization of the public sphere in the latter part of the last century. Elsewhere he has argued that a concomitant process, the scientization of politics, further served to mystify practical discourse on sociopolitical issues. Thus, for example, the professionalization of planning with the introduction of technical terms and standards, bureaucratic and legal devices, may be seen to have led to merely token public involvement in many important planning matters.[3] These two central elements in Habermas's analysis of advanced capitalism are presented as underlying causes of a current tendency toward the generation of legitimation crises:

State intervention and planned scientific and technological progress can serve to regulate the imbalances and conflicts which result from a process of production governed by the imperatives of capital investment . . . only . . . at the cost of producing a conflict, which, for the time being, can be kept latent. This conflict has the following form: on the one hand, the priorities set under economic imperatives cannot be allowed to depend on a general discursive formation of the public will—therefore politics today assumes the appearance of technocracy. On the other hand, the exclusion of consequential practical questions from discussion by the depoliticized public becomes increasingly difficult. . . . Because of this, a chronic need for legitimation is developing today. (Habermas 1974b, p. 5)

For Habermas, true legitimation may be achieved only through the repoliticization of the public sphere; that is, a genuine consensus should be sought through a process of discursive will formation concerning all issues of importance for society and conducted according to the rules of a communicative or practical form of rational decision making. The historical reference for this view lies in the liberal model of the public sphere, and it should be remembered that planning decisions are closely tied to its development through the genesis of the public local inquiry process in the enclosure movement. Concomitantly the analytic reference for Habermas's argument is contained in his theory of universal pragmatics, the analysis of the rational foundations of everyday speech acts.

Practical Discourse: The Ideal Speech Situation

Following J. L. Austin, John Searle, and Stephen Toulmin, Habermas analyzes speech acts in order to discover how a competent speaker forms acceptable sentences in utterances. Habermas argues that communicative competence is tied to the speaker's ability to succeed (or fail) in his or her use of speech acts, and this in turn is a consequence of what is described as their "generative power," which works to compel a hearer to take up an interpersonal relation with the speaker (Habermas, 1970, 1979b).

According to Habermas four different kinds of speech act are related to four corresponding validity claims (*Geltungsansprüche*), which are thematically stressed in every utterance. Related to communicative speech acts is an underlying claim that what the speaker says is understandable. It is implicit in each utterance that the interlocutors can reach an understanding purely in the sense that what is being spoken is comprehensible to the participants, and consequently the validity claim underlying the communicative speech act is realized immanently in communication. With respect to representative speech acts, the corresponding validity claim is that of sincerity or truthfulness. It is implicit in the utterance that the speaker is saying what he or she believes to be true and is sincere. The veracity of an individual can be realized immediately through assurances or through consistency in behavior. The underlying validity claim that relates to regulative speech acts is that it is correct and appropriate for the speaker to be uttering the words that he or she does—or, to put this another way, that the normative context of the utterance is legitimate. This normative dimension to speech may be grounded immediately in the convictions of the interactants. Conversely recourse may be made to a discursive examination of the rightness of the normative context, in which case a practical discourse would be necessary. Finally, constative speech acts imply an underlying validity claim to the truth of an utterance. Apart from the certainty of the interlocutors as to the experiential source of the truth claim, recourse may be made to a theoretical discourse in which evidence could be brought to bear in support of the claim.

It is fundamental to Habermas's thesis that everyday speech is based on a background consensus provided through the reciprocal raising and recognition of the four validity claims. Where those claims cannot be substantiated immediately, there must be recourse to a process of mediation; that is, the claims to appropriateness and truth must be substantiated in some form of discourse, the former in practical discourse, the latter in theoretical discourse. Practical discourse is of fundamental importance to the successful repoliticization of the public sphere, where practical questions concerning activities of the state can be examined. As Habermas states:

Practical questions . . . are posed with a view to the acceptance or rejection of norms, especially norms for action, the claims to validity of which we can support or oppose with reasons. Theories which in their structure can serve the clarification of practical questions are designed to enter into communicative action. Interpretations which can be gained within the framework of such theories . . . can only be translated into processes of enlightenment which are rich in political consequences, when the institutional preconditions for practical discourse among the general public are fulfilled. (Habermas 1974b, p. 3)

What, then, are the institutional preconditions for practical discourse? Habermas provides the basis of an answer to this question in his concept of the ideal speech situation (*ideale Sprechsituation*), which lays down a number of criteria intended to ensure that the consensus that emerges from practical discourse serves generalizable, and not particular, interests. Thus the general symmetry requirement suggests that the structure of a system of communication is free from both internal and external constraints only when for all participants to a discourse there is equal opportunity to select and employ speech acts. Now we can specify the requirement with regard to each of the speech act categories outlined (see table 1).

First, all potential participants to a discourse must have the same chance to employ communicative speech acts, that is, to initiate and perpetuate the discourse. They must be able to raise questions and provide answers within the discursive context. With reference to the underlying validity claims of speech, this requirement demands in its simplest form that participants prove understandable.

Second, all potential participants must have the same chance to employ representative speech acts, to express attitudes, feelings, and intentions. This serves to ensure freedom from internal constraints on discourse by requiring that participants are both honest and sincere to themselves and to others. The underlying validity claim relating to representative speech acts therefore demands that participants are sincere in their arguments.

Third, all potential speakers must have equal chance to use regulative speech acts; they must be equally able both to command and oppose, permit and forbid arguments. Similarly they must have equal opportunity both to make and accept promises and provide and call for justifications. This requirement guarantees that there are no one-sidedly binding norms in operation. If we refer once again to the underlying validity claim, it is clear that this requirement serves to ensure that interlocutors raise fully appropriate arguments with respect to the relevant normative context.

Table 1
Underlying validity-claims of speech

Speech act	Communicatives	Representatives	Regulatives	Constatives
Validity claim	Comprehensibility	Truthfulness	Appropriateness	Truth
Grounding (1)	Immanent	Assurances	Conviction	Certainty
(2)			Practical discourse	Theoretical discourse

Finally, all potential participants to the discourse must have equal opportunity to use constative speech acts. This requirement ensures the equal opportunity to provide interpretations and explanations and also to problematize any validity claims so that in the long run no one view is exempt from consideration and criticism. Thus the corresponding underlying validity claim of speech requires that all arguments be truthfully grounded.

Habermas maintains that these formal properties, derived from his formal analysis of the rational foundations of everyday speech, alone guarantee that a rationally grounded consensus can emerge from practical discourse: "A reasonable consensus can eventually be distinguished from a false one only in respect to an ideal speech situation" (Habermas 1973a, p. 257). Only to the extent that a decision is reached owing to the force of the better argument can it be argued that communication has taken place free from domination.

A preliminary reading of the features of the ideal speech situation may lead one to form the opinion that together they merely represent an idealistic, normative conception for political discourse (Therborn 1971, Woodiwiss 1978). However, Habermas himself notes that it is doubtful whether the ideal speech situation can be empirically attained because of external political and internal psychological constraints on the participants. But this is not in fact a problem, since what is being suggested is that it is the supposition of the ideal speech situation: its use as a rational standard against which existing discourses can be judged, which is important. In this sense the model of the ideal speech situation should be used counterfactually as a critical measure of the existence of constraints on communication.

The ideal speech situation is neither an empirical phenomenon nor a mere construct, but rather an unavoidable supposition reciprocally made in discourse. This supposition can, but need not be counterfactual; but even if it is made counterfactually, it is a fiction that is operatively effective in the process of communication. Therefore I prefer to speak of an anticipation of an ideal speech situation. . . . This anticipation alone is the warrant which permits us to join to an actually attained consensus the claim of a rational consensus. At the same time it is a critical standard against which every actually realized consensus can be called into question and checked. (Habermas 1973a, p. 258)

Before I attempt to utilize the model of the ideal speech situation to call into question and check the "consensus" that emerged out of a recent example of public participation in the development of nuclear energy in Britain, I want to stress the following points. First, the model of the ideal speech situation is the formal description of those democratic properties that the public sphere strove to attain in the eighteenth and nineteenth centuries in Britain. In this sense Habermas's model is grounded in historical analysis. Second, the British public local inquiry system (of which the Windscale Inquiry is a prominent but by no means atypical example) arose during and as part of that public sphere. Third, the ideal speech situation is further grounded analytically through Habermas's discussion of universal pragmatics: the rational foundations of everyday speech. It is the formal conditions of possible consensus formation, of practical discourse, which provide legitimatory force for political decisions today (Habermas 1979b, p. 184). Fourth, as a consequence, we are at once presented with both a normative model for the conduct of political discourse and an incisive model of social criticism, which, as Habermas revealed in a recent interview, remains faithful to the very foundations of critical theory: "I need the ideal speech situation in order to reconstruct the normative foundations of Critical Theory" (Horster and Reijen 1979, p. 41).

We can now turn to an empirical application of the model, specifically to a consideration of the public local inquiry into the proposal to construct a thermal oxide reprocessing plant (THORP) for waste nuclear fuel, at Windscale, Cumbria, in 1977. This inquiry was held to consider several issues of sociopolitical importance, and the communicative process that took place at the inquiry may be interpreted as a form of practical discourse.

Public Local Inquiry at Windscale

In June 1976 British Nuclear Fuels Limited (BNFL), a state-owned limited company, submitted a formal application to the local authorities in Cumbria, England, to build a commercial-scale nuclear waste reprocessing plant at their Windscale works. Several national and international issues of a controversial nature were being raised, and responding to pressures from several sources, the secretary of state for the environment, Peter Shore, called in the application on December 22, 1976, so that a public local inquiry could be held.

The Windscale Inquiry was conducted by Mr. Justice Parker, assisted by two technical assessors, from June 14, 1977, until November 4,

1977—100 days of inquiry in all. The major objectors to the proposal included the Friends of the Earth (FOE), the Town and Country Planning Association (TCPA), the Windscale Appeal Group (WAG), the Oxford Political Ecology Research Group (PERG), and the Socialist Environment and Resources Association (SERA). It is impossible to summarize the many and varied arguments presented at the hearing. Generally the inquiry was officially held to consider "the implications of the proposed development for the safety of the public and for other aspects of the national interest" (Parker Report 1978, para. 1.2).

It is important to note that it was not until these terms of reference were announced on April 4, 1977, that objectors were certain that discussion of issues relating to the national interest was permissible at the hearing. Thus they had a little over two months in which to prepare their cases. The inquiry took place as scheduled and was followed by the publication of a written report by Mr. Justice Parker on March 6, 1978, which recommended that construction of THORP should begin without delay. By contrast the accompanying ministerial decision was in fact to refuse the application; however, this proved to be merely a procedural device in order to allow the House of Commons to debate the issue in the light of the Parker Report, for it was argued that a parliamentary as opposed to a ministerial decision was necessary for such an important issue. On May 15, 1978, parliamentary approval for THORP was obtained. Thus in less than two years BNFL had gained permission for its plans through what appeared to be the most democratic of available procedures: a public hearing and a parliamentary decision.

I now wish to examine some specific issues raised at the hearing and recorded in the Windscale Inquiry transcripts, which lend support to the view that the communication process that occurred at the Windscale public inquiry was in fact systematically distorted and that the subsequent decision to allow the construction of THORP did not reflect a genuine consensus on the issue and was not reached solely due to the force of the better argument. To do this we can analyze the discourse that took place in terms of the four major requirements of the ideal speech situation, all of which must be met if the consensus that emerges from a practical discourse is to be genuine.

Communicatives

To what extent were the participants at the inquiry equally able to initiate and perpetuate discourse, that is, to raise issues and provide appropriate answers? To what extent were they able to make their arguments understood? A major limitation on the ability of the objectors to raise and develop their arguments was their lack of financial resources. No state finance is made available to objectors at British public local inquiries, and this proved to be a significant feature of the Windscale Inquiry where the main objectors had very limited funds available for undertaking research and hiring legal counsel. In comparison, BNFL, as a state-financed company, had much greater financial reserves. This imbalance affected the chances of an equal presentation of arguments at the inquiry. For example, when the inspector demanded details of alternative energy proposals that might fill the supposed energy gap resulting from a decision not to press ahead with the development of nuclear energy, objectors were unable to undertake the necessary research to provide support for their arguments. This was in part due to the financial constraints and in part a consequence of the fact that the question was being put only on the thirteenth day of the inquiry itself. Objectors had neither the time nor the finance to meet the inspector's request, and Mr. Kidwell for FOE stated that to attempt to do so "would greatly lengthen the Inquiry, and it is not something on which we feel able to embark" (Windscale Inquiry Transcripts, Day 17, July 7, 1977, p. 98).

A similar example arose with the question of the economic viability of the THORP project. During the inquiry the participants were led to believe that economic arguments were of central interest to the hearing. All concerned expended a great deal of time and effort in presenting their respective cases; however, Parker later decided in his report, on which the final parliamentary decision was based, that any evidence of the unsatisfactory economic performance of THORP need not count against the proposal and thereby lead to a refusal of planning permission. Conversely Parker argued that a financially profitable plant would be a much more acceptable proposition. Thus evidence of financial advantage would count in favor of the proposal, whereas any evidence of financial disadvantage would not count against it. This effectively emasculated the arguments of objectors who had questioned

THORP's economic reliability, arguments they had taken a great deal of time and money to research and present.

Objectors were often at a disadvantage in presenting their cases because they were unable to afford to hire legal counsel to present their cases and undertake cross-examination of other parties' witnesses. This resulted in several examples of confusion on the behalf of objectors over the correct procedure to be used in cross-examination and consequently in their inability to present their cases unproblematically. On several occasions the inspector was obliged to offer guidance, of which the following is a typical example:

The Inspector: Forgive me for interrupting you but this is not the time for making a speech. . . . I must remind you that the object of cross-examination is simply to establish facts. Arguments will follow. I know it is difficult because you are not an expert in the subject and the tendency is to bring in a great deal of argument. You must try and restrict yourself at this stage to seeking facts and then we will have the argument later. (Windscale Inquiry Transcripts, Day 8, June 23, 1977, p. 3)

This advice was given to Mr. Taylor of PERG, although similar warnings were given to Dr. Little of Ridgeway Consultants and to Mr. Sedley of SERA. The point to be made here is that the formalized, legal nature of the hearing restricted the ability of all the participants to make their cases equally understood. Although it may be true that all arguments were later given time for fuller development at the inquiry, clearly participants who were able to afford to hire counsel were at a distinct advantage in being able to present their cases according to the formal rules of the occasion. Those objectors with less sufficient resources were less able to make their arguments understood.

Representatives

The second requirement of the ideal speech situation relates to the ability of participants to discourse to express themselves sincerely and to have equal opportunity to represent fully their attitudes and opinions on particular issues. All speakers must be free from both internal and external constraints on their arguments.

With regard to internal constraints, it was argued at the inquiry that the pro-nuclear lobby failed to present a wholly truthful account of affairs within the industry. One suggested reason for this is the existence of a massive institutional commitment to the unbridled development of nuclear energy, a point raised by Andrew Dudman of the local branch of FOE at the inquiry:

I think the building of THORP will make the Fast Breeder Reactor programme more likely because of the *momentum of high technology*. By this, I mean the tendency for high technology to develop without benefit of rational judgements but by its own logic. This is due to the vast sums of money involved, long lead-times, questions of prestige which make political decisions like admitting mistakes or changing one's mind, difficult or impossible, and perhaps most of all to the human factor which here has two aspects in particular:
a) the technology is so advanced that the only relevant advice that the government can get is from the technologists involved, and
b) the technologists so involved are characteristically committing themselves . . . wholeheartedly and unquestioningly to the solution of a great technical problem. (Windscale Inquiry Transcripts, Day 61, September 8, 1977, pp. 7–8)

As a result the fundamental characteristic of the nuclear industry that emerges is one of overall consensus, a state of affairs that is highly improbable for no scientific process can develop without some controversy and disagreement (Kemp 1977).

With regard to external constraints on the ability of speakers to represent their arguments fully, the evidence of certain parties was said to be constrained by financial and other interests. Thus, on the one hand, Brian Wynne of the Network for Nuclear Concern argued that the particular interests of BNFL in developing a profitable reprocessing plant may well overcome more universal, generalizable interests in reliable safety standards. On the other hand, John Tyme, for the National Centre for Alternative Technology, stated that he was having difficulty in obtaining witnesses from two separate sources:

The first is Government Departments and Government Agencies. Here, sir, we find that witnesses are refused the opportunity of providing you with evidence. The second source, sir, is private firms. We are finding, sir, that what amounts to the ever proliferating contracts associated with the Atomic Energy Authority are inhibiting firms from giving evidence before you, sir, the Tribunal, lest they lose either contracts in mind or possible contracts way in the future. (Windscale Inquiry Transcripts, Day 61, September 8, 1977, p. 1)

This leads us to consider whether actual witnesses to the inquiry were prevented from giving their evidence sincerely due to external pressures and constraints placed on them or if such pressures prevented certain witnesses from appearing. Following from this it can be argued that the second requirement of the ideal speech situation was not met at the Windscale Inquiry in that the participants were not equally able to represent their attitudes and opinions on the issues fully and sincerely due to the existence of both internal and external constraints on communication.

Regulatives

The third requirement refers to the need for all participants to practical discourse to have the equal chance to command and oppose, permit and forbid arguments. The fundamental restriction on the implementation of this particular rule within the British public local inquiry context is the existence of the Official Secrets Act and related legislation. Members of the nuclear industry can be prevented from giving evidence in public if their testimony is thought to contravene the Act, and indeed the objectors at the Windscale Inquiry were well aware of the possible use of confidentiality as an excuse to disguise issues and prevent certain facts and arguments from being scrutinized:

Kidwell: My clients I must say will be readily receptive of a considered judgement by the government that some area of information falls within the Official Secrets Act if such areas exist.
    We may view with much more scepticism the claim by BNFL to confidentiality of information. It would not be the first time an inquiry has found itself handicapped by unnecessary and successive secrecy on the part of the nuclear agents. (Windscale Inquiry Transcripts, Day 1, June 14, 1977, pp. 27–28)

Clearly BNFL and the government were in a privileged position in terms of their ability to restrict access to information in their possession, whether covertly or overtly, and appeals to the need for security and to the legitimacy of the Official Secrets Act were a primary mechanism through which this privilege was maintained. Thus despite the inspector's statement that "care must be taken to ensure that all possible information can be produced and considered" (Windscale Inquiry Transcripts, Day 25, July 19, 1977, p. 2), he nevertheless proceeded to deliver a carte blanche to BNFL by restricting discussion of the safety of plutonium containers as follows: "remember always that once there is an item deductions can be made, and something which looks harmless in itself may be very far from harmless" (Windscale Inquiry Transcripts, Day 27, July 21, 1977, p. 49). The significance of this type of argument was not lost on Mr. Aylesbury, who stated for WA: "I would confine myself to a comment on our behalf that what is secret is not necessarily safe, and clearly on behalf of the Appeal I wish to express our continuing worries about the fuel plutonium transportation, but obviously I cannot take up the particular lines any further" (ibid., p. 50).

Clearly there was not an equal chance for all participants at the Windscale Inquiry to employ regulative speech acts since the establishment enjoyed the privilege of being able to forbid arguments through the device of appeals to confidentiality and the need for security, supported by the relevant legislation.

Constatives

The final requirement of the ideal speech situation demands that all participants to the discourse should have equal opportunity to put forward or criticize statements, explanations, interpretations, and justifications so that in the long run no one view is exempt from consideration and criticism.

On the one hand, certain arguments were exempt from consideration at the inquiry, and on the other hand, certain arguments actually presented at the inquiry were either omitted from or misrepresented in the inspector's report on which the final parliamentary decision was based. Thus not only did concerns for confidentiality and security inhibit the consideration of certain issues, but perhaps more important, according to established inquiry procedure, government policy itself was exempt from discussion. Indeed some confusion did exist at the inquiry as to the exact policy position of the government with respect to both reprocessing and the development of a commercial fast breeder reactor, and it was not until the fifty-fifth day of the inquiry that the government's position was clarified. Even then this position could not be debated by those who wished to do so. Perhaps the clearest, albeit indirect discussion of the development of government policy on these issues came from Andrew Dudman of FOE, who argued that the nuclear establishment was confused about policy and was singleminded in its determination to achieve the fast breeder reactor.

Finally, several arguments were either omitted from the inspector's report or, worse, misrepresented in it. For example, PERG later argued that their evidence on major hazards and the safety risks accompanying the development of THORP was distorted by the inquiry:

> The treatment of PERG's hazard evidence by legal counsel and the Inspector provided us with a salutary lesson concerning the workings of the legal mind. In the, perhaps naive, belief that the proceedings of the Inquiry were meant to illicit truth, our witness Thompson agreed under cross examination with two propositions:
> (i) It is possible that THORP may be made acceptably safe. . . .
> (ii) That the accident analyses carried out by him were not predictions of risk under realistic conditions. . . .
> It was not altogether surprising to us that legal counsel should seek answers under cross examination which, taken out of context, were convenient to their case. We were saddened that the Inspector should quote the same answers, also out of context and without their important qualifications, in paras 11.16 and 11.17 of his report. (PERG 1978, p. 5)

This is just one example of many similar omissions and misrepresentations in the report. It is arguable, therefore, that the truthful grounding of arguments both at the inquiry itself and in the subsequent parliamentary debate was hindered through misrepresentation and distortion. In other words the fourth requirement of the ideal speech situation was also not met by the public local inquiry at Windscale.

Conclusion

The communication process that occurred at the Windscale Inquiry and in the subsequent decision to proceed with the development of THORP, when analyzed in terms of the ideal speech situation, may be said to have been subject to systematic distortion. Each of the four requirements of distortion-free practical discourse was transgressed in some manner, and as a consequence, it can be argued that any assumed consensus emerging from the decision was in fact a false one. This may appear to be a surprising statement in view of the fact that a parliamentary decision was taken on the issue. But it should be remembered that the parliamentary decision was in fact based on the findings of the Parker Report, which contained distortions of events at the inquiry and was a reflection of the imbalances and inequalities evident at the inquiry itself. The consensus that emerged was an apparent and not a true one; legitimacy for the decision was achieved not through the force of the better argument but through the systematic distortion of communication; and those interests that prevailed were not generalizable interests but those of state and capital in proceeding with the development of a mode of energy production designed to lower unit costs and lessen the possibilities for industrial action by the working class. Nuclear energy is seen on the one hand as a possible technical fix for the declining profits of capitalism and on the other hand as a means for wresting control over energy production from such disparate but potentially disruptive elements as the mineworkers and the oil-exporting countries of the Middle East.[4]

It may be argued that the use of the ideal speech situation as a critical standard in such cases is an idealistic and impossibly demanding yardstick. I have attempted to demonstrate, however, that the ideal speech situation is not idealistic but is historically grounded in the criteria of openness, impartiality, and rationality that gained importance during the development of the public sphere with the enclosure movement and formally grounded in Habermas's analysis of the rational foundations of everyday speech. The requirements of a truly rational consensus are therefore not merely utopian and arbitrary but follow from historical precedent and from the notion that only with the promise of attaining an underlying rational consensus can practical discourse and everyday speech continue to take place successfully.

Finally, this leads us to a consideration of the relevance of a critical theoretic approach to the analysis of planning (as well as other important sociopolitical) issues today, for critical theory provides the potential for exploding the myths surrounding institutionalized political decision making. History and linguistic analysis show that public hearings may not be as open, impartial, and rational as they are claimed to be, and the legitimacy of political processes may be questioned if systematically distorted communication enables the domination of particular interests (of state and of capital) over more generalizable interests. There has been a recent tendency in British politics to justify controversial government decisions in advance by claiming them to be subject to the outcome of a public inquiry. Evidence I have presented would suggest, however, that this is merely another move in the attempt to depoliticize the public sphere by appealing to the democratic nature of public hearings in order to gain justificatory force when the legitimacy of such an appeal may well be suspect. Clearly continued research into the communicative processes of practical decision making in both planning and other sociopolitical areas will help to throw further light on the true nature of politics in advanced capitalism. Thus to employ critical theoretic terminology, such groups as political activists, environmentalists, and political scientists should beware of the scientization of politics and attempts to depoliticize the public sphere through such means as the use of mystifying terminology, bureaucratic rules, and the distortion of communication. The theoretical work of Jürgen Habermas provides a form of social criticism that guards against these possibilities and reaffirms the need for rational, truly democratic political decision making by enabling the demystification of the interested, ideological constraints and conditions that surround public hearings.

Notes

Many thanks to the Town and Country Planning Association for allowing me to have access to their transcripts of the Windscale Inquiry and to the University of Wales for financial support. Thanks also to Karin Schubert for her assistance with translations and to John Forester for some useful comments and criticisms.

1. See, for example, *Guardian*, December 19, 1979; *Western Mail*, June 27, 1979. On PWR development in Britain see Kemp et al. (1984) and Purdue et al. (1984).

2. Evidence was given to the Galloway Hills People's Inquiry by the Town and Country Planning Association: *Town and Country Planning* (June 1980), pp. 49, 200–203. The main objection to the formal public local inquiry was that the terms of reference excluded any discussion of the dumping of nuclear waste and its ramifications. The inquiry was to consider an application for test drilling and nothing more.

3. Arnstein (1971) has developed a ladder of citizen participation, of which tokenism is a central element.

4. This has become clear from the revealing leak of cabinet minutes, quoted in Campbell (1980). The following statement is attributed to David Howell, the energy minister: "[The nuclear] programme would not reduce the long term requirement for coal. But [it] would have the advantage of removing a substantial proportion of electricity production from the dangers of disruption by industrial action by coal miners or transport workers" (Campbell 1980, p. 468).

References

Arnstein, S., 1971. "A Ladder of Citizen Paticipation in the United States." *Journal of the Royal Town Planning Institute* 57:176–182.

Ash, M., 1977. "Energy and Form: The Windscale File." *Town and Country Planning* (November): 469–477.

Benn, T., 1979. *Arguments for Socialism.* London: Jonathan Cape.

Breach, I., 1978. *Windscale Fallout: A Primer for the Age of Nuclear Controversy.* Harmondsworth: Penguin.

Bugler, J., 1977. "Nuclear Civil War." *New Statesman*, November 4, pp. 603–604.

Bugler, J., 1978a. "The Windscale Verdict." *New Statesman*, March 10, pp. 309–310.

Bugler, J., 1978b. "Windscale: A Case Study in Public Scrutiny." *New Society*, July 27, pp. 183–186.

Campbell, C., 1980. "The Nuclear Cage." *New Statesman*, March 28, pp. 464–469.

Cooke, P. N., and R. V. Kemp, 1980. "Normative Structures: Their Role in the Analysis of Communicative Content in Public Policy-Making." Department of Town Planning Working Paper No. 3. Cardiff: University of Wales Institute of Science and Technology.

Curtler, W. H. R., 1920. *The Enclosure and Redistribution of Our Land.* Oxford: Clarendon.

Dreitzel, H. P., ed., 1970. *Recent Sociology*, Number 2. New York: Macmillan.

Elliot, D., P. Coyne, M. George, and R. Lewis, 1978. *The Politics of Nuclear Power.* London: Pluto Press.

Ganz, G., 1974. *Administrative Procedures.* London: Sweet and Maxwell.

Gonner, E. C. K., 1912. *Common Land and Enclosure.* London: Macmillan.

Habermas, J., 1965. *Strukturwandel der Öffentlichkeit. Untersuchungen zu einer Kategorie der bürgerlicher Gesellschaft.* 2 Aufl., Berlin: Neuwied.

Habermas, J., 1970. "Toward a Theory of Communicative Competence." In H. P. Dreitzel, ed., *Recent Sociology.* New York: Macmillan.

Habermas, J., 1971. *Toward a Rational Society.* London: Heinemann.

Habermas, J., 1973a. "Wahrheitstheorien." In H. Fahrenbach, ed., *Wirklichkeit und Reflexion, zum Sechzigsten Geburtstag fur Walter Schutz.* Pfullingen.

Habermas, J., 1974a. "The Public Sphere: An Encyclopedia Article." *New German Critique* 3:49–55.

Habermas, J., 1974b. *Theory and Practice.* London: Heinemann.

Habermas, J., 1976a. *Legitimation Crisis.* London: Heinemann.

Habermas, J., 1976b. "Some Distinctions in Universal Pragmatics." *Theory and Society* 3:155–167.

Habermas, J., 1979a. "Conservatism and Capitalist Crisis." *New Left Review* 115:73–84.

Habermas, J., 1979b. *Communication and the Evolution of Society.* London: Heinemann.

Hall, D., 1978. "Windscale Inquiry Report." *Town and Country Planning* (May):246–250.

Held, D., 1978. "Extended Review on Jürgen Habermas." *Sociological Review* 26:183–194.

Held, D., 1980. *Introduction to Critical Theory: Horkheimer to Habermas.* London: Heinemann.

Held, D., and L. Simon, 1976. "Habermas' Theory of Crisis in Late Capitalism." *Radical Philosophers' News Journal* 6:1–19.

Hohendahl, P. U., 1979. "Critical Theory, Public Sphere and Culture, Jürgen Habermas and His Critics." *New German Critique* 16:89–118.

Horster, D., and W. van Reijen, 1979. Interview with Jürgen Habermas. *New German Critique* 18:29–43.

Kemp, R., 1977. "Controversy in Scientific Research and Tactics of Communication." *Sociological Review* 25:515–534.

Kemp, R., 1980. Planning, Legitimation, and the Development of Nuclear Energy: A Critical Theoretic Analysis of the Windscale Inquiry." *International Journal of Urban and Regional Research* 4:350–371.

Kemp, R., T. O'Riordan, and M. Purdue, 1984. "Investigation as Legitimacy: The Maturing of the Big Public Inquiry." *Geoforum* 15:477–488.

McCarthy, T. A., 1973. "A Theory of Communicative Competence." *Philosophy of the Social Sciences* 3:135–156.

McCarthy, T. A., 1978. *The Critical Theory of Jürgen Habermas.* Cambridge: MIT Press.

Parker, Hon. Mr. Justice, 1978. *The Windscale Inquiry* (The Parker Report). London: Her Majesty's Stationery Office.

Patterson, W. C., 1976. *Nuclear Power.* Harmondsworth: Penguin.

Pearce, D., L. Edwards, and G. Beuret, 1979. *Decision Making for Energy Futures.* London: Macmillan.

Political Ecology Research Group (PERG), 1978. "The Windscale Inquiry and Safety Assessment." *Oxford Report,* no. 4.

Purdue, M., R. Kemp, and T. O'Riordan, 1984. "The Context and Conduct of the Sizewell B Inquiry." *Energy Policy* 12:276–282.

Royal Commission on Environmental Pollution, 1976. Sixth Report: *Nuclear Power and the Environment* (Flowers Report). London: Her Majesty's Stationery Office.

Saville, J., 1969. "Primitive Accumulation and Early Industrialization in Britain." In R. Miliband and J. Saville, ed., *The Socialist Register.* London: Merlin.

Searle, G. J., 1978. "Lessons from the Windscale Inquiry." Paper presented to U.K. Area Group of Committee O of the International Bar Association. London, April 28.

Smith, P. J., 1977. "One Hundred Days at Windscale." *New Society,* November 24, 405–407.

Stott, M., and P. Taylor, 1980. *The Nuclear Controversy.* London: Town and Country Planning Association and Political Ecology Research Group.

Therborn, H., 1971. "Jürgen Habermas: A New Eclecticism." *New Left Review* 67:69–83.

Thompson, E. P., 1968. *The Making of the English Working Class.* Harmondsworth: Penguin.

Town and Country Planning Association (TCPA), 1978. *Planning and Plutonium.* London: TCPA.

Town and Country Planning Association (TCPA), 1980. "Policy by Stealth." *Town and Country Planning* 49:200–203.

Woodiwiss, T., 1978. "Critical Theory and the Capitalist State." *Economy and Society* 7:175–192.

Wraith, R. E., and G. B. Lamb, 1971. *Public Inquiries as an Instrument of Government.* London: Allen and Unwin.

Critical Theory and Planning Practice

John Forester

Introduction: Practical Planning Theory

This paper introduces "critical theory" for use in planning contexts.[1] In particular, the "communications theory of society" developed by Jürgen Habermas will be applied to planning practice. To dramatize the case, it will be argued that a critical theory of planning practice can be not only empirical, interpretive, and normative in its content, but that it can be practical as well.[2] Why practical? Critical theory may help us anticipate and correct for (a) obstacles to effective design review and democratic planning processes, (b) undeserved resentment and mistrust of planners, and (c) unintentionally counterproductive technical planning practice.

This work is based on eighteen months of regular observation of a metropolitan city planning department's office of environmental review, whose responsibility it was to assess building plans for the city, review them for "significant adverse environmental impact," and then issue either a "negative declaration" or a requirement of an environmental impact report. Some cases reviewed were obviously without significant impacts; a few others clearly required environmental impact reports. Most proposals, though, fell in between those two groups. In these cases, the planners had to check the likely impacts quite carefully and often negotiate with the project sponsor or developer for design changes to assure minimal adverse environmental impacts. In such cases the "review planner" was reviewing, to be sure, but he or she was also participating in project planning and redesign. By using simple examples from this context, it can be shown that a "critical theory of planning practice" may be at once practical, factual, economical, and ethically instructive as well.

In a nutshell, the argument is as follows: critical theory gives us a new way of understanding action, or what a planner does, as attention-shaping (communicative action), rather than more narrowly as a means to a particular end (instrumental action).[3] If planners do not recognize how their ordinary actions may have subtle communicative effects, the planners may be well-meaning but counterproductive nonetheless. They may be sincere but mistrusted, rigorous but unappreciated, re-assuring yet resented. Where they intend to help, planners may create dependency; where they intend to express good faith, they may raise expectations unrealistically. These problems are not inevitable, though. By recognizing the practical, communicative character of planning actions, we can suggest strategies to avoid these problems and improve practice as well. In addition, we can understand structures of action, e.g., the organizational and political contexts of planning practice, as structures of selective attention, and so systematically distorted communication. Developers and neighborhood residents are likely to withhold information, for example; access to information and the ability to act on it (i.e., expertise) are unequally distributed; the agendas of decision making (and planning department work programs as well) are politically and selectively structured; the ability of citizens to participate effectively is unequally distributed.[4]

Such a view leads us to ask a more specific set of questions of the planner than the ones we've always asked before about whose ends or interests are being served. Now we ask, how does the planner politically shape attention and communicate? How does the planner provide or withhold information about project alternatives to affected people? Does the planner speak in a way that people can understand, or are they mystified? Does the planner encourage people to act or rather discourage them with a (possibly implicit) "leave it to me"? What can planners do to prevent unnecessary, disabling distortions of communication: how can they work to enable learning, participation, and self-determination?

The Critical Communications Theory of Society: An Overview

Only an overview of Habermas's communications theory of society can be presented here. In the remainder of the paper, Habermas's arguments will be developed and applied in the context of planning practice. Significant other aspects of his work cannot be discussed in this brief paper though; such work treats, for example, the limits of instrumental rationality, the relationships between knowledge and interest, and the development of moral identity.[5]

Habermas's communications theory of society in effect treats social and political-economic structures as operative communication structures. These relations of power and production not only transmit information, but they communicate political and moral meaning; they seek support, consent, trust, sacrifice, and so forth. The critical content of the theory is centered in the analysis of the systematically but unnecessarily distorted communications which shape the lives of citizens of advanced industrial societies. In the United States, citizens are faced with such influences when politicians or administrators pretend a political problem to be simply a technical one; when private, profit-seeking interests (such as the nuclear construction or pharmaceuticals industries) misrepresent benefits and dangers to the public; when professionals (such as physicians, planners, or social workers) create unnecessary dependency and unrealistic expectations in their clients; or when the established interests in a society avoid humanitarian social and economic policies (such as comprehensive health services) with misleading rhetoric and falsehood, e.g., "the public sector is always, inevitably, less efficient than the private sector." Such distortions of pretense, misrepresentation, dependency-creation, and ideology are communicative influences with immobilizing, depoliticizing, and subtly but effectively disabling consequences. To isolate and reveal the debilitating power of such systematically distorted communications, Habermas seeks to contrast these with the ordinary, commonsense communication of mutual understanding and consensus which makes any shared knowledge possible in the first place.

The spinal element of Habermas's critical communications theory lies in this contradiction between the disabling communicative power of bureaucratic or capitalistic, undemocratic institutions on the one hand, and the collective enabling power of democratic political criticism, mutual understanding, and self-determined consensus on the other. By undertaking a detailed analysis of the requirements of the ordinary mutual understanding which makes any shared political criticism or technical analysis possible, Habermas establishes a critical reference point, the possibility of politically unobstructed discussion and common sense (technically, intersubjectivity), to which he can then contrast the distorting communicative influences of concrete productive relations and the structure and policies of the state. It is crucial to note, here, that some distortions of communication (e.g., imperfect information) are inevitable, necessarily present in the structure of any political economy; this is true of face-to-face communication as well. Nevertheless, many distortions are not inevitable; they are artificial, and thus the illusions they promote may be overcome. Such distortions are, for example, the deceptive legitimation of great inequalities of income and wealth, the consumer ideologies inherited and generated from the organization of capitalist productive relations, the manipulation of public ignorance in the defense of professional power, and the oppressive racial, ethnic, and sexual type-casting to which vast segments of our population are subjected daily. Politically debilitating distortions of communication are political artifacts and not natural necessities. These are the target of Habermas's critical communications theory.[6]

Habermas thus sets the stage for an empirical political analysis exposing the subtle ways that a given structure of state and productive relations functions: (1) to legitimate and perpetuate itself while it seeks to extend its power; (2) to exclude systematically from decision-making processes affecting their lives particular groups defined along economic, racial, or sexual lines; (3) to promote the political and moral illusion that science and technology, through professionals and experts, can "solve" political problems; and so (4) to restrict public political argument, participation, and mobilization regarding a broad range of policy options and alternatives which are inconvenient to (incompatible with) the existing patterns of ownership, wealth, and power. Habermas assesses the problems of distorted communications not only at an interpersonal level but also at the level of social and political-economic structure. In this way, he begins to fulfill the critical tasks of revealing how the citizens of advanced capitalistic societies may remain not only ignorant of their own democractic political traditions, but also oblivious to their own possibilities for corrective action—as they are harangued, pacified, misled, and ultimately persuaded that inequality, poverty, and ill health are either problems for which the victim is responsible or problems so "political" and "complex" that they can have nothing to say about them. Habermas argues that democratic politics or planning requires the consent that grows from processes of collective criticism, not from silence or a party line.

John Forester

The critical impulse in Habermas's work, then, depends upon a two-pronged analysis. To show that the political-economic structure, understood as a communications structure, is systematically but unnecessarily distorted, first he must develop an answer to the question, "distorted from what?" His theory of "universal pragmatics," discussed below, addresses this problem. Secondly, the critical communications theory must suggest how existing social and political-economic relations actually operate as distorted communications, obscuring issues, manipulating trust and consent, twisting fact and possibility. Habermas has devoted less attention to this second problem (the empirical research into these systematic distortions of communication) than he has to preparing the groundwork for such research. Tables 1 and 2, though (presented and discussed later in this article), identify basic types of distorted communication which subvert understanding and knowledge at face-to-face, organizational, and political-economic or structural levels of analysis. The power of Habermas's work is to carry forward the classical Marxian "critique of ideology" into a subtle and refined analysis of the structurally, systematically distorted communication and language-use which constitute, mediate, and take expression in the concrete, historical social relations of production, politics, and culture. Although these paragraphs have provided only a simplified overview of Habermas's communications theory, some of the finer points can now be elaborated and applied to planning practice.

Planning Practice as Attention-Shaping: Communicative Action

In practice any action works not only as a tool but also as a promise, shaping expectations. Planners may be effective not because they put words on paper, but because they may alter expectations by doing so. The planner's formality may tell a city resident more than the actual information provided. The quality of the communication counts; without it, technical information would never be trusted, and cooperation would be impossible. With no one listening, effective work in the planning office would grind to a halt.

Consider a local planner's description (to a neighborhood group) of a proposed shopping center project. If he or she describes the project in predominantly economic terms, the audience will see something different than if it is described in mostly political terms. And again, they would see something different if he or she describes the project in the most simple ordinary language—as if doing a Sunday supplement story about the proposed shopping center. But each of these descriptions would be about the same project. Which account should be given? Which account should be believed?[7] Choices must inevitably be made.

The problem is this: the planner's ordinary description of a project (or of a meeting, of what someone said, etc.) is a communicative action in itself. Like all action, it depends upon intentions and interests, and an audience. Without an audience, the description would be like a play on opening night when no one came, and it would be absolutely uninteresting and worthless, almost by definition, without intentions and interests setting it up. But with interests making something worth describing, intentions making the describing worth doing, and an audience to listen, the planner's description of a project may actually help get ordinary work done.

Planners do much more than describe, of course. They warn others of problems; they present information to other staff (and neighborhood residents, developers, and others); they suggest new ideas; they agree to perform certain tasks or meet at certain times; they argue for particular efforts; they report relevant events; they offer opinions; and they comment upon ideas and proposals for action. These are only a few of the minute, essentially pragmatic, communicative acts which planners perform all the time. These acts are the "atoms" out of which any bureaucratic, social, or political action is constructed. When they are verbal, we can call these acts "speech acts."[8] If these social acts were not possible, we couldn't even ask one another "what did the project sponsor say?" Precisely because such communicative acts are effective, the phrase "watch out—he doesn't like planners" has meaning. The pragmatic meaning is: you watch out.[9] Without these elementally communicative acts, the intelligibility and common sense of our ordinary social world could not exist. Planning problems would be inexpressible; practical action would be impossible.[10]

These elementary communicative actions are at the heart of the possibility of any ordinary, cooperative working relationships—in everyday life, in planning, in political movements, and in society generally. Communicative acts are fundamental to practical life; they come first. Without them there is no understanding, no common sense, no shared basis even for disagreement or conflict.[11] Without shared, commonly structured communicative abilities (i.e., "communicative competence") we would not be able to say "Hello" and be understood. And the planner would not be able to say, "The meeting's Wednesday at 7:30 — come prepared" and be understood either. These communicative acts are ordinary, often just taken for granted, but they are politically potent as well.[12] The planners' speech acts perform both technical and political work.

From Enabling Rules to Organizing Practices

Enabling Rules

These essential communicative acts of ordinary planning practice don't just happen. They do not grow automatically from natural conditions. They are not biological. They are social actions, working through languages we can speak together. Words and noises don't just come from our mouths; we speak. We tell, or ask, or promise, or greet, or argue. We act. And when we speak, we don't just make noises, we participate in a structured form of social action, which is already normative and rule-structured.[13] And it's not up to us to decide whether or not we want to follow the rules of ordinary language use — if we want someone else to understand what we say, what we promise, or warn of, or call attention to, or ask. If we want to tell someone that a project review meeting is likely to be especially important, we can't just make up a special word to get the point across — we must try hard to say what we mean, using the language, and whatever frame of reference we share. If we want to be understood when we speak practically, we must follow (or put into use, or work through) the rules structuring ordinary language — or what we really mean to say won't be what anyone listening thinks we mean. The rules here are not restrictions; they enable us to know what one another means.[14] They help me know that "please check out the proposal" isn't likely to mean "we're all done with it."[15] We can communicate pragmatically — though there are exceptions — because we presuppose and anticipate, when speaking, that a set of implicit rules will ordinarily be followed in real life.[16]

We ordinarily (but not always!) try and expect others:[17]

1. to *speak comprehensibly*; if we didn't ordinarily presuppose this norm to be in effect, we'd expect babble and never listen;

2. to *speak sincerely*; if we did not presuppose this norm, generally, we'd never trust anyone we listened to—or even trust that we could check with someone else to see what was really meant;[18]

3. to *speak legitimately*, in context; we don't expect building developers to give biblical interpretations in front of the Planning Commission or clergy to propose planned unit developments before their congregations; and

4. to *speak the truth*; if we didn't generally presuppose this norm, we'd never believe anything we heard, even if we had no doubt of the speaker's sincerity, if we knew the best of intentions were involved. We'd never be able to check or test the truth of a story or hypothesis if we generally expected falsehood to pervade communication. Only by presupposing and mutually fostering this norm of "truth" do we make it possible for each other to tell the difference between reality and ideology, between fact and sheer fantasy. Those skeptical about this norm of truth might consider if they presume less when they speak of the realities of poverty, sexism, or cruelty. (Of course exceptions to the generally presupposed norm exist. We can lie, but even the lie only works because the listener is ordinarily bound by the norm to expect truthfulness in ordinary communication.)

These norms of pragmatic communication are usually taken for granted. They are part of the subtle foundations of common sense. If we violate them, or when we do, we face puzzlement, mistrust, anger, and disbelief.[19] As these pragmatic norms are broken, our shared experience and our social and political world disintegrate.[20] These problems have special importance in planning for two reasons. First, since planners often have little formal power or authority, the effectiveness of their communicative acts becomes all the more important. Second, planners serving the public face particular special, private, or class interests (e.g., corporate development interests) which may work systematically to violate these norms of ordinary communication. Planners then face the results; a community group snowed by a developer's consultant, an inquisitive citizen confused by apparently "necessary" public works cutbacks, a working-class community organization led to accept delays as wealthier neighborhoods receive more attention from city government. Planning staff members need to anticipate the practical effects not only of the class-based communicative actions of others, but of their own communicative practices as well.

Meaning More (in Practice) Than Intended

When planners tell a neighborhood group about a proposed project, they inevitably communicate more than they intend.[21] They may lapse into bureaucratic language and so confuse and mystify people.[22] They may present information but have no way of knowing what it will really mean to the audience. They may be trying to please, but their professional or formal manner may lead residents to doubt their sincerity. Pragmatically effective communication is never guaranteed.[23] The four norms of "universal pragmatics" are just that: they are pragmatic guides and standards for practice.[24] As they are violated, mutual understanding, trust, and cooperation will suffer. We can take these four norms of ordinary communication, our universally presupposed pragmatic abilities, and pose them, then, as practical questions for planning practice.

1. Is the planner's communication *comprehensible*, so others can understand what in fact is happening around them or to them?

2. Is the planner's communication offered *sincerely* and uttered in good faith, or are the listeners being manipulated, misled, fooled or misguided?

3. Is the planner's communication *legitimate*, given the planner's role and the participation of other interested parties, or is the planner taking advantage of professional status unfairly? (If a planner tells a developer or community organization member, "you'll have to live with this design, there's nothing you can do," this may be, for example, a personal judgment in professional clothes.)

4. Is the planner's communication *true*? Can we believe it, bet on it? Is there evidence supporting it? What do other accounts of the situation say? Are the listeners being offered information upon which they can act, or are they being misinformed, however unintentionally?

Practical Distortions of Communication: Political Costs and Corrective Strategies

In bargaining or other adversarial situations, for example, planners won't be expected to "tell the whole truth, and nothing but the truth." When planners must present arguments as advocates for a particular proposal, or when they must argue for budgetary needs, others may expect the ordinary norms of communication discussed above to be violated by the planners, but they will also expect (in order to compensate) to be able to check what the planners say with others, e.g., friends or contacts in other agencies whom they expect *not* to violate these basic norms.[25] This latter expectation makes any checking possible.[26] Thus, in those conventional situations when bargaining or adversarial behavior is expected to result in exaggeration, mistruth, or misrepresentation, the ordinary pragmatic norms nevertheless make possible compensating checking strategies which protect us from being misled, from "being snowed." In these situations, the four questions of comprehensibility, sincerity, legitimacy, and truth become more, rather than less, important. If we are generally to trust and rely upon planners as responsible public servants, it will be crucial to know not only when and why insincerity and falsehood may at times be justified, but also to know what results such practices have.[27] These questions are particularly important because of the bureaucratic and political pressures operating upon planners:[28] planners will often feel compelled to be less frank or open than they might wish, but then they should not be surprised when they find members of the public at times suspicious, resentful, or angry.

These four questions ask how the four norms of ordinary communication are met or violated in planning practice, but this is only a slight beginning. The planners' distortions are certainly no more important or influential than the systematic structural distortions of communication which planners and their clients both face. Consider: the politically selective channeling of information; the unequally distributed ability to engage in political and planning processes (of citizens with or for whom the planning staff work); the professional status (or stigma) of the planner's deeds; conflicting interpretations of cases and significance; scarce information and fluid networks of contacts; and a maze of bureaucratic rules for the uninitiated to navigate. We are led to ask of the organizational structure of private interests and public agencies how they foster or retard open, unmanipulated communication (and so participation) by affected persons. When ordinary communication is structurally but unnecessarily or deliberately distorted, responsible political action will be crippled.[29]

The socially and politically structured distortions of communication we face every day—as citizens and as planners—can now begin to be recognized and assessed (table 1). For each entry in table 1 we can ask a practical question: "How can planners work with others to prevent such distortions of communication?" Table 2 suggests strategies of response, "exposing" or correcting the distortions of table 1.

These strategies of response are varied, but they can be summarized in one word—"organizing." This is the planner's pragmatic response to a political reality of effectively disabling distortions of ordinary communication: the careful, political organization of attention and action which corrects or seeks to eliminate these distortions.[30] Not only do these strategies address the basic obstacles to open democratic political processes, they are also pragmatic as well. They seek concretely to marshal information, to cultivate support, to work through informal channels, to use expertise discriminately, and so forth.[31] Thus, the analysis of the distortion or violation of the norms of ordinary communication leads logically to questions of response.

On Practice: Enabling (Organizing) and Disabling Practice

Now what of local planning practice? Where's the practical payoff for planners? As we broaden our understanding of the planner's action (from technical to communicative), we come to understand the practical organizational problems planners face a little differently. We come to understand that problems will be solved not by one expert, but by pooling expertise and non-professional contributions as well; not by formal procedure alone, but by informal consultation and involvement; not predominantly by strict reliance on data bases, but by careful use of trusted "resources," "contacts," 'friends"; not through formally rational management procedures, but by internal politics and the development of a working consensus; not by solving an engineering equation, but by complementing technical performance with political sophistication, support-building, liaison work, and, finally, intuition and luck. Only in the most isolated or most routine cases will future-oriented planning proceed "one, two, three."[32]

Critical Theory and Planning Practice

Table 1
How we experience distortions of communication

Practical level	Norms of pragmatic communication			
	Comprehensibility	Sincerity	Legitimacy	Truth
Face to face	Lack of sense ambiguity confusion "What?"	Deceit, insincerity "Can I trust him?"	Meaning out of context "Is this right?"	Misinformation "Is this true?"
Organizational (e.g., hospital proposing expansion)	Public exclusion by jargon "What's this mean?	Rhetorical reassurances; expression of false concern; hiding of motives "Can we trust?"	Unresponsiveness; assertion of rationalizations; professional dominance "Is this justified?"	Information withheld; responsibility obscured; need misrepresented "Is this true?"
Political-economic structure	Mystification complexity "Do you think *they* understand what that means?"	Misrepresentation of the public good "That's their line."	Lack of accountability; legitimation by line, not by active participation "Who are they to say?"	Policy possibilities obscured, withheld, or misrepresented; ideology as: public ownership is always inefficient "What they never tell us about is . . ."

Table 2
Responses correcting distortions of communication: organizing practices of planners

Practical level	Distortion type (pragmatic norm violated)			
	Comprehensibility	Sincerity	Legitimacy	Truth
Face to face[a]	Revealing meaning	Checking intentions	Determining roles and contexts[b]	Checking evidence
	"What does that mean?"	"Does she mean that?"	"I don't need to accept that . . ."	"I'll check to see if this is really true."
Organizational[c]	Minimizing jargon; creating public review committees	Organizing counter-advocates; checking with contacts, networks	Making decisions participatory; checking with affected persons	Utilizing independent/critical third party expertise
	"Clean up the language so people can understand it."	"Check with Stu to see if we can trust them on this."	"What's the neighborhood association had to say about this?"	"Check the data and calculations to see if these figures are really correct."
Political-economic structure[d]	Demystification; counter-skills	Exposing unexpressed interests	Democratizing the state; politicizing planning[c]	Institutionalizing debate, political criticism
	"All this really means is . . ."	"Of course they say that! They're the big winners if no one speaks up."	"Without political pressure, the bureaucracy will continue to serve itself . . ."	Democratizing inquiry; politicizing planning[f]: "we have to show what can be done here."

a. For an analysis of the problems of distorted communication and political response at the level of face to face interaction see "Listening: The Social Policy of Everyday Life (Critical Theory and Hermeneutics in Practice)" (Forester 1980b).

b. R. R. McGuire writes, "... insofar as systems of rules and norms contribute to systematically distorted communication, insofar as they exist as systematic barriers to discursive will formation, they are irrational. ... And insofar as [communication structures] create a fiction of reciprocal accountability, concomitantly creating ideologies by sustaining the 'legitimacy' of these very structures they are irrational ... and hence illegitimate—involving no moral obligation" (1977).

c. Several sources provide insight and suggestions for those seeking to correct distortions of communication at the organizational level: Harold Wilensky (1967), Needleman (1974), Saul Alinsky (1971); also helpful may be Guy Benveniste (1977) and Paulo Freire (1974, 1970).

d. The political economic ethic or vision of "opening communications" is the ethic of the critique of ideology. Embodied in actions seeking to correct distorted communication, the distortion of attention to actual possibilities, this is a call for political organizing, for democratizing public policy.

e. To politicize planning does not mean to grind planning to a halt. This is the poisonous misreading of politics that perpetuates a narrow, technically-focused, politically inept planning practice. To politicize planning along the lines called for by critical theory means to broaden the basis of consideration of alternatives, to foster participation and spread responsibility to non-professional citizens; to balance the reliance upon technique with the attention to regular political debate and criticism. See Pitkin (1972).

f. "The ultimate objective of repoliticization ... should be to resurrect the notion of democracy, which is far too important an ideal to be sacrificed to capitalism. ... The problem is not that capitalist societies accumulate, but the way in which they do it. In order for the beneficiaries of accumulation to remain a narrow group, a boundary is established beyond which democracy is not allowed to intrude. ... [T]he time has come to think, not about demolishing accumulation, but about democratizing it. The way to eliminate the contradictions between accumulation and legitimation is to apply the principles of democracy to both—to give people the same voice in making investment and allocation decisions as they theoretically have in more directly political decisions" (Wolfe 1977, p. 346).

The planner's technical acts may be instrumentally skilled, but nevertheless politically inept. A formal economic calculation may be impeccably performed, but the planner's client may "not really trust the numbers." Any technical action (calculating a solution, making a demographic prediction, reviewing architectural plans for flaws) communicates to those it serves, "this solution (etc.) serves your needs" or "now, this much done, you may still wish to . . . (change this parameter, devise another scenario, look and see for yourself)." In planning contexts, this meta-communicative character of technical action has often been overlooked.[33] Its practical implications, particularly its costs, have often been neglected. The most well-meaning professional activities of planning staffs have at times communicated, if unintentionally, "leave the analysis to me; I'll give you all the results when I'm through; you can depend on me." At times this has reflected an agreed-upon division of labor. At other times the political and practical consequences of such (often implicit) communication has been to separate planners and planned-for, to reduce the accessibility to information of those affected by plans, to minimize the planner's capability to learn from design review criticism, to engender public mistrust for planning staff, and to reinforce the planner's apprehension of what seems to be necessarily disruptive public participation. As long as this practical communicative dimension of (even the most technical) planning is ignored, planners will pay such costs.[34]

This practical communicative dimension of planning practice involves much more than how clearly the planner writes or speaks.[35] *What* the planner chooses to say—and not to say—is pragmatically, and politically, crucial. If the planner, for example, takes the role of the "informed technocrat" and chooses to emphasize the technical aspects of a problem while ignoring its political dimensions, the planner's own understanding of his or her appropriate role may lead to a serious misrepresentation of that problem. Ideologies, of course, are distortions of communication in precisely this sense. They are distortions not because they are unclear, but because they are indeed clear; but they so misrepresent social and political reality that they may obscure alternatives, cover up responsibility, encourage passivity and fatalism, and justify the perpetuation of inequity and suffering.

Echoing the work of Karl Mannheim and John Dewey, Habermas's argument implies that such distortions are increasingly likely in planning if planners become more removed from a democratic planning process which encourages political debate, the criticism of alternative problem definitions, and the collective construction of new design and policy proposals.[36] Thus, the sensitivity to distorted communication by planners leads not only to attention to matters of clarity, "cleaning up communications," but also to the appropriate, inevitably political roles of planning staff: do they foster or thwart informed public participation; do they pre-empt or enable public debate and argument; do they encourage or discourage design and policy review and criticism?

Planning organizations may—against all their best intentions—immobilize or disable public political participation and action. By ignoring the effects of bureaucratic language, planning organizations may perpetuate the exclusion of all but those who already "know the language." If they are not perceived to speak truthfully, planning organizations will breed distrust, suspicion, and a growing hostility to professional public servants—to say little of the possible cooperation that will be poisoned. More subtly, if planning organizations pre-empt community involvement by defining problems as overly technical or as too complex for non-professionals to understand, they may, again against their best intentions, engender political passivity, dependency, and ignorance.[37] And if they do not systematically search for design alternatives and possible political solutions through regular processes of community consultation, expertise pooling, and project reviews running from "brainstorming" to "collective criticism," planning organizations are likely to "satisfice" too quickly or inefficiently, and miss real program or design opportunities.

Ironically, then, technically oriented planning may effectively but unintentionally communicate to the public, "you can depend on me; you needn't get involved; I'll consult you when appropriate." This message may simplify practice in the short run, but it may also lead to inefficiency and waste in general. It counterproductively may separate planners from the political constituency they serve, weakening them both before the designs and agendas of powerful economic forces in their neighborhoods and cities.[38] It may subvert the accountability of planners and serve to keep affected publics uninformed rather than politically educated about events and local decisions affecting their lives. Planning which is predominantly technical in focus may also neglect its political friends. When action is at stake—not to mention the planners' jobs themselves, of course—this can be costly. We may find opportunities to improve planning productivity and efficiency, then, not simply by appealing to community involvement, but by calling attention to the minute, practical communications which function either to discourage or alternatively encourage cooperative, constructive, trusting, supportive organizational and community bases for the actions of planners. Technical work should not be seen in a vacuum, then. To avoid the counterproductive "leave it to us" messages that these acts may meta-communicate, planners have several options, as indicated in table 3.

The statement "planning is political" need not be the end of discussion; it may be a fruitful beginning. By anticipating the interests and commitments of affected groups, planners may build political support in addition to producing technically sound documents. To be effective, rigorous analysis must be used (if not always appreciated) by politically influential groups or the staff of other agencies; technical analysis in planning cannot stand alone. Numerous studies show that the "technician" role of planning analysis is often frustrating and ineffectual if divorced from the pragmatic considerations of political communication: lobbying, maintaining trust and "an ear," addressing the specific concerns of the decision-making audiences as well as those inherent in the projects themselves, and so on.[39] Paying attention to the practical communications that structure the planning process can save wasted time and effort; otherwise, technical reports may be destined to end up on the shelf.

Nevertheless, the strategies indicated above are not without their problems. How much information should be given to which groups, and when? What can planners do to prevent such information from being ignored, misinterpreted, or manipulated? What organizational and political forms of community planning, widespread participation, and design review might be both democratic and efficient? These are not new questions for planners—but the analysis of systematically distorted communication provided by critical theory allows these questions to be asked and answered in new ways. In particular these ways include: (1) clarifying the ordinary norms of practical communication; (2) identifying the essential types of disabling distortions to be corrected; (3) clarifying the planner's role in perpetuating or seeking to correct such distortions; and (4) locating within a political-economic structure of power and ideology—treated as a structure of systematically distorted communication of assurance, threat, promise, and legitimation—the pragmatic and political communicative character of planning practice.

Table 3
Communicative strategies complementing planners' technical work

Complementing their technical work, planners can:

1. cultivate community networks of liaisons and contacts, rather than depending on the power of documents, both to provide and disseminate information;

2. listen carefully to gauge the concerns and interests of all participants in the planning process to anticipate likely political obstacles, struggles, and opportunities;

3. notify less-organized interests early in any planning process affecting them (the more organized groups whose business it is to have such information won't need the same attention);

4. educate citizens and community organizations about the planning process and the "rules of the game";

5. supply technical and political information to citizens to enable informed, effective political participation;

6. work to see that community and neighborhood, nonprofessional organizations have ready access to public planning information, local codes, plans, and notices of relevant meetings, and consultations with agency contacts, "specialists" supplementing their own "in-house" expertise;

7. encourage community-based groups to press for open, full information about proposed projects and design possibilities;

8. develop skills to work with groups and conflict situations, rather than expecting progress to stem mainly from isolated technical work;

9. emphasize to community interests the importance of effective participation in informal processes of project review, and take steps to make such design-change negotiation meetings equitable to professionally unsophisticated groups;

10. encourage independent, community-based project reviews and investigations;

11. anticipate external political-economic pressures shaping design decisions and compensate for them—soliciting "pressure we can use" (e.g., countering vested anti-public interests) rather than minimizing external pressure altogether.

(These actions are all elements of "organizing" practices, practically mobilizing concerned and affected persons, in addition to technically calculating problem solutions.)

Each of the entries in tables 1, 2, and 3 ought to be regarded as an illustration pointing to practical, political research questions. Such questions are *empirical* as they question the forms and effects of disabling or enabling communication; they are *interpretive* as they question the meanings and myths generated by alternative organizational forms and professional practices; and they are *normative* as they question the political and moral responsibilities of professionals, bureaucrats, and citizens alike. If the organizing strategies listed in table 3 are considered as isolated ideas, they are nothing new. Only if they are understood and carried out in the context of the structural analysis of systematically distorted communication illustrated in tables 1 and 2 can they be seen in a new light, focused upon new goals and objectives, and put into practice in increasingly sensitive and effective ways.

Conclusion

Practical organizing strategies (suggested in table 3) may provide options for planners seeking to improve local planning practice and avoid the disruptive, frustration-producing problems of organizationally distorted communications (suggested in table 1). Planning actions are not only technical, they are also communicative: they shape attention and expectations. These communicative effects are often unintentional, but they are pragmatic nevertheless; they make a difference. Presenting technical information to a community organization, a planner's manner may communicate as much as his or her words.

These practical communicative effects can be counterproductive for planners if they are ignored. Alternatively, if they are recognized, planners can complement their technical activities with strategies (suggested in table 2) designed to open effective communication to those persons and groups affected by proposed projects and plans. These practical communication strategies may be organizationally economical as they reduce the unnecessary disruption of the planning process, as they cultivate support for planners' actions, and as they reduce the likelihood that planners' efforts will be washed away by the larger political process in which any planning is embedded. Finally, the focus on the pragmatic aspects of such communicative planning actions can be rooted in the recent literature of critical theory, especially as developed in the writings of Jürgen Habermas. Significantly, a critical theory of planning practice, barely indicated here, calls our attention

(a) *empirically* to concrete communicative actions and organizational and political-economic structures, (b) *interpretively* to the meanings and experiences of persons performing or facing those communicative actions, and (c) *normatively* to the respect or violation of fundamental social norms of language use, norms making possible the very intelligibility and common sense of our social world. By recognizing planning practice as normatively rule-structured communicative action which distorts, covers up, or reveals to the public the prospects and possibilities they face, a critical theory of planning aids us practically and ethically as well. This is the contribution of critical theory to planning: pragmatics with vision—to reveal true alternatives, to correct false expectations, to counter cynicism, to foster inquiry, to spread political responsibility, engagement, and action. Critical planning practice, technically skilled and politically sensitive, is an organizing and democratizing practice.

Notes

This essay was originally published in the *Journal of the American Planning Association* (July 1980) and is reprinted here with slight changes with permission. An earlier version, prepared for a conference on planning theory and practice at Cornell University in April 1979, appears in *Urban and Regional Planning in an Age of Austerity* (Pierre Clavel, John Forester, William Goldsmith, eds.), Pergamon Press, 1980.

Thanks for comments on this draft to Simon Neustein, Bruce Fink, Jim Dorris, and John Friedmann.

1. By "critical theory" I refer predominantly to the work of Jürgen Habermas and the interpreters of his recent work (1970, 1971, 1973, 1975, 1979). Excellent interpreters of Habermas's critical theory are Richard Bernstein (1976), Thomas McCarthy (1978), and Trent Schroyer (1973).

2. Bernstein completes his review of the apparent restructuring of modern social and political theory with the challenge: "An adequate social and political theory must be *empirical, interpretive,* and *critical*" (1976, p. 235).

3. For one distinction between instrumental and communicative action, see Habermas (1970, p. 91 and following). Also important for an understanding of the concepts of systematic structuring of attention (e.g., distortions of communication) is Berger and Luckmann (1966).

4. See Steven Lukes (1974) for the treatment of the structural distortions of communications and information considered by E. E. Schattschneider, Peter Bachrach, and Morton Baratz; Murray Edelman's work (1971, 1978) provides another view of distorted communications. Schroyer (1973) and Claus Mueller (1973) are attempts to bridge Habermas's analysis of communicative action and its distortions (on the one side) and the more traditional treatments of power and political structure (on the other side). See also, for example, the lengthy introduction of Habermas (1973). Cf. Alvin Gouldner's very narrow reading of systematic distortions of

communication as "censorship" (1976). Cf. also Paulo Freire's powerful and moving *Pedagogy of the Oppressed* (1970), which provides many fascinating parallels with Habermas's work.

5. See note 1, above.

6. Such distorted communications mediate, in Marxist terms, the contradictions between working and ruling classes, between the means of production and the social relations of production, between labor and capital. In ordinary terms, these distortions hide from citizens the end results of their labor, the possibilities of collective improvement now existing in modern cooperative organization and technology, and the social costs of the private control of investment and labor.

7. This question is especially important to the extent that the listener has no opportunity to engage the speaker and question the given description—thus enabling a richer account to be given. But when the listener is uninformed and trusting, even the recourse to conversation and interaction may not change matters. The offered account, selective as it must be, will effectively stand (e.g., the planner may say to the community organization member/developer, "There's just nothing much you can do.") It's helpful to remember, of course, that planners are not omniscient, and that such statements, like others, may or may not be actually true.

8. The classic analysis of "speech acts" appears in the work of John Austin (1961), and more recently, John Searle (1969).

9. Non-verbal communication counts, too, but must be developed in another paper. In face-to-face interaction, non-verbal communication takes the form of tone, gesture, deadpan or lively facial expressions. At the organizational level, non-verbal communication is effective in the structuring of agendas, meetings, work-programs, and the character (e.g., more or less formal, comprehensible, encouraging) of the planning or policy formulation process. At both levels, what remains unsaid may be as important, and effective, as what is said. See, e.g., Paul Watzlawick et al. (1967). See also note 33.

10. Habermas calls the theory of these speech acts "the theory of universal pragmatics": universal because all social communication seems to depend on the structure and possibility of such acts, and pragmatic because these acts are concretely practical—they make a difference in our lives. See his (1979) "What Is Universal Pragmatics?" See also note 9, above.

11. See, for example, Karl Otto Apel's "The Priori of Communication and the Foundation of the Humanities" in Dallmayr and McCarthy (1977).

12. Paul Watzlawick shows that even a threat depends upon effective communication; the minimal conditions for a threat to be successful are that it must "get through" and be believable (1976, p. 107ff).

13. See, for example, Cavell (1969), especially the essay "Must We Mean What We Say?" Cf. Pitkin (1972).

14. See Searle (1969) for the difference between *regulative* and *constitutive* rules. Charles Taylor develops some of the political implications of these differences for politics and the study of politics in his "Interpretation and the Sciences of Man," in Dallmayr and McCarthy (1977).

15. "Please check out the proposal" may have many non-literal practical meanings too, of course. It may mean, "this proposal isn't documented properly," for example. But our understanding of such non-literal meanings presupposes we know how to apply the ordinary rules of language-use. Otherwise, we wouldn't, at the first level, be able to recognize the literal meaning, its possible implications, and then at the second level, its fit or possible mis-fit with the context of its use (i.e., whether or not we should take it literally).

16. Extended analysis of such presupposition and anticipation of the "universal pragmatic" norms of speech can be found in McCarthy (1978). Jeremy Shapiro (1976) is also helpful.

17. See Habermas's "What Is Universal Pragmatics?" (1979, p. 2). Note that these ordinary expectations are *not* prescriptive rules; this analysis does not implore planners, "Tell the truth! Be right! Be sincere! Be clear! Always and forever!" Nevertheless, we may investigate just how planners act by exploring the truth, legitimacy, sincerity, and clarity of their communications.

18. This "sincerity" condition differs from the "truth" condition which follows. Sincerity refers to the genuine expression of the speaker's intentions; truth refers to the fit or misfit of statements or representations of reality with the reality supposedly represented. A speaker may be sincere or insincere; a statement may be true or false. (One might say that an expression, as an indication of a speaker's intentions, is sincere or insincere.) A physician may be utterly sincere in prescribing a medication to alleviate certain symptoms, but the medication may nevertheless not work; a planner may be wholly sincere in saying that a certain widening of a street will draw twice the existing traffic flow, but the widening may not actually have those consequences. In each case, the speaker is sincere, but what is said is not true. Insincerity threatens and subverts trust; mistruth weakens and subverts knowledge. Consider as examples fads in political movements, popular psychology, or the misuse of the women's movement in commercial advertising.

19. "Since our ability to cope with life depends upon our making sense of what happens to us, anything which threatens to invalidate our conceptual structures of interpretation is profoundly disruptive" (Marris 1975, p. 13).

20. Fred Dallmayr argues that the violation and respect of these universal pragmatic norms of communication may be taken to ground a "communicative ethics" and a normative political vision (1974). Forester develops the implications of a "communicative ethics" for planning (1980a). See also Trent Schroyer (1973, pp. 162–163) for the argument that Habermas's critique of systematically distorted communications is a refined form of the classical critique of ideology.

21. Cavell distinguishes the semantic meaning of an uttered sentence from the pragmatic meaning of the same utterance, and he argues that as speakers and actors we are responsible for both. Good intentions are not enough; pragmatics count (1969).

22. From the journal of a young planner in California: "Sitting in Environmental Review Committee meetings, I notice how the applicants interact with the Committee—the 'slickies' know the genre. They speak with professional language, e.g., 'that's correct' for 'that's right.' Others come in and get bounced around by the strange terminology and the unfamiliar process. What a humiliating experience for them. . ." (Personal correspondence, fall 1978).

23. Cf. a public health department director, facing a planning commissioner's proposal of additional formal interagency meetings: "What you're proposing is a formal structure that'll look great on paper, but won't be operational. What we need is ongoing informal consultation and communication so we know what each other's doing—that's what works!" (K.G., Tompkins County Comprehensive Health Planning Subarea Council, 3/21/79).

24. "The normative foundation of a critical theory is implicit in the very structure of social action that it analyzes" (Bernstein 1976, p. 213).

25. To the extent that neither of these two expectations (one that the situation at hand is one in which the norms of communication are likely to be broken, a second that methods and means of checking, to compensate, are available) exists in the listener, a planner's (or any speaker's) violation of the ordinary norms of communication will be particularly dangerous and oppressive.

26. It is important to make clear, especially to those holding that conflict is everpresent in social and political life, that the propositon, *P*, that all interactions are so conflictual to be

untrustworthy sources of misrepresentation, is untenable, for then not only would checking the truth of any one position be impossible, but it would be impossible for the proposition P itself to be credible, for there to be any consensus that P was trustworthy or true. Compare the discussion of the "norm of truth" in the text.

27. See Bok (1978) for an extended discussion.

28. Assessing the distorted communications prevalent in modern bureaucracies, Ralph Hummel argues that bureaucratic organizations are characterized not by two-way communication, but by one-way information. "Bureaucracy separates man from his language. . . . The 'language' through which a bureaucracy speaks to us is not a language designed for problem-solving. Bureaucratic language is a language for passing on solutions. . ." (1977, pp. 157–159).

29. See, e.g., Mueller (1973).

30. The normative goal or ideal of organizing and opening communications ought not be dismissed as romantic or utopian, a call for infinite gentleness or listening forever—for it is a practical call to prevent noise, misinformation, unnecessary ambiguity, the misleading elevation or lowering of citizens' expectations. See Forester (1982).

31. We must beware, when we speak of opening communications, that this is not understood so narrowly as "getting more citizen input," getting more bodies to meetings. This is precisely how "input" misleads us, for it is not input, but responsibility and constructively critical political participation that are at issue.

32. See for example, Benveniste (1977).

33. When the context of a planner's description or evaluation is technical, that description or evaluation may have a pragmatic political effect in addition to that of its technical message. Paul Watzlawick writes, "The paramount communicational significance of context is all too easily overlooked in the analysis of human communication, and yet anyone who brushed his teeth in a busy street rather than in his bathroom might be quickly carted off to a police station or a lunatic asylum—to give just one example of the pragmatic effects of nonverbal communication" (1967, p. 62).

34. Ivan Illich argues, "Paradoxically, the more attention is focused on the technical mastery of disease, the larger becomes the symbolic and non-technical function performed by medical technology" (1977, p. 106).

35. Such a "clarity criterion" falls under only the first of the four universal pragmatic norms discussed above: comprehensibility, sincerity, legitimacy, and truth.

36. See, for example, Karl Mannheim (1950, 1949) and John Dewey (1927).

37. Jeffry Galper (1975) writes of professional social work practices: "In every interaction in which we engage, we encourage certain responses in others and discourage other responses. Workers who are themselves politicized . . . will offer suggestions and interpretations from this perspective. . . . [These interpretations] must clearly be offered in service to the client and not in service of political ends that are somehow separate from the situation and well-being of the client."

38. Cf. Galper: "In one sense, the virtual death of a formal welfare state organizing role is a benefit because it forces us to develop the organizing role for persons in all service-delivery positions" (1975, p. 217). In the face of fiscal conservatism and austerity budgets, planners, too, must work as organizers. See Clavel, Forester, Goldsmith, eds. (1980).

39. See, for example, Arnold Meltsner (1976) and Norman Krumholz et al. (1975); cf. the analysis of interviews with local planners in Baltimore by Howell Baum, School of Social Work and Community Planning, University of Maryland, Baltimore, Maryland 21201. (See also the sources cited in note c to table 2.)

References

Alinsky, Saul, 1971. *Rules for Radicals*. New York: Vintage Press.

Austin, John, 1961. *How To Do Things with Words*. London: Oxford University Press.

Benveniste, Guy, 1977. *The Politics of Expertise*. 2d edition. San Francisco: Boyd and Fraser.

Berger, Peter, and Thomas Luckmann, 1966. *The Social Construction of Reality*. New York: Anchor Press.

Bernstein, Richard, 1976. *The Restructuring of Social and Political Theory*. Philadelphia: University of Pennsylvania Press.

Bok, Sissela, 1978. *Lying*. New York: Pantheon.

Cavell, Stanley, 1969. *Must We Mean What We Say?* New York: Scribners.

Clavell, Pierre, John Forester, and William Goldsmith, eds., 1980. *Urban and Regional Planning in an Age of Austerity*. New York: Pergamon Press.

Dallmayr, Fred, 1974. "Toward a Critical Reconstruction of Ethics and Politics." *Journal of Politics* 37:926–957.

Dallmayr, Fred, and Thomas McCarthy, eds., 1977. *Understanding and Social Inquiry*. Notre Dame: Notre Dame Press.

Dewey, John, 1927. *The Public and Its Problems*. Denver: Henry Holt and Co.

Edelman, Murray, 1978. *Political Language*. New York: Academic Press.

Edelman, Murray, 1971. *Politics as Symbolic Action*. New York: Academic Press.

Forester, John, 1982. "Planning in the Face of Power." *Journal of the American Planning Association*, Winter, 67–80.

Forester, John, 1980a. "What Do Planning Analysts Do? Planning and Policy Analysis as Organizing" *Policy Studies Journal* 9:595–604.

Forester, John, 1980b. "Listening: The Social Policy of Everyday Life (Critical Theory and Hermeneutics in Practice)." *Social Praxis* 7:219–232.

Freire, Paulo, 1974. *Education for Critical Consciousness*. New York: Seabury Press.

Freire, Paulo, 1970. *Pedagogy of the Oppressed*. New York: Seabury Press.

Galper, Jeffry, 1975. *The Politics of Social Services*. Englewood Cliffs, N.J.: Prentice-Hall.

John Forester

Gouldner, Alvin, 1976. *Dialectic of Ideology and Technology*. New York: Seabury Press.

Habermas, Jürgen, 1979. *Communication and the Evolution of Society*. Boston: Beacon Press.

Habermas, Jürgen, 1975. *Legitimation Crisis*. Boston: Beacon Press.

Habermas, Jürgen, 1973. *Theory and Practice* Boston: Beacon Press.

Habermas, Jürgen, 1971. *Knowledge and Human Interests*. Boston: Beacon Press.

Habermas, Jürgen, 1970. *Toward a Rational Society*. Boston: Beacon Press.

Hummel, Ralph, 1977. *The Bureaucratic Experience*. New York: St. Martin's Press.

Illich, Ivan, 1977. *Medical Nemesis*. New York: Bantam Books.

Krumholz, Norman, et al., 1975. "The Cleveland Policy Planning Report." *Journal of the American Institute of Planners* 41, 5: 298–304.

Lukes, Steven, 1974. *Power: A Radical View*. London: Macmillan.

Mannheim, Karl, 1950. *Freedom, Planning and Democratic Planning*. New York: Oxford University Press.

Mannheim, Karl, 1949. *Man and Society in an Age of Reconstruction*. New York: Harcourt.

Marris, Pater, 1975. *Loss and Change*. New York: Anchor Press.

McCarthy, Thomas, 1978. *The Critical Theory of Jürgen Habermas*. Cambridge: MIT Press.

McGuire, R. R., 1977. "Speech Acts, Communicative Competence, and the Paradox of Authority." *Philosophy and Rhetoric* 10(1): 30–45.

Meltsner, Arnold, 1976. *Policy Analysts in the Bureaucracy*. Berkeley: University of California Press.

Mueller, Claus, 1973. *The Politics of Communication*. New York: Oxford University Press.

Needleman, Carolyn, and Martin Needleman, 1974. *Guerrillas in the Bureaucracy*. New York: Wiley.

Pitkin, Hanna, 1972. *Wittgenstein and Justice*. Berkeley: University of California Press.

Schroyer, Trent, 1973. *The Critique of Domination*. Boston: Beacon Press.

Schutz, Alfred, 1970. *Phenomenology and Social Relations*, ed. Helmut Wagner. Chicago: University of Chicago Press.

Searle, John, 1969. *Speech Acts*. London: Cambridge University Press.

Shapiro, Jeremy, 1976. "Reply to Miller's Review of Habermas's *Legitimation Crisis*." *Telos* 27 (Spring) 170–176.

Watzlawick, Paul, 1976. *How Real Is Real?* New York: Vintage Press.

Watzlawick, Paul, et al., 1967. *Pragmatics of Human Communication.* New York: Norton Press.

Wilensky, Harold, 1967. *Organizational Intelligence.* New York: Basic Books.

Wolfe, Alan, 1977. *Limits of Legitimacy.* New York: Free Press.

V

Models of Policy Analysis

Critical Evaluation of Public Policy: A Methodological Case Study

Frank Fischer

Critical theory has always stressed the need for a link between theory and practice. It is generally agreed, however, that its own connection to practice has remained quite abstract. The practical concerns of public policy evaluation are a case in point. The connection between the epistemological categories of critical theory and the practical objectives of policy evaluation have largely gone unexplored. For this reason policy analysts have mainly dismissed critical theory as a philosophical project of little relevance to their immediate concerns. The purpose of this chapter is to address this misconception through a methodological case study of Project Head Start, a compensatory educational program for disadvantaged children. The task is to show that the epistemological components of a critical theory have direct methodological bearing on the politics of policy evaluation.[1] The discussion also demonstrates the import of these connections for a "post-empiricist" reconstruction of the social and policy sciences.

Social Relevance as a Methodological Issue

The search for an alternative methodology for the social and policy sciences began during the latter half of the 1960s, essentially as a response to the political turmoil generated by the public policies of the Great Society. The fact that an increasing reliance on social and political research to plan and legitimate policies was sometimes accompanied by violent challenges to political authority became a source of both consternation and embarrassment to many social scientists.[2]

In sharp contrast to the self-confidence exhibited in the early 1960s by empirically oriented social scientists, the latter half of the decade brought polemical discussion and speculation about the relevance of their research to actual political problems. Complaints emanated from both ends of the political spectrum. On the right, those oriented toward the priorities of the established power structure increasingly lamented the failure of the social sciences to provide usable knowledge for social guidance and control, while on the left, those oriented toward the causes of the poor and of minorities accused the social sciences of ideological distortion and manipulation.

During periods of normative malaise, as Karl Mannheim pointed out, the academic community is often compelled to confront the epistemological issues that underlie competing political perspectives.[3] In the late 1960s and early 1970s, in disciplines such as political science and sociology, political disagreements gave rise to vitriolic epistemological debates about the role of relevance in science. In particular, these debates focused attention on the relation of knowledge to power. Who controlled the production of knowledge? And for what purpose was it employed? One result of this debate was an increasing recognition of the emergence of technocracy and the forms of social and political control associated with it.

The power of technocracy is based on a positivistically oriented empirical conception of knowledge, which is reflected in a growing inventory of operational techniques such as cost-benefit analysis, operations research, systems analysis, strategic plannning, and computer simulations.[4] Emphasizing the tenets of value-neutral objectivity, empirical operationalism, and professional expertise, modern technocracy stands or falls with the ideology of scientism. Thus, as Habermas explains, knowledge under technocracy "is defined by what the sciences do and can . . . be explicated through the methodological analysis of scientific procedures."[5] In this way, methodological research can take the form of politics at the level of theory.

The fact that empiricists frequently violate their own methodological principles should not blind us to the strategic value of their textbook precision. More than any other factor, their grip on mainstream social science is the result of their ability to say what their method is— indeed, to say it with remarkable exactitude. Moreover, it has permitted them to present their adversaries with an uncompromising demand. To those who argue for other methods of obtaining knowledge, they insist on an account of their procedures.[6]

Those who assumed the challenge have generally defined methodological research as the search for a postempiricist paradigm.[7] They have raised fundamental questions about the validity of the fact-value dichotomy and the principle of ethical neutrality, which have long informed the methodology of the social and policy sciences. In sharp contrast to the view that values are emotive responses (matters of personal conviction, taste, or faith) that lie beyond the reach of rational assessment, postempiricists argue that even the constitution of a fact, let alone a theory, is inherently tied to value assumptions lodged (explicitly or implicitly) in the foundations of the researcher's theoretical and ideological orientation. Beyond the narrow emphasis on empirical research, an adequate postempiricist methodology would have to place primary emphasis on the study of the theoretical and normative structures that guide data collection and assessments.

The search for an alternative methodology followed several separate avenues. First, there was a phenomenological orientation drawn largely from sociology. For researchers who followed this path, a relevant social science must place primary emphasis on the social actor's normative point of view. Patricia Carini and David Schuman, for example, argued that the investigator must get inside the social situation to grasp the actor's interpretations of events.[8] Carini concentrated on the elaboration of sophisticated methodological procedures for "unobtrusive" observation, while Schuman offered a detailed account of the effects of education on everyday life. Both argued that researchers must evaluate effectiveness in terms of the impressions and outlooks of the client group rather than in terms of quantitative indicators alone.

At the same time there was a resurgence of social and political philosophy. While political theorists agreed about the need to begin with the social actor's subjective viewpoint, they insisted on pushing the level of analysis beyond the relativity inherent in the social actor's own commonsense interpretations of everyday exerience. The task must also include the explication of fundamental value principles on which this experience was organized.

In this respect the critical theory of the Frankfurt school began to attract special attention. As a thoroughgoing attempt to link philosophy and science, fact and value, the work of Max Horkheimer, Theodor

Adorno, and Herbert Marcuse, followed by that of Habermas, represented a major effort to construct a theory capable of relating philosophical critique and political interpretation to everyday self-awareness. Habermas's work, which began to appear in English in the early 1970s, is a comprehensive attempt to ground epistemologically the categorical framework of this project, a critical theory and method intended to promote political consciousness and self-actualization.[9]

These phenomenological and philosophical critiques of mainstream social science methodologies raised profound epistemological issues about the empiricist treatment of the normative character of the social world. As Richard Bernstein has succinctly summarized, "they posed questions about fundamental categorical distinctions between 'theory and practice,' where 'practice' is understood as the technical application of theoretical knowledge; the distinction between empirical and normative theory, where the former is directed toward description and explication of what *is*, while the latter deals with the clarification and justification of what ought to be; the distinction between descriptive and prescriptive discourse; and the distinction between fact and value."[10]

Many mainstream social scientists were willing to accept the normative character of the problem but not the phenomenological or philosophical solutions. They were disturbed by the antiempiricism of the interpretively oriented approaches, and they advanced a third orientation closely aligned to the methodological tenets of scientific naturalism, a long-standing approach to normative theory.[11] Rather than turning to the methods of social interpretation and political critique, which offered no scientific procedures for judging among competing hypotheses, the proper response was to increase the empirical rigor of social and policy science through the adoption of a naturalistic systems framework.[12] As a rigorous teleological methodology, systems analysis shifted the empirical focus from a narrow efficiency orientation to a broader perspective emphasizing the multiple evaluation criteria of complex phenomena.[13]

Supported by a rigorous statement of systems theory and its empirical methodology, the technocratic conception of social science managed to maintain its hold on the disciplines. However, the fact that the phenomenological and philosophical approaches succeeded in staking out valid contributions suggested that something more was involved than was readily apparent. The strident tone of the debate subsided, but the problem continued to linger.

The Politics of Methodology: The Case of Head Start

The nature of this intellectual turmoil can be illustrated by anchoring these competing methodological perspectives to specific types of political arguments that emerge in a particular policy debate. For this purpose, I employ the arguments that arose in response to the findings reported in the Westinghouse Learning Corporation's evaluation study of Project Head Start.[14]

As a compensatory educational program for disadvantaged children, Head Start was a prototype of the Johnson administration's War on Poverty. To the leaders of the Democratic party it appeared as a panacea, "a quick, easy solution for the embarrassing, ever dangerous, problems of poverty, hunger, malnutrition, and explosive political alienations" that found expression in the urban riots of the 1960s.[15] Not only was the program essentially noncontroversial, and thus relatively safe in traditional political terms, it was also a reasonably inexpensive major social program. Opening in 1965, Head Start listed the following among its objectives:

Improving the perceptual, conceptual, and verbal skills of disadvantaged children.

Developing cultural and educational curiosity.

Providing better medical and dental care to poor children.

Assisting in improving the self-discipline of disadvantaged children.

Enlarging the sense of personal dignity and self-worth.

Developing a socially responsible attitude toward the community and the larger society in both the children and their parents.

Initial expectations were high. Educational psychologists spoke in glowing terms of the anticipated outcomes. (Some seemed to believe that several years of educational neglect might be compensated for in the short space of several summer sessions.) This interest and excitement was reflected in the early enrollment figures; in the first summer, more than five times the number of children initially anticipated were enrolled.

Three and a half years after the program opened its doors, negative reports began to appear. The first evaluation studies of the educational effects of the program failed to confirm the initial expectations. As Harrell Rodgers put it, "the studies showed that the . . . educational

gains tended to be small, especially for children who had not participated in year-round programs."[16] The most significant of these studies
was commissioned by the federal government. Conducted by the
Westinghouse Learning Corporation of Ohio University, a policy research organization specializing in educational affairs, the study became
the subject of a major political controversy.

The controversy was instigated by Richard Nixon, who had based
his presidential campaign in part on the "failures" of the War on
Poverty. In 1969 as part of his continuing emphasis of this theme,
Nixon presented the negative findings of the Westinghouse Report in
his economic opportunity message to the Congress on national television. Proclaiming the program "a proven failure," he triggered an
intense debate that ricocheted through Congress, the executive branch,
educational circles, and the communities of the poor. Had the research
organization in fact demonstrated the failure of the program? Did the
evidence really show that participation in Head Start had no long-
term results? Many leading social scientists were skeptical. Steeped in
the empirical techniques of mainstream social science, they questioned
whether the evaluators had used proper methodological procedures.
Were the statistical samples properly chosen? Did the empirical instruments accurately measure reading achievements? Was the ex post
facto research design inherently faulty?[17]

Equally interesting was another group of social scientists who raised
a different kind of question.[18] Supported by many leaders of poor
communities, they argued that the evaluation study employed the
wrong criteria. In basing their conclusions on a measurement of reading
scores alone, the Westinghouse evaluators showed that they had failed
to understand the nature and purpose of Head Start. The legislation,
they argued, had posited improved reading scores as only one of the
program's objectives. Equally important was the provision of socially
relevant experiences for ghetto children, such as an enlargement of
their sense of personal dignity and self-worth and the development
of socially responsible attitudes. Many sociologists and psychologists
argued that these social experiences were critical for the transition
from poverty to the middle class. Only through the experiential as-
similation of mainstram social values could these disadvantaged children
successfully function in middle-class institutions. Thus, to judge the
Head Start program a failure based on narrowly conceived empirical
measurements of individual reading scores was a methodological error.

Instead of objectively amassing empirical data from test scores, evaluators must develop subjectively relevant measures of social progress derived from first-hand experience with the disadvantaged community and its children; they must, in short, assume a phenomenological orientation.

There was a third type of argument that pertained more to the development of socially responsible attitudes toward the larger society.[19] Concerned about theoretical and ideological principles, these critics maintained that, regardless of outcomes or consequences (whether based on objective reading scores or on community-related standards), empirical measurement was an insufficient ground for judging Head Start a failure. In this view, Head Start had been designed to facilitate a basic value that must extend to all citizens in a democratic system: the right to equal opportunity. Thus, the final evaluation of such a program must rest on a normative commitment to the equal opportunity principle, regardless of its secondary or indirect consequences for other dimensions of the social system. Compensatory programs like Head Start are designed to nurture long-term harmony and stability in the social order and must be judged accordingly.

Because of the ideological foundations of this argument, in the pragmatic realm of public policy it was sometimes advanced through implicit assumptions rather than stated premises.[20] We can, however, more or less reconstruct it as follows. Equal opportunity is one of the basic legitimating principles of liberalism. In this system educational institutions (designed for social mobility through the principle of merit) are the primary vehicles for the realization of equal opportunity. Thus, in a society marked by growing social inequalities, educational programs for disadvantaged children are of critical importance. Without programs such as Head Start, explicitly designed to give material meaning to the opportunity principle, the social system is left vulnerable to what Habermas calls a "legitimation crisis." To avert the social and political turmoil that can result from a general collapse of belief systems, compensatory programs must ensure adequate socialization of disadvantaged children, the potentially problematic citizens of the future generation. At this level of analysis reading scores are of secondary importance; the program's primary contribution must be measured in terms of its basic contribution to social legitimacy. Indeed one of the primary factors that confers this legitimacy is the very existence of the program.

The foregoing arguments shared two common assumptions, one political and one methodological. All three—the empirical probe, the phenomenological concern about social relevance, and the ideological justification of equal opportunity—reflected a political concern that the Westinghouse study would be used to eliminate Head Start. As one source put it, they "feared that Congress or the Administration [would] seize upon the report's generally negative conclusion as an excuse to downgrade or discard the Head Start program."[21] These fears were justified. While the Nixon administration was never able to eliminate the Head Start program entirely, the program budget was continuously cut. As Harrell Rodgers puts it, the Westinghouse Report's "negative findings were basically accepted at face value and cost Head Start much of its support in Congress."[22]

In the social sciences the phenomenologically and philosophically oriented arguments also shared a methodological concern. For these positions the issue was how to fit the Westinghouse data into alternative theoretical and normative frameworks. No longer could empirical data based on objective criteria be offered as value-neutral evidence. Evaluators would have to recognize that criteria such as reading scores are indicators drawn from a particular conception of social life.

Comprehensive Rationality

There would appear to be little common ground among these competing perspectives. It was difficult for trained observers, let alone the average editorial reader, to form an intelligent opinion about Head Start. How to make sense of the situation became a prominent part of the public debate.

In the face of this turmoil, it is not surprising that the issue in methodological circles began to shift away from the question of "which methodological orientation is right?" to "what is the relationship among them?" Much of this reconceptualization can be attributed to Habermas's epistemological contribution.

In the late 1960s and early 1970s, Habermas began to establish a theoretical relationship between various types of knowledge and the needs and interests of particular social and political institutions.[23] Specifically, the component parts of the methodological debate in the social sciences—empirical, phenomenological, and philosophical— emerged from his analysis as "cognitive strategies" required for maintaining a stable, enduring social system. Fundamentally, society is built on these three types of knowledge, which inform the institutions that organize the basic categories of social reality: work, social interaction, and power. Each of these spheres of activity generates a form of rational knowledge that is required for social maintenance in the sphere itself, as well as in the overall system. Each of these interests serves as a particular viewpoint for apprehending one dimension of the social totality. Knowledge generated from these viewpoints is the product of their cognitive categories, which establish the methodological strategies that systematically guide inquiry; that is, they specify the modes of discovering knowledge relevant to each sphere, as well as the warrants for rational evaluation of the particular knowledge claims offered within them.

More recently Habermas has attempted to elaborate and refine his theory of comprehensive rationality by incorporating the knowledge-constituting categories of empirical and normative discourse into a theory of "communicative competence." This involves an attempt to link these modes of discourse to the structure of ordinary language and the process of argumentation. Drawing on the work of Stephen Toulmin, Habermas shows that "substantial arguments" are "pragmatic unities" that situate ordinary language sentences in relation to the basic social categories of reality (work, interaction, and power) and their respective cognitive strategies (empirical, phenomenological, and philosophical methodologies).[24]

For our present purposes, we need only recognize that a comprehensive system of rationality is a multimethodological system. As a postempirical model, it not only incorporates but also transcends its empirical data by interpreting their meaning both in the specific phenomenological context of action and as a fundamental critique of society's normative principles and axioms. In these terms a critical evaluation is one that explicates (for the purposes of discourse) the full range of empirical and normative assumptions that contribute to a particular judgment, from manifest to latent, from concrete to abstract.

While the theory of cognitive interests provides a rational basis for relating the competing methodologies to one another, we must still explore how these cognitive orientations might be employed as an integrated assessment procedure at the practical level of argumentation and evaluation. Beyond the demonstration that all three modes of rationality are component parts of a comprehensive theory of rationality, the viability of the contribution for the practice of policy evaluation will ultimately depend on our ability to specify the logical connections that integrate these cognitive strategies within the framework of a specific discourse, such as the Head Start debate. What is needed is a method of logic designed to clarify the structures and functions of the different propositions that constitute a comprehensive evaluation argument.

The objective is to translate the epistemological requirements of the three modes of inquiry into a unified framework for the discursive assessment of policy arguments. As a metastructure such a framework would provide a logical basis for judging the soundness, strength, or conclusiveness of an argument. By clarifying the nature of an evaluation's propositions, it would guide an assessment of the relevance of the different types of objections that might be validly offered as criticisms in the various phases of a discourse.

Although Habermas does not explore this more practical level of the problem, he again provides an initial insight. Pointing to Toulmin's work on "substantial arguments," Habermas maintains that the progress of knowledge takes place through explanations or justifications based on a nonpositivistic (nondeductive) "informal" logic.[25] This suggests that the place to begin the search for a logic of a unified methodology capable of interconnecting validity claims of the basic cognitive strategies is in the structural form of the substantial argument.

Toulmin's study of arguments is addressed to the problems that arise from an overreliance on the classical syllogism as a mode of inference.[26] Where positivists argue that explanations that fail to approximate the ideals of the formal syllogism are imperfect or incomplete, Toulmin has shown that such a model rests on a limited conception of logic appropriate only to various stages of inquiry, both scientific and normative. An argument in a particular "substantial" context that fails to fulfill the requirements of the formal syllogism need not be judged incomplete or irrational. Its rationality can be properly judged only by the rules of inquiry appropriate to its own context (or "knowledge domain" in Habermas's terms).

Toulmin provides a six-element representation of the logical structure of a substantial argument (figure 1). As a scheme for mapping out arguments, the elements D, W, and C parallel the model of the formal syllogism. The principal difference between the classical form and the

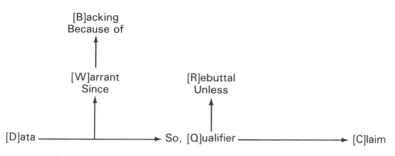

Figure 1. The structure of arguments.

substantial model is based on the introduction of Q, R, and B. Q and R express the tentative and contextual character of substantial arguments; Q expresses the degree of cogency or force attributed to a claim, while R specifies the contextual conditions under which the acceptability of the claim can be challenged. B reflects the demand for discursive redemption of the warrant. While in the classical syllogism the warrant (as major premise) tautologically establishes universal proof of the claim, in the substantial argument good reasons must be given to back a warrant. This opens the possibility of a second form of argument required to justify the use of the warrant.[27]

This second form of argument differentiates a comprehensive methodology from the conventional approach in the social sciences. Where rationality in the positivist's assessment of social action culminates with evidence on the technical efficiency of means, a comprehensive evaluation includes the justification of the warrant. But what does this form of argument look like? Beyond the pursuit of B, Toulmin has not schematically worked out this line of the model. For this purpose we can turn to the work of Paul Taylor, also writing in the informal logic tradition.[28] Taylor has sketched out the informal logic of a complete evaluation argument, that is, the way in which we give good reasons to justify a particular judgment. The remainder of this chapter will present this logic of evaluation and use it to demonstrate two essential points. First, it provides a more comprehensive, multimethodological model of rationality, which pursues the reasons given to support a judgment from the empirical evidence on technical efficiency, through the norms of the situation, to the abstract philosophical principles that back the warrant. Second, and more important for our present purposes, the method can be applied in practice for policy evaluation, as I shall illustrate with the Head Start arguments.

A Logic for Critical Evaluation

The logic of evaluation is concerned with two questions: What does it mean to evaluate something? How can such evaluations be justified? Specifically this logic focuses on the rules implicitly or explicitly followed in an attempt to judge a rule or standard to be good, to justify a goal as right, or to show that a decision to take an action ought to be made.[29]

A critical evaluation is one that systematically examines the full range of empirical and normative assumptions that contribute to a particular judgment. In this section I show how the probe of the logic of evaluation extends from concrete empirical questions to abstract normative issues concerning the subject's way of life. Specifically, this range of questions is structured around four phases that interrelate two fundamental levels of evaluation. First-order discourse, consisting of verification and validation, involves decision making based on principles fixed in the value system governing the particular decision-making process in question. In second-order discourse, composed of vindication and rational social choice, evaluation turns to questions about the acceptability of the value system itself. Each of the four phases has specific requirements that must be fulfilled in making a complete justification of a value judgment. For a reason to be considered a "good reason," it must meet all of the requirements of the four-phased probe.[30]

It is also important to note that evaluative discourse can be initiated by a problem emerging in any of the four phases of inquiry. For the purposes of systematic presentation, however, it is helpful to examine them in a formal order ranging from first- to second-order discourse.

Technical Verification of Program Objectives

Verification is the most familiar of the four phases. It is addressed to the basic empirical questions that have monopolized the attention of social and policy scientists. At this level an evaluator must seek answers to problems revolving around the three following types of questions:

Does the evaluatum (program) empirically fulfill its stated objective(s)?

Does the empirical analysis uncover secondary effects that offset the program objectives?

Does the program fulfill the objectives more efficiently than alternative means available?

The questions of technical verification (specifically concerned with measuring the efficiency of consequences) are quite familiar in policy evaluation methodology. They rest on the problems of observation, experimentation, measurement, and hypothesis testing. In Habermas's terminology, they are "empirical-analytic" questions that are organized and pursued through the analytic logic of the formal syllogism (D, W, and C) in Toulmin's model.

We recognize these concerns to be the ones that triggered the Head Start debate. The initial question raised about the Westinghouse evaluation involved empirical methodology: Was the control group adequate? Was sufficient attention paid to program variations? Was the sample random? The correspondence between technical verification in the logic of evaluation and this issue in the Head Start debate is direct and requires little further elaboration. Before passing to the next phase of the logic, however, I should add an interesting political footnote to the debate about the Westinghouse evaluation.

Even though the Westinghouse Report was widely criticized, Congress and the President basically accepted its findings and proceeded to cut the Head Start budget. At least this was the case until the advent of the Carter administration. Although it received much less fanfare than the Westinghouse study, further academic research now began to reveal different conclusions. In fact, new studies showed that participation in Head Start did improve reading and other cognitive skills. As an expert in the Office of Child Development explained, new evaluations offered "compelling evidence that early intervention works, [and] that the adverse impact of a poverty environment on children can be overcome by appropriate treatment."[31]

Most important, the new findings reflected the development of more sophisticated methodologies for measuring program outcomes. The early critics of the findings were thus correct in their initial judgments: the Westinghouse study had not adequately measured the program. This point was not lost on Democratic party politicians. Touting the legacy of Great Society programs, the Carter administration used these new results to restore part of the Head Start budget. Methodological research thus bore directly on the political outcome.

Frank Fischer

Situational Validation of Policy Goals

Criticisms directed at the technocratic conception of policy evaluation largely derive from a failure to extend evaluation beyond the verification of program objectives. From technical verification the logic of evaluation leads to questions of validation, concerned with whether the particular goals (from which the objectives are derived) are relevant to the situation. At this level, evaluation turns from the methodological principles of empirical verification to the logical rules of first-order normative discourse. As a process of reasoning that takes place within an adopted value system, the focus of discussion here centers around the following questions:

Is the objective or goal (standard or rule) relevant? Can it be justified or grounded by an appeal to principles or to established causal knowledge?

Are there circumstances in the situation that require an exception to be made to the goal?

Are two or more goals equally relevant to the situation?

Does the value system governing the evaluation place higher precedence on one of the conflicting goals? Or does it make contradictory prescriptions in such a situation?

Because they are concerned with relevance and situational circumstances, the questions of validation share a number of central concerns with the phenomenological conception of social science. Here we shall simply indicate the key connecting points. The phenomenologist's concepts of social relevance and the logic of the situation are the lifeworld counterparts to validation's questions about relevant standards and the circumstances of the situation. Being concerned with the social actor's cognitive reality (constructed from subjective experience), the phenomenologist's task is to explicate the actor's relevant rules and standards as employed in social decisions. Where the good-reasons approach focuses on the logical structures of everyday arguments, the phenomenological social scientist pursues an empirical description of the specific logics utilized by particular actors to shape the meaning and purpose of the situation under observation.[32]

Pursuing the Head Start illustration in the context of situational validation, we can begin with the recognition that those who criticized the Westinghouse conclusions for failing to employ socially relevant criteria in their study addressed issues at the level of situational validation. Countering the conclusion that Head Start failed, minority leaders and academic researchers raised two types of criticisms. The first concerned the use of multiple criteria. Minority leaders argued that the Head Start study was too narrowly conceived. They questioned the validity of reading scores as the sole criterion for judging the overall success of a program designed to improve the life opportunities of socially deprived children. Head Start was also designed to teach other types of socially relevant knowledge, such as personal health, self-discipline, and socially responsible attitudes toward the community.

Others, particularly academic researchers, focused on the methodological issues raised by the particular learning situation. Often drawing on the holistic techniques of phenomenological social scientists, they argued for the use of experience-related criteria for the contextual and longitudinal measurement of cognitive skills. If the general purpose of the program is to provide children with both the cognitive and the social skills necessary to function successfully in mainstream middle-class institutions, an evaluation must follow their life situation from Head Start into those institutions. In short, the educational development of these children must be monitored contextually through a progression of institutional situations.[33]

These turned out to be much more than partisan criticisms, as had often been suggested during the initial Head Start debate. Indeed, educational experts have attributed most of the new findings to the introduction of just these methodological improvements. Especially important was the use of new experience-related teaching techniques and their socially based measurement criteria. Even more impressive were the results achieved through longitudinal measurement: "The studies showed that Head Start is very successful in cutting down in the rate of school failure, in improving IQ scores and reading achievement, and in helping children gain self-confidence. . . . The earlier and the more exposure children had to Head Start, the greater the gains they tended to make and maintain."[34]

Systems Vindication of Value Orientations

At this point, we shift from first- to second-order discourse. The systems vindication of a value subsystem requires that the evaluation process

Frank Fischer

step outside the value orientation from which the standards and rules are drawn in the course of validation and examine their overall implications for the larger social system.

In systems vindication reasoning shifts from the logical mode of argumentation back to empirical inquiry. By requiring justification of the adoption of the value system as a whole, this phase of the logic asks whether the consequences of this commitment further specific ideals and whether living in accordance with the system is consistent with the desired way of life. Systems vindication is principally a "pragmatic test." A value system is demonstrated to have instrumental value when it is shown to be pragmatically successful in furthering certain ends of the larger system; it has contributive value if it is an essential component of the system as a whole. Deliberation here revolves around two basic questions:

Do the practical consequences resulting from a commitment to the value system facilitate the realization of the ideals of the accepted order?

Do other value systems, which reflect interests and needs in the social system as a whole, judge the consequences (as benefits and costs) to be distributed equitably?

Vindication is an empirical evaluation. Scientific knowledge and techniques are required for valid predictions of the instrumental or contributive role of a value system in realizing the ideals of a given social order. In the mainstream methodological debate, vindication reflects the concerns advanced by the advocates of the systems perspective. As a shift from the micro to the macro levels of evaluation, Habermas refers to the systems approach as "second-order technical knowledge." His purpose is to designate the relation of the more comprehensive systems framework to the first-order technical analysis of means to ends. At this level the kinds of issues examined include the physical, social, and psychological consequences that result from a specific way of life and the relevance of specific value systems to particular social situations or circumstances.

Although the empirical complexity of the questions raised in vindication are often beyond the capabilities of existing social science methodologies, it is nonetheless possible to locate the concerns of this level of evaluation in policy debates. In the case of Head Start the most salient issue at this level has been the controversy about the culture of poverty. Essentially an extension of the issue raised in situational validation, it has often taken the following form: If social researchers can empirically demonstrate that ghetto children are socialized into value systems that lack instrumentality for the American way of life, it can be argued that socially relevant experiences must be the primary criteria for the evaluation of compensatory educational programs such as Head Start.

The culture of poverty, as defined by Oscar Lewis, refers to a lower-class value system that denigrates hard work, discipline, and ambition and sacrifices future rewards for immediate gratification. The outcome is poverty resulting from slothfulness. Passed from parent to child, this value system perpetuates a "cycle" of poverty. Unable to participate in the dominant achievement-oriented culture of U.S. society, these lower social classes are incapable of pulling themselves out of their predicament.[35]

Much of the policy justification for compensatory programs such as Head Start can be traced to the argument that a culture—or more precisely a subculture—of poverty blocks the life chances of disadvantaged children. In the case of the Head Start debate, however, few of the program's critics raised empirical questions about the validity of the phenomenon per se. More typically the critics of such compensatory programs took a different line of attack. For example, Edward Banfield, a leading social scientist who supported the attack on Great Society programs, not only accepted the culture of poverty thesis but argued that the very severity of the problem put it beyond reach of government programs such as Head Start.[36] A primary source of governmental policy failures in this area, according to Banfield, was located in the unwillingness and inability of liberal reformers to address the deeper cultural differences that entrench urban poverty. Solutions effectively designed to penetrate the problem at this level would have to be massive in scope. Anything short of total intervention amounts to mere situational change, with only temporary ameliorative effects. Massive intervention, Banfield argued, is politically unacceptable to the power structure. Given existing political structures and decision rules, particularly interest group politics and incrementalism, such policy intervention would not only be too costly, it would also rest on values outside the political culture. Banfield thus rejected government antipoverty programs because they cannot be vindicated by the dominant political values of the system. At this point, he rested his case.

In the urban literature this view has been identified as a new realism based on the hard facts of the political system.

Banfield's position has been attacked from numerous liberal quarters. One such assault criticized Banfield's treatment of existing political institutions as frozen. Timothy Hennessey and Richard Feen attributed this treatment to his underlying political philosophy. Banfield, they argued, "rejects out of hand the possibility that the opinion makers' propensity to imagine a future may lead them to a view of the facts decidedly different from [his]—namely an alarming deterioration in the social and political climate in American cities which in turn impels them to use considerable skill to design realistic programs to alleviate the problem."[37]

This argument opens the way for a different line of discourse. Fundamental to the logic of evaluation is the possibility of an alternative vision of political culture. Evaluation halts at vindication only if all parties agree on the answer to the question, "Do you accept this political way of life?" It is, indeed, on this point that Banfield's most truculent critics have launched their objections. This recognition of alternative visions of a political way of life moves the argument from vindication to the next and final phase of the evaluation process, rational social choice. At this stage evaluation shifts attention from the existing or "real" culture to the pursuit of an ideal culture.

Rational Social Choice

Disparities between the standards of equity and the empirical consequences of a particular social system encountered in vindication trigger political debate about the social system itself, which ultimately leads to the philosophical concerns of the fourth level of evaluation. The transition from systems vindication to rational social choice raises the following types of questions:

Do the fundamental ideals that organize the accepted social order provide a basis for an equitable resolution of conflicting judgments?

To what extent can an unequal distribution of benefits be shown to be advantageous to all needs and interests?

If the social order is unable to resolve value system conflicts, do other social orders equitably prescribe for the relevant interests and needs that the conflicts reflect?

What is the empirical or speculative evidence that supports the justification of an alternative social order?

At the level of rational social choice, an attempt is made to establish a basis for the choice of one way of life over another. Rational choice, as employed here, is not to be confused with the decisionistic rational choice theories that have proliferated in the managerially oriented social sciences in recent years. Here it refers to the task of the classical conception of political philosophy: the construction of models of the rational way of life. Based on the identification and organization of specific values—such as equality, freedom, or community—these models can serve as a basis for the adoption of evaluative standards and norms.

The notion of rational choice in the selection of a way of life is a conceptual ideal. In describing the ideal, we must state the conditions for any person to render a fully rational choice. For this purpose we must include at least three primary conditions: freedom, impartiality, and enlightenment. To the extent that a model of a way of life is chosen in a manner that approximates these conditions, it can be legitimately employed as a basis for criteria utilized in justifying value judgments.

Each of these conditions only sets up an ideal toward which the processes of choice must be oriented. No actual choice can ever be completely free, fully enlightened, or altogether impartial; hence no choice made among alternative ways of life can be fully rational. In the real world of political conflict, argumentation at this level of evaluation characteristically takes the form of ideological debate.

Questions of rational social choice are part of the traditional concern of the philosopher. The work of John Rawls, for example, has revived general interest in the classical problems of rational social choice and in the process has become a source of heated controversy in political as well as scholarly journals.[38] Rawls is concerned with developing a method for determining the type of social order a "rational person" would choose and the reasons that would be given for that decision. To uncover the nature of such an order, he establishes a fundamental situation called the "original position." Free of distracting circumstances, the original position is a methodological device designed to assist social actors in making rational choices about values. Like Habermas's "public sphere," the device permits the participants to establish hypothetically

Frank Fischer

a social order in which each person agrees to certain basic rights and principles. In turn, these values and principles can be used as a basis for the critique of the extant social system. As Habermas explains, such critique is aimed at explicating both manifest and latent ideologies and domination in the exercise of social and political power.[39]

During the period of the Head Start debate, political philosophers, influenced by Rawls's theory of justice, focused on a number of issues that bear directly on the evaluation of compensatory educational programs. Of particular importance were the principles of equal opportunity and the nature of an egalitarian society.[40]

Those in the Head Start controversy who argued that evaluation must ultimately rest on ideological principles were essentially arguing at this level. More specifically, the exchanges regarding the relative importance of reading scores and socially relevant standards had a second-order counterpart in a debate that focused on the nature of the good society. One group contended that the good society emerges from the long-term social benefits of a meritocratic system based on the values of individual competition and native skill (generally measured as IQ). Another group stressed the advantages of pursuing an egalitarian social order founded on the values of community and fraternity. While to many observers these arguments seemed to have little practical import for the immediate issues in the debate arising from the Westinghouse evaluation, on closer examination they are essentially the theoretical counterparts of the more practical concerns surrounding the project. In short, those advocating a meritocratic social order were presenting second-order philosophical reasons for emphasizing the importance of reading scores as the primary measure of progress. Those representing the egalitarian cause were offering a second-order justification for the first-order emphasis on socially relevant standards.

One of the most interesting studies that illustrates the nature of argumentation at this level was conducted by Samuel Bowles and Herbert Gintis. In *Schooling in Capitalist America*, Bowles and Gintis sought to show that the principle of equal opportunity cannot be realized through compensatory education programs in a capitalist social order.[41] At the level of systems vindication they provided an impressive array of historical data to demonstrate that commitment to the equal opportunity principle has not led to greater equality in capitalist societies. The primary function of this principle is not, they assert, social justice but rather the facilitation of social control. By blurring the class divisions that constitute the basic realities of the educational system, belief in the principle serves as a powerful stabilizing force in capitalist societies.

Where others (such as Banfield) reject equal opportunity as an idealistic principle, Bowles and Gintis use it at the level of rational social choice to call for alternative egalitarian institutions. Rather than rejecting the equal opportunity principle because it clashes with extant political values, they employ the principle as the basis for a critique of the real values of capitalism. For them, equal opportunity can be achieved only by a radical change brought about by the adoption of socialist value principles. In short, they call for a new way of life.

Integrating Themes

I have attempted to weave together three themes: the arguments of the Head Start debate, their methodological counterparts in the mainstream social sciences, and a multimethodological logic of a critical evaluation. One way to emphasize these comparisons is to use a diagram. Following Toulmin's model, I have sketched the logical framework of a comprehensive-critical evaluation in figure 2.

A critical judgment as presented here is one that has been pursued progressively through the four phases of evaluation. The formal logic of an empirical assertion moves from D to C, mediated by a warrant backed by normative and empirical assumptions. In normal discussion these assumptions generally serve as a background consensus and are called into question only during disputes. The task of a comprehensive-critical evaluation is to make explicit these assumptions through a progressive critique extending from validation to rational social choice. It is here that we can understand Habermas's classical Aristotelian contention that in the last instance an empirical statement must be judged by its intentions for the good and true life. As reflected through the logical link of an empirical assertion to the level of rational social choice, a full delineation of the logic of an evaluative argument discloses its meaning and implications for the pursuit of a particular conception of the ideal society.

We can also show the relationship of the Head Start policy arguments and their methodological counterparts to figure 2. In the case of the policy arguments, the purpose is to illustrate how the seemingly dis-

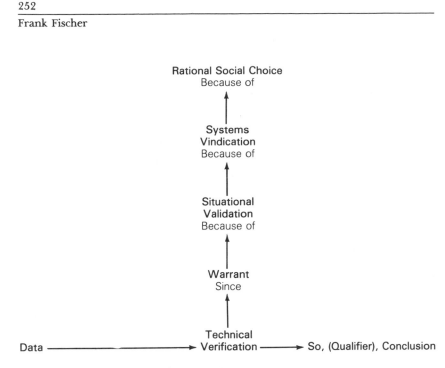

Figure 2. The logical structure of critical evaluation.

parate criticisms that emerged in response to the Westinghouse evaluation are in fact different aspects of a comprehensive evaluation.

In actual debate, most critics appear to be talking past one another. Each has chosen a specific dimension of the Head Start program as the crucial issue on which the debate is seen to turn. But as the logic of evaluation makes clear, each of these orientations is only part of a full assessment of the question. From the perspective of the methodology presented here, evaluators would present not only their empirical findings but also the full range of assumptions on which their criteria (norms and standards) were based. This would provide the basis for a systematic critical debate that would explore the full range of issues, from evidence to principles. In table 1, the issues at each level of the Head Start debate are related to their level of evaluation. The table also shows the relationship of their respective methodological orientations to the logic of evaluation.

Concluding Comments

The nature of the critical evaluation method offered here is bound to generate controversy, especially among critical theorists. Some have

Table 1
Head Start arguments and methodological issues

Head Start arguments	Methodology of critical evaluation	Methodological debate
Principle of equal opportunity	Rational social choice	Political philosophy
Culture of poverty	Systems vindication	Systems perspective
Socially relevant experiences	Situational validation	Phenomenological approach
Measuring reading scores	Technical verification	Empirical analysis

argued that an effort to pin down the logic of a critical social science is a violation of its basic objective, an emancipatory discourse for political self-determination. In this view the very attempt to say what the rules of such a method are is to introduce intellectual constraints. For this reason it is important to be clear about what I have attempted here. While such criticisms are indeed relevant to the processes of critical reflection, the task has not been to offer specific methodological procedures for this level of evaluation. Instead, the purpose has been to clarify the logic of the relationship between critical reflection and the phenomenological and empirical modes of inquiry in evaluative discourse. In the context of a struggle to supplant the dominant technocratic patterns in the social and policy sciences, the ability to specify the logical connections between empirical and normative discourse in specific policy arguments is essential to open and expand the scope of the mainstream dialogue.

Few political science and sociology departments teach critical theory, let alone integrate its components into their methodology courses. In the absence of methodological specification, critical social science will continue to be relegated to the softer side of the curriculum—philosophy and the history of ideas. For some, especially philosophers and intellectual historians, this will present no particular problem. But for those engaged in the trenches of mainstream social science— teaching subjects such as policy evaluation, urban planning, or research methodology—much depends on the attempt to bring the concepts of critical theory into the disciplines. If we are to train a new generation of social scientists to reject positivism and technocracy, we must be able to provide alternative methodologies for science and decision making.

The effort here has been designed to address this need. In this regard one of its most important advantages for a methodological politics is its ability to undermine the technocratic conception of knowledge on its own terms. By systematically relating the normative questions of phenomenology and political philosophy to the deductive syllogism of the empirical sciences, technical-instrumental knowledge is reduced to a component of a larger inferential process. Moreover, its relationship to questions about the good life is schematically portrayed.

Empiricists typically dismiss phenomenological and philosophical analyses by suggesting that they are concerned with other types of questions and concerns. By implication, empirical and normative theories can therefore be developed in relative isolation, a reality reflected in the departmental character of the modern curriculum. The methodological error behind this separation is clarified, however, by a full delineation of the logic of evaluation. The modes of inquiry—empirical science, phenomenology, and political philosophy—are shown to be interrelated components of a comprehensive-critical judgment. Each has its own type of data and internal logic, but none can stand entirely alone. As coexisting perspectives on the same social reality, they are the components of a larger inferential process. Integrating the range of normative and empirical perspectives, the methodological framework suggests the dimensions of a postempiricist theory of rationality.

At this stage the method is advanced more as a project than as a finished product. As an exploration of relatively uncharted territories, it is designed to open a new direction and to expand the contemporary academic dialogue. Ultimately, of course, the value of the method will depend on its usefulness as an alternative tool for the critical assessment and evaluation of policy arguments. In the interim, its discussion is aimed at encouraging others to join in and take up the methodological challenge.

Notes

1. The methodological framework presented here is based on insights drawn from Jürgen Habermas's critical theory. He established the agenda and developed the direction. But the

proposed method is in no way the product of explicit textual exegesis. As a suggestive beginning, it is a synthesis of interrelated contributions by Habermas, Stephen Toulmin, and Paul Taylor.

2. For a general discussion, see Frank Fischer, *Politics, Values, and Public Policy: The Problem of Methodology* (Boulder, Colo.: Westview Press, 1980), pp. 1–64.

3. Karl Mannheim, *Ideology and Utopia* (New York: Harcourt, Brace and World, 1936), pp. 13–54.

4. Wolf V. Heydebrand, "Technocratic Corporatism," in *Organization Theory and Public Policy*, ed. Richard Hall and Robert Quinn (Beverly Hills: Sage, 1983), pp. 93–114.

5. Jürgen Habermas, *Knowledge and Human Interest* (Boston: Beacon Press, 1972), p. 67.

6. See Richard J. Bernstein, *The Restructuring of Social and Political Theory* (New York: Harcourt Brace Jovanovich, 1976). Bernstein formulates the empiricist position in this way: "Whatever disagreements there may be about the characteristics of the natural sciences, mathematics and logic, there can be no doubt that these disciplines are the exemplars of warranted knowledge. One of the depth motivations for restricting the domain of legitimate knowledge to these disciplines or those which have been molded upon them, was the revulsion against the belief that there are other forms of knowledge and other means of gaining knowledge. Positivists claimed that when we examine these other pretenders to knowledge, we discover they lack what is characteristic of scientific knowledge: rational prcedures for testing, validating and rejecting hypotheses."

7. Ibid., p. xvi.

8. Patricia F. Carini, *Observation and Description: An Alternative Methodology for the Investigation of Human Phenomena* (Grand Forks, N.D.: University of North Dakota Press, 1975); and David Schuman, *Policy Analysis, Education, and Everyday Life* (Lexington, Mass.: D. C. Heath and Co., 1982).

9. See Martin Jay, *The Dialectical Imagination* (Boston: Little, Brown, 1973); and Jürgen Habermas, *Theory and Practice* (Boston: Beacon Press, 1973).

10. Bernstein, *Restructuring*, p. 173.

11. On the limitations of the phenomenological and philosophical approaches, see David Easton, "Commentary on Lane's Paper," in *Integration of the Social Sciences Through Policy Analysis*, ed. James C. Charlesworth (Philadelphia: American Academy of Political and Social Science, 1972), p. 92. Easton argued that the critics were correct about the failure of the social sciences to deal with value orientations but were wrong in their responses. Phenomenology and philosophy, in this view, were inferior solutions because they provided no procedures for judging among competing hypotheses. For Easton and other empiricists, they offered little more than a return to the earlier philosophical methods of intuition and speculation. Some complained that they simply represented a revived liberal arts program.

12. For a discussion, see Fischer, *Politics*.

13. George J. Graham, Jr., and Scarlett G. Graham, "Evaluating Drift in Policy Systems," in *Problems of Theory in Policy Analysis*, ed. Phillip M. Gregg (Lexington, Mass.: D. C. Heath and Co., 1976), pp. 77–87. Macroevaluation, Graham explains, "links the determinants and the consequences of social policy, including comparative investigation of the relationship between policy processes and such system characterizing variables as the social structure, political institutions (political pluralism, groups, parties), governmental policy making and policy executing structures, and constitutional and ideological constraints." The systems-level of evaluation is introduced to establish "parameters and clarify the limitations that will invariably constrain

and reduce available courses of public action." As a macroevaluative framework, the systems perspective provides a means for techniques pursued under the rubric of policy analysis. Such an orientation offers the methodological basis for a more informed assessment of value goals than the standard conception of means-ends analysis.

14. *The Impact of Head Start: An Evaluation of the Effects of Head Start on Children's Cognitive and Affective Development*, Study by the Westinghouse Learning Corporation (Athens: Ohio University, July 12, 1969).

15. Harrell Rodgers, "Head Start—Where Are the Headlines Now?" *Dissent* (Spring 1979): 234.

16. Ibid., p. 235.

17. Walter Williams and John W. Evans, "The Politics of Evaluation: The Case of Head Start," in *Evaluating Social Programs*, ed. Peter Rossi and Walter Williams (New York: Seminar Press, 1972), pp. 249–264; see also M. S. Smith and J. S. Bissell, "Report Analysis: The Impact of Head Start," *Harvard Educational Review* 40 (Winter 1970): 51–105.

18. Williams and Evans, "The Politics of Evaluation."

19. See Edmund W. Gordon, "Guidance in the Urban Setting," in *Opening Opportunities for Disadvantaged Learners*, ed. Harry Passow (New York: Teachers College Press, 1972), p. 213.

20. The best guide to the general outline of this argument is Samuel Bowles and Herbert Gintis, *Schooling in Capitalist America* (New York: Basic Books, 1976). For a guide to the political arguments in support of the initiation of the Head Start program, see "Head Start, A Retrospective View: The Founders," in *Project Head Start*, ed. Edward Zigler and Jeanette Valentine (New York: Free Press, 1979), pp. 43–134. As president, Lyndon Johnson announced plans to extend the project with these words: "We have reached a landmark not just in education, but in the maturity of our democracy. The success of this year's Head Start program—and our plans for the years to come—are symbols of this nation's commitment to the goal that no American child shall be condemned to failure by the accident of his birth."

21. *New York Times*, cited by Williams and Evans, "Politics of Evaluation," p. 263; and Walter Williams, *Social Policy Research and Analysis* (New York: American Elsevier Publishing Company, 1971), pp. 103–130.

22. Rodgers, "Head Start," p. 235.

23. Jürgen Habermas, *Knowledge and Human Interest* (Boston: Beacon Press, 1971), pp. 301–317; also see Thomas McCarthy, *The Critical Theory of Jürgen Habermas* (Cambridge: MIT Press, 1978), for the best methodological explication and interpretation of Habermas's project.

24. In reference to substantial arguments, see Jürgen Habermas, *Legitimation Crisis* (Boston: Beacon Press, 1975), p. 107.

25. Ibid.

26. Stephen Toulmin, *The Uses of Argument* (Cambridge: Cambridge University Press, 1958).

27. Ibid.

28. Paul W. Taylor, *Normative Discourse* (Englewood Cliffs, N.J.: Prentice-Hall, 1961).

29. Ibid.

30. For a detailed guide to these phases of evaluation, see Fischer, *Politics*.

31. Bernard Brown, "Long-Term Gains from Early Intervention: An Overview of Current Research" (Paper presented at the 1977 annual meeting of the American Association for the Advancement of Science, Denver, Colorado, February 23, 1977).

32. See Fischer, *Politics*.

33. Barbara Dillion Goodson and Robert D. Hess, "The Effects of Parent Training Programs on Child Performance and Parent Behavior" (Paper presented at the 1977 annual meeting of the American Association for the Advancement of Science, Denver, Colorado, February 23, 1977).

34. Rodgers, "Head Start," p. 235.

35. Oscar Lewis, *Five Families: Mexican Case Studies in the Culture of Poverty* (New York: Basic Books, 1959). The debate over this hypothesis triggered the publication of a number of controversial studies, including the Moynihan Report and Banfield's *Unheavenly City*. U.S. Department of Labor, Office of Policy Planning and Research, *The Negro Family*, prepared by Daniel Patrick Moynihan (Washington, D.C.: Government Printing Office, 1965); and Edward C. Banfield, *The Unheavenly City: The Nature and Future of Our Urban Crisis* (Boston: Little, Brown, 1970).

36. Banfield, *Unheavenly City*.

37. Timothy M. Hennessey and Richard H. Feen, "Social Science as Social Philosophy: Edward C. Banfield and the 'New Realism' in Urban Politics," in *Varieties of Political Conservatism*, ed. Matthew Holden, Jr. (Beverly Hills: Sage, 1974), p. 29.

38. John Rawls, *A Theory of Justice* (Cambridge, Mass.: Belknap Press, 1971).

39. Habermas, *Knowledge and Human Interest*, p. 310.

40. See, for example, James Fishkin, *Justice, Equal Opportunity and the Family* (New Haven: Yale University Press, 1983). On compensatory education and Head Start, see pp. 68-74.

41. Bowles and Gintis, *Schooling in Capitalist America*.

The Policy Analysis–Critical Theory Affair: Wildavsky and Habermas as Bedfellows?

John Forester

Introduction

Policy analysis and critical theory might seem to be unlikely marriage partners, but that may simply be because they haven't met yet. This paper will introduce the two to one another, but it takes no responsibility for the outcome of the relationship. Whether or not there's a match here depends upon far more than any introduction can do.

The combination of critical theory and policy analysis might raise eyebrows for yet other reasons. Considering the work of Aaron Wildavsky (1979) as paradigmatic here, policy analysis seems quite earthy, pragmatic if not celebrating realpolitik, proud of realism, boasting of relevance, utility, access to power, and political savvy.[1] Critical theory, in contrast, seems rarified, systematic and philosophical but not practical, doubting realism as naiveté, warning that our commonplace sentiments may be mere liberal ideology; here we may consider the work of Jürgen Habermas (1970, 1973, 1975, 1979), for example.[2] The policy analyst speaks of feasibility, costing out alternatives, impact analysis, and market solutions; the critical theorist speaks of systematically distorted communications, speech acts, practical claims-making, and someone named "Hermene-U-Tics." Is it possible that these two animals live in the same world and care about the same things?

The policy analyst and the critical theorist are also each a bit envious of the other; for each, the other's strength is their own weakness. The policy analyst is strong on organizational and budgetary analysis, but rather blind to many of the systematic philosophical and ethical problems nested in the impressive-sounding claims of their products: policy analyses and evaluations (for a discussion of these problems see MacRae 1976, Fischer 1980, Churchman 1979). The critical theorist is strong on philosophy and ethics, strong on the dangers of a tempting pragmatism and so-called professional ethics, but rather weak in the analysis of concrete organizations and institutions that carry out policies in practice.[3] In the abstract, each needs the other; in the concrete, each has little patience with the other's style.

Yet the analyst hungers for more powerful ways of understanding political action and the significance of alternative government actions; "costs and benefits" are only poorly measured, and the difficulties of interpreting the significance of the various possible outcomes of differing policy proposals present recurring, unavoidable problems (see, e.g., Rein 1976, Dunn 1981). If the critical theorist can help the policy analyst watch out for important problems, for obstacles to implementation, for likely sources of poor information, the analyst may listen (see Forester 1980, 1982a). The critical theorist is far from self-sufficient either: critical theory works supposedly to inform the possibilities of emancipatory, freedom-seeking political action; yet the analysis of institutional conditions that enhance or thwart such action, such "praxis," again presents recurring, unavoidable problems to be faced (see, e.g., Cohen 1979, Honneth 1979). If the policy analyst can help the critical theorist understand questions of the organizational dynamics of power and the strategic side of interorganizational conflict, the theorist may listen (see, e.g., Lukes 1974).

The Personalities

There are still other reasons for these two to be interested in one another. Both the policy analyst and the critical theorist say nobly that they are interested in the conditions of social and political learning (see Lindblom and Cohen 1979, ch. 2, Wildavsky 1979, ch. 10, Habermas 1979, ch. 3). Both say that they seek to improve the quality of citizens' interactions that are shaped, regulated, and structured by public policymaking and state action. The policy analyst is concerned with efficiency and redistribution; the critical theorist is concerned with the same tension, altered a bit: the dialectic between technological progress and social learning, between the development of the forces of production and that of the relations of production (see Habermas

1979, ch. 4). The optimism of each is the pessimism of the other. The analyst hopes that productivity will enable ever more distribution through the workings of markets; the critical theorist despairs that ever greater private capital accumulation may only tighten the control of corporate capital upon labor and then export dependency as imperialistic aid (see O'Connor 1979). The analyst periodically fears that "politics" will replace "markets," thus enormously increasing the demands for governance in the polity (see Lindblom 1977, part two). The critical theorist, in contrast, hopes that social and labor movements will coalesce to democratize investment decision-making in the society (see Wolfe 1977). Then the effective governing of the polity by capital may be wrestled away and transformed into legitimate processes of political participation and membership.[4] The analyst wants the market to solve as many problems of decision-making as possible; the critical theorist, however, wants democratic politics to govern investment decisions. The analyst has the market, however, imperfect, as it now exists to work with; the critical theorist has democratic traditions to appeal to, some socialist experience to evaluate critically, and a better day to look forward to and work toward. Yet these days, though the policy analyst has several lovers in Washington, the critical theorist is more likely to be enjoying other pleasures.

Friends of both know the secrets being kept here, of course. The policy analyst worries about market imperfections and the nagging problems of being "second-best," which in the market may be far, far from best (see, e.g., Lancaster and Lipsey 1956–57). The critical theorist worries about the assessment of legitimacy, and the problems of distinguishing a true from false consensus or manipulated agreements from truly consensual ones (this is the problem forcefully raised, if hardly finally resolved, by Habermas 1975, part III). Naturally, each projects their worries as skepticism toward the other.

To the analyst who argues that market interactions should distribute services, the critical theorist cries that the market is often rigged, imperfect, subject to horrendous information imperfections and problems of monopoly, to say nothing of the exploitation of labor and the appropriation of surplus. To the critical theorist who argues that truly democratic politics would solve the analyst's problems, or that the correction of ideological distortions of communication could solve policy problems, the analyst asks simply, "How? How will you 'democratize' the state's agencies and all of the economy as well? Where's the experience that shows this can be done? Do you even have an articulate democratic theory of administration? A notion of 'democratizing' (replacing?) large-scale bureaucracies? Show me!"

The Rub

The policy analyst is unabashedly and proudly a liberal, classically conservative and distrustful of government. The critical theorist is humbly and faithfully a democrat, attuned to the responsibilities of membership and watchful for the domination of either the many by the few or the few by the many. Both share but hide one deep wish: to avoid the embarrassment they each feel in knowing that "liberal democracy" is a contradiction in terms, and that liberal democracies are contradictions in deed. If such opposites always attracted one another, this would surely be a match made in heaven. Yet here on earth, the two visions pull in quite different directions (see Burton and Murphy 1980).

Skeptical of politics, the policy analyst will trade a bit of democracy (not quite sure what it means) and a lot of participation (sure enough what that means!) for a well-functioning market. The critical theorist is appalled, of course. The theorist, in contrast, linking exchange to commodification to exploitation, will gladly trade a lot of market (knowing well enough what it means) and a lot of consumer sovereignty (not quite sure what that means) for more pervasive democratic decision-making. To adapt from Isaac Kramnick, the analyst as liberal will pursue safety and the "freedom to choose," even when information about what's to be had is quite poor; the critical theorist as democrat will pursue the health of the polity and the responsible virtues of democratic membership, even when notions of health may be contested.[5] Both argue to take their own risks—and to define those risks to be taken by members of society at large.

Who imposes risks upon whom? Ultimately, which risks are borne by the public is a question of power. While it may reflect little on the ultimate merits of their arguments, today policy analysts bask in the light of the powerful in office; thus they may be quite tempted to entertain the illusion that the risks and market imperfections that they condone and accept for the public at large are somehow justified or "legitimate." (A recent popular account is Halberstam 1972.) Yet they hardly need a critical theorist of any sophistication to ask the embarrassing question, "since when did established 'might' make 'right'?" Policy analysts inevitably face the question of the legitimacy of various public policy options, whether they appeal to "let the market decide" or not (see Schaar 1970, 1981).

Rejecting "politics" supposedly, the policy analyst acts on the fear of bureaucratic or authoritarian domination by appealing to market interactions of diverse consumers presumably able to make decisions about their wants and needs for themselves (see "Two models" in Lindblom 1977; also Wildavsky 1979, especially ch. 5). Political interactions between citizens, representatives, decision-makers, and administrators are thought too complex, too unwieldy, and certainly not feasible to recommend in practice. Market interactions, then, are deemed a good substitute by the policy analyst, and a substitute with a morally ironic advantage: the market diffuses, if not avoids, political responsibility, diminishing the moral burdens upon decision-makers and spreading these not to citizen participants of political structures but rather to consumers, each presumably a sovereign unto (traditionally) himself. (For related discussions of liberalism, see Lowi 1969, Leiss 1976, Hirsch 1976, Marcuse 1964.) Self-deception is rampant here, the critical theorist thinks. Consumer sovereignty is a myth; and the private and corporate control of investments profoundly affecting citizens' health, safety, and quality of life hardly produces conditions of political freedom.

As one might have already gathered, there is no easy match here: some excitement and passion perhaps, but when the time comes to part company, there will be little love lost. These two have common problems, but that will not keep them together. The struggles between market advocates and democrats will persist, certainly as long as the control of capital remains in corporate hands, democratically unaccountable, and perhaps they will confront us as well after any democratization of investment (and accumulation) that might be achieved.[6]

The Tasks Remain

If it is true that these struggles will persist regardless of the most fundamental (re)structuring of relations of power and authority in society, then we should ask what there is to be learned from the passions and conflicts of the arranged meeting bringing policy analyst and critical theorist together. For indeed, though the romance of the two was fated not to be, we may have much to learn from the arguments at hand. Pulling politically in two quite different directions, the critical theorist and the policy analyst nevertheless share a fundamental interest in the practical political evaluation of public policy proposals. However much the analyst celebrates or the critical theorist despairs that particular policies must now be understood within the context of capitalist domestic and world market relations, the concrete tasks of policy analysis remain.

As the policy analyst knows only too well, myriad complexities often threaten to overwhelm any hope of producing analyses of great precision and accuracy (see, e.g., Rein 1976, Fischer 1980). Information about past policies is difficult enough to get; information about future consequences of not one but several alternative proposals is almost impossible to obtain in any detail. Aggregate economic forecasts may be made, and demographic projections computed, but intervening variables of all sorts threaten to make any precise disaggregated predictions barely credible. These are problems of gathering adequate facts.

To make matters worse, the criteria by which to evaluate the significance of various future outcomes are multiple, incommensurable, not easily quantifiable, and logically conflicting. Are health benefits for an unemployed poor person worth as much, more, or less than the housing assistance for elderly widows? Even if there is no choice to be made between the two, how are such potential results of policy adoption (e.g., in alternative budget allocations) to be "measured" and compared? As Jan Dekema writes, such comparisons of incommensurables leads us beyond the consideration of transforming the "value," whatever that is, of each outcome into utilities—to practical political considerations of political identity and direction (see Dekema 1981). As the analysts' utility-measuring apparatus becomes evermore inadequate in the face of such complexity, political and moral decisions are called for. Here the insights of the critical theorist may help us to understand just what, and how much is at stake in policy analysis.

Policy as Productive and Reproductive, "Cogitative" and "Interactive"

For like the policy analyst, the critical theorist understands that policies shape and remake structures of action and "interaction," as Wildavsky puts it.[7] Policies may produce direct results or services as, for example, when public health nurses are paid by taxpayers' dollars to provide citizens with nursing care. Policies may also, however, set the stage upon which citizens then buy and sell, offer and accept services, and so on—as when physicians' services are reimbursed by public dollars for Medicare and Medicaid patients. Either way, policy making shapes personal experience. In the first case policies are directly productive; in the second case the policies are reproductive, for they reproduce a set of economic, professional, or political positions or roles. Tariffs, for example, may protect the economic status of manufacturers; government reimbursement for medical care reinforces the traditional power of the physician to control patients' medical care (lay practitioners, for example, may not be reimbursed); and civil rights legislation seeks to protect the basic political status of citizens supposedly entitled to certain rights by the constitution. Policies thus may produce direct results, but they reproduce social, political, and economic status, rights, and roles as well.

Policy analysts like Wildavsky speak of the productive/reproductive distinction as that between policy in pursuit of "cogitation" (policy seeking a comprehensive, cognitive "problem-solving" decision regarding what to produce for whom at what time and in what quantities) and policy in pursuit of "interaction" (policy seeking to establish a framework of interaction in which citizens can decide, supposedly by and for themselves, what they want and need and how they will spend their time, energy, and resources accordingly) (see Wildavsky 1979, ch. 5; cf. Lindblom and Cohen 1979). Wildavsky suggests that every policy may well combine elements of both cogitation and interaction, thus productive elements and reproductive ones as well.[8] This insight might suggest to critical theorists that policies ought not be distinguished as productive *or* reproductive, but that in practice they combine both aspects: a policy then might not only achieve one instrumental, productive outcome, but it might well also serve to reproduce particular concrete economic, political, and social institutional relations.

While the productive side of policy development is usually quite visible in terms of the instrumentally intended outcomes desired, the reproductive side of policymaking may be far less visible, far more subtle, but every bit as important. Can these reproductive dynamics of policy development be assessed systematically? Here, actually, the critical theorist may be quite practically helpful, for the critical theorist can provide an analysis of "interaction" that applies a powerful and systematic theory of ordinary communicative action.

The Policy Analysis of "Interaction" and "Learning"—and Distinguishing the Two

Somewhat curiously sharing Wildavsky's policy analytic insight, critical theorists recognize that the problems of political interaction, or politically staged interaction via policymaking, are closely connected to the evaluation of the conditions that enable social and political learning.[9] Liberals have long celebrated the market as a learning mechanism; and so too have democratic theorists, organizers, and "their" policy analysts alike sought to articulate an account of democratic political interactions that would represent a politically coherent alternative learning process (see Pateman 1970, Walzer 1980). Critical theory may help here as well.

Suspicious of markets, though, the critical theorist is quick to point out to the policy analyst that the mere fact of policy-created "interaction" ought not be equated with social, political, or economic "learning" in any dignified and nontrivial sense of the latter term. For if learning is to refer to some enhanced competence for action and self-understanding among members of the affected public, then the simple existence of *any* interaction will not constitute learning.[10] If a policy encouraging oil exploration reproduces consumer-monopolist interactions on the market, consumers and suppliers may exchange signals, but little learning will take place. Indeed, in the absence of antitrust efforts, market information under these conditions will be quite distorted, imperfect, and misrepresentative of "true costs of production"— a fact that the consumer will never learn as a participant in a monopoly-dominated interaction. Where policies produce or influence interaction, then, there is not yet necessarily learning.

To the extent that social, political, and economic learning are valued, then, the analysis of those conditions that facilitate learning must be distinguished from, and not confused with, the analysis of the form and content of citizens' interactions.[11] Forms of "interaction" and "learning" may coincide, but they very well may not. It is one thing to say that entitlement to third-party reimbursement for medical care may extend coverage (interaction) to persons unable to pay for that care themselves; it is another thing to point out that such reimbursement "hides" from patient and physician alike the costs of providing particular services (an issue of learning). Thus, policy analysts face two analytical problems:

1. First, they must be able to assess the character of interactions fostered, protected, encouraged, or structured (reproduced) by policy development.

2. Second, they must then be able to isolate the influences enabling or thwarting actual social, political, and economic learning.

If critical theorists are right that policy analysts like Wildavsky may fail to distinguish clearly the dynamics of interaction from the precarious contingency of genuine learning processes, then the burden falls to the critical theorists to provide the required analyses here. Let us consider each problem in turn.

The Critical Theorist's Contribution to the Analysis of Interaction

While policy analysts seem to list quite easily different kinds of inter-actions (bargaining, voting, market exchange, negotiation, arbitration, and so on) produced by policies, there seems to be little systematic analysis by policy analysts of many of these forms of interaction (how-ever much attention *has* been paid to one of these forms: market interactions).[12] Critical theorists, on the other hand, might consider these various sorts of interaction as more or less imperfect progeny of a paradigm type of social action: that one oriented to reaching mutual understanding, what critical theorists call "communicative ac-tion."[13] To provide the foundation for an analysis of policy-promoted interactions more generally, let us consider briefly the ideal-typical and paradigmatic case of ordinary communicative action.

In communicative action, one person seeks to gain another's under-standing. Here, the critical theorist's analysis of "speech acts" (promises, offers, threats, and questions, for example), suggests that all com-municative action, and thus derivatively interaction, depends for its successful performance on the ability or competence of speakers (actors) to make and offer for acceptance, doubt, or rejection, to listeners (other actors) four inseparable but analytically distinct claims:

i. That what is said is true (or refers to something truly existing);

ii. That what is said is properly in context—that it is legitimately said;

iii. That the speaker is sincere, means what he or she says; and

iv. That the utterance is clear and meaningful in the language at hand.

Writing a check in a grocery store, for example, works as successful communicative action only if the grocer correspondingly accepts:

i. The "truth claim" that "there's money to cover this in the bank" (whether this is explicitly uttered or not);

ii. The "legitimacy claim" that the check is issued properly by a reputable bank, or that the check is indeed a proper mechanism of payment (thus it is not accepted in the "express—no checks" line!);

iii. The "sincerity claim" that the person writing the check does mean to pay, and thus will not go to the nearest telephone and ask the bank to stop payment on the check; and finally

iv. The "comprehensibility or meaningfulness" claim that the writing of a signature on a particular piece of paper indeed counts as writing a check, so that the act is intelligible, independent of the other judgments regarding truth, legitimacy, and sincerity.

This analysis of communicative action becomes particularly interesting for the purposes of policy analysis if we now ask a specific practical question. What happens not from the speaker's point of view in communicative action, but from the listener's point of view? What do we find? As truth claims are ordinarily accepted by citizens, their *knowledge and beliefs* are changed. As citizens accept or reject legitimacy claims, they grant or withhold their *consent* to others' actions. Similarly, as sincerity claims are accepted or doubted, so *trust* is given or withheld. And finally, as meaning claims are ordinarily accepted, so is citizens' *attention* directed selectively. The critical theorist's reconstruction of ordinary communicative action, thus, points to the heart of social action and "interaction" more generally: the recreation in everyday life of particular relations of belief-construction, consent-granting, trust-giving, and attention-investment. If we generalize from the paradigm case, then, we see that what is at stake in all policy-promoted interactions are the contingent, vulnerable, and perhaps distorted, practical productions of citizens' knowledge or ignorance, consent or resistance, trust or suspicion, and attention or neglect.[14]

Consider an example. In New York State, the policy providing work-men's compensation insurance to workers injured at the workplace produces a direct, if questionably sufficient, benefit—the payment to the worker (when one is awarded)—but the policy also reproduces a particular structure of social and political-economic interactions as well. First, the legislation not only purports to provide just and fair compensation, but it proscribes legal suits by the injured worker against the employer.[15] Socializing employers' risk, then, the legislation hinders the ability of workers to call legally and morally into question the responsibility of their employers to maintain safe and decent working conditions. Second, because the legislation creates supposed "market incentives" rather than worker-employer negotiations to mitigate or prevent future injuries or illnesses, the policy provides a safety valve for worker-employer conflict, but it does little to promote trust and mutual learning among the parties at hand (see extensive discussion in Berman 1978, ch. 4). Third, because it avoids addressing the dif-ficulties of measuring and attempting to provide compensation for occupationally related diseases, the operation of the legislation works to distract attention from workers' vulnerability to such disease, and it directs attention instead to the problems of accidents, injuries, and individual accommodation and adjustment (Berman 1978, ch. 4).

Vulnerable at work, then, workers covered by workmen's com-pensation may nevertheless receive some compensation just as they simultaneously give up the ability to sue parties who may be responsible for their injury; their trust in the employer's good will to prevent future injuries may be minimal, hardly fostered by policy; and their attention is then directed to the (in)adequacies of after-the-fact com-pensation rather than to altered relations of control, design changes, or safety measures that might be instituted in the workplace. Without providing any mechanism for discussion and learning about hazards in each specific workplace, the legislation thus reinforces:

1. Workers' lack of knowledge, their ignorance of health conditions affecting their lives (until it is too late and they show up filing workmen's compensation claims);

2. Their distrust of employer "cooperation," and their increased sense of worker-employer conflict;

3. Their impotence and lack of control regarding the conditions of their work; and

4. Their inability to pay attention to problems of industrial disease and available workplace health and safety preventive measures.

Once again, then, we may see, here, that just as in all communicative action, what is at stake in the forms of interaction produced by public policies is the practical day-to-day management, or reproduction, of citizens':

1. Beliefs, knowledge, or ignorance;

2. Consent or deference, informed or not so;

3. Trust and relations of cooperation or, alternatively, of suspicion, rivalry, and distrust; and

4. Attention-payment and relative neglect (cf. Forester 1982a,b).

If policy analysts regard the interactions produced by policies to include activities as apparently diverse as bargaining, negotiation, voting, and buying and selling on the market, they run a particular ironic risk. Analysts may successfully find interactive mechanisms to avoid the responsibility of detailed policy specification (Wildavsky's "cogitation"), but by so delegating decision-making responsibility to interactive processes in the larger society, they may be peculiarly unable to evaluate and assess the actual consequences of so diffusing that responsibility. It is one thing to appeal ideologically to the multitudes of citizen decision-makers, consumer-sovereigns, or voters, that might now make decisions by and for themselves, but it is another task, and still the task of policy analysts, to teach us about the collective, public, and social consequences of alternatively available policy interactions. To do this, though, policy analysts require at the very least a systematic account of such interactions, and this is precisely what the critical theorist's analysis of communicative action provides. Policy analysis that recognizes the centrality of "interaction" must therefore rest upon a powerful theory of action, and that theory of action is the heart of the critical theorist's concern.

Policy Analysis and the Inevitable Judgment of Legitimacy

Yet the analysis of interaction is not yet an assessment of social learning. Thus, policy analysts need to be able to assess the ways in which policies encourage or hamper social and political learning, given that policies may structure citizen interactions in any of a number of ways.[16]

Clearly, citizens do not "learn" through interactions in which information is systematically distorted, for example, by monopolists distorting price signals or by political ideologists misrepresenting the
likely costs, benefits, and virtues of their favored proposals. When
industrial polluters dismiss claims that their toxic wastes may be causing
health problems, or when they hire consultants to do the same, the
intelligent citizen might well be skeptical. Yet so far there is interaction,
query, claim, and skepticism, but there is not yet any appreciable
learning (except perhaps that the company may not be cooperative
in furnishing chemical lists complete with itemized toxic effects). If
the mere existence of interaction does not suffice to promote learning,
the critical theorist may again have something practical to contribute
to the complex evaluative work of policy analysis.

The difficult issue here is this one: how can we distinguish true
social, political, and economic learning from manipulation, deliberate
distortion, rigged negotiations, stacked votes, and so on? Answering
this question requires an analysis of the *legitimacy* of learning interactions, or conversely, analysis of the avoidable institutional barriers
to relatively open, undistorted, and uncoerced social and political discourse. Thus it is easy to see why policy analysts have been reluctant
to distinguish carefully the mere existence of "interaction" from the
achievement of relations of genuine "learning." For doing so requires
nothing less than a workable account of political legitimacy, an account
that can distinguish legitimate constraints upon social and political
interactions from those that are due to monopoly, the abuse of power
or authority, deliberate deceit, negligence, and so on. Until policy
analysts can produce such an account, their appeal to substitute both
"interaction" and "learning" for policymakers' or policy analysts'
"cogitation" or "problem-solving" (not to say "planning," *pace* Wildavsky) will actually not democratize that responsibility for decision-
making. Rather it will diffusely obscure that responsibility, by failing
to distinguish its exercise in legitimate rather than illegitimate (rigged,
monopolistic, or "stacked") interactions.[17] This appeal to "interaction"
and "learning" will remain conceptually incoherent, confusing mere
interaction (and thus perhaps manipulated and coercive interactions)
with actual social and political learning. Until policy analysts come to
grips, then, with their own necessary judgments of the legitimacy or
illegitimacy of the particular forms and contexts of interactions encouraged by various policy alternatives, these analysts will effectively

be unable to distinguish the "learning" one does when faced with scientific reports of chemical hazards from the "learning" one does when faced with a supervisor's demand for cover-up: "Keep quiet about that accident or you'll get fired!"

If by "interaction" and "learning" policy analysts can mean legitimate *or* illegitimate exchanges of information or practical communications (offers, signals, threats, arguments, bribes, and so on), then anything goes, and when anything goes, surely democratic politics and public political responsibilities are the first to go. If "interaction" and "learning" encompass and mean everything, legitimate or illegitimate, then they mean nothing (cf. Wildavsky 1973). And the style of policy analysis founded upon such "interaction" and "learning" will mean less— however rhetorically powerful its advocates may be. Without an account of political legitimacy, policy analysis can only blow in the winds issuing from whomever wields power on the one hand, and from the analyst's own ad hoc hunches about "what is right" or legitimate on the other. That this is politically dangerous for all those citizens who might wish to be informed by—or who will be affected by—such analysis should be patently obvious.

The problem of legitimacy in policy analysis, then, will not go away; it is far from being the only important issue facing the analyst, but it demands attention nonetheless. Without a coherent position regarding this problem, the policy analyst may hardly be distinguished from an intellectual mercenary.

The Contribution of Critical Theory to the Analysis of Policy-Promoted "Learning"

Let us consider, then, whether or not critical theory can provide any practical help here.

Critical theory makes a clear analytical distinction between interaction and sociopolitical and scientific learning. This is the distinction Habermas (1979, ch. 1) makes between communicative action and discourse. As we suggested above, the critical theorist's account of interaction is rooted in a model of pure communicative action. Just as the paradigm case of pure communicative action is structured in terms of four claims to be offered, doubted, accepted, or rejected, so can we understand social and political interaction more broadly to raise, however contingently and precariously in different circumstances, those same claims. Without an actor's successful performance in establishing all of those claims with a listener, the most simple understanding and making sense together would be endangered. When we reject a truth claim we do not believe the other; when we reject a sincerity claim, we do not trust the other. When we reject a meaning claim we are confused or puzzled by the other. When we reject a legitimacy claim, we refuse to grant the other the right to say what's said (or in saying that, to do what might have been intended to have been done: offering to sell us the Brooklyn Bridge—cheap!). The more that these claims are uncertain, the more we need to learn about them. In any one interaction, all of these claims are present; and since all of these claims depend upon the performance (the practical communicative competence) of the speakers, they are all perpetually contingent, never guaranteed, vulnerable to challenge, precarious as they form the basis of ordinary interaction (see Forester 1981b). Social and political learning, then, will only be possible if citizens can freely test or check these claims—without coercion or compulsion operating to bias or invalidate their findings.

Critical theorists argue that in the act of making any of the four claims that constitute communicative action, the speaker, oriented to reaching mutual understanding, anticipates the in-principle possibility of *showing* the particular claim to be justified—showing this on the basis of argument, that is, without coercing their listeners. At the risk of using terms here that have been severely romanticized and misinterpreted, critical theorists argue that in all communicative action oriented toward the achievement of mutual understanding about a point in question, speakers anticipate the (counterfactual) possibility of an "ideal speech situation" in which their claims could be established or validated on the merits of the force of the better argument alone, that is, in a discussion, a discourse, free from domination.[18]

Such an ideal speech situation is an idealization, of course; it does not, nor could it, strictly, exist empirically. It is rather an abstract but operative anticipation, explainable most simply as follows. Let us say that Wildavsky and I (or either of us) seek to reach an understanding with others about planning. We claim that "planning" is a terribly ambiguous concept in the domain of public affairs. One part of what we *mean* by that claim, then, is not only that others who care to listen could in principle come and check the validity of what we say, but also that were they able to do this without coercion or threat, thus evaluating our argument only on its own merits, they would accept our claim. This is a simple and weak enough assumption. The anticipation of an "ideal speech situation" may be not much more complicated than the assumption we may more explicitly make at different times (and perhaps act upon as well), then, that independent, "third-party" consultants, auditors, or analysts might evaluate a claim without being swayed by systematic compulsion, threat, coercion, ideology, or manipulation.

Let us now consider social, political, and scientific learning simply about claims of factual truth and normative legitimacy. In practice, when citizens doubt, challenge, or wish to learn about truth claims, they may appeal to scientific findings, research, and scientific discourses to attempt to establish the truth or falsity of the questioned claim. To the extent that these scientific discourses are free from political manipulation and systematic bias or ideology, to that extent then can those discourses be considered to structure genuine social learning about issues of truth and falsity, issues of what really is so, given the best arguments now available. Similarly, when actors doubt, challenge, and seek to learn about the dubious rightness of legitimacy claims, they seek discourses in which they hope to evaluate and establish the validity of those claims on the basis of the best available arguments. And again, to the extent that actually existing forms of discourses (e.g., debates, appeal procedures, courts of law, and administrative hearings) are not "stacked" or rigged, but are free from systematic distortion, then to that extent can those discourses be considered to structure practically social and political learning about the rightness and propriety of normative political or moral claims.

In both cases of calling factual (truth) and normative (legitimacy) claims into question, citizens step outside of their immediate contexts of interaction and seek recourse to domination-free discourses to check and learn about the validity of the uncertain claims. Where citizens have *no* recourse to such discourses, analysts will discover *not* the social and technical learning that can check, test, evaluate, and refine ongoing patterns of interaction and claims-making, but rather they will discover *policy traps*. Without institutionalized possibilities of learning, citizens will be ignorant rather than more knowledgeable, subordinate rather than authoritative, cynical rather than cooperative, and confused rather than increasingly aware of the issues affecting their lives.[19]

John Forester

Consider a final example. Both institutional forms of interaction and learning can be expected to differ across various policy sectors. The policy creating the Occupational Safety and Health Administration (OSHA), for example, also structures particular patterns of interaction between workers on the shop floor, industrial management, and OSHA inspectors. A detailed retrospective policy analysis might reveal, then, the particular effects of the OSHA legislation upon the practical claims-making activities that constitute those patterns of interaction: the policy's reproduction of particular patterns of knowledge, consent, trust, and awareness — of workers and employers alike. The policy analysis might also show that the OSHA legislation explicitly addressed citizens' and workers' problems of social and scientific learning in two ways. First, by establishing the National Institute for Occupational Safety and Health (NIOSH), the OSHA legislation encouraged the investigation, checking, testing, and eventually the classification of scores of hazardous and dangerous substances about which all too little was known by anyone. The establishment of NIOSH was one step enabling workers to draw upon scientific studies funded neither by the manufacturers of the chemicals in question nor by other special-interest groups. Second, the OSHA legislation led to the specification of rules structuring griev-ance processes accessible to workers wishing to call into question claims about the safety of work processes or work environments. How well these two institutional learning processes work, of course, must be a central concern for any policy analysis of OSHA.

Conclusion

Besides producing some services directly, then, policymaking not only stages and structures practical claims-making interactions (diagnoses, entitlements, incentives, and so on), but it also structures, inhibits, or facilitates citizens' learning, their recourse to technical-scientific and legal-political discourses. Thus, as we have argued above, policymaking may both profoundly shape citizens' knowledge or ignorance, consent or resistance, trust or suspicion, and attention or neglect, and it may also enhance or restrict their abilities to learn as it provides (or fails to provide) the institutional mechanisms for social, political, and sci-entific learning.

The policy-shaped patterns of "interaction," then, must be sharply distinguished from policy-produced "learning processes." Each of these faces of policy must be studied. The analysis of restrictions upon citizens' learning, and the subsequent qualification of results, must be distinguished from the policy analyst's other empirical research questions asking how a given policy structures citizens' knowledge, consent, trust, and attention, the substantive content of citizens' "interactions."

By applying an analysis of communicative action that provides a framework for the assessment of both policy-structured "interactions" and "learning processes," the critical theorist specifies two lines of questions for the policy analyst: empirical research questions about policy-structured interactions, and equally essentially but more philosophical and "cogitative" questions about the more or less legitimate, open or distorted, working of whatever "learning processes" the policy promotes. Critical theory, then, provides policy analysts with: (1) a framework for the analysis of policy-produced direct outcomes and policy-reproduced "interactions" (as practical claims-making), and (2) a related analysis of those policy-enhanced mechanisms enabling citizens to call into question and learn about any of the interactive claims that they confront. As these policy-structured learning mechanisms might expose systematic distortions of "interaction," they may provide in part the avenues for the learning, the sociopolitical and technological-scientific progress, desired by citizens, policymakers, and policy analysts as well.

If this argument has merit, some few changes might result. Perhaps when next they meet, the policy analyst will feel a little less reticent to talk about issues of legitimacy and distorted interactions, and perhaps the critical theorist will be less reticent to talk about concrete organizational behavior. They still might not like one another, but they might both learn something about what they are doing.

Notes

This essay was first published in the *Journal of Public Policy*, volume 2, part 2, May 1982. It is based on a paper presented at the 1981 Conference of the American Political Science Association, New York City. The author wishes to thank Kieran Donaghy, Frank Fischer, William Goldsmith, Donald Moon, Simon Neustein, Stephen White, and Aaron Wildavsky for their comments.

John Forester

1. For a closely parallel analysis, see Lindblom and Cohen (1979). Where Wildavsky contrasts "cogitative" or "intellectual" or "planning" styles of analysis and problem-solving against "interactive" or "political" styles, Lindblom makes the parallel distinction between comprehensive, planned or political decision-making on the one hand and interactive or market-styled decision processes on the other. They both intend a sharp distinction, if ultimately the distinguished terms are nevertheless complementary, between any single decision-maker's "solution" ("planning" for Wildavsky and "politics" for Lindblom) and the interactive solutions worked out by a plurality of independent decision-makers, whether on the market or in voting processes ("markets" for both Lindblom and Wildavsky, and "politics," i.e., bargaining, negotiation, voting, and so on, for Wildavsky). As Wildavsky acknowledges in his introduction (footnote, page 11), his and Lindblom's work have much in common. Cf. here also Lindblom (1977).

2. The best secondary works on Habermas's critical theory are Bernstein (1976), McCarthy (1978), and Held (1980). For an application to the practice of planning analysts, see Forester (1982a,b, 1983) and "Critical Theory and Planning Practice" (this volume).

3. For sensitive discussions of the necessity to situate the critical theoretical analysis of communicative action and communicative distortions, see Misgeld (1976) and Wellmer (1976).

4. Consider here the closing lines of Lindblom's recent major work (1979, p. 356): "It has been a curious feature of democratic thought that it has not faced up to the private corporation as a peculiar organization in an ostensible democracy. Enormously large, rich in resources, the big corporations, we have seen, command more resources than do most government units. They can also, over a broad range, insist that government meet their demands, even if these demands run counter to those of citizens expressed through their polyarchal controls. Moreover, they do not disqualify themselves from playing the partisan role of a citizen—for the corporation is legally a person. And they exercise unusual veto powers. They are on all these counts disproportionately powerful, we have seen. The large corporation fits oddly into democratic theory and vision. Indeed, it does not fit."

5. From a lecture at Cornell University, Fall 1980.

6. While I have not studied this in detail historically, recent Yugoslav and Chinese experience seems to suggest as much.

7. Wildavsky (1979, p. 12) writes, "My preference for interaction rather than cogitation, for more 'asking' and less 'telling', for politics over planning, is not meant to protect interaction from scrutiny as if it were a dogma. On the contrary, skepticism should extend especially to interaction—how it develops, what sustains it, why it produced outcomes, its class and ideological biases, when it should be changed—precisely because we begin by intending to rely on it. In a word, the main task of responsible intellectual cogitation is to monitor, appraise, modify, and otherwise strengthen social interaction." As we will see below, Wildavsky leads us to, but does not himself answer, two questions that naturally follow such a statement; (a) how are we to understand the substantive content of "interaction" (i.e., what is at stake in interaction, beyond "preferences"?), and (b) must not interaction and learning processes be distinguished, and if so, how?

8. "If the reader will allow me my preference for two-thirds politics and one-third planning, this hybrid of social interaction and intellectual cogitation may be called policy analysis" (Wildavsky 1979, p. 124).

9. Though Habermas (1979) hardly focuses upon policymaking or state action, with the exception of the last chapter, the whole book addresses the problems of developing a systematic, historical account of social learning that would integrate social action (chapter 1), moral development (chapter 2), the historical development of normative structures (chapter 3), the dialectic of the forces and social relations of production (chapter 4), and political legitimacy and democratic

theory (chapter 5). See Forester (1981a). Wildavsky writes, somewhat analogously, for example, "Analysts should value policies by the extent to which they permit learning, the ease by which errors are identified, and the motivation produced by organizational incentives to correct error" (Wildavsky 1979, p. 392). And on the next page, he continues, "When we as citizens are deprived of our errors we also lose our capacity for self-correction, for self-improvement by moral development."

10. Wildavsky (1979, p. 125) recognizes, but does not develop, the implications of these problems. He writes, "Action outside the rules (monopoly, for instance) may not be socially desirable. The classical conditions of the marketplace—competition, information, internalization of costs— must be satisfied for prices to represent optimal choices. If not, governmental intervention may be justified to restore competition, to provide as public information that which is not in the interest of any firm to supply privately, and to arrange compensation when the behaviour of one party imposes burdens on another that, like pollution, cannot be alleviated through the marketplace. All these market imperfections depend upon theoretical schemes for recognition and for correction." Once corrected the liberal market will do fine, presumably; with anti-trust legislation as well?

11. Again, Wildavsky (1979, p. 124) recognizes, but does not explore in any systematic way, the role of the "rules of the game" structuring the quality of social interaction. He writes, "Where there is agreement that these conditions [e.g., monopoly: JF] (and their subsequent consequences) break the rules for decent decision-making, they are regarded as imperfections in the respective arenas and institutions. Rules for regulating interaction (such as conditions for allowing monopoly or of specifying who may vote) are subject to change, both through evaluation and intervention, so as to improve interaction. Social interaction may be preferred to intellectual cogitation as a style of analysis without the need to accept only current modes. Indeed the stress on correcting error suggests that alteration in interaction is desirable." Critical theory may help us clarify which such alterations in interaction and the social capacity for learning may be desirable, as we see below.

12. Lindblom and Cohen (1979, p. 25) write, "Needing investigation are those forms of interaction that serve some significant problem-solving function in society, as for example, voting, delegation, some forms of political negotiation, and market interactions do, even if some people may see the same interactions as creating problems, as is again the case with voting and markets."

13. Habermas's analysis of communicative action appears in the difficult essay "What Is Universal Pragmatics?" chapter one of Habermas (1979). McCarthy's discussion of Habermas's theory of communicative action is extensive and helpful (McCarthy 1978). For an application to organizational analysis, see Forester (1983).

14. The political and practical implications of such management of belief, consent, trust, and attention are developed in Forester (1982a,b, 1983) and "Critical Theory and Planning Practice" (this volume).

15. The New York State Workmen's Compensation Law states in Section 11, Article 2 ("Exclusiveness of Remedy"), Subdivision 21, "Compensation as exclusive remedy—Generally": "The remedy provided by this chapter for an employee engaged in the employment enumerated therein is exclusive and in full substitution for an action for damages." Followed by legal precedents dating from 1916 and directly below, as follows: "This chapter was designed to assure to workingman protection against loss of earning power through injury sustained in his employment, regardless of how injury occurred or what brought it about, and in return for such new and comprehensive liability the employer is accorded relief from all other liability on account of such injury. *William* v. *Hartshorn*, 1946, 296 NY, 49 69 N.E. 2nd 557." If this is not sufficiently clear, another case example follows: "Under this chapter, immunity from suit for damages has been vouchsafed to an employer and to a co-employee responsible for injuries suffered by a workman as a result of an industrial accident in covered employment. *Maxarredo* v. *Levine*, 1948, 274 App. Div. 122, 80 N.Y.S. 2nd 237."

John Forester

16. Again Wildavsky (1979, p. 397) recognizes such problems in principle, but he devotes little sustained attention to the influences threatening to distort interactions. Still, he writes, sensitively but perhaps too easily, "Social interaction is efficacious only when autonomous individuals establish reciprocal social relationships. Individual moral development requires a balance between autonomy and reciprocity, citizen and community, which, at the public level, is the task of policy analysis." I have tried to clarify these problems of anticipatable distortion in Forester (1980a, 1982a, 1982b).

17. Again, while both Lindblom and Cohen (1979) and Wildavsky (1979) mention this problem and recognize that it exists, they hardly address it. Even if this problem constitutes only "one third" of the policy analyst's work, as Wildavsky suggests (see note 8), i.e., subjecting interaction to scrutiny (see note 7), Wildavsky would be the first to acknowledge that two-thirds of a movie ticket doesn't get you in the door. This theoretical "third" represents the necessary and essential contribution of political philosophy, political theory as it is called, to the practical work of policy analysts and to the discipline of policy analysis.

18. Thomas McCarthy puts it this way: "The very act of parcipating in a discourse of attempting discursively to come to an agreement about the truth of a problematic statement or the correctness of a problematic norm, carried with it the supposition that a genuine agreement is possible. If we did not suppose that a justified consensus were possible and could in some way be distinguished from a false consensus, then the very meaning of discourse, indeed of speech, would be called into question." In "Translator's Introduction," Habermas (1975, p. xvi).

19. Habermas's analysis of social learning at the social structural level appears in Habermas (1979, ch. 3). Departing from Habermas's analysis there, I would argue that learning in the dimensions of truth and comprehensibility (attention investment) claims constitutes technological-scientific learning, while learning in the dimensions of rightness and sincerity claims constitutes legal-moral learning. If this argument holds, then the reconstruction of communicative action (the so-called "universal pragmatics") allows an *integration* of the level of analysis of social action and interaction with the level of analysis of systematic production and reproduction, or systemic development of the forces of production on the one hand, and the social relations of production on the other.

References

Berman, D., 1978. *Death on the Job*. New York: Monthly Review Press.

Bernstein, R., 1976. *The Restructuring of Social and Political Theory*. Philadelphia: University of Pennsylvania Press.

Burton, D., and B. Murphy, 1980. "Democratic Planning in Austerity: Practice and Theory." In P. Clavel et al., eds., *Urban and Regional Planning in an Age of Austerity* (New York: Pergamon).

Churchman, C. W., 1979. *The Systems Approach and Its Enemies*. New York: Basic Books.

Cohen, J., 1979. "Why More Political Theory?" *Telos* 40.

Dekema, J., 1981. "Incommensurability and Judgement." *Theory and Society* 10: 521–546.

Dunn, W., 1981. *Public Policy Analysis*. Englewood Cliffs, N.J.: Prentice-Hall.

Fischer, J., 1980. *Politics, Values, and Public Policy*. Boulder, Colo.: Westview Press.

Forester, J., 1980. "Listening: The Social Policy of Everyday Life (Critical Theory and Hermeneutics in Practice)." *Social Praxis* 7(3–4).

Forester, J., 1981a. "Selling You the Brooklyn Bridge and Ideology" (review of Habermas's *Communication and the Evolution of Society*). *Theory and Society*, September.

Forester, J., 1981b. "Hannah Arendt and Critical Theory: A Critical Response." *Journal of Politics*, February.

Forester, J., 1982a. "Critical Reason and Political Power in Project Review Activity." *Policy and Politics* 10(1).

Forester, J., 1982b. "Planning in the Face of Power." *Journal of the American Planning Association*, Winter.

Forester, J., 1983. "Critical Theory and Organizational Analysis." In G. Morgan, ed., *Beyond Method* (Los Angeles: Sage).

Habermas, J., 1970. *Toward a Rational Society*. Boston: Beacon Press.

Habermas, J., 1973. *Theory and Practice*. Boston: Beacon Press.

Habermas, J., 1975. *Legitimation Crisis*. Boston: Beacon Press.

Habermas, J., 1979. *Communication and the Evolution of Society*. Boston: Beacon Press.

Halberstam, D., 1972. *The Best and the Brightest*. New York: Random House.

Held, D., 1980. *Introduction to Critical Theory*. Berkeley: University of California Press.

Hirsch, F., 1976. *Social Limits to Growth*. Cambridge: Harvard University Press.

Honneth, A., 1979. "Communication and Reconciliation: Habermas's Critique of Adorno." *Telos* 39 (Spring).

Leiss, W., 1976. *The Limits of Satisfaction*. Toronto: University of Toronto Press.

Lindblom, C., 1977. *Politics and Markets*. New York: Basic Books.

Lindblom, C., and D. Cohen, 1979. *Usable Knowledge*. New Haven: Yale University Press.

Lowi, T., 1969. *The End of Liberalism*. New York: W. W. Norton.

Lukes, S., 1974. *Power: A Radical View*. New York: Macmillan.

McCarthy, T., 1978. *The Critical Theory of Jürgen Habermas*. Cambridge: MIT Press.

MacRae, D., 1976. *The Social Function of Social Science*. New Haven: Yale University Press.

Marcuse, H., 1964. *One-Dimensional Man*. Boston: Beacon Press.

Misgeld, D., 1976. "On Critical Theory." In J. O'Neill, ed., *On Critical Theory* (New York: Seabury).

O'Connor, J., 1979. "The Democratic Movement in the United States." *Kapitalistate*.

Pateman, C., 1970. *Participation and Democratic Theory*. Cambridge: Cambridge University Press.

Rein, M., 1976. *Social Science and Public Policy*. New York: Penguin.

Schaar, J., 1970. "Legitimacy in the Modern State." In P. Green and S. Levinson, eds., *Power and Community* (New York: Pantheon).

Schaar, J., 1981. *Legitimacy in the Modern State*. New Brunswick, N.J.: Transaction Books.

Walzer, M., 1980. *Radical Principles*. New York: Basic Books.

Wellmer, A., 1976. "On Critical Theory." In J. O'Neill, ed., *On Critical Theory* (New York: Seabury).

Wildavsky, A., 1973. "If Planning Is Everything, Maybe It's Nothing." *Policy Sciences*.

Wildavsky, A., 1979. *Speaking Truth to Power*. Boston: Little, Brown.

Wolfe, A., 1977. *The Limits of Legitimacy*. New York: Free Press.

VI

Critical Historical Studies

Corruption of Freedom in America

Trent Schroyer

In the introduction to *Theory and Practice*, Jürgen Habermas has suggested that between the levels of valid theory and prudent political strategies there is a mediating sphere where the organization of enlightenment processes requires insight into specific contexts. The intention of this chapter is to apply Habermas's crisis theorems to the history of the institutions and political culture of the United States. In the course of attempting to do this, I found myself both trying to apply Habermas's categories and posing questions to their applicability—especially where the American context differed from that of Continental Europe. In this sense the following is an attempt to think with and against Habermas's critical theory in reconstructing the foundations for normative politics (ethical principles that mediate between theory and practice) in the American context.

Marxism and the American Context

Why has a sustained radical movement not been realized in the American context? This reality has not been explained by radicals in general and Marxist socialists in particular.[1] Despite recurrent economic, political, and legitimacy crises, American radicalism has remained a marginal and sporadic event in American history. Why?

Perhaps a clue is to turn the question around: Is there a negative affinity between the American sociocultural context and Marxist socialism? When Americans dream of a better world, why have socialist symbols failed to provide bridges between existing and possible worlds?

Can it be that "socialism," or its moral equivalent, is actually contained within the utopian concept of "Americanism" itself?[2]

My thesis is that the origins of the American social identity discloses a "cultural surplus" that anticipates a society in which individual participation and autonomy of communities constitute the common public good. By "cultural surplus" I mean traditional cultural symbols that retain their capacity to anticipate utopian alternatives to existing realities.

The American cultural surplus has also been reified to legitimate a social conservatism that reduces local autonomy to an accommodating and affirmative particularism (as in Reagan's idea of a New Federalism) or to an antimodern authoritarianism (as in the evangelical right's reaction to the separation of church and state). The following will argue that these images are ideological distortions of a more critical American political culture. Ideological distortions of cultural surplus sever present events from historical remembrance of more universal and reflexive ideals. Ideologies present oversimplified explanations that transform complex social causations into quasi-natural processes to which we must realistically adapt—for example, the transition from the Carter administration's foreign policy, based on "economic interdependence" and "human rights," to the Reagan administration's "realism" that identifies world leadership with military power and the "free market" as the global mechanism of progress for all. This signals a major ideological shift in the planetary meaning of "Americanism." This return to "realism" has renewed the slogan of the "containment of communism" in a context where less developed countries are increasingly unable to realize Western models of economic development and political modernization.

This return to ideology has happened simultaneously with a reactivation of enforced secrecy and suppression of public information.[3] Thus the current American ideology construction indicates a real loss of the open society meaning of democracy, as well as a shared sense of planetary sociality for which the American cultural surplus has always played a "social imaginary" role.[4]

The Reagan administration has effectively revitalized a new version of American "realism," which has, since Hamilton's opposition to Jefferson, seen state formation as the real institution building and to which democracy was always an abstract moral ideal.[5] Like American Marxism, American realism has always viewed theory and ethical beliefs as abstractions that degenerate in practice into utopianism and sentimentalism. The realists, like the Marxists, focus on the "real" constellations of power and view "practical action" as that which is essential for fundamental institution building and problem solving. For both, moral "idealism" remains the recurrent (superstructural) waves of reform, revival, and cultural renewal that are often inconsistent with the "real" causes that make them possible.[6] In this way the Reagan administration has been successful in recasting the normative force of Americanism in the future "world society" as a renewal of economic liberalism. Needless to say, there are other versions of "Americanism." For example, a post–World War II English perspective captures another image:

U.S. citizenship is something as unique as it is extraordinary; it differs radically from what is understood in Europe as "nationality." The United States is a fragmentary, most imperfect, and in some respects grotesque advance-copy of a future world-order. It is a Brotherhood rather than a "people." Americans have something more than nationality. In its place they have what amounts almost to a religion, a "way of life." It is one of the most important spiritual phenomena in the world today. . . . American citizenship takes with it of course a whole system of ethics and politics; of puritan ethics and revolutionary politics.[7]

Thus Wyndham Lewis suggests that in taking in persons from all nations, the United States has formed a spirit of revolutionary universalism that foreshadows, even if imperfectly, a world society. But the content of the American "revolutionary universalism" is precisely what is at stake in any reconstruction of an American cultural surplus, and this has not been adequately achieved by American realists—or Marxists.

American Marxists have tended to reduce normative structures and cultural traditions to social relations of production and thereby to underestimate the dialectical importance of moral-ethical expectations and sociocultural experimentation. Thus the "production paradigm"[8] locates the "progressive" dynamic of modern society in the "labor process" and represents the wage-labor contract as undermining all traditional social identity. Critique, as analysis of class-controlled production process, posits "political" means ("class struggle") and ends ("socialist revolution") that remain abstractions in the American ethos. Hence the question returns: is the Marxist revolutionary ideal, formed in the struggles to overcome the *ancien régime*, an inappropriate model of liberation in the American context?

In retrospect it is clear that Marx's theory was limited by its formulation in the utopian phase of the initial institutionalization of liberal capitalism in England. Only in such a context could its conception of political mediation be reduced to a supplementary function of capital accumulation. As many contemporary critics have argued, capitalism cannot be analyzed with this theoretically limited concept of political process. State interventions go far beyond any particular instrumental use by the capitalist class and become increasingly significant as a generalized medium of control, as well as an institutionalization of socialized legal constraints on extensions of the logic of commodities. Not only have capitalist "social relations" become—in contrast to the nineteenth-century liberal state—"repoliticalized," but the legitimacy of their operations has also become, as Jürgen Habermas has argued, a crucial sphere for their transformation.[9]

Today the centrality of public discourse about the legitimacy of state regulations that protect (even if partially) individual economic security and environmental quality from being totally reduced to the logic of commodification has become obvious. In these spheres a "repoliticalization" of the relations of production has transformed the functional neutrality of the liberal construction of natural law. Because the prepolitical sphere of economic liberty can no longer be regulated by exchange alone but is also stabilized by systematic intervention of administrative power, the relationship of human and political rights changes. Under these conditions purely formal bourgeois human rights can be interpreted as political rights to genuine participation. Where liberty was once conceived as the possessive individualist right to hold and exclude others from the use and disposition of property, today the right to liberty extends to the right to an income or a job, as well as to equal opportunity to develop one's self.[10]

President Reagan's efforts to overturn state regulations and recommodify the noncommodity spheres (for example, land and labor) while massively escalating military expenditures provide the problem situations for linking the new social movements. Learning how to relate the images of liberation from the peace, ecology, and feminist movements will be more concrete if the latent cultural surplus of the American tradition can provide general principles of law and ethical consciousness that point beyond the instrumentalism of free market exchange as well as the law and order mentality inherent in an American civil religion.[11] Therefore the following attempts to reconstruct a cultural surplus as part of a different critical comprehension of the central contradiction of American development: the contradiction of an open democratic society with the authoritarian forms of statism essential for maintaining the "free enterprise system."

There is a limit to ideological constructions; cultural traditions and normative structures have semantic and contextual referents that cannot be totally manipulated. The irony of ideology constructions is that once institutionalized and accepted as the basis for social consensus, their utopian moment, or cultural surplus, may become realized.[12] Historically social and political norms, in becoming the basis for social interaction, create reciprocal expectations that define the meaning of social reality. While a new political cultural construction might be attempted by the state, it cannot be invented abstractly. Ideology constructions are constrained by what already exists in national traditions. When past political culture constructions realize themselves in institutional forms, their utopian contents can be taken for "truth" by social actors. Historical social integrations contain a standard of moral consciousness that has social consequences and can become, in an unintended way, a force for liberation when the utopian content is actualized.

American Crises and Ideology Constructions

As a background framework, it is useful to outline some of the most important American political realignments that emerged as responses to societal crises:

1. The "revolutionary period" of American history: the formation of a unified polity and the debate about the forms of federalism for a republic. Ratification of the Constitution over the opposition of a majority of anti-Federalists represented an evasion of the first legitimacy crisis of the new Republic and established the American ideology.

2. The Civil War realignment beginning in 1856, which presupposed the expressive moral-political discourse surrounding the issues of slavery or free states in the West, as well as the issue of the desirable type of sociopolitical order. This crisis was the final result of a series of early questions of legitimacy beginning in Jefferson's era and continued by Jacksonianism.

3. The realignment beginning in the 1890s brought about by the impact of the growing concentration of capital. This culminated in the progressive era's substitution of a corporate ideology for both economic and political spheres for a new ideology of American "community." These events provided the principles and programs for the critical realignment of 1932, which, in the context of the depression, institutionalized the New Deal's contributions to the corporate state. This entire period of transition to organized capitalism was effectively the evasion of the third and longest period of "crisis."

4. The contemporary ongoing crisis period that began in the 1960s represents the end of liberal pluralism in the context of an economic, fiscal, and legitimacy crisis. Reaganomics is a strategy for the reindustrialization of the American economy and also intends to dismantle the New Deal. The new "social contract" it would like to impose by force (due to economic revitalization "necessities") would retain the affluent American dream for the few while requiring austere social discipline from the many.

Each of these pivotal periods in American history represents a fundamental choice that redefined the American social identity. Each crisis period generated oppositional or third party movements and was accompanied by intensified social conflicts. In these events the political capacity to achieve "consensus" also required a political symbolism of revitalization presided over by a charismatic leader—Washington, Lincoln, Teddy Roosevelt, and Franklin Roosevelt. Today Reagan aspires to this role. As I will show, an unrecognized cost of the American ideology is that after each successful political realignment, decision making shifted more and more to "elites" while mass participation became less significant.

The purpose of the schema is to indicate that the fourth and contemporary American crisis represents the exhaustion of all the past revitalizations of American society. The post–Civil War's economic liberalism (which Reagan hopes to revive in a new way) is no longer a creditable account of a society where the state's stabilizing functions have not only become massive and essential for the economic growth but also ineffectual in overcoming structural poverty and unemployment. Nor is the neoconservative "revolution" against "big government" able to change the scale of government substantially or return real autonomy to the local levels. Despite the claim of returning "appropriate responsibilities" to local government, the actual consequences have been to undermine the possibilities for local immunity from higher-level decisions, as well as for chances to initiate and implement new policy in such areas as clean air, voting rights, and implementation of local and regional economic development. In the last area, Reagan has claimed that local autonomy would undermine national interests.[14]

By forcing the national goal the Reagan administration is undermining the rights of local and regional governments to pursue their own strategies for balancing development and the quality of life (an example is acid rain legislation). Because higher levels of government ultimately draw their legitimacy from local decisions about the best scale at which to provide goods and services and implement policy, the neoconservative practice in key policy areas contradicts its supposed advocacy of decentralized local democratic government. The neoconservative "revolution" in government has not reversed the long-term tendency toward less local autonomy but has in fact intensified its transformation into bureaucratic apparatus for the goals of the federal government.

In these current efforts to avoid crisis we seen manifested once again the unique ability of American politics to aim for a system goal of imperialistic expansion and economic growth while justifying it by the ideological manipulation of the American cultural surplus. In American history since the Constitution, ideology and political goals and motives have been split off from each other and in practice have been inconsistent. Republicans actualize economic liberalism, progressive liberals yearn for "community," and "conservatives" stand for laissez-faire.

What we must remember is the original nation-forming process because its foundation myths and symbols have been used again and again in the legitimations of political realignments. Before each of the pivotal crises lies 150 years of colonial history, during which the primary symbols that defined the American social identity were fused. Initiations into the "New World" were ritual events that generated narratives explaining differences from the "Old World." Much of the dialectic of American political culture has been the ever-renewed explaining of the greater purity, virtue, or higher mission of the American nation over that of England and Europe. In this project the construction of foundation myths and creation narratives was inescapable.

The cultural origins of America begin in the situational applications of Calvinist political theology and radical Whig republicanism to the colonial experience to the natural context. What is common to all the colonies was the awesome encounter with the untamed land and native peoples whose spontaneous wildness was both inspiring and terrible. Indeed colonial ambivalence about "savagery" was the central trauma of the pre-Revolutionary period. Fear of the sensuousness of Indian sensibility—especially the test of the female Christian soul by "possession"—was the central theme of the captivity sermons (and exorcisms) in early colonial social life.[15] Surrender to Indian "savagery" and the wilderness they exemplified was viewed by most colonists as the essence of evil defilement. Hence the challenge of the howling darkness of the wilderness was the need to "civilize" and bring salvation to the Indian by missionary activity and/or the musket.

The other side of the encounter with the wilderness was experienced in the first real "stable natural communities" of the "Old West," that is, the lands first developed inland from the coasts: the Shenendoah and Hagerstown valleys of the south to the Mohawk Valley of backwoods New England. Here the "steady farmer" had an autochthonic sense of belonging to the land. Today it is important to remember the great difference between the "Old West's" practice of "inhabitation," which involved a primordial sense of imitating creation by shaping and dwelling in a place, and the violent exploitation of the land now viewed as the "frontier ethic" (or the "cowboy ethic" of James Watt's commodity view of "natural resources"). For the Old West—the focus of Frederick Jackson Turner's frontier thesis of the American character—inhabiting the land was a communal act of creation, of becoming one with the land in order to sustain both the community and the land.[16]

Transformation of the narrative of frontier settlement into a "cowboy" justification of the logic of commodification distorts its relevance as an original land ethic and its commonality with contemporary reassertions of the need for sustainable "natural communities" that can be protected by local community autonomy. It is this original community land ethic that a contemporary Jeffersonian defends:

A healthy culture is a communal order of memory, insight, value, work, conviviality, reverence, aspiration. It reveals the human necessities and the human limits. It clarifies our inescapable bonds to the earth and to each other. . . . A culture cannot survive long at the expense of either its agriculture or its natural sources. . . . The word "agriculture," after all, does not mean "agriscience," much less "agribusiness." It means "cultivation of land." And "cultivation" is at the root of the sense of both "culture" and "cult." The ideas of tillage and worship are thus joined in culture. And these words come from an Indo-European root meaning both "to revolve" and "to dwell." To live, to survive on the earth, to care for the soil and to worship, are all bound at the root of the idea of a cycle. . . . If we corrupt agriculture we corrupt culture, for in nature and within certain invariable social necessities, we are one body.[17]

European Origins of the American Political Culture

Early American political culture is unique in two ways. First, it is the most traditional of all modern Western societies in the sense that it was an attempt to renew the fundamental ideals of European civilization against their corruption in the Old World. Second, the untamed land and the indigenous peoples provided a latent "other" in the formation of the American social identity whose "wildness" exerted an ambivalent attraction-repulsion on the content of the American myth of foundation.

Early American political culture is derived from seventeenth- and eighteenth-century radical republicanism, which opposed the emergence of commercial society and "moveable property."[18] The version of this aristocratic civic humanism most important for the early colonists was the Radical Whigs' "Country ideology" as expressed by James Harrington and others. But this political culture was also mixed with a Calvinist moral practice of conscience and covenant.[19] The resulting colonial political forms were pragmatic and unstable in that they aspired to unite a politics of civic virtue with a Christian millennialist moral vision. Perhaps the most accurate expression of this unique combination is "apocalyptic Whiggism."

American social identity begins in the dilemmas of colonial identity, as this was formed within the long history of colonial and European conflicts.[20] For example, during the transition from James II to William and Mary, numerous colonial rebellions were based on the claims to the "rights of Englishmen," and yet these same traditions were used to express the differences of the colonial identity.[21] Colonial social identities were then convergent through the common problem of balancing English republicanism and the reality of subordination to the mercantilist strategy of the court ideology of empire. The rapid mobilization of the colonial peoples after the Stamp Act could occur only because of a common social situation they had already shared and that permitted rapid development of a new nation and political consciousness in the Revolutionary period.

In the Revolutionary context, the ambiguities of colonial identity were solved by selecting the country Whigs' republicanism, whose more radically democratic intentions had not been realized in England and thus defined the purity and the difference of American virtue. It is important to remember that the radical country Whigs had conceived a political society as having material and moral-ethical preconditions. Loss of these preconditions was a corruption of freedom. Corruption is essentially a conception of political alienation that the radical Whigs extended in response to the financial revolution (circa 1694) that promoted the commodification of the sociopolitical institution of property.

"Corruption" means the destruction of the preconditions that make political participation possible. It indicates an undermining of civic virtue resulting from the loss of freehold land, the victory of moveable property, and the moral-ethical consequences of the commercial process of specialization and division of labor. This early critique of modernity was developed as a civic humanist critique of corruption as early as 1698. Republican civic humanism could reconcile "liberty" with equality only insofar as equals had nothing to fear from political action or opinion. In the English context, this meant independent freehold of land and the right to defend this with arms; today, the right to a job? The republican paradigm of civic virtue resisted the growth of trade and credit as the emergence of a momentous corruption that would spread fear for security from one level of society to all.[22] They also believed that the "monied interest," whose increasing power rested on the new "moveable" forms of property, also corrupted government to act in its exclusive interest. As a reaction to the dynamic of commercial capitalism, the country Whigs ironically and defensively radicalized a political culture that normatively established a notion of the common good.

The historical watershed for corruption was the Glorious Revolution of 1688, when transition to William and Mary also meant the foundation of a major war effort that required an explosive development of the credit and banking system of the realm. This escalation of corruption was irreversible, since land increasingly became valued in terms of the rates of interest, and it was no longer possible to maintain an agrarian republic centered on the independent warrior-citizen. The radical Whig ideology, however, having developed as a dual critique of absolutism and modernity, became that version of English republicanism that had an affinity to the American colonial situation. The central problem confronting early American political theorists was how to reconcile the growing importance of credit systems and its inevitable specialization and division of social labor with the maintenance of a political and moral society. The resolution of this antinomy of virtue and empire, of civic participation, and self-interested pursuit of wealth was the founding of the American nation. The context of this founding was deeply concerned with problems posed by the conflict of classical politics and liberal contract theory, which I believe the liberal and Marxist interpretations have oversimplified and reduced. Implicit in the origins of the American political culture is, I believe, a residual cultural surplus. Although it is true that the framers of the Constitution believed that they had gone beyond classical politics by grounding government in the "social contract," they also held (perhaps inconsistently) that they had created a foundation that would promote the civic virtue essential for preserving this new political order. The actual complex of liberal and classical political elements in the foundation is a controversial and crucial interpretive problem.

The story has been told in ways that stress the liberal conception of property as a prepolitical natural right and as the contractual ground of individual interest and social harmony. On this account the theorists of the new social contract (Locke and Hobbes) had been dominant in their belief that the natural order, including civil society and government, is one of harmony that is oriented to the securing of wealth. Here the "political" has been submerged into a systemic political-economic view of society, and human nature is conceived as fundamentally oriented to the "prudent" pursuits of increasing wealth and avoiding the terror of nature (the fate of poverty).[23] In this construction the protection of property is essential for the authority of the entire society; its pursuit provides the motive for all citizens and the legitimate function for the government. Scarcity or the inability to satisfy material needs is the source of human society, and the role of the government is therefore to provide "justice"—that is, security of property and contract. As a result the concerns with civic virtue become unnecessary because the origin of society is the ever-renewed pursuit of self-interest for which government is a mechanism that secures the rules for the incessant game of wealth maximization. The common good is not achieved by discourse about the ends of a good society but by the unintended result of individual self-interest (the self-regulating process of the market) and the self-corrective mechanisms of government. The notion of civic virtue, and of civic participation essential to maintain it, becomes unnecessary.

This view, however, which justifies the perspectives of contemporary liberalism, neoconservatism, and Marxism on the origins of the American nation, is deficient. The notion of corruption retains a real content in relation to the founding and provides an appropriately immanent category for the critique of American society. The inversions of the constitutional framers and the subsequent growth of the American state can be expressed more appropriately in an American vernacular.

The American Myth of Foundation

In ancient Rome, all institutions were seen as having been founded by the will of a heroic leader.[24] Foundations tied the institution to its origin; the beginning is the law in itself to which historic change of the institution always returns. The American founding fathers assumed two great classical models of founding or new beginnings: that of the Hebrew exodus from Egypt and Aeneas's wandering before the founding of Rome. Both are, as Hannah Arendt says, legends of liberation, and both indicate that the phases of liberation and the foundations of freedom are not identical.

The events of liberation and foundation in America had a complexity that is usually interpreted in terms of their result. My thesis here is that the Revolutionary situation was an origin that signified a normative intention lost by the result. It was the unique convergence of classical republicanism (civic humanism of the radical Whigs) and the political theology of Calvinist Christianity that together formed an originating and transitory political culture in which both traditions anticipated (although we will see in diferent ways) a society where public action was viewed as essential for sustaining political freedom and individual moral development. Only insofar as persons could be independent and free from fear could public virtue be achieved. In other words the common good, as that constitutionally secured end that political participation free from fear is essential for the Republic, is an immanent positive notion of freedom. In the contemporary context this would suggest that material equality (as material independence and the equal opportunity for personal autonomy) and the institutionally open possibility for establishing the habit of public virtue by being able to sustain political participation are the conditions that constitute freedom.

The cultural surplus inherent in the nation-forming process of the Revolutionary context, however, was ideologically distorted in the act of founding what is today a growing American statism. To make this argument, in this section I will focus on the expectation of civic humanism in the next public theology. The crucial point is that soon after the act of foundation, these two traditions emerged as antagonists and have continued to be so until today's reactivation of the Christian "moral majority" around the issues of social conservatism. Reconstructing the originating union of politics and religion in America is the key to their relation today.

The Federalist victory in the struggle to ratify the Constitution has some aspects of a counterrevolution in that the positive notion of freedom was muted and distorted into a form of government not expected by classical republicans. The Federalists had created a representative democracy and justified it in republican and "federalist" rhetoric; for many the difference has never been noted.[25] The result undermined the trend toward participatory democracy, or as Alexander Hamilton put it, the whole power lies "in the hands of the *representatives* of the people." In the discourse of that day the truest perception may have been that of Patrick Henry who argued that the federal Constitution was not a real federalism of states but a pseudo-construction: "What right had they to say, *We, the people?* My political curiosity, exclusive of my anxious solicitude for public welfare, leads me to ask: who authorized them to speak the language of *We, the people*, instead of, *We, the states?*"[26]

Ultimately this inversion of the republican ideal of federalism into a unit of liberal pluralism distorted classical political ends into liberal mechanisms for civil society. This was aided by the religious fervor too. In the ratification struggle the Federalists effectively made analogies to the Americans as a chosen people who had a millenarian mission.[27] Proof of "electness" was linked to the legendary energy of frontier life and the classic republican image of the warrior-citizen. These converging metaphors legitimated the compromise of 1787, as they had the compromise of the Northwest Ordinance, which provided new territory for pursuing republican independence.[28] Thus the classic republican concern for securing the agricultural character of the Republic was met by this compromise on the national land domain. Theoretically it also resolved the republican contradiction of empire and corruption by idealizing the frontier hero, who as potential everyman could renew equal liberty in new states to the west.

The regional elites supported the ratification of the Constitution because it was a compromise that consolidated their power at the national level and limited the political potentials for local challenges to their economic and political power. The security won by the constitutional foundation was the protection of "property" against majority rule democracy or the securing of a weak state against the possibility of rule by popular democratic participation.

American fear of "excessive democracy" originated in post-Revolutionary America where constitution writing in every state and county had become a national preoccupation. The Federalists maintained that too much power had been given to state legislatures and not enough to the senate and governors of the states. Or, more generally, the political process was too dependent on the permanent input of every town meeting and convention.[29]

Here then is the central contradiction of American society: in the foundation for American freedom is an immanent conflict between state formation and the practice of democracy, which has been intensified by each of the past pivotal crises. In the American founding is a fundamental corruption of freedom, which thereafter systematically distorted a recognition of the need for civic participation as the essential precondition for freedom.

The anti-Federalists, however, recognized the aristocratic and counterrevolutionary intention of the Constitution, seeing it as a turning aside of the popular democratic and egalitarian politics of the Revolutionary era.[30] The Federalists had, "in the name of 'the people' . . . engineered a conservative counter-revolution and erected a nationalistic government whose purpose in part was to thwart the will of 'the people' in whose name they acted."[31] But ratification of the Constitution over the opposition of the anti-Federalists was not easy; in Massachusetts the ratification vote was 187 to 168; in Virginia, 89 to 79. The anti-Federalist opposition was a profound statement of early American republican political sentiment, and though translated into the Bill of Rights, the importance of that opposition as an expression of American political theory has not yet been realized. The Federalists came from behind and won due to superior national organization and manipulative use of the media.

The mythic elements and ideological distortions of the American foundation must be remembered today as a pseudo-compromise of the 1780s.[32] The deep sense of tragedy expressed by the anti-Federalists is the most significant indicator of this reality. The Federalist victory had undermined local participation and secured the power of regional elites. For Robert Morris, John Jay, Alexander Hamilton, and other Federalists, to say "all power is in the people and not in the state governments" was recognized by many anti-Federalists for what it was: ideology.

The framers of the Constitution had promoted the superior virtue of the American foundation as being grounded in the consent of the people and renewed as legitimate by democratic elections of representatives. By institutionalizing James Madison's dual federalism, they had supposedly mediated interest politics by a system of the division and balancing of power—since Montesquieu had established that only "power arrests power." That is, only by creating the conditions under which power can be multiplied and powerless impotence avoided can a union of equals be established. By analogy, founding a "federal republic" meant reconciling the legal rights of self-determination of each state not only with the centralized advantages of a monarchy in foreign affairs but also the balancing of power between the branches of government and the states themselves. Hence the republican notion of checks and balances was to make it possible to generate power and permit minorities to react against established interests. What was to be avoided, Madison explains in Federalist No. 47, is both governmental tyranny and moral tyranny: "The accumulation of powers legislative, executive, and judiciary, in the same hand whether of one, a few or many, and whether hereditary, self-appointed, or elective, may justly be pronounced the very definition of tyranny."

It was this antistatist diffusion of the possibility of majority rule that makes the Republic appear democratic. Less obvious is that it also prohibits the realization of equal liberty because it limits the scope of civic participation. The actuality then of the "sovereignty of the people" is that a weak state is accepted as the cost of securing that democratization will never go to the point of prevailing over that "natural aristocracy" (who supposedly would be able to discern the best interest of the society).[33] The most sympathetic interpretation is that the framers of the Constitution, except Hamilton, did not recognize that their half-step toward state formation would foster an identity of individual interest and economic self-interest and eventually undermine what remained of the republican elements of political civic virtue. What was concealed and/or confused by the founders was that civic participation becomes unnecessary for individual self-interest especially where the end of politics becomes inseparable from economic self-interest.

Where citizens rely on representatives, their experience in civic affairs atrophies and they become, as Alexis de Tocqueville warned, oriented to judging political affairs only in terms of their private economic interests. Where a people understand liberty and equality only in economic terms, they will fail to understand that the economic and political ends of the public realm are often in conflict and the practice of civic virtue will decline and cannot be replaced by laws alone.[34]

Nonetheless there remain normative justifications for civic participation in the American political origins, ones that go beyond the liberal identification of politics with the private egoistic sphere. For example, in the second constitution (the Bill of Rights), especially the Ninth Amendment and Article 4.4 of the Constitution that guarantees every state in the Union a republican form of government, there is a residue of radical republicanism that can be cited for a renewal of freedom in historically new situations. The Ninth Amendment was the suggestion of Madison who, in his correspondence with Jefferson in 1788, confronted the problem that the anti-Federalists had feared: the securing of rights not enumerated by the Bill of Rights and possibly endangered at later situations. Thus, the curious contentlessness of the Ninth Amendment: "The enumeration in the Constitution of certain rights shall not be construed to deny or disparage others retained by the people."

Because of the Ninth Amendment, the meaning of "due process' of law is extended to those practices of autonomous personal and social life already enjoyed in open democratic society and that cannot arbitrarily be denied.[35] From this leverage point, it is possible for social actors to extend the sphere of guaranteed freedoms to claim the preexisting rights of a quality environment, self-determining control over their bodies, and so forth. These are the preexisting substantial spheres of liberty rooted in the values of a constitutionally protected common good. In this way there is a residual primacy of politics behind everyday life in America that was signified in the origins of the American nation.

The legal formulation of the Ninth Amendment is unique and not consistent with Anglo-American common laws that depend on precedent. Its origin has been traced to Thomas Jefferson's consultations in Paris with physiocratic theorists (the Abbé de Mably and Dr. Richard Gem), the results of which were sent to Madison in March of 1789. The physiocratic document is an argument for the supremacy of the judicial to "guard the deposit of the laws" and is exactly parallel to Madison's formulations when presented as the Ninth Amendment in the Bill of Rights (June 1789). This is an enlightenment legal methodology which, as Justice William Douglas argued in *Griswold* v. *Connecticut*, strenthens the possibilities of using legal process for democratizations against the corruptions of contemporary corporatism. Thus, the Ninth Amendment and Article 4.4 of the Constitution are essential for securing the conditions of public virtue and provide a general principle of law that resists suppression of unnamed rights and defines "due process" in new situations. This enlightenment legal doctrine returns to Roman civil law, in contrast to Anglo-American legal method, and implied that existing law is an imperfect expression of natural law and must be interpreted as an analogy in new situations to mirror more perfectly the natural law. On these grounds, Justice Douglas argued in *Griswold* that the Bill of Rights in its totality guarantees a right of privacy as a general principle of law and its extension to other corrupted rights is possible. The force of the Ninth Amendment is stronger if Article 4.4 of the Constitution is also understood as an intent to secure the preconditions for republican virtue in all states.

By this interpretation the concept of federalism retains a normative sense that is rooted in a consensual social compacting in the classical sense of mutual promise and obligations (an ethically based concept of law) and not the modern contractarian protection of the egoistic individual. The classical theory of a mutual contract is based on a "consociation," an ethical principle of reciprocity that presupposes equality. On the other hand the modern social contract (that of Hobbes) is where the safety of every individual is protected by the state. The Lockean concept of the social contract is a mixture of the classical and modern concepts and remains a controversially inadequate expression of the American practice of social compacting. Thus Hannah

Trent Schroyer

Arendt distinguishes between the two kinds of "social contract" in the seventeenth century, the one found in Locke's *Treatise on Civil Government* where individuals resign their power to higher authority in exchange for protection of life and property, and the other a mutual contract by which people bind themselves together in order to form a community based on reciprocity and equality.[36] The actual content of the latter is a promise that is the ethical foundation of government. Those who give their "consent" covenant and combine together by an act of mutual promise do not merely secure their individual economic entitlements.

On this interpretation the sovereignty of the American people also resides in the mutual consent of people within each state to combine and as people of one nation to elect an executive. Thus the moral-ethical foundation of dual federalism presupposes the consensus that creates the power of the state. If this power is perceived as illegitimate, there is an ethical ground for contesting the constituted power. That is, the forming of covenants, compacts, and constitutions from the original Mayflower compact to the Declaration of Independence and the Articles of Confederation assumed that the power resided in the people and that delegated power can be revoked.[37]

It is precisely this potential for the democratization of public policy formation that has been repeatedly denied in practice and systematically undermined by the American foundation's counterrevolution against civic participation. Today an ongoing formation of the American state has accelerated the equation of public discourse with those societal reorganizations essential to achieve greater economic growth. This escalation of corruption was qualitatively transformed in the nineteenth century by the transfer of the Lockean defense of individual private property to corporate units. This represents an ideological transfer of the original republican rights of the agrarian farmer's home and tools to the right of corporate enterprise to make economic decisions unconstrained by political authority.[38] The reality of the internal organization of the corporation as hierarchical and despotic and increasingly committed to the aggressive use of its resources to influence political processes can be exposed as an escalation of corruption.

This ideology transfer from individual rights of an agrarian society to the rights of economic corporations received its systematic legitimacy during the so-called progressive era. The Reagan state is now engaged in the systematic closure of previously available public information in ways that secure the asymmetric power of "corporate persons" against "natural persons"—that is, citizens. Contrary to the neoconservative promise to "get government off the backs of the citizens," Reagan's turn to secrecy by limiting the scope of the Public Information Act, rewriting the classification of government documents, and subjecting government officials to lifelong censorship actually increase the power of corporate persons over natural citizens in the market. In the name of "national security" American citizens are being asked to participate in their own political alienation and give up their right to information that is essential for rational action in the economy and public policy formation.[39]

Actions to overcome colonization of communities and enforced dependence of individuals have been local struggles that challenge the rights and antidemocratic privileges of "corporate persons." For example, in Vermont and Maine, formation of state energy boards selected from local energy districts has begun a type of public planning outside of the administrative structures, which may be a model for public research and planning. Another example is the effort to create an Appalachian Mountain Authority, which, unlike other state energy planning groups, is a public forum responsible only to local groups. In these public formations, the leverages of federalism are a structural potential for substantive democratization in America in that they are a legal leverage for flexibility against the state and corporate system.[40] The very spaciousness of the country, the large distances between urban centers, permits an ongoing capacity of local and even state governments to become bastions for cultural politics of dissenting and/ or countercommunities.[41]

This potential for building local power bases is also central to the various forms of "green politics," which make up the American bioregional movement. This movement advocates a revitalization of local and regional civic participation as essential for the reinhabitation of bioregions. The notion of a bioregion is inherent in the history of American regional planning, as well as in the patterns of settlement of the indigenous American peoples. Ecologically the notion of a bioregion is an assertion that the opposition of town and country is irrelevant now that the potentials of ecological catastrophe force a rethinking of how human settlement is related to global ecology.

Religion and Enlightenment

Ratification of the U.S. Constitution fused the charter myth of foundation and soon acquired that unique quality of the mixed Anglo-American legal and religious traditions: divinity. The Constitution became the source and central icon of an American political religion, or civil religion, that had its justification in the Anglo-American inseparability of law and religion. It is this element of generalized lowest common denominator ethos of foundational law and nonspecific concept of divinity that has transformed the political meaning of democracy in America into a vague melding of the public and private values, that is, into a religion of democracy—a civil religion. The critical open process meaning of democracy that encourages public discourse and genuine compromise becomes reduced in a civil religion to a confusion of the political, religious, and moral—that is, to an acceptance of the sacred mission of the polity that does not discriminate critically, to a "conviction of consensus."[42]

How is it possible to develop a critical consciousness about inherent coercion in the body politic where religion is affirmatively oriented to individual or collective redemption?[43] This is the question put by the Marxist critique of religion to the American origins. The following tries to argue that rightly reconstructed religion can be a source of critique itself.

The sociocultural moment of Western civilizational processes is constituted as an event-structure where fundamental symbols of meaning, connected to the initial series of founding events, supply a surplus beyond what is signified. Future events are interpreted in terms of the promised meaning of founding events. Rebellions, reform, and new beginnings depart from new situations that are reevaluations of the promise of the initial semantic surplus.

Paul Ricoeur has argued that the Western tradition has a unique retelling form that cannot be reduced to synchronic systems.[44] Understanding of the covenant at Sinai is essential to securing the legitimacy of the new Christian covenant, to the Reformation, and to the founding of the New World. Material determinants and the power of social constellations also force cultural reinterpretations, but they do not determine the semantic meaning given to new situations. A cultural surplus is reinterpreted by actors seeking to discover the "true" meaning of new events as resymbolications of the founding symbols. A fundamental intentionality is set up by the founding events (such as the exodus from Egypt) that thereafter establishes a signifying unity that is itself essential to maintaining the continuity of historical social and personal identity.

Cultural surplus has a peculiar dialectic that has been described as "lordship and bondage." For example, the Hebrew liberation was a turning of the world upside down that required a new "servitude" to the law of Yahweh.[45] The new covenant of Christianity promised salvation from the bondage of the body and mortality in the conversion to Christ (who is now "the lord"). In the metaphor of the world-turned-upside-down, as represented in the dialectic of lordship and bondage, there is a fundamental cultural surplus that has been used again and again in Western history to resymbolize the meaning of liberation and redefine the symbolic telos for attaining the perfect community. From the beginning Judeo-Christian traditions envisioned a perfect community in which freedom could be reconciled with justice. But the symbolizations of the old and new (Christian) covenants differed, as illustrated by the two-fold meaning of the term *presence* (*Parousia*), which can mean the possibility for immediate conversion or an expected second coming at the end of history.[46] Individual conversion or millenarian expectations define the radical hope for liberation, for a realization of the "not-yet-present."

Creation of the semantics of liberation from bondage, from servitude and captivity can be seen as the unique cultural innovation of the ancient Hebrews. While other archaic states maintained their social identity through a cosmological scheme of religiocultural practices open to reinterpretations as empires rose and fell, as in ancient Egypt, only the Israelites conceived of their social identity as inseparable from a transcendent mission. Whereas other archaic empires maintained their hierarchical class societies by justifying the essential function of cosmic mediation by divine kingship, only the Israelite covenant with Yahweh conceived of the identity of the Israelite as servitude to the Lord whose covenanted promise of liberation defines the identity and mission of the nation.[47] The Christian covenant, which begins with Christ's death on the cross, differs in that the Judaic eschatology of end-time is now defined as existing outside of history. Christians are an eschatological community in themselves. The complex history of the ongoing use of these messianic eschatologies for rebellions and renewals that return to the semantic surplus of liberation cannot be

expanded on here. Suffice it to say that the modern amnesia of traditions has lost the dialectic of lordship and bondage, which is now
remembered in secular social theory as a Hegelian reflection that was
important for Marx.

I believe it can be shown that the cultural retelling of the "revealed"
order of history in ever new situations has been the political function
of a theologically based cultural surplus from at least the age of Caesar
Augustus up to the modern era. In the modern era the ideology of
equality of exchange (supposedly) eclipsed theological dialectics as the
primary cultural form for justification of social power and idealization
of the good life. In Marx's critique of capitalist domination, the notion
of the universal proletariat continued this cultural surplus in "secular"
terms in that the proletariat's liberation is the precondition for freedom.
Here the symbol of the world-turned-upside-down finds new re-
statement. Continuity of the cultural surplus is in the ongoing power
of negative reason to deny the immediacy of idolatry and hierarchical
privilege. In the struggle of wage labor and capital, in the overturning
power of money, and in the universal suffering of the proletariat, the
promise for an apocalyptic community is renewed in the new symbol
of the socialist revolution. Continuity of Western cultural surplus was
recognized by the early Marx when he asserted that the critique of
religion is the beginning of all critique. Today there is a real need for
critical demythologizations that deny the pseudo-explanatory while
recovering the sense in which theological discourse has always depicted
a fundamental structure of justice as intrinsic to the practice of religious
life. What has been happening in South American liberation theology
and European political theology may be paradigmatic for how the
American religious traditions can be critically recovered.[48]

The basic insight of Judeo-Christian eschatology that makes a "redemptive critique" more than a delusion of personal salvation is the
theological principle that "power" paradoxically emerges from need,
not sociopolitical status.[49] In the face of terror and fear of death, the
servants can act on a reversal of the domination ascribed to them by
their master(s). Call it sacrifice, martyrdom, or anything else, it is also
a resistance to bonds of slavery based on an insight into true reciprocity,
friendship, community, and love. Freedom is a critical choice made
again and again in every human life; the universal situation of being
a child is a testament to this common structure of human existence.

The question is whether eschatological insight can be "consciousness raising." If this means that the liberatory intentions of religious practice are openly expressible at the level of discourse, too, then the answer is complex. The early monastic movements, the poor people's movements beginning in the twelfth century, the fourteenth-century theologically based revolts guided by John Wyclif and his disciple Jan Hus, and the Puritan revolution of the seventeenth century brought into focus the dominations of the church and king, the popular right to tyrannicide, and the political theory of popular sovereignty. Indeed a "new history of political theory" defines a radical scholastic tradition traceable from Duns Scotus through William of Ockham to the conciliarist struggles to control the papacy and was also extended to "civil society," especially in the Lutheran and Calvinist debates about the right to resistance.[50] The origins of modern political theory of resistance and revolution can be traced to the debates of civic humanism (classic republicanism) and their dialectic within radical scholasticism and the Reformation.

In these events the cultural surplus of the Judeo-Christian mission of world community was used to oppose the ideology of church or absolute state. Indeed the Reformation itself can be seen as consistent with this idea of mission and with the rebellions implied by the implicit concept of freedom as personal fulfillment. Marxists, too, readily equate this cultural dynamic with the ideology of the *ancien régime* and see only the social irrationality of the personal delusion of salvation.[51] Today the actual relations are more complex and become more relevant as critical movements with communities of faith develop their own critical encounters with modernity. Many questions have not been faced by Marxist criticism about the relations of totalizing critique and modern theological renewals by Karl Rahner, Bernard Lonergan, Paul Tillich, and others. In these renewals authority is not based dogmatically on the structures of the church but in the processes of persuasion of the mind. Surely the origins of modern political and scientific theory can be traced to the Judeo-Christian cultural surplus as a *maieutic* for the transvaluations of authority in the light of reason.

In practice, however, the relations between religion and enlightenment are more complex. The best that can be said is that they are not necessarily in contradiction. This is especially true of the relations of Radical Whiggism, Calvinist political theology, the enlightenment-based new religion, and the evangelical reactions in America. The following reconstruction tries to separate these components in the context of American origins.

1. *Prerevolutionary period: Political theology* American political culture differentiated itself from England after the Glorious Revolution. In this nation-forming process, political theology and the political compulsiveness of radical republicanism created a unique political culture. Colonial rebellions against English authority were culturally both a manifestation of the political quest for public virtue and a fundamental instance of the Calvinist reforming conscience at work.[52] This convergence of two traditions defines the unique intention of the American revolutionary origin.

2. *The Revolutionary period: Fusion of the American nation* The Calvinist influence on early American culture is direct and profound; in 1776, 75 to 85 percent of the colonists could trace their religious background to one form or other of the Calvinist form of reformation.[53] Anglo-American puritanism had fused Christian charity and civic virtue into a form of introspective conversion and fraternal covenant that politicized the "individualism" of conversion. These early traditions thus linked individualism and community into a social concept of humanity that promoted political action as few other Christian churches or sects had done and reinforced the republican ideology of public virtue as the common good of the American social community.

3. *The new religion as legitimation of the foundation for freedom* There is no mention of a Supreme Being, or Christianity, in the Constitution, and this signals an enlightenment universalism that has been called the "new religion." For example, Jefferson's phrasing in the Declaration of Independence of the "laws of nature" and "nature's God" makes explicit the synthesis of enlightenment rationalism and a deistic understanding of theism. This "new religion" was effectively institutionalized by the Constitution, the Bill of Rights, and the evolution of juridical practice, but it has been understood in at least two different ways: first, as Jefferson, Madison, and others understood it (the new religion) and, second, as a travesty that denied the identity of Christianity and the common law, a position held by the evangelical reaction.

4. *Evangelical reactions to the new religion* Starting with Jonathan Edwards and the first wave of revivalism and then more clearly in the second great awakening (circa 1795), the initial Puritan intention to build

Christian societies was transformed into a personal, private discipline of the inner life of the soul. Evangelical revivalism reinforced the pietistic elements of Christianity. From this perspective, the separation of church and state was seen as the work of "infidels" and the Declaration of Independence as "atheistic." In both cases, it was viewed as the work of Jefferson, "one of the greatest enemies that Christianity ever had . . . in America."[54]

The task of comprehending how these moments formed and changed over time can be approached retrospectively. If we begin with an explication of the late states, the earlier phases of this cultural transformation can be more clearly recognized. This genealogy is essential because only the later evangelical reactions construe salvation in pietistic and privatized forms that recreates the early Christian tendency to retreat from this world into a separate community. By focusing on the fear-inducing drama of good and evil in each soul, an affinity between privatized religion and the pessimism of possessive individualism becomes possible. But it is important to realize that this affinity was not constitutive of the American national mission, and thus it is this later antienlightenment thrust that has to be explained.

The key to the antienlightenment movement of mainstream Christianity in America is also part of the refutation of contemporary neoconservative accounts of cultural modernism. I am persuaded that Sidney Mead is correct in his claim that the evangelical mainstream of American Christianity was in opposition to both the early Calvinist political theology and the "new religion" too. If so, then American culture since the beginning of the nineteenth century has been in contradiction with the social structure. What Daniel Bell believes is a result of cultural modernism was begun by the evangelical privatization of religion. A large part of the distortion in the American political culture can be traced back to this evangelical reaction against the premises of the Declaration of Independence and the Constitution. Where the beliefs of religious practice contradict the normative structures of the legal-juridical framework (or where the culture is in opposition to the social structure), a distortion of American social consciousness was shaped that became a major factor in American history. An indicator of this distortion is the charge that Jefferson's "atheistic philosophy" and its "untrue maxim . . . that sovereignty resides in the people" brought on the Civil War.[55] From this perspective the Civil War was a contest between God and Jeffersonianism in that the idea of government by the consent of the people led to the "pretentious usurpations of states' rights." In these interpretations democratic government is not a matter of rights but of "expediency, prudence and providence." The evangelical movement was therefore one of the forms of legitimation for increasing centralization of government, as well as being a mystifying cultural component that concealed the formation of the American ideology.

This begins with Anglo-American antideism stimulated by the equating of Jacobin France and enlightenment philosophies and given an organizational form by the founding of the London Missionary Society in 1795.[56] At the same time rumors of a world conspiracy of the Masonic order were used to stigmatize the anti-Federalist democratic clubs that emerged in the 1790s. The movement back to Christian orthodoxy and against the "new religion" became part of the antirepublican strategy of the high Federalist establishment. The Federalist anti-Jacobin crusade not only resulted in the Alien and Sedition Acts but also supported the regressive orthodox movement against enlightenment universalism. Today as American "education for freedom" puts forth the Federalist Papers as fundamental evidence for a revolution made by "free men," it is also important to remember that the Federalists themselves helped to demolish the enlightenment-grounded republicanism, replacing it with a Christianized democratic ethos that is a distortion of the American revolutionary intention. The resulting vulgarized political culture substituted patriotic moralism for conscience politics and began the substitution of local voluntary associations for weak political institutions that neoconservatives now claim to be "mediating structures."

This period of vulgarization and regression in American culture stimulated European reflections on American degeneracy. As the French naturalist comte de Buffon implied, in America the evolutionary tendency is from civilization to barbarism; the American environment has a regressive effect on animals and people. This impression is perhaps warranted by the emergent cultural contradiction of evangelical reaction and the rational foundations of the Republic. Instead of republicanism, the reactionary polity envisioned was a Christian democracy. Instead of a political theology identified with public virtue and rational persuasion, the emerging evangelical religions (Methodism, Baptism, and others) featured a voluntaristic emotionalism that identified belief and personal conversion. In retrospect the entire "genteel tradition" can be viewed as an exorcism of encircled fear: fear of Europe, the Negro slave, popular passion, and the Indian. This cultural schizophrenia has been most perceptively recognized by Mark Twain, who claimed the American passion for morality rested on a fundamental fear of being found out and corresponded to the American admiration for the open amorality of the successful.[57]

This contradiction between the republican foundations and privatized religious practice, however, remained invisible because the myth of foundation legitimated a union of nationalist mission and religious nationalism. The difference between an enlightenment, "new religion" version of the American civil religion and its later evangelical transformation needs more clarification. The close resemblance of evangelical mission and the earlier political theology can be seen in John Adams's view of the Revolution "as merely the opening of a grand scheme and design in Providence for the illumination of the ignorant, and the emancipation of the slavish part of mankind all over the earth." It is also evident in Andrew Jackson's belief that God had charged the United States with the unique responsibility of preserving freedom for the benefit of the human race. Thus the symbol of a sacred American mission in history was the eschatological kernel of the American nationalist religion. To "manifest destiny" is the calling of America; to overturn all blocks to this end is an intrinsic element of the American "nationalistic theology." This belief first emerged in colonial America, where the self-image of the American people as a chosen people implied that they were to complete the Reformation and begin a regeneration of the world.[58] But the Calvinist political theology understood this in terms of a political covenant that in the earlier phase was also seen as implying the need for public virtue and common sense. The later evangelical reaction saw this mission in terms of a separatist Christian (even Protestant) mission. This evangelical version went so far as to deny the senses in which the Constitution and Bill of Rights effectively disestablished all religion and hence desectarianized American society.

It is important today to remember that America was the first "post-Christendom" nation that moved beyond Locke's principle of tolerance by creating a context of religious freedom. Where laws disestablish religion, the normative order of a religious culture shifts to the liberty of conscience itself. This "law" replaces any particular religious form and becomes ethically the "common law" and morally the "common sense" of the social order.[59] The common law and the ongoing renewal of legal institutions therefore establish a fundamental moral meaning to religious pluralism. In practice, this has meant that the history of U.S. Supreme Court decisions on freedom of religious conscience has moved beyond a theistic Christian foundation to a more universalistic definition of "no established religion." This implies that all tradition-alisms can be overcome in "due process." To the degree that any particular religion is denied, the law as a universalistic structure does become a moral guide. The American legal system, then, differentiates the legitimate moral order from any particular type of religious and moral ideology and yet by doing so becomes an institution that performs a role approximating a new "secular theology." Yet this enlightenment universalism of the juridical process was (and is) not understood or accepted by religious groups. This universalistic foundation has been fought since the rule of disestablishment itself and continuing up to the contemporary opposition to the Supreme Court's *Schempp* decision, which prohibits school sponsorship of a particular form of moral education.

The American nation is defined by the union of enlightenment universalism, the social contract based on a social compact (the re-publican tradition), and the notion of individuality inherent in the religious notion of conscience. This tripartite synthesis defines the original intention of the American foundation and the origin of the idea of an American nation. All differences in socioeconomic, cultural, and regional identities are bridged by this fundamental cultural surplus that ties the nation's identity back to this beginning as an origin defining its end.

Conclusion: Sociocultural Resources for Democratization in America

If we hypothetically assume the legitimacy crisis dynamic as context, the relevant question is this: Where are these conflicts casting forward a postconventional moral-ethical consciousness? Habermas holds that only the cultural residues of science, "post-auratic art," and univer-salistic morality provide potential leverages against the trends toward technocratic corporatism. Supposedly these remaining vital components of culture represent normatively legitimate needs that cannot be satisfied completely within the corporatist tendencies. These spheres provide ideal values with normative foundations today and can result in oppositional practices that further realize these potentials.

But if we put this theory in the American context, there are additional sources for forms of moral-ethical consciousness that go beyond the instrumentalism of equivalent exchange or the law and order mentality of conventional morality. If we ask where are the symbolic structures or context encouraging a postconventional self-consciousness that discriminates between norm maintenance and norm making or between universal ethical principles and the self-interested competitive egocentrism of the corporate gamesman, we have to include the traditional American cultural surplus. These motivational complexes are open to critical reconstruction and critique, but this must be done hermeneutically and not by attempting to reconstruct exclusively in terms of economic class relations such social movements as various versions of Jeffersonian agrarian decentralization, or antiparty movements, the abolitionists, women's suffrage, and agrarian populism. From the perspective of the American cultural surplus, Marxist socialism is simply a variation of technocratic corporatism and fundamentally insensitive to the American vision of the reciprocity of free social community and individual moral development. If we recover the original intentions of American libertarianism with sufficient care, we will, I believe, recognize that the traditional civic ethic provides some universal principles for political participation, as well as converging with the notion of rational consensus as developed analytically by communicational ethics.

Notes

1. See *Failure of a Dream?*, ed. J. M. Laslett and Seymour Martin Lipset (Garden City, N.Y.: Doubleday, 1974), which reflects on this question.

2. Leon Samson, *Toward a United Front* (New York: Farrar and Rinehart, 1935), and Warren I. Susman's comments in this thesis in *Failure of a Dream?*, pp. 443ff.

3. See Floyd Abrams, "The New Effort to Control Information," *New York Times Magazine*, September 25, 1983, which sees the closure of information as a threat to the First Amendment. This view is also shared by James Coleman who suggests the necessity of a political theory of information rights. See Coleman's *The Asymmetrical Society* (Syracuse, N.Y.: Syracuse University Press, 1982), pp. 153ff.

4. See Cornelius Castoriadis, *Crossroads in the Labyrinth* (Cambridge, Mass.: MIT Press, 1984), for the concept of the "social imaginary," which seems to me to strengthen and add another dimension to the idea of cultural surplus.

5. See Norman Jacobson, "Political Realism and the Age of Reason," *Review of Politics* (1953).

6. For example, George Shulman's "The Pastoral Idyll of Democracy," *Democracy* (Fall 1983), uses a term—*Pastoral*—that fails to see that the city-country opposition is outdated in an international world economy whose dynamics shape a global ecology crisis. Reasserting the difference between work and politics and the "fundamental reality of workers engaged collectively in the production of life" (p. 49) is important but no more so than the recognition of how normative judgments and cultural values are excluded in "realistic" (technocratic) decision making. A similar expression of the limits of the "production paradigm" of Marxism is Stanley Aronowitz's proclamation that Habermas's communication theory is just new-style Kantianism and should not be "confused with the liberatory project" as well as "who cares about social integration anyway." See Aronowitz's review in *Village Voice Literary Supplement*, May 8, 1984, and his later response to Andrew Arato's letter, June 12, 1984.

7. Wyndham Lewis, *America and Cosmic Man* (London: Nicholson and Watson, 1948).

8. For the distinction between the communications and production paradigms of critique, see Gyorgy Markus's important article, "Practical-Social Rationality in Marx: A Dialectical Critique," *Dialectical Anthropology* 4, no. 4 (December 1979) and no. 5 (1980). Markus achieves an incisive critique of Marx's concept of socialism as separating the realm of necessity (the centralized apparatus of material-technical production) from the communal self-government of associated producers that posits the social goals for development (the realm of freedom). This institutional separation of technical and sociopolitical decisions continues the bourgeois separation of economics and politics as institutionally segregated spheres and, in socialist practice, has been subject to the same type of reification of technical-economic imperatives that conceals domination as in capitalist societies. See part I, p. 275.

9. Jürgen Habermas, *Legitimation Crisis* (Boston: Beacon, 1973).

10. See the essays by C. B. McPherson and Charles Reich in Virginia Held, ed., *Property, Profits and Economic Justice* (Belmont, Calif.: Wadsworth Publishing Co., 1980). For an analysis of the economic imperatives for such a guaranteed job project to provide full employment and economic recovery, see Lester Thurow, *The Zero-Sum Society* (New York: Basic Books, 1980).

11. The crucial linking movement may well be the feminist movement. See Riane Eisler and David Loye, "The Hidden Future," *World Futures* 19 (1983): 123–136, and Birgit Brock-Utne, "The Relationship of Feminism to Peace and Peace Education," *Bulletin of Peace Proposals* 15 (1984).

12. See Claus Offe, *Industry and Inequality* (London: Edward Arnold, 1976), p. 13.

13. See Walter Dean Burnham, "Revitalization and Decay," *Journal of Politics* 38 (August 1976); also see William Appleman Williams's *America Confronts a Revolutionary World: 1776–1976* (New York: William Morrow), pp. 113ff.

14. See Gordon Clark, "A Theory of Local Autonomy," *Annals of the Association for American Goegraphers* 74 (1984), for an effort to provide a conception of local autonomy in terms of the variables of immunity and initiative.

15. See Richard Slotkin's *Regeneration through Violence* (Middletown, Conn.: Wesleyan University Press, 1973), and Frederick Turner, *Beyond Geography: The Western Spirit against the Wilderness* (New York: Viking Press, 1980).

16. See John Opie, "Frederick Jackson Turner, The Old West and the Formation of a National Mythology," *Environmental Review* 5 (Fall 1981), and William Cronon, *Changes in the Land: Indians, Colonists and the Ecology of New England* (New York: Hill and Wang, 1983).

17. Wendell Berry, *The Unsettling of America: Culture and Agriculture* (San Francisco: Sierra Club, 1977).

18. Most comprehensive in its recovery of this political tradition of civic humanism is J. G. A. Pocock's *The Machiavellian Moment: Florentine Political Thought and the Atlantic Republican Tradition* (Princeton: Princeton University Press, 1975); also Gordon S. Wood, *The Creation of the American Republic* (New York: W. W. Norton, 1972). That this tradition had an impact on the early enlightenment has also been argued by Franco Venturi, *Utopia and Reform in the Enlightenment* (Cambridge: Cambridge University Press, 1971).

19. Robert Bellah, *The Broken Covenant* (New York: Seabury, 1975); also see Daniel Bell, "The End of American Exceptionalism," in N. Glazer and I. Kristol, eds., *The American Commonwealth* (New York: Basic Books, 1976), pp. 193ff.

20. David B. Davis, "Cultural History and the American Identity," in W. S. Dillon, ed., *The Cultural Drama* (Washington, D.C.: Smithsonian Institution Press, 1974).

21. David S. Lovejoy, *The Glorious Revolution in America* (New York: Harper and Row, 1972); also see Seymour Martin Lipset, *The First New Nation* (Garden City, N.Y.: Doubleday, 1967).

22. Cf. Ernst Vollrath, "That All Governments Rest on Opinion," *Social Research* 43 (Spring 1976). Also see Sheldon Wolin, "Analysis of Fear as the Fundamental Emotion of Liberalism," in *Politics and Vision* (Boston: Little Brown, 1960), pp. 314ff.

23. Nicholas Xenos, "Classical Political Economy," *Humanities in Society* 3 (Summer 1980).

24. J. G. A. Pocock, *The Ancient Constitution and the Feudal Law* (New York: Norton, 1967).

25. Cf. Wood, *Creation*.

26. In Morton Borden, ed., *The Anti-Federalist Papers* (East Lansing, Mich.: Michigan State University Press, 1965–1967).

27. Ernest Tuveson, *Redeemer Nation* (Chicago: University of Chicago Press, 1968), pp. 120ff.

28. Formulation of this policy had been forced by the state of Maryland's refusal to ratify the Articles of Confederation due to the claim that "equality" must be reconciled with empire. Consequently Virginia ceded its territory north and west of Ohio on the condition that it be held in a common fund, a national domain, to be formed into new independent "republics." This republican fantasy was, however, in response to the growing momentum of land speculation in the northwest; hence, Jefferson's ordinance of April 23, 1784 (which became the Northwest Ordinance of July 13, 1787), designated seven states and conditions for statehood (slavery excluded).

29. Remembering that nine of every ten adults at that time were farmers, ratification of the Constitution represented a "compromise" between the men of wealth in the cities and on the land (especially in the South). The same opposition continued in later American history as the difference between Jeffersonians and "federalists," although this division was mediated by the regional factor, which was related directly to slavery. It is important to remember today that the Federalists tended to be rich and more favorable to commerical expansion, while the anti-Federalists, or "true" federalists, put greater emphasis on local retention of power by the people and on the political structures needed for generating real and not forced consensus.

314

Trent Schroyer

30. See Jackson Turner Main, *The Antifederalists: Critics of the Constitution* (Chicago: Quadrangle, 1961), pp. 184ff.

31. Merrill Jenson, *The Articles of Confederation* (Madison: University of Wisconsin Press, 1963), pp. 165, 245.

32. For the concept of pseudo-compromise, see Habermas, *Legitimation Crisis.*

33. See Sheldon Wolin, "The Idea of the State in America," *Humanities in Society* 3 (1980).

34. Alexis de Tocqueville, *Democracy in America*, ed. P. Bradley (New York, 1966), 1:93.

35. See Mitchell Franklin, "The Ninth Amendment as Civil Method and Its Implications for a Republican Form of Government," *Tulane Law Review* 11 (1966): 487; see also Laurence Tribe, *American Constitutional Law* (Mineola, N.Y.: Foundation Press, 1978), pp. 570ff.

36. See Hannah Arendt, *On Revolution* (New York: Viking, 1966), pp. 168ff., for an elaboration of two kinds of social contract.

37. The question reinforced by the ferment of religious subcultures was the issue of the "sovereignty of the people." Distorted by the representative inversion, the Constitution evades the question of how to assert the sovereignty of the people. When is civil disobedience justified? Or how can the First Amendment be applied to cases where the executive and/or legislative political decisions need to be contested? The limits of Supreme Court review in the so-called political question doctrine is the crucial test in the American policy's claim to "sovereignty of the people." See Tribe, *American Constitutional Law*, pp. 15–19, 307ff., 1149ff.

38. See Robert Dahl, "On Removing Certain Impediments to Democracy in the United States," *Dissent* (Summer 1979).

39. See James Coleman, *The Asymmetric Society* (Syracuse, N.Y.: Syracuse University Press, 1982).

40. For a discussion of the relevance of local and regional forms of public energy planning, see Robert Engler, *The Brotherhood of Oil* (Chicago: University of Chicago Press, 1977), pp. 199ff.

41. See Robert Wiebe, *The Segmented Society* (New York: Oxford University Press, 1975), who argues "what has held Americans together is their capacity for living apart!" But it is also this which permits greater social experimentation with new public formation than is possible in Europe. For example, the land trust movement in America provides an alternative use of the privileges of "corporate persons."

42. See D. J. Boorstin, *The Genius of American Politics* (Chicago: University of Chicago Press, 1953), p. 157.

43. See Jürgen Habermas, "Consciousness Raising or Redemptive Critique," *New German Critique* 17 (Spring 1979).

44. See Paul Ricoeur, *The Conflict of Interpretations* (Evanston: Northwestern University Press, 1974), pp. 27ff.

45. See Abraham Rotstein, "The World Turned Upside Down," *Canadian Journal of Political and Social Theory* (Spring–Summer 1978).

46. Rudolf Bultmann, *Primitive Christianity* (Cleveland: Meridian, 1966).

47. Ernst Bloch, *Atheism in Christianity* (New York: Herder and Herder, 1972); Walter Benjamin, *Illuminations* (New York: Schocken, 1969).

48. See *Liberation, Revolution and Freedom*, ed. Thomas McFadden (New York: Seabury Press, 1975), and Dorothee Soelle, *Political Theology* (Philadelphia: Fortress Press, 1974).

49. I first encountered the idea that "power comes from need" from William Murion's unpublished manuscript, "The Dynamic of Christianity," to be published as *Getting Religion*. More recently this has been elaborated imaginatively by Elizabeth Janeway in *The Powers of the Weak* (New York: Morrow Quill, 1981).

50. See Quentin Skinner, *The Foundation of Modern Political Thought* (New York: Cambridge University Press, 1978), vols. 1–2, for a rewriting of the origins of modern political theory that roots it in the movement of Catholic Counciliarism and the theological critiques of papal tyranny.

51. The dialectic of lordship and bondage can be decoded as a reflection on the dynamic of redemptive critiques that are at the same time consciousness-raising critiques. Such a mediation has yet to be achieved but falls within the scope of the critique of religion. But to do this requires that the "neutralization of religion by modernity" thesis be reexamined. This means that Habermas's "motivation crisis theorem" does not fit the American context; the role of traditional cultural universal remains central to the American political culture.

52. See Alan Heimert, *Religion and the American Mind* (Cambridge: Harvard University Press, 1966); or for a different interpretation, see Rhys Isaac, "Preachers and Patriots," in Alfred F. Young *The American Revolution* (De Kalb: Northern Illinois University Press, 1976). See also the editor's comment on this issue on p. 456, suggesting that the possible convergence of millenialists and radicals may yet be discovered to be a significant factor in the American revolution.

53. Sydney Ahlstrom, *A Religious History of the American People* (New Haven: Yale University Press, 1972), pp. 124ff.

54. Sidney Mead, *The Old Religion in the Brave New World* (Berkeley: University of California Press, 1977), pp. 98ff.

55. Ibid., p. 102. The charge was made by Horace Bushnell, the Protestant prophet of nineteenth-century "progressive orthodoxy," who influenced Christian educational thinking in ways that helped bring to an end the influence of an earlier union of Calvinism and Scottish moral philosophy.

56. Henry May, *The Enlightenment in America* (New York: Oxford University Press, 1976), p. 265.

57. Quoted in Wilson Carey McWilliams, *The Idea of Fraternity in America* (Berkeley: University of California Press, 1973), p. 450.

58. Robert N. Bellah, *The Broken Covenant: American Civil Religion in Time of Trial* (New York: Seabury Press, 1975).

59. See May, *Enlightenment*, pp. 341ff., for an account of the special affinity of Scottish thought and the American foundations. The Scottish enlightenment and its philosophy of "common sense" was of fundamental importance to the legal thought of Americans.

Modern and Postmodern Architecture

Jürgen Habermas

The exhibition "The Other Tradition: Architecture in Munich from 1800 to the Present" offers an opportunity to consider the meaning of a preposition. This preposition has inconspicuously become part of the dispute on postmodern or late-modern architecture. With the prefix *post* the protagonists wish to dismiss the past, unable as yet to give the present a *new* name: To the recognizable problems of the future, they—that is to say, we—do not yet have the answer.

At first the expression *postmodern* had only been used to denote novel variations within the broad spectrum of the "late-modern," when it was used during the 1950s and 1960s in the United States for literary trends that intended to set themselves apart from earlier modern writings. Postmodernism only became an emotionally loaded, outright political war cry in the 1970s, when two contrasting camps seized the expression. On the one hand the "neoconservatives," who wanted to rid themselves of the supposedly subversive contents of a "hostile culture," in favor of reawakened traditions; on the other hand, certain *critics of economic growth*, for whom the New Architecture (*Neues Bauen*) had become the symbol of the destruction brought on by modernization. Thus for the first time architectural movements that had shared the theoretical position of modern architecture—and had rightfully been described by Charles Jencks as late-modern—happened to

This lecture was presented in December 1981 at the exhibition "The Other Tradition: Architecture in Munich from 1800 to the Present" and was first published in the *Süddeutsche Zeitung* of 5–6 December 1981. The present translation by Helena Tsoskounoglou was first published in *9H* (London), no. 4 (1983).

have been dragged into the "conservative" wake of the 1970s, paving the way for an intellectually playful yet provocative repudiation of the moral principles of modern architecture.

In Opposition to Modernism

It is not easy to disentangle the frontiers for all parties agree in the critique of the soulless "container" architecture, of the absence of a relationship with the environment and the solitary arrogance of the unarticulated office block, of the monstrous department stores, monumental universities and congress centers, of the lack of urbanity and the misanthropy of the satellite towns, of the heaps of speculative buildings, the brutal successor to the "bunker architecture" — the mass production of pitch-roofed doghouses, the destruction of cities in the name of the automobile, and so forth. . . . So many slogans with no disagreement whatsoever!

Indeed what one side calls *immanent criticism*, the other side considers to be the *opposition to the "modern."* The same reasons that encourage the one side to a critical continuation of an irreplaceable tradition are sufficent for the other side to proclaim a postmodern era. Furthermore these opponents draw contrasting conclusions according to whether they confront the evil in terms of cosmetics or in terms of criticism of the system.

Those of a *conservative disposition* satisfy themselves with a stylistic cover-up of that which nonetheless exists, either like the traditionalist von Branca or like the pop-artist Venturi, who transforms the spirit of the Modern Movement into a quotation and mixes it ironically with other quotations, like dazzling radiant neon light texts. The radical *antimodernists*, on the other hand, tackle the problem at a more fundamental level, seeking to undermine the economic and administrative constraints of industrial constructions. Their aim is a de-differentiation of the architectural culture. What the one side considers as problems of style, the other perceives as problems of the decolonization of lost human habitats. Thus those who wish to continue the incompleted project of the shaken Modern Movement see themselves confronted by various opponents who agree only inasmuch as they are determined to break away from modern architecture. Modern architecture which has even left its mark on everyday life, after all, is still the first and only unifying style since the days of classicism. It has developed out of both the organic as well as the rationalistic origins of a Frank Lloyd Wright and an Adolf Loos, and flourished in the most successful works of a Gropius and a Mies van der Rohe, a Le Corbusier and an Alvar Aalto. It is the only architectural movement to originate from the avant-garde spirit: it is equivalent to the avant-garde painting, music, and literature of our century. It continued along the traditional line of occidental rationalism and was powerful enough to create its own models; in other words, it became classic itself and set the foundations of a tradition that from the very beginning crossed national boundaries. How are such hardly disputable facts reconcilable with the fact that in the very name of this International Style, those unanimously condemned deformations that followed World War II could have come about. Might it be that the real face of modern architecture is revealed in these atrocities, or are they misrepresentations of its true spirit?

The Challenge of the Nineteenth Century to Architecture

I should like to attempt a provisional answer by: (1) listing the problems that faced architecture in the nineteenth century, (2) giving an account of the programmatic answers that the Modern Movement offered in response to the problems, (3) pointing out the kind of problems that could not be solved by this program. Finally, (4) these considerations should help to make a judgment on the suggestion, which this exhibition attempts to make (presuming its intentions have been correctly understood), How good is the recommendation to adopt the modern tradition unerringly and to continue it critically instead of following the "escapist movements" that are currently dominant: be it tradition-conscious "neohistoricism," the ultramodern "stage-set" architecture that was presented at the Venice Biennale in 1980, or the "vitalism" of simplified life in anonymous, deprofessionalized, vernacular architecture? The industrial revolution and the accelerated social modernization that followed introduced a new situation to nineteenth-century architecture and town planning. I would like to mention the three best-known challenges:

the qualitatively new requirements in architectural design;

the new materials and construction techniques; and finally

the subjugation of architecture to new functional, above all economic, imperatives.

Industrial capitalism created *new interest spheres* that evaded both courtly-ecclesiastical architecture and the old European urban and rural architectural culture. The diffusion of culture and the formation of a wider, educated public, interested in the arts, called for new libraries and schools, opera houses and theaters. However, these were conventional tasks. Entirely different is the challenge presented by the transport network, which was revolutionized by the railway; not only did it give a different meaning to the already familiar transport structures, the bridges and tunnels, but it also introduced a new task: the construction of railway stations. Railway stations are characteristic places for dense and varied as well as anonymous and fleeting encounters, in other words, for the type of interactions that were to mark the atmosphere of life in the big cities, described by Benjamin as overflowing with excitement but lacking in contact. As the motorways, airports, and television towers have shown, the development of transport and communication networks has initiated innovations time and again.

This also applied to the development for commercial communication. It not only created the demand for a new scale of warehouses and market halls, but introduced unconventional construction projects as well: the department store and the exhibition hall. Above all, however, industrial production with its factories, workers' housing estates, and goods produced for mass consumption created new spheres of life into which formal design and architectural articulation were not able to penetrate at first.

In the second half of the nineteenth century those mass products for daily use that had escaped the stylistic force of the traditional arts and crafts were the first to be perceived as an aesthetic problem. John Ruskin and William Morris sought to bridge the gap that had opened between utility and beauty in the everyday life of the industrial world by reforming the applied arts. This reform movement was led by a broader, forward-looking architectural notion that accompanied the claim to form, from an architectural point of view, the *entire* physical environment of bourgeois society. Morris in particular recognized the contradiction between the democratic demands for universal participation in culture and the fact that, within industrial capitalism, increasing domains of human activity were being alienated from the creative cultural forces.

The second challenge to architecture arose from the development of *new materials* (such as glass and iron, steel and cement) and *new methods of production* (above all the use of prefabricated elements). In the course of the nineteenth century the engineers advanced the techniques of construction, thereby developing new design possibilities that shattered the classical limits of the constructional handling of planes and volumes. Originating from greenhouse construction, the glass palaces of the first industrial exhibitions in London, Munich, and Paris, built from standardized parts, conveyed to their fascinated contemporaries the first impression of new orders of magnitude and of constructional principles. They revolutionized visual experience and altered the spectators' concept of space, as dramatically as the railway changed the passengers' concept of time. The interior of the centerless, repetitive London Crystal Palace must have had the effect of a transcendence of all known dimensions of designed space.

Finally, the third challenge was the capitalist *mobilization* of labor, real estate, and buildings, in general of all *urban living conditions*. This led to the concentration of large masses and to the incursion of speculation in the field of private housing. The reason for today's protests in Kreuzberg and elsewhere originates in that period. As housing construction became an amortizable investment, so decisions about the purchase and the sale of estate, about construction, demolition, and reconstruction, about renting and vacating property were freed from the ties of family and local tradition, in other words they made themselves independent of use-value considerations. The laws of the building and housing market altered the attitude toward building and dwelling. Economic imperatives also determined the uncontrolled growth of cities. Out of these arose the requirements of a kind of town planning that cannot be compared to baroque city developments. The way these two sorts of functional imperatives, those of the market with those of communal and state planning, intersect, and the way they entangle architecture in a new system of subordinations, is demonstrated in a grand style by the redevelopment of Paris by Haussmann, under Napoleon III. The architects played no noteworthy parts in these plans.

Jürgen Habermas

Failure of Historicism, Modernism's Answer

In order to understand the impulse from which modern architecture developed, one has to bear in mind that the architecture of the second part of the nineteenth century was not only overwhelmed by this third requirement of industrial capitalism, but, although the other two challenges were recognized, it has still not mastered them. The arbitrary disposition of scientifically objectified styles, having been torn from their formative context, enabled historicism to sidestep into an idealism that had become impotent, and to separate the field of architecture from the banalities of everyday bourgeois life. By setting utilitarian architecture free from artistic demands, a virtue was made of the necessity of the new domains of human concerns that had been alienated from architectural design. The opportunities offered by the new possibilities of technical design were only grasped in order to divide the world between architects and engineers, style and function, impressive facades on the exterior and autonomous spatial disposition in the interior. Thus historical architecture did not have much more to set against the immanent dynamic of economic growth, to the mobilization of urban living conditions, to the social plight of the masses, than the escape into the triumph of spirit and culture over the (disguised) material bases.

In the reformist tendencies of the *Jugendstil*, from which modern architecture emerged, the protest was already raised against this falsity, against an architecture of repression and symptom formation. It was no coincidence that, in the same period, Sigmund Freud developed the foundations of his theory of neurosis.

The Modern Movement took on the challenges for which nineteenth-century architecture was no match. It overcame the stylistic pluralism and the differentiations and subdivisions with which architecture had come to terms. It gave an answer to the alienation from culture and industrial capitalist domains with the claim for a style that would not only make a mark on prestige buildings, but would also penetrate everyday practice. The spirit of modernism was to participate in the totality of social manifestations. Industrial design was able to take up the reform of the applied arts: the functional design of utility buildings was able to take up the engineering skills demonstrated in transport and commercial buildings; the concept of commercial quarters was able to take up the models of the Chicago School. Over and above that, the new architectural language seized on the exclusive fields of monumental architecture, of churches, theaters, law courts, ministries, town halls, universities, spas, etc. On the other hand it expanded into key areas of industrial production, into settlements, social housing, and factories.

What Does Functionalism Really Mean?

The New Style could certainly not have penetrated into all spheres of life had modern architecture not assimilated the second challenge, that is, the immensely widened range of technical design possibilities with a determined aesthetic approach. The term *functionalism* incorporates certain key notions—principles for the construction of rooms, for the use of materials and methods of production and organization. Functionalism is based on the conviction that forms should express the use-functions for which a building is produced. But the expression *functionalism* also suggests false concepts. If nothing else, it conceals the fact that the qualities of modern buildings result from a consistently applied autonomous system of aesthetic rules. That which is wrongly attributed to functionalism it owes in fact to an aesthetically motivated constructivism, following independently from new problem definitions posed in art. Through constructivism, modern architecture followed the experimental trail of avant-garde painting.

Modern architecture found itself at a paradoxical point of departure. *On the one hand* architecture has always been a use-oriented art. As opposed to music, painting, and poetry, architecture cannot escape from its practical contextual relations of colloquial speech. These arts remain tied to the network of common practice and everyday communication. It is for that reason that Adolf Loos considered architecture, together with anything else that serves a purpose, to be excluded from the sphere of art.

On the other hand architecture is dominated by the laws of modern culture—it is subject, as is art in general, to the compulsion of attaining radical autonomy. The avant-garde art that freed itself from perspective perception of the object and from tonality, from imitation and harmony, and that turned to its own means of representation, has been characterized by Adorno with key words like *construction, experiment,* and *montage.* According to Adorno the paradigmatic works indulge in an esoteric absolutism, "at the expense of real appropriateness, within which functional objects, as for example bridges and industrial facilities, seek their own formal laws. . . . On the contrary, the autonomous work of art, functional only within its immanent teleology, seeks to attain that which was once called beauty." Thus Adorno contrasts the work of art, functioning "within itself" with the use-object, functioning for "exterior purposes." However, modern architecture, in its most convincing examples, does not comply with the dichotomy outlined by Adorno. Its functionalism rather *coincides* with the inner logic of a development of art. Above all, three groups worked on the problem that had arisen out of cubist painting: the group of purists around Le Corbusier, the constructivists around Malevitch, and in particular, the De Stijl movement (with van Doesburg, Mondrian, and Oud). Just as de Saussure had analyzed language structures at that time, the Dutch Neoplasticists, as they called themselves, investigated the grammar of the means of expression and design of the most general techniques used in the applied arts in order to incorporate them in a total work of art involving the comprehensive architectural articulation of the environment. In Malevich's and Oud's very early house plans one can see how those objects of the functionalist Bauhaus architecture emerge from the experimental approach using pure means of design. It is precisely in Bruno Taut's catch-phrase, "what functions well, looks good," that the *aesthetic significance of functionalism*, expressed so clearly in Taut's own buildings, is lost.

While the Modern Movement recognized the challenges of the qualitatively new requirements and the new technical design possibilities, and while it essentially responded correctly, it reacted rather helplessly to the pressures of the market and the planning bureaucracies.

The broadened architectural concept that had encouraged the Modern Movement to overcome a stylistic pluralism that stood out against everyday reality was a mixed blessing. Not only did it focus attention on the important relations between industrial design, interior design, and the architecture of housing and town planning, but it also acted as a sponsor when the theoreticians of the New Architecture (*Neues Bauen*) wanted to see total forms of life completely subjugated to the dictates of their design tasks. However such totalities extend beyond the powers of design. When Le Corbusier finally managed to realize his design for a "unité jardin verticale," it was the communal facilities that remained unused or were eradicated. The utopia of preconceived forms of life that had already inspired the designs of Owen and Fourier could not be filled with life, not only because of a hopeless under-estimation of the diversity, complexity, and variability of modern aspects of life, but also because modernized societies with their functional interdependencies go beyond the dimensions of living conditions that could be gauged by the planner with his imagination. The crisis that has become apparent today within modern architecture can be traced back not to a crisis in architecture itself, but to the fact that it had readily allowed itself to be overburdened.

The Compulsion of the System, Architecture and the Will to Life

Moreover, modern architecture, with the indistinctions of functionalist ideology, was poorly armed against the dangers brought about by the post–World War II reconstruction, the period during which the International Style broadly asserted itself for the first time. Gropius certainly emphasized the close relations that architecture and town planning had with industry, commerce, politics, and administration. In those early days he already perceived the character of the process of planning. However, within the Bauhaus, these problems only appeared in a "format," which was tailored only to didactic purposes. Furthermore, the success of the Modern Movement led the pioneers to the unjustified expectation that "unity of culture and production" could be achieved in another sense as well. The economic and politicoadministrative limitations to which the design of the environment was subjected appeared in this transfigured viewpoint to be a mere question of organization. When in 1949 the American Architects Association sought to insert in its statutes the condition that architects should not operate as building contractors, Gropius protested—not against the insufficiency of the means, but against the purpose and reason for the proposal. He persisted in his belief: "Art, that has become a cultural factor in general, will be in a position to give the social environment the unity, which will be the true basis for a culture embracing every object, from a simple chair to a house of prayer." Within this grand synthesis, all the contradictions characterizing capitalistic modernization, especially in the field of town planning, disappear—the contradictions between the requirements of a structured environment on the one hand, and the imperatives shared by money and power on the other.

Jürgen Habermas

Restoration of Urbanity?

No doubt that development met with a linguistic misunderstanding. Those means that are suitable for a certain purpose are called *functional*. In this sense one can understand functionalism as seeking to construct buildings according to the measure of the users' purposes. The term *functional*, however, also characterizes decisions that stabilize an anonymous relation of activities, without the system's existence having necessarily been called for or even noticed by any of the participants. In this sense, what is considered as "system-functional" for the economy and administration—for example, an increase in the density of inner city areas with rising prices in real estate and increasing tax revenues—by no means has to prove to be "functional" in the background of the lives of both inhabitants and neighboring residents. The problems of town planning are not primarily problems of design, but problems of controlling and dealing with the anonymous system-imperatives that influence the spheres of city life and threaten to devastate the urban fabric.

Today everyone is talking about recalling the traditional European city. However, as early as 1889, Camilo Sitte, who was one of the first to compare the medieval town with the modern city, had warned against such forced lack of constraints. After a century's criticism of the large city, after innumerable, repeated, and disillusioned attempts to keep a balance in the cities, to save the inner cities, to divide urban space into residential areas and commercial quarters, industrial facilities and garden suburbs; private and public zones; to build habitable satellite towns; to rehabilitate slum areas; to regulate traffic most sensibly, etc.—the question that is brought to mind is whether the actual *notion* of the city has not itself been superseded. As a comprehensible habitat, the city could at one time be architecturally designed and mentally represented. The social functions of urban life, political and economic, private and public, the assignments of cultural and religious representation, of work, habitation, recreation, and celebration could be *translated* into use-purposes, into functions of temporally regulated use of designed spaces. However, by the nineteenth century at the latest, the city became the intersection point of a *different kind* of functional relationship. It was embedded in abstract systems, which could no longer be captured aesthetically in an intelligible presence. The fact that from the middle of the nineteenth century till the late 1880s, the great industrial exhibitions were planned as big architectural events reveals an impulse that seems touching today. While for the purpose of international competition, arranging a festive and vivid display of their industrial products in magnificent halls for the general public, the governments literally wanted to set the stage for the work market and bring it back within the limits of the human habitat. However, not even the railway stations, which had brought their passengers into contact with the transport network, could represent the network's functions in the same way as the city gates had once represented the actual connections to the nearby villages and neighboring towns. Besides, airports today are situated way outside cities, for good reasons. In the characterless office buildings that dominate the town centers, in the banks and ministries, the law courts and corporate administrations, the publishing and printing houses, the private and public bureaucracies, one cannot recognize the functional relations whose point of intersection they form. The graphics of company trademarks and of neon-light advertisements demonstrate that differentiation must take place by means other than that of the formal language of architecture. Another indication that the urban habitat is increasingly being mediated by systemic relations, which cannot be given concrete form, is the failure of perhaps the most ambitious project of the New Architecture. To this day, it has not been possible to integrate social housing and factories within the city. The urban agglomerations have outgrown the old concept of the city that people so cherish. However, that is neither the failure of modern architecture, nor of any other architecture.

Perplexity and Reactions

Assuming this diagnosis is not absolutely wrong, then it first of all merely confirms the dominating perplexity and the need to search for new solutions. Of course, it also raises doubts as to the reactions that have been set off by the disaster of the simultaneously overburdened and instrumentalized architecture of the Modern Movement (*Neues Bauen*). In order at least provisionally to orient myself within the complex terrain of countermovements, I have distinguished three tendencies that have one thing in common: contrary to the self-critical continuation of the Modern Movement, they break away from the Modern Style. They want to dissolve the ties of the avant-garde formal language and the inflexible functionalistic principles; programmatically, form and function are to be separated once again.

On a trivial level, this holds true for neohistoricism, which transforms department stores into medieval rows of houses, and underground ventilation shafts into pocketbook-size Palladian villas. As in the past century, the return to eclecticism is due to compensatory needs. This traditionalism falls under the heading of political neoconservatism, not unknown to Bavaria, insofar as it redefines problems that lie on a *different level*, in terms of questions of style, thus removing it from the consciousness of the public. The escapist reaction is related to a tendency for the affirmative: all that remains should stay as it is. The separation of form and function also applies to the *Postmodern Movement*, which corresponds to Charles Jencks's definitions and which is free of nostalgia—whether it is Eisenmann and Graves, who autonomize the formal repertoire of the 1920s artistically, or whether it is Hollein and Venturi, who, like surrealist stage designers, utilize modern design methods in order to coax picturesque effects from aggressively mixed styles. The language of this stage-set architecture indulges in a rhetoric that still seeks to express in ciphers systemic relations that can no longer be architecturally formulated. Finally, the unity of form and function is broken in a different way by the *Alternative Architecture* that is based on the problems of ecology and of the preservation of historically developed urban districts. These trends, often characterized as "vitalistic," are primarily aimed at closely linking architectural design to spatial, cultural, and historical contexts. Therein survive some of the impulses of the Modern Movement, now obviously on the defensive. Above all, it is worth noting the initiatives aiming at a communal "participatory architecture," which designs urban areas in a dialogue with the clients. When the guiding mechanisms of the market and the town planning administration function in such a way as to have dysfunctional consequences on the lives of those concerned, failing the "functionalism" as it was understood, then it only follows that the formative communication of the participants be allowed to compete with the media of money and power.

However, the nostalgia for de-differentiated forms of existence often bestows upon these tendencies an air of antimodernism. They are then linked to the cult of the vernacular and to reverence for the banal. This ideology of the uncomplicated denies the sensible potential and the specificity of cultural modernism. The praise of anonymous architecture, of architecture without architects, has a price, which this vitalism, having become critical of the whole system, is willing to pay— even if it has another "Volksgeist" in mind, as, for example, the one whose transfiguration in its time brought the monumentalism of the Führer-architecture to its ultimate completion.

A good deal of truth also lies in this form of opposition. It takes on the unanswered problems modern architecture had left in the background—that is to say—the colonization of the human habitat by the imperatives of autonomized systems of economic and administrative processes. However, it will only be possible to learn something from all of these oppositions if we keep one thing in mind: At a certain fortunate moment in modern architecture, the aesthetic identity of constructivism met with the practical spirit of strict functionalism and cohered informally. Traditions can only live through such historic moments.

Contributors

Ben Agger
Department of Sociology
State University of New York at Buffalo
Buffalo, New York

Frank Fischer
Department of Political Science
Rutgers University–Newark College
Newark, New Jersey

John Forester
Department of City and Regional Planning
Cornell University
Ithaca, New York

Peter Grahame
Department of Sociology
Trent University
Peterborough, Ontario

Jürgen Habermas
Faculty of Philosophy
University of Frankfurt
Frankfurt, West Germany

Daniel C. Hallin
Department of Political Science
University of California, San Deigo
La Jolla, California

Ray Kemp
Sizewell Inquiry Review Project
University of East Anglia
Norwich, England

Timothy W. Luke
Department of Political Science
Virginia Polytechnic Institute and State University
Blacksburg, Virginia

Dieter Misgeld
The Ontario Institute for Studies in Education and Department of
Educational Theory
University of Toronto
Toronto, Ontario

John O'Neill
Department of Sociology
York University
Toronto, Ontario

Trent Schroyer
School of Environmental Studies
Ramapo College
Mahwah, New Jersey

Stephen K. White
Department of Political Science
Virginia Polytechnic Institute and State University
Blacksburg, Virginia

Index

Index